Henrik Ibsen

Henrik Johan Ibsen was the pioneer who opened new frontiers of modern drama and violated all the unwritten taboos of the nineteenth-century theater.

He was born in Skien, a small Norwegian timber port, in 1828, into a prosperous family which in a few years lost almost all of its resources. Ibsen's father, overwhelmed by the disaster, lived in a state of skulking despair, while his mother drove herself into the devotions of an impersonal pietism. These scenes of despondency from his childhood recur in Ibsen's dramas, his parents serving as models of human wreckage. At fifteen Ibsen left Skien and found work as a druggist's apprentice, and, soon after, began to write poems that ridiculed important local citizens. In 1848 *Catilina,* his first play, was published; *The Burial Mound* (1850) was the first of his plays to be performed. Neither attracted much public attention.

In 1851 Ibsen was hired by the Norwegian Theater in Bergen as a director, writer, and producer. He disliked the work and left, but not before involving himself in over 145 productions. Returning to Oslo in 1857, he married in 1859 and spent the next few years in great financial difficulty. Having received little recognition as a playwright, he left Norway for Italy in 1864, beginning what became a twenty-seven-year expatriation.

When his play *Brand* (1865) was published in Copenhagen in 1866, it was judged both a commercial and artistic success, and this, along with his next work, *Peer Gynt* (1867), gave him some of the prominence he sought. With each succeeding play he moved further into a more experimental realm, the "drama of ideas." *A Doll's House* (1879) and *Ghosts* (1881) aroused much public outcry for their iconoclasm. In *An Enemy of the People* (1882) Ibsen made controversy the very core of the action. With *The Wild Duck* (1884) he was on the threshold of a new naturalistic style of playwriting for which Chekhov became celebrated many years later.

In spite of his lifelong rebelliousness and frequent clashes with public opinion, Ibsen returned to Norway in 1891. He died in Oslo in 1906.

ASK YOUR BOOKSELLER FOR BANTAM CLASSICS BY THESE INTERNATIONAL WRITERS

Aristophanes
Dante Alighieri
Honore de Balzac
Fyodor Dostoevsky
Alexandre Dumas
Euripides
Gustave Flaubert
Johann Wolfgang von Goethe
Jacob and Wilhelm Grimm
Homer
Victor Hugo
Henrik Ibsen
Franz Kafka
Pierre Choderlos de Laclos
Gaston Leroux
Niccolo Machiavelli
Thomas Mann
Karl Marx and Friedrich Engels
Guy de Maupassant
Plato
Edmond Rostand
Marquis de Sade
Sophocles
Marie-Henri Beyle de Stendhal
Leo Tolstoy
Ivan Turgenev
Jules Verne
Virgil
Voltaire
Johann David Wyss
Emile Zola

Hedda Gabler

AND OTHER PLAYS

by

Henrik Ibsen

BANTAM BOOKS
NEW YORK   TORONTO   LONDON   SYDNEY   AUCKLAND
A · BANTAM · CLASSIC

HEDDA GABLER AND OTHER PLAYS
A Bantam Classic Book / July 1995

"Tea Leaves," Paxton. Courtesy of
The Metropolitan Museum of Art.

ISBN 0-553-21447-0

Published simultaneously in the United States and Canada

Bantam Books are published by Bantam Books, a division of Bantam
Doubleday Dell Publishing Group, Inc. Its trademark, consisting of
the words "Bantam Books" and the portrayal of a rooster, is Regis-
tered in U.S. Patent and Trademark Office and in other countries.
Marca Registrada. Bantam Books, 1540 Broadway, New York, New
York 10036.

PRINTED IN THE UNITED STATES OF AMERICA

OPM   0   9   8   7   6   5   4   3   2   1

Contents

~

Peer Gynt

(1867)

Characters

AASE, *widow of John Gynt, a peasant.*

PEER GYNT, *her son.*

Two Old Women with corn-sacks.

ASLAK, *a blacksmith.*

Wedding Guests, a Steward at the Wedding, a Fiddler, etc.

A Stranger and his Wife.

SOLVEIG *and little* HELGA, *their daughters.*

The Owner of Hægstad Farm.

INGRID, *his daughter.*

The Bridegroom and his Parents.

Three Cowherd Girls.   A Woman in Green.

The TROLL KING.   *Several Trolls of his Court.*

Troll Boys and Girls.   Two Witches.

  Hobgoblins, Brownies, Elves, etc.

An Ugly Urchin.   A Voice in the Gloom.

  Birds' Cries.

KARI, *a cotter's wife.*

Mr. Cotton

MONSIEUR BALLON

HERR VON EBERKOPF

HERR TRUMPETERSTRAALE

       tourists.

A Thief and a Receiver of Stolen Goods.

ANITRA, *daughter of a Bedouin Chief.*

Arabs, Female Slaves, Dancing Girls, etc.

The Statue of Memnon (with song).

  The Sphinx at Gizeh (dumb).

PROFESSOR BEGRIFFENFELDT, *Ph.D., in charge of the Lunatic Asylum at Cairo.*

Lunatics with their Keepers.

HUHU, *a language-reformer from the Malabar coast.*

HUSSEIN, *an Eastern Secretary of State.*

A Fellah, carrying a royal mummy.

A Norwegian Skipper and his Crew.

A Strange Passenger.

A Priest.

A Funeral Party.

A Button-Moulder.

A Thin Man.

The action, which begins in the early years of the century and ends somewhere about our own day {1867}, takes place partly in the Gudbrandsdal and on the surrounding mountain-tops, partly on the coast of Morocco, in the Sahara Desert, in the Cairo Lunatic Asylum, at Sea, etc.

Act I

~

Scene I

Scene.—*The wooded mountain-side near* AASE'S *farm, with a stream rushing past. On the farther bank stands an old mill. It is a hot summer's day.* PEER GYNT, *a sturdy youth of twenty, comes down the path, followed by his mother* AASE, *who is short and slight. She is scolding him angrily.*

AASE.　　Peer, you're lying!

PEER GYNT (*without stopping*).　　No, I'm not!

AASE.　　Well, then, will you swear it's true?

PEER GYNT.　　Swear? Why should I?

AASE.　　Ah, you daren't! Your whole tale's a pack of lies!

PEER GYNT.　　Every blessed word is true!

AASE (*facing him*).　　I wonder you can face your mother! First of all, just when the work is at busiest, off you go to prowl about the hills for weeks after reindeer in the snow; come back with your clothes in rags, game-bag empty—and no gun! Then you have the cheek to think you can make your mother swallow such a pack of lies as this about your hunting!—Tell me, then, where you found this precious buck?

PEER GYNT.　　West of Gendin.

AASE (*with a scornful laugh*).　　I dare say!

PEER GYNT.　　I was leeward of the blast, and behind

a clump of trees he was scraping in the snow for some moss——

AASE (*as before*).   Oh, yes, no doubt!

PEER GYNT.   I stood and listened, held my breath, heard the scraping of his hoof, saw the antlers of his horns; then upon my belly crawled carefully between the rocks; peeped from cover of the stones— Such a buck, so sleek and fat, I suppose was never seen!

AASE.   I expect not!

PEER GYNT.   Then I fired! Down the buck came on the ground! But the moment he had fallen I was up astride his back, on his left ear got my grip and was just in act of thrusting with my knife into his gullet just behind his head—when, hi! with a scream the ugly beggar scrambled up upon his feet. From my hand his sudden back-throw jerked my hunting-knife and scabbard, pinned me to his loins and held me by the legs between his antlers like a pair of mighty pincers; then he rushed with bounds gigantic right along the ridge of Gendin!

AASE (*involuntarily*).   Christ in Heaven——!

PEER GYNT.   Have you ever been upon the ridge at Gendin? Fully half a mile it stretches, at the top as sheer and narrow as a scythe-blade. Looking downward—past the slopes and past the glaciers, past the grey ravines and gullies—either side you see the water wrapped in dark and gloomy slumber half a mile at least beneath you. Right along it he and I clove our passage through the air. Never rode I such a steed! Far ahead the peaks were sparkling as we rushed along. Beneath us in the void the dusky eagles fell away like motes in sunshine; you could see the ice-floes breaking on the banks, yet hear no murmur. But the sprites that turn us dizzy danced and sang and circled round us— I could hear and seemed to see them!

AASE (*swaying as if giddy*).   Heaven help us!

PEER GYNT.   On a sudden, on the precipice's edge, from the hole where it lay hidden almost at the reindeer's feet, up a ptarmigan rose, cackling, flapping with its wings in terror. Then the reindeer, madly swerving, gave a bound sky-high that sent us plunging o'er the edge and downwards. (AASE *totters and grasps a tree-trunk*. PEER GYNT *continues*.) Gloomy precipice behind us!—Fathomless abyss below us! First through clouds of mist we hurtled, then a flock of gulls we scattered wheeling through the air and screaming. Downward still and ever downwards! But beneath us something glistened whitish, like a reindeer's belly. Mother, 'twas our own reflection mirrored in the lake beneath us, rushing up, it seemed, to meet us just as swiftly and as madly as we downwards rushed towards it.

AASE (*gasping for breath*).   Peer! God help me——! Tell me quickly!

PEER GYNT.   Buck from air and buck from water met with mighty splash together, scattering the foam around us. Then at last we somehow managed to the northern shore to struggle; Buck, he swam and dragged me after—so I got home——

AASE.   But where's the reindeer?

PEER GYNT.   I expect he's where I left him—— (*Snaps his fingers, turns on his heel and adds*): If you find him, you may keep him!

AASE.   And your neck you haven't broken? Nor your legs? Nor smashed your backbone? Praise and thanks to God be given for His goodness that has saved you! There's a rent across your breeches, it is true; but that is scarcely worth a mention when one thinks what the harm might well have been from a leap like that of yours—— (*She suddenly pauses, stares at him with open mouth, seems to struggle for speech and at last breaks out.*) Oh, you lying little devil!—Christ above us, what a liar! All that rigmarole you told me is the tale of Gudbrand Glesnë that I heard when I was twenty. 'Twas to him that all this happened, not to you, you——

PEER GYNT.   Yes, it did; history repeats itself.

AASE.   Lies, I know, can be so furbished and disguised in gorgeous wrappings that their skinny carcasses not a soul would recognize. That's what you've been doing now, with your wonderful adventures—eagles' wings, and all that nonsense—making up a pack of lies, tales of breathless risk and danger, till one can no longer tell what one knows and what one doesn't.

PEER GYNT.   If a man said that to me, I would beat him to a jelly.

AASE (*in tears*).   Would to God that I were dead and buried in the cold black earth! Prayers and tears have no effect. You're a hopeless ne'er-do-well!

PEER GYNT (*in tears*).   Dearest pretty little mother, every word you say is true; so be gay and happy——

AASE.   Pshaw! Don't talk nonsense. How could I be happy, if I wanted to, with such a pig as you for son? Don't you think it's pretty hard for a poor weak widow never to feel anything but shame? (*Weeps again.*) How much is there left of all that your grandfather enjoyed in his days of comfort? Where are the well-filled money-bags left by good old Rasmus Gynt? 'Twas your father emptied them, pouring money out like sand—buying land in all directions—gilded coach to ride about in. Where's the stuff so freely wasted at the famous winter banquet, when each guest sent glass and bottle crash against the wall behind him?

PEER GYNT.   Where are the snows of yesteryear?

AASE.   Hold your tongue when I am speaking! See the farm-house—scarce a window but is smashed and stuffed with dish-clout; scarce a hedge or fence is standing; no protection for the cattle from the wind and wet; the meadows and the fields all lying fallow; every month distraint on something——

PEER GYNT.   That's enough of dismal wailing! Often when our luck's been drooping it has grown as strong as ever.

AASE.   Where it grew, the soil is poisoned. Peer, you certainly don't lack good opinion of yourself. You are just as brisk and bumptious, just as pert, as when the Parson who had come from Copenhagen asked you what your Christian name was, telling you that where he came from lots of men of highest station would be glad to be as clever; and your father was so grateful for his amiable praises that a horse and sledge he gave him. Ah, me! All went well in those days. Parsons, Captains and such people, dropping in to see us daily—filling up with drink and victuals until they were nearly bursting. But it's when your fortunes alter that you get to know your neighbours. Since the day when "rich John Gynt" took the road with pedlar's pack, not a soul has e'er been near us. *(Wipes her eyes with her apron.)* You're a stout and strapping fellow—you should be a staff supporting your old mother in her troubles. You should work the farm for profit and look after all the little that your father left behind him. *(Weeps again.)* Heaven knows, it's precious little use you've been to me, you rascal. When you are at home, you're loafing by the fire, or grubbing idly in the ashes and the embers; when you're in the town you frighten all the girls you meet at dances, so that I'm ashamed to own you—fighting with the lowest tramps——

PEER GYNT *(moving away from her).*   Let me be!

AASE *(following him).*   Can you deny you were foremost in the brawling in that dog-fight of a scrimmage down at Lundë? Who but you cracked the blacksmith Aslak's arm? Or at any rate disjointed one of his ten fingers for him?

PEER GYNT.   Who has stuffed you up with that?

AASE (*hotly*).   Why, the cotter heard his howls!

PEER GYNT (*rubbing his elbow*).   Yes—but it was I that howled.

AASE.   What!

PEER GYNT.   Yes, mother, *I* got thrashed.

AASE.   What?

PEER GYNT.   Well, he's a lusty chap.

AASE.   Who is?

PEER GYNT.   Aslak—as I felt!

AASE.   Shame! I'd like to spit upon you! To let such a scurvy swiller, such a worthless drunken rascal, beat you! (*Weeps again.*) Often I've endured shame and scorn on your account, but that this disgrace should happen is the very worst of all. If he *is* a lusty fellow, need that mean you're a weakling?

PEER GYNT (*with a laugh*).   Well, it doesn't seem to matter if I beat, or if I'm beaten—either way you start your wailing. You may cheer up——

AASE.   Are you lying now again?

PEER GYNT.   Yes, just this once; so you may as well stop crying. (*Clenches his left hand.*) See, 'twas with this pair of pincers that I bent the blacksmith double, while my right hand was my hammer——

AASE.   Oh, you brawler! You will bring me to my grave by your behaviour!

PEER GYNT.   Nonsense! You're worth something better—better twenty thousand times! Little, homely, dainty mother, just believe what I am saying. All the town shall do you honour; only wait till I have done something—something really great!

AASE (*contemptuously*). You!

PEER GYNT. Who knows what lies before him!

AASE. If you ever know enough to mend your breeches when they're torn, 'tis the most that I could hope for!

PEER GYNT (*hotly*). I'll be a King, an Emperor!

AASE. Oh, God help me! Now he's losing what was left him of his wits!

PEER GYNT. Yes, I shall! Just give me time!

AASE. Of course! As the old proverb runs, "Everything comes to him that waits."

PEER GYNT. Mother, you shall see.

AASE. Be quiet! You are as mad as mad can be. After all, it's true enough something might have come of you if you'd thought of something else but your stupid lies and nonsense. Hægstad's daughter fancied you, and you might have won the game if you'd rightly gone to work——

PEER GYNT. Do you think so?

AASE. The old man is too weak to stand against her. He is obstinate enough in a way; but in the end it is Ingrid takes the lead, and where *she* goes, step by step the old hunks comes stumbling after. (*Begins to cry again.*) Ah, Peer—a richly dowered girl, heir to his lands, just think of it. You might, if only you had liked, in bridegroom's finery be dressed instead of in these dirty rags!

PEER GYNT (*quickly*). Come on, I'll be a suitor now.

AASE. Where?

PEER GYNT. Why, at Hægstad!

AASE. Ah, poor boy, the right of way is barred to you.

PEER GYNT. What do you mean?

AASE. Alas, alas! You've lost the moment—lost your chance——

PEER GYNT.   How's that?

AASE (*sobbing*).   While you were on the hills, riding your reindeer through the air, Mads Moen went and won the girl.

PEER GYNT.   What? He? That guy the girls all laugh at?

AASE.   Yes. Now she's betrothed to him.

PEER GYNT.   Just wait till I have harnessed up the cart—— (*Turns to go.*)

AASE.   You needn't take the trouble. The wedding is to-morrow.

PEER GYNT.   Pooh! I'll get there by this evening.

AASE.   Fie! Do you want to make things worse? Just think how everyone will mock us!

PEER GYNT.   Cheer up! All will turn our right. (*Shouting and laughing at the same time.*) No, mother! We won't take the cart; we haven't time to put the mare in.

{*Lifts her off her feet.*

AASE.   Let me alone!

PEER GYNT.   No, in my arms you shall be carried to the wedding!

{*Wades out into the water.*

AASE.   Help! Help! Oh, Heaven protect me!—Peer, we'll drown——

PEER GYNT.   Oh, no, we shan't—I'm born to meet a better death.

AASE.   That's true; you'll probably be hanged. (*Pulls his hair.*) You beast!

PEER GYNT.   You'd best keep quiet, for just here the bottom's smooth and slippery.

AASE.   Ass!

PEER GYNT.   Yes, abuse me if you like, words don't do any harm. Aha! The bottom's sloping upwards now——

AASE.   Don't lose your hold of me!

PEER GYNT.   Gee up! We'll play at Peer and Reindeer now! *(Prances.)* I am the reindeer, you are Peer!

AASE.   I'm sure I don't know what I am!

PEER GYNT.   See here, now—here's an even bottom. *(Wades to the bank.)* Now give your steed a pretty kiss to thank him for the ride you've had.

AASE *(boxing his ears)*.   That's the thanks I'll give him!

PEER GYNT.   Wow! That's a scurvy sort of tip.

AASE.   Put me down!

PEER GYNT.   Not till we get to where the wedding is afoot. You are so clever, you must be my spokesman— talk to the old fool—tell him Mads Moen is a sot——

AASE.   Put me down!

PEER GYNT.   And tell him, too, the sort of lad that Peer Gynt is.

AASE.   Yes, you may take your oath I will! A pretty character I'll give you! I'll draw a faithful portrait, too,— and all your devil's pranks and antics I'll tell them of—in every detail——

PEER GYNT.   Oh, will you!

AASE *(kicking him in her temper)*.   I won't hold my tongue till the old man sets his dog upon you, as upon a tramp!

PEER GYNT.   Ah, then I think I'll go alone.

AASE.   All right, but I shall follow you!

PEER GYNT.   Dear mother, you're not strong enough.

AASE.   Not strong enough? I'm so worked up that I could smash a heap of stones! Oh, I could make a meal of flints! So put me down!

PEER GYNT.   Yes, if you promise——

AASE.   Nothing! I'm going there with you, and they shall know the sort you are!

PEER GYNT.   Oh, no, you won't; you'll stay behind.

AASE.   Never! I'm going there with you.

PEER GYNT.   Oh, no, you aren't.

AASE.   What will you do?

PEER GYNT.   I'll put you on the mill-house roof!

{Puts her up there. She screams.

AASE.   Lift me down!

PEER GYNT.   If you will listen——

AASE.   Bah!

PEER GYNT.   Now, little mother, listen——

AASE *(throwing a bit of turf thatch at him)*.   Lift me down this moment, Peer!

PEER GYNT.   If I dared I would, indeed. *(Goes nearer to her.)* Remember to sit still and quiet—not to kick your legs about, nor the tiles to break or loosen—or an accident may happen, and you might fall off.

AASE.   You beast!

PEER GYNT.   Don't shift!

AASE.   I wish you'd been shifted up the chimney, like a changeling!

PEER GYNT.   Mother! Shame!

AASE.   Pooh!

PEER GYNT.   You should rather give your blessing on my journey. Will you?

AASE.   I'll give you a thrashing, big as your are!

PEER GYNT.   Oh, well, good-bye! Only have patience, mother dear; I shan't be long *(Is going; but turns, lifts a warning finger and says):* But don't forget you mustn't try to move from there!

{Goes.

AASE. Peer!—Heaven help me, he is gone! Reindeer-rider! Liar! Hi! Will you listen?—No, he's off over the meadows. *(Screams.)* Help! I'm giddy!

> {*Two* OLD WOMEN, *with sacks on their backs, come down the path towards the mill.*

FIRST OLD WOMAN. Who's that screaming?

AASE. Me!

SECOND OLD WOMAN. Why, Aase, you have had a lift in life!

AASE. One that won't do me much good—I'll be booked for heaven directly!

FIRST OLD WOMAN. Pleasant journey!

AASE. Fetch a ladder! Get me down! That devil Peer——

SECOND OLD WOMAN. What, your son?

AASE. Now you can say you have seen how he behaves.

FIRST OLD WOMAN. We'll bear witness.

AASE. Only help me—help me to get straight to Hægstad——

SECOND OLD WOMAN. Is he there?

FIRST OLD WOMAN. You'll be revenged; the blacksmith's going to the party.

AASE *(wringing her hands).* Oh, God help me! My poor boy! They will murder him between them!

FIRST OLD WOMAN. Ah, we know that lot quite well; you may bet that's what will happen!

SECOND OLD WOMAN. You can see she's lost her senses. *(Calls up the hill.)* Eivind! Anders! Hi! come here!

A MAN'S VOICE. What?

SECOND OLD WOMAN. Peer Gynt has put his mother up upon the mill-house roof!

SCENE II

SCENE.—*A little hill covered with bushes and heather. The high-road, shut off by a fence, runs at the back.* PEER GYNT *comes down a foot-path, goes quickly up to the fence, and stands looking out over the landscape beyond.*

PEER GYNT.　　Yonder lies Hægstad. I shall soon be at it. (*Climbs half over the fence, then stops and considers.*) I wonder if Ingrid's sitting all alone there? (*Shades his eyes and looks along the road.*) No, folk with gifts are swarming up like midges. Perhaps I had better turn and go no farther. (*Draws his leg back over the fence.*) There'll be their grins behind my back for certain—whispers that seem to burn their way right through you. (*Moves a few steps away from the fence and begins absently plucking leaves.*) If only I'd a good strong drink inside me—or could just slip into the house unnoticed—— Or if no one knew me——. No, some good strong liquor would be best; their laughter wouldn't hurt then.

> {*Looks around suddenly as if startled, then hides among the bushes. Some* COUNTRY FOLK, *carrying presents, pass along the road on their way to the wedding.*

A MAN (*in conversation*).　　With a drunkard for father, and a poor thing of a mother——

A WOMAN.　　Yes, it's no wonder the boy is such a wastrel.

> {*They pass on. After a little,* PEER GYNT *comes forward, blushing with shame, and peeps after them.*

PEER GYNT (*softly*).　　Was it of me they gossiped? (*With a forced shrug.*) Oh, well, let them! Anyway they can't kill me with their gossip. (*Throws himself down on the heather slope and for some time lies on his back with his hands under his head, staring up into the sky.)* What a curious cloud! That bit's like a horse, and there is its rider and saddle and bridle, and behind them an old crone is riding a broomstick. *(Laughs quietly to himself.)* That's mother! She's scolding and screaming "You beast! Hi! Peer, come back!" *(Gradually closes his eyes.)* Yes, now she is frightened.—There rides Peer Gynt at the head of his henchmen, his charger gold-shod, silver-crested his harness. Peer carries gauntlets and sabre and scabbard, wears a long coat with a fine silky lining. Splendid the men in his retinue following; but there's not one sits his charger as proudly, not one that glitters like him in the sunshine. The people in groups by the wayside are gathered, lifting their hats as they stare up in wonder; the women are curtseying, everyone knows it is Kaiser Peer Gynt and his thousand retainers. Half-guinea pieces and glittering shillings are strewn on the roadway as if they were pebbles; rich as a lord is each man in the parish. Peer Gynt rides over the seas in his glory; Engelland's Prince on the shore is awaiting, and Engelland's maidens all ready to welcome him. Engelland's nobles and Engelland's Kaiser rise from their seats as he deigns to approach them. Lifting his crown, speaks the Kaiser in welcome——

ASLAK THE SMITH *(to some others, as they pass by on the other side of the fence).*   Hullo! Look here! Why, it's Peer Gynt the drunkard!

PEER GYNT *(half rising).*   What, Kaiser——!

ASLAK *(leaning on the fence and grinning).*   Get up on your feet, my young fellow!

PEER GYNT.   What the devil——? The blacksmith! Well, pray, what do *you* want?

ASLAK *(to the others).*   He hasn't got over our spree down at Lundë.

PEER GYNT *(springing up).*   Just let me alone!

ASLAK.   That I will. But, young fellow, what have you done with yourself since we parted? It's six weeks ago. Have the troll-folk been at you?

PEER GYNT.   I can tell you I've done something wonderful, Aslak.

ASLAK (*winking to the others*).   Let's hear it then, Peer!

PEER GYNT.   No, it won't interest you.

ASLAK.   Shall we see you at Hægstad?

PEER GYNT.   You won't.

ASLAK.   Why, the gossip says there was a time you were fancied by Ingrid.

PEER GYNT.   You dirty-faced crow!

ASLAK.   Now don't get in a temper! If the girl *has* refused you, there surely are others. Remember the goodly John Gynt was your father! Come along to the farm! There'll be girls at the wedding as tender as lambkins and widows well seasoned——

PEER GYNT.   Go to hell!

ASLAK.   You'll be sure to find someone who'll have you. Good evening. I'll give the bride all your good wishes!

> {*They go off, laughing and whispering.* PEER *stands for a moment looking after them, then tosses his head and turns half round.*

PEER GYNT.   Well, Ingrid at Hægstad may wed whom she pleases, for all that I care! I shall be just as happy! (*Looks down at his clothes.*) Breeches all torn—all dirty and tattered. If only I had something new to put on me—— (*Stamps his foot on the slope.*) If I only could carve at their breasts like a butcher and tear out the scorn and contempt that they show me! (*Looks round suddenly.*) What was that? Who is it that's laughing behind there? I certainly thought that I heard——. No, there's no one. I'll go home to mother. (*Moves off, but stops again and listens in the direction of Hægstad.*)

The dance is beginning! *(Stares and listens; moves step by step towards the fence; his eyes glisten; he rubs his hands down his legs.)* How the girls swarm! Seven or eight of them there for each man! Oh, death and damnation, I must go to the party!— But what about mother, sitting up there on the roof of the mill-house——? *(His eyes wander towards the fence again; he skips and laughs.)* Haha! I can hear them out dancing a Halling! Guttorm's the boy—how he handles his fiddle! Hear it sparkle and flash like a stream at a waterfall! And think of the girls—all the pick of the neighbourhood—— Yes, death and damnation, I'm off to the party!

{Vaults over the fence and goes off down the road.

SCENE III

SCENE.—*The courtyard of the farm at Hægstad. The farm buildings are at the back. A number of guests are assembled, and a lively dance is in progress on the grass. The* FIDDLER *is seated on a table. The* STEWARD *stands in the doorway. Cookmaids pass to and fro between the buildings. The older folk are sitting about, gossiping.*

A WOMAN *(joining a group of guests who are sitting on some logs).*   The bride? To be sure she is crying a little, but that's not a thing that is out of the usual.

The Steward *(to another group).*   Now then, my friends, you must empty your noggins!

A MAN.   Ah, thank you kindly—you fill up too quickly!

A YOUTH *(as he flies past the* FIDDLER, *holding a girl by the hand).* That's the way, Guttorm! Don't spare your fiddle-strings!

THE GIRL. Scrape till it echoes out over the meadows!

OTHER GIRLS (*standing in a ring round a youth who is dancing*). That's a good step!

A GIRL. He's lusty and nimble!

THE YOUTH (*dancing*). The roof here is high and the walls far apart, you know!

> {*The* BRIDEGROOM *comes up whimpering to his* FATHER, *who is standing talking to some others, and pulls at his jacket.*

THE BRIDEGROOM. Father, she won't! She is not being nice to me!

HIS FATHER. What won't she do?

THE BRIDEGROOM. She has locked herself in.

HIS FATHER. Well, you must see if you can't find the key.

THE BRIDEGROOM. But I don't know how.

HIS FATHER. Oh, you are a nuisance!

> {*Turns to the others again. The* BRIDEGROOM *drifts across the courtyard.*

A BOY (*coming from behind the house*). I say, you girls! Now things will be livelier! Peer Gynt's arrived!

ASLAK (*who has just come on the scene*). Who invited him?

THE STEWARD. No one did.

> {*Goes into the house.*

ASLAK (*to the girls*). If he should speak to you, don't seem to hear him.

A GIRL (*to the others*). No, we'll pretend that we don't even see him.

{PEER GYNT *comes in, hot and eager, stops in front
of the group and rubs his hands.*

PEER GYNT.   Who is the nimblest girl of the lot of
you?

A GIRL *(whom he has approached).*   Not I.

ANOTHER.   Nor I.

A THIRD.   No, nor I either.

PEER GYNT *(to a fourth).*   Then *you* dance with me,
for want of a better.

THE GIRL *(turning away).*   I haven't time.

PEER GYNT *(to a fifth).*   You, then.

THE GIRL *(moving away).*   I'm off homeward.

PEER GYNT.   Homeward to-night? Are you out of
your senses?

ASLAK *(after a little in a low voice).*   Peer, she has taken
an old man to dance with.

PEER GYNT *(turning quickly to another man).*   Where
are the disengaged girls?

THE MAN.   Go and look for them.

{*He moves away from* PEER GYNT, *who has suddenly
become subdued. He glances furtively and shyly at the
group. They all look at him, but no one speaks. He
approaches other groups. Wherever he goes there is a
sudden silence; when he moves away, they smile and look
after him.*

PEER GYNT *(in a low voice).*   Glances—and thoughts
and smiles that are cutting—jarring on one like a file on a
sawblade!

{*He sidles along by the palings.* SOLVEIG, *holding little* HELGA *by the hand, comes into the courtyard with
her* PARENTS.

A MAN *(to another, close to* PEER GYNT).   These are
the newcomers.

THE OTHER.   Living out westward?

FIRST MAN.   Yes, out at Hedal.

THE OTHER.   Ah, yes—of course they are.

> {PEER GYNT *advances to meet the newcomers, points to* SOLVEIG *and addresses her* FATHER.

PEER GYNT.   May I dance with your daughter?

THE FATHER.   You may; but before that we must go indoors and give our hosts our greetings.

> {They go in.

THE STEWARD (*to* PEER GYNT, *offering him a drink*).   As you're here, I suppose you must wet your whistle.

PEER GYNT (*looking fixedly after the newcomers*). Thanks, I'm for dancing. I don't feel thirsty. (*The* STEWARD *leaves him.* PEER GYNT *looks towards the house and laughs.*) How fair she is! Was there ever a fairer? Eyes glancing down at her shoes and white apron—and the way she held on to her mother's skirt, too—and carried her prayer-book wrapped in a kerchief——! I must have a look at her!

> {Is going into the house, but is met by several YOUTHS coming out.

A YOUTH.   What, off already? Away from the dance?

PEER GYNT.   No.

THE YOUTH.   You're on the wrong road, then!

> {Takes him by the shoulders to turn him round.

PEER GYNT.   Let me get past!

THE YOUTH.   Are you frightened of Aslak?

PEER GYNT.   I, frightened?

THE YOUTH.   Remember what happened at Lundë!

> {The group laugh and move off to where the dancing is going on. SOLVEIG comes to the door.

SOLVEIG.   Are you the boy who wanted to dance with me?

PEER GYNT.   Of course I am. Can't you tell by the look of me? Come on!

SOLVEIG.   But I mustn't go far—mother said so.

PEER GYNT.   Mother said? mother said? Were you only born yesterday?

SOLVEIG.   Don't laugh——

PEER GYNT.   Is it true you are almost a kiddie still. Are you grown up?

SOLVEIG.   I shall soon be confirmed, you know.

PEER GYNT.   Tell me your name—then we can talk easier.

SOLVEIG.   My name is Solveig. Tell me what yours is.

PEER GYNT.   Peer Gynt.

SOLVEIG (*drawing back her hand from his*).   Oh, heavens!

PEER GYNT.   Why, what is the matter?

SOLVEIG.   My garter's come loose; I must tie it more carefully. (*Leaves him.*)

THE BRIDEGROOM (*pulling at his* MOTHER'S *sleeve*). Mother, she won't—

HIS MOTHER.   She won't? What won't she do?

THE BRIDEGROOM.   Mother, she won't——

HIS MOTHER.   What?

THE BRIDEGROOM.   Unbar the door to me!

HIS FATHER (*in a low and angry voice*).   You're only fit to be tied in a stable, sir!

HIS MOTHER.   Poor boy, don't scold him—he'll be all right presently.

{A YOUTH *comes in, with a crowd of others who have been dancing.*

THE YOUTH.   Brandy, Peer?

PEER GYNT.   No.

YOUTH.   Just a drop!

PEER GYNT.   Have you got any?

YOUTH. Maybe I have. (*Pulls out a flask and drinks.*) Ah, that's got a bite to it! Well?

PEER GYNT. Let me try it. (*Drinks.*)

SECOND YOUTH. And now have a pull at mine!

PEER GYNT. No.

YOUTH. Oh, what rubbish! Don't be a simpleton! Have a drink, Peer!

PEER GYNT. Well, give me a drop of it. (*Drinks again.*)

A GIRL (*in an undertone*). Come, let's be off.

PEER GYNT. Why, are you afraid of me?

YOUTH. Do you think there is any that isn't afraid of you? You showed us what you could do, down at Lundë.

PEER GYNT. I can do better than that if I'm roused, you know!

YOUTH (*whispering*). Now he is getting on!

OTHERS (*making a ring round* PEER). Come on, now—tell us, Peer, what you can do?

PEER GYNT. Oh, I'll tell you to-morrow——

OTHERS. No! Tell us to-night!

A GIRL. Can you show us some witchcraft, Peer?

PEER GYNT. Ah, I can conjure the Devil!

A MAN. My grandmother, she could do that long before I was born, they say.

PEER GYNT. Liar! What *I* can do, no one alive can do. Why, once I conjured him into a nutshell, right through a worm-hole!

OTHERS (*laughing*). Of course—we can guess that!

PEER GYNT. He swore and he wept and promised to give me all sorts of things——

ONE OF THE GROUP. But had to go into it?

PEER GYNT. Yes; and then, when I'd stopped up the worm-hole, Lord! if you'd heard him buzzing and rumbling!

A GIRL.   Fancy!

PEER GYNT.   'Twas like a great bumble-bee buzzing.

THE GIRL.   And pray have you got him still in the nutshell?

PEER GYNT.   No, the old Devil got right clean away again. It is his fault the blacksmith dislikes me.

A BOY.   How's that?

PEER GYNT.   Because I took him to the smithy and asked the smith to crack the nutshell for me. He said he would. I laid it on the anvil; but you know Aslak's very heavy-handed, and with a will he laid on the hammer——

A VOICE FROM THE GROUP.   Did he kill the Devil?

PEER GYNT.   No, he laid on stoutly, but the Devil looked after himself and just vanished through ceiling and walls in a flame of fire.

SEVERAL VOICES.   And Aslak——?

PEER GYNT.   Stood there with his hands well roasted. And since that day we have never been friendly.

{General laughter.

VOICES.   That's a fine rigmarole!

OTHERS.   Easily his best one!

PEER GYNT.   Do you suggest that I made it up?

A MAN.   Oh, no, I know you didn't; for I've heard the story told by my grandfather——

PEER GYNT.   Liar! It happened to me, I tell you!

THE MAN.   Oh, well—that's all right.

PEER GYNT (*tossing his head*).   Pooh! I can ride through the clouds on horseback! There are lots of fine things I can do, I tell you!

{Roars of laughter again.

ONE OF THE GROUP.   Peer, let us see you ride clouds!

OTHERS.   Yes, dear Peer——!

PEER GYNT. Oh, you won't need to beg me so humbly—one day I'll ride like a storm o'er the lot of you! The whole countryside shall fall at my feet!

AN OLDER MAN. Why, now he's raving!

ANOTHER. Yes, the great booby!

A THIRD. The braggart!

A FOURTH. The liar!

PEER GYNT (*threatening them*). Just wait and you'll see, then!

A MAN (*half drunk*). Yes, wait and you'll get your jacket well dusted!

OTHERS. A good sound drubbing! A nice black eye, too!

> {*The crowd disperses, the older ones angry and the younger ones laughing and mocking him.*

THE BRIDEGROOM (*edging up to* PEER). Peer, is it true you can ride through the clouds, then?

PEER GYNT (*shortly*). Anything, Mads! I'm the boy, I can tell you!

THE BRIDEGROOM. I suppose you've a coat that will make you invisible?

PEER GYNT. An invisible hat, do you mean? Yes, I have one. (*Turns away from him.* SOLVEIG *comes across the courtyard leading* HELGA *by the hand.* PEER GYNT *goes to meet them, looking happier.*) Solveig! Ah, I am glad you have come to me! (*Grasps her wrists.*) Now I shall swing you round most nimbly!

SOLVEIG. Oh, let me go!

PEER GYNT. Why?

SOLVEIG. You look so wildly.

PEER GYNT. The reindeer grows wild when summer's approaching. Come along, girl! Come, don't be sullen!

SOLVEIG (*drawing back her arm*). No—no, I daren't.

PEER GYNT.   Why?

SOLVEIG.   No, you've been drinking.

> {*Moves away a little, with* HELGA.

PEER GYNT.   I wish I had stuck my knife in the lot of them!

THE BRIDEGROOM (*nudging* PEER'S *elbow*).   Can't you help me to get in there where the bride is?

PEER GYNT (*absently*).   The bride? Where is she?

THE BRIDEGROOM.   In the loft.

PEER GYNT.   Oh, is she?

THE BRIDEGROOM.   Oh, come, Peer—dear Peer—you might try to!

PEER GYNT.   No, you must manage to do without me. (*A thought strikes him. He says, softly and meaningly*): Ingrid! The loft! (*Goes up to* SOLVEIG.) Have you made up your mind, then? (SOLVEIG *turns to get away, but he bars her path.*) I look like a tramp, and so you're ashamed of me.

SOLVEIG (*hastily*).   Oh, no, you don't; that isn't the truth.

PEER GYNT.   It is. And it's because you think I am fuddled; but that was for spite, because you had hurt me. Come along, then!

SOLVEIG.   I daren't, if I wanted to.

PEER GYNT.   Who are you frightened of?

SOLVEIG.   Mostly of father.

PEER GYNT.   Your father? Oh, yes—he's one of the solemn ones! Sanctimonious, isn't he? Answer me!

SOLVEIG.   What shall I say?

PEER GYNT.   Perhaps he's a preacher? And you and your mother the same, I dare say? Are you going to answer me?

SOLVEIG.   Let me alone.

PEER GYNT.   I won't! (*In a low but hard and threat-*

ening voice.) I can turn myself into a troll! I shall come and stand by your bed at midnight; and if you hear something that's hissing and spitting, don't you suppose it's your cat you are hearing. It is I! And I'll drain your life blood out of you; and your little sister—I'll eat her up, for I turn to a werewolf whenever the night falls, your loins and your back I'll bite all over—— *(Changes his tone suddenly and entreats her anxiously.)* Dance with me, Solveig!

SOLVEIG *(looking darkly at him)*.   Ah—now you are horrid.

                              {*Goes into the house.*

THE BRIDEGROOM *(drifting up to* PEER *again)*.   I'll give you an ox, if you'll help me!

PEER GYNT.   Come!

          {*They go behind the house. At the same moment a crowd comes back from dancing, most of them drunk. Noise and confusion.* SOLVEIG, HELGA *and their* PARENTS *come out to the door.*

THE STEWARD *(to* ASLAK, *who is in the front of the crowd)*.   Be quiet!

ASLAK *(pulling off his coat)*.   No, here we'll settle the matter. Peer Gynt or I shall get a thrashing.

SOME OF THE CROWD.   Yes, let them fight!

OTHERS.   No, no, let them argue!

ASLAK.   No, we must fight; we want no arguing.

SOLVEIG'S FATHER.   Be quiet, man!

HELGA.   Will he hit him, mother?

A BOY.   It's better fun with his lies to tease him!

ANOTHER.   Kick him out, I say!

A THIRD.   No, spit in his face!

A FOURTH *(to* ASLAK*)*.   Are you backing out?

ASLAK *(throwing away his coat)*.   I'll murder the beggar!

SOLVEIG'S MOTHER (*to* SOLVEIG). You see now what they think of the booby.

{AASE *comes in, with a cudgel in her hand.*

AASE. Is my son here? He shall have such a drubbing! Just wait and you'll see what a thrashing I'll give him!

ASLAK (*turning up his shirt-sleeves*). No, *your* little body's too weak for that.

VOICES Aslak will thrash him!

OTHERS. Slash him!

ASLAK (*spitting on his hands and nodding to* AASE). Hang him!

AASE. What? Hang my Peer? Just try, if you dare! This old Aase's got teeth and claws!—Where is he? (*Calls across the courtyard.*) Peer!

THE BRIDEGROOM (*running in*). Oh, God in Heaven! Come, father! Mother!

HIS FATHER. Why, what's the matter?

THE BRIDEGROOM. Oh, Peer Gynt! I——!

AASE (*with a scream*). What? What? Have you killed him?

THE BRIDEGROOM. No, Peer Gynt——! Look, up there on the hillside!

VOICES. With the bride!

AASE (*letting her cudgel fall*). The beast!

ASLAK (*in amazement*). Where the hill is steepest he's climbing, by God—like a mountain goat!

THE BRIDEGROOM (*in tears*). And carrying her under his arm like a pig!

AASE (*shaking her fist at* PEER). I wish he would fall and——! (*Screams anxiously.*) Take care of your footing!

INGRID'S FATHER (*coming out bareheaded and white with rage*). I'll have his life for his rape of the bride!

AASE. No, may God punish me if I let you!

Act II

Scene I

SCENE.—*A narrow track high up on the mountain-side. It is early morning.* PEER GYNT *comes hurriedly and sulkily along the path.* INGRID, *wearing some of her bridal ornaments, is trying to hold him back.*

PEER GYNT.   Get away!

INGRID (*in tears*).   What, after this? Where to?

PEER GYNT.   Anywhere you like.

INGRID (*wringing her hands*).   What deceit!

PEER GYNT.   It's no use railing. We must go our own ways—both.

INGRID.   Think what binds us two together!

PEER GYNT.   Oh, the devil take all thinking! And the devil take all women—except one——!

INGRID.   And who is she?

PEER GYNT.   She's not you.

INGRID.   Who is it, then?

PEER GYNT.   Get you back to where you came from! Go back to your father!

INGRID.   Dearest——

PEER GYNT.   Pshaw!

INGRID.   You surely can't be meaning what you say.

PEER GYNT.   I can and do.

INGRID.   To ruin me and then forsake me?

PEER GYNT.   Well, what have you got to offer?

INGRID.   Hægstad farm, and something more.

PEER GYNT.   Is your prayer-book in your kerchief?
Where's your mane of hair all golden? Do you glance down
at your apron? Do you hold on to your mother by her skirt?
Come, answer!

INGRID.   No; but——

PETER GYNT.   Shall you go to Confirmation very
shortly?

INGRID.   No, but, dearest——

PEER GYNT.   Are your glances always bashful? If I
beg, can you deny me?

INGRID.   Christ! I think he's lost his senses——!

PEER GYNT.   Does one feel a holy feeling when one
sees you? Answer!

INGRID.   No, but——

PEER GYNT.   Then what matter what you offer?

> *{Turns to go.*

INGRID *(confronting him).*   Remember it's a hanging
matter to forsake me now.

PEER GYNT.   So be it.

INGRID.   Rich you may be, and respected, if you take
me——

PEER GYNT.   I can't do it.

INGRID *(bursting into tears).*   Oh, you tempted——

PEER GYNT.   You were willing.

INGRID.   I was wretched.

PEER GYNT.   I was mad.

INGRID *(threateningly).*   You'll pay a heavy price for
this!

PEER GYNT.   I should call the heaviest cheap.

INGRID.   Is your mind made up?

PEER GYNT.   Like stone.

INGRID.   Very well. You'll see who'll win.

{Goes down the hill.

PEER GYNT *(is silent for a little; then suddenly calls out).*   Oh, the devil take all thinking! And the devil take all women!

INGRID *(turns head and calls up mockingly).*   All but one!

PEER GYNT.   Yes, all but one!

{They each go their way.

SCENE II

SCENE.—*By a mountain lake, on boggy moorland. A storm is blowing up.* AASE, *in despair, is calling and searching in every direction.* SOLVEIG *can scarcely keep pace with her. Her* PARENTS *and* HELGA *are a little way behind.* AASE *beats the air with her arms and tears her hair.*

AASE.   Everything's against me with the might of anger! The skies and the water and the hateful mountains! Fogs from the skies are rolling to mislead him—treacherous waters will delude and drown him—mountains will crush or slip away beneath him——! And all these people! They are out to kill him! By God, they shall not! I can't do without him! The oaf! To think the devil thus should tempt him! *(Turns to* SOLVEIG.*)* Ah, my girl, one simply can't believe it. He, who was always full of lies and nonsense—he, who was only clever with his talking—he, who had never done a thing worth telling—he——! Oh, I want to laugh and cry together! We were such friends in our needs and troubles. For, you must know, my husband was a drunkard, made us a byword in the neighbours' gossip, brought all our good estate to rack and ruin, while I and Peerkin sat at home together—tried to forget—we knew no better counsel; I was too weak to stand up stoutly to it. It is so hard to face the fate that's coming; and so one tries to shake one's sorrows off one, or do one's best to rid one's mind of thinking. Some fly to brandy, others try romancing; so we found comfort in the fairy stories all about trolls and princes and such cattle— tales, too, of stolen brides—but who would ever think that such stories in his mind would linger? *(Becomes terrified again.)* Ah, what a screech! A nixie or a kelpie! Peer! Oh, my Peer!—Up there upon the hillock——! *(Runs up on to a little hillock and looks over the lake.* SOLVEIG'S PARENTS *come up to her.)* Not a thing to be seen!

THE HUSBAND *(quietly).* It is worst for him.

AASE *(in tears).* Oh, Peer! my Peer! My own lost lamb!

THE HUSBAND *(nodding his head gently).* Aye, lost indeed.

AASE. Say no such thing! He is so clever; there's no one like him.

THE HUSBAND. You foolish woman!

AASE. Oh, yes, oh, yes, I may be foolish, but he is fine!

THE HUSBAND *(always quietly and with a gentle expression).* His heart is stubborn; his soul is lost.

AASE *(anxiously).* No, no! God's not so hard as that!

THE HUSBAND. Do you think he feels the weight of his sinning?

AASE *(hastily).* No—he can ride through the air on a reindeer!

THE WIFE. Christ! Are you mad!

THE HUSBAND.   What are you saying?

AASE.   There's nothing that is too great for him. You'll see, if only he live to do it——

THE HUSBAND.   'Twould be best to see him hang on the gallows.

AASE (*with a scream*).   Good God!

THE HUSBAND.   When he's in the hangman's clutches perhaps his heart may turn to repentance.

AASE (*confusedly*).   Your talk will make me dazed and giddy! We must find him!

THE HUSBAND.   Save his soul.

AASE.   And body! We must drag him out if he's in the marshes, and ring church bells if the trolls have got him.

THE HUSBAND.   Ah! Here's a track——

AASE.   May God repay you if you help me aright!

THE HUSBAND.   'Tis our Christian duty.

AASE.   All the others are naught but heathens! There was only one that would come and wander——

THE HUSBAND.   They knew him too well.

AASE.   He was too good for them. (*Wrings her hands.*) And to think—to think his life is in danger!

THE HUSBAND.   Here's a footprint.

AASE.   That's the way we must go, then!

THE HUSBAND.   We'll scatter and search below the pastures.

{*He and his wife go on.*

SOLVEIG (*to* AASE).   Tell me some more.

AASE (*wiping her eyes*).   About my son?

SOLVEIG.   Yes. Tell me everything!

AASE (*smiling and holding her head up*).   Everything? 'Twould weary you!

SOLVEIG.   You'd be sooner wearied with telling me, than I with hearing.

SCENE III

SCENE.—*Low treeless hills below the higher mountains, whose peaks show in the distance. It is late in the day, and long shadows are falling.* PEER *comes running in at full speed, and stops on a slope.*

PEER GYNT.   They're after me now—the whole of the parish! And everyone's taken his stick or his rifle. The old man from Hægstad is leading them, howling. It has soon got abroad that Peer Gynt is the quarry! A different thing from a fight with the blacksmith! This is life! All my muscles are strong as a bear's. (*Swings his arms about and leaps into the air.*) To overthrow everything! Breast a waterfall! Strike! Pull a fir-tree up by the roots! This is life! It can harden and it can exalt! To hell with all my trumpery lying!

{THREE COWHERD GIRLS *run across the hill, shouting and singing.*

THE GIRLS.   Trond of Valfjeld! Baard and Kaare! Listen, trolls! Would you sleep in our arms?

PEER GYNT.   Who are you shouting for?

THE GIRLS.   Trolls! Trolls! Trolls!

FIRST GIRL.   Trond, come lovingly!

SECOND GIRL.   Come, lusty Baard!

THIRD GIRL.   All the beds in our hut are empty!

FIRST GIRL.   Love is lusty!

SECOND GIRL.   And lustiness love!

THIRD GIRL.   When boys are lacking, one plays with trolls!

PEER GYNT.   Where are your boys, then?

THE GIRLS (*with a burst of laughter*).   They can't come!

FIRST GIRL.   Mine called me dearest sweetheart, too, now he is wed to an elderly widow.

SECOND GIRL.   Mine met a gipsy wench up at Lien, now they are both on the road together.

THIRD GIRL.   Mine made an end of our bastard brat, now on a stake his head is grinning.

ALL THREE.   Trond of Valfjeld! Baard and Kaare! Listen, trolls! Would you sleep in our arms?

PEER GYNT (*leaping suddenly among them*).   I'm a three-headed troll, and the boy for three girls!

THE GIRLS.   Can you tackle the job?

PEER GYNT.   You shall see if I can!

FIRST GIRL.   To the hut! To the hut!

SECOND GIRL.   We have mead!

PEER GYNT.   Let it flow!

THIRD GIRL.   This Saturday night not a bed shall be empty!

SECOND GIRL (*kissing Peer*).   He gleams and glitters like glowing iron!

THIRD GIRL (*kissing Peer*).   Like a baby's eyes from the blackest tarn!

PEER GYNT (*dancing with them*).   Dismal bodings and wanton thoughts, laughter in eyes and tears in throat!

THE GIRLS (*making long noses at the mountain-tops, and shouting and singing.*)   Trond of Valfjeld! Baard and Kaare! Listen, trolls! Did you sleep in our arms?

> {*They dance away over the hills with* PEER GYNT *between them.*

SCENE IV

SCENE.—*Among the mountains. The snowy peaks are gleaming in the sunset.* PEER GYNT *comes in, looking wild and distraught.*

PEER GYNT.   Palace o'er palace is rising! See, what a glittering gate! Stop! Will you stop!—It is moving farther and farther away! The cock on the weather-vane's lifting its wings as if for a flight—into rifts of rock it has vanished, and the mountain's barred and locked. What are these roots and tree trunks that grow from the clefts of the ridge? They are heroes with feet of herons—and now they are vanished away. A shimmer like strips of rainbow my sight and mind assails. Are they bells that I hear in the distance? What's weighing my eyebrows down? Oh, how my forehead's aching—as if I'd a red-hot band pressing—! But who the devil put it there I don't know! (*Sinks down.*) A flight o'er the ridge at Gendin—romancing and damned lies! Over the steepest walls with the bride—and drunk for a day—hawks and kites to fight with—threatened by trolls and the like—sporting with crazy lasses—damned romancing and lies! (*Gazes upwards for a long time.*) There hover two brown eagles; the wild geese fly to the south; and I have to trudge and stumble knee-deep in mud and mire. (*Springs up.*) I'll go with them! Cleanse my foulness in a bath of the keenest wind! Up aloft I'll lave my stains in that glittering christening-font! I'll away out over the pastures; I'll fly till I'm pure and clean—fly o'er the ocean waters, o'er the Prince of Engelland's head! Ah, you may stare, you maidens; I'm flying, but not to you. It's no use your waiting———! Yet I might swoop below——— Why, where are the two brown eagles? They've gone to the devil, I think! See, there's the end of a gable, it's rising bit by bit; it's growing out of the rubbish—see, now the door stands wide! Aha! I recognize it, the grandfather's farm new built! Gone are the clouts from the casements and the fence that was tumbling down; lights gleam from every window; they are feasting there within. Listen! The Parson's tapping his knife upon his glass; the Captain's hurled his bottle and broken the mirror to smash. Let them waste and let them squander! Hush, mother—there's plenty more! It's rich John Gynt that is feasting; hurrah for the race of Gynt! What's all the bustle and rumpus? What are the cries and shouts? "Where's Peer?" the Captain is calling—the Parson would drink my health—go in, then, Peer, for the verdict; you shall have it in songs of praise: Great, Peer, were thy beginnings, and in great things thou shalt end.

> [*He leaps forward, but runs his nose against a rock, falls and remains lying on the ground.*

SCENE V

SCENE.—*A mountain-side, with trees in full leaf through which the wind is whispering. Stars are twinkling through the branches. Birds are singing in the treetops.* A WOMAN IN GREEN *crosses the slope. After her follows* PEER GYNT, *performing all sorts of amorous antics.*

THE WOMAN IN GREEN (*stopping and turning round*). Is it true?

PEER GYNT (*drawing his finger across his throat*). As true as my name is Peer; as true as that you are a lovely woman! Will you have me? You'll see how nice I can be; you shall never have to weave or to spin; you shall be fed till you're ready to burst; I promise I never will pull your hair——

THE WOMAN IN GREEN.   Nor strike me, either?

PEER GYNT.   No; is it likely? We sons of kings don't strike our women.

THE WOMAN IN GREEN.   A king's son?

PEER GYNT.   Yes.

THE WOMAN IN GREEN.   I'm the Dovrë-King's daughter.

PEER GYNT.   Are you really? Well, well! How suitable!

THE WOMAN IN GREEN.   In the mountains my father has his castle.

PEER GYNT.   And my mother a larger one, let me tell you.

THE WOMAN IN GREEN.   Do you know my father? His name's King Brosë.

PEER GYNT.   Do you know my mother? Her name's Queen Aase.

THE WOMAN IN GREEN.   The mountains reel when my father's angry.

PEER GYNT.   If my mother begins to scold, they totter.

THE WOMAN IN GREEN.   My father can kick to the highest rafters.

PEER GYNT.   My mother can ride through the fiercest river.

THE WOMAN IN GREEN.   Besides those rags have you other clothing?

PEER GYNT.   Ah, you should see my Sunday garments!

THE WOMAN IN GREEN.   My week-day garments
are gold and silver.

PEER GYNT.   It looks to me more like tow and
grasses.

THE WOMAN IN GREEN.   Yes. There's just one
thing to remember: we mountain folk have an ancient custom; all that we have has a double shape. So when you come
to my father's palace it would not be in the least surprising
if you were inclined to think it merely a heap of ugly stones
and rubbish.

PEER GYNT.   That's just the same as it is with us!
You may think our gold all rust and mildew and mistake
each glittering window-pane for a bundle of worn-out clouts
and stockings.

THE WOMAN IN GREEN.   Black looks like white,
and ugly like fair.

PEER GYNT.   Big looks like little, and filthy like
clean.

THE WOMAN IN GREEN (*falling on his neck*).   Oh,
Peer, I see we are splendidly suited!

PEER GYNT.   Like the hair to the comb—or the leg
to the breeches.

THE WOMAN IN GREEN (*calling over the hillside.*)   My
steed! My steed! My wedding steed!

> {*A gigantic pig comes running in, with a rope's end for
> a halter and an old sack for a saddle.* PEER GYNT
> *swings himself on to its back and seats the* WOMAN
> IN GREEN *in front of him.*

PEER GYNT.   Houp-là! We'll gallop right into the
palace! Come up! Come up, my noble charger!

THE WOMAN IN GREEN (*caressingly*).   And to think
I was feeling so sad and lonely—one never can tell what is
going to happen!

PEER GYNT (*whipping up the pig, which trots off*).   Great
folk are known by the steeds they ride!

SCENE VI

SCENE.—*The Royal Hall of the King of the Trolls. A great assembly of* TROLL COURTIERS, BROWNIES *and* GNOMES. *The* TROLL KING *is seated on his throne, with crown and sceptre. His children and nearest relations sit on either side of him.* PEER GYNT *is standing before him. There is a great uproar in the hall.*

TROLL COURTIERS.   Slay him! The Christian's son
has tempted the fairest daughter of our King!

A YOUNG TROLL.   Let me slash him on the fingers!

ANOTHER.   May I tear his hair out for him?

A TROLL MAIDEN.   Let me bite him on the buttocks!

TROLL WITCH (*with a ladle*).   Let me boil him down
for broth!

ANOTHER (*holding a chopper*).   Shall he toast on a spit
or be browned in a kettle?

THE TROLL KING.   Quiet! Keep calm! (*Beckons to his
counsellors to approach him.*) We must not be too boastful.
Things have been going badly with us lately; we don't feel
sure if we shall last or perish, and can't afford to throw away
assistance. Besides, the lad is almost without blemish, and
well-built, too, as far as I can gather. It's true enough that
he has only *one* head; but then my daughter hasn't more than
one. Three-headed Trolls are going out of fashion; two-

headed even, nowadays aren't common, and *their* heads usually are not up to much. *(To* Peer Gynt.) And so, my lad, it's my daughter you're after?

Peer Gynt.   Yes, if she comes with a kingdom for dowry.

The Troll King.   You shall have half while I am living and the other half when I am done for.

Peer Gynt.   I'm content with that.

The Troll King.   But stop, young fellow, *you've* got to give some pledges also. Break one of them, and our bargain's off and you don't get out of here alive. First, you must promise never to give thought to aught except what within these hills is bounded; shun the day, its deeds, and all the sunlit places.

Peer Gynt.   If I'm called King, 'twill not be hard to do it.

The Troll King.   Secondly—now I'll see how far you're clever———

{Rises from his seat.

The Oldest Troll Courtier *(to* Peer Gynt*)*. Let's see if you've got a wisdom tooth that can crack the nut of our monarch's riddle!

The Troll King.   What is the difference between Trolls and Men?

Peer Gynt.   There isn't any, as far as I can gather; big trolls would roast and little ones would claw you—just as with us if only we dared do it.

The Troll King.   True; we're alike in that and other things, too. Still, just as morning's different from evening, so there's a real difference between us, and I will tell you what it is. Out yonder under the skies, men have a common saying: "Man, to thyself be true!" But here, 'mongst Trolls, "Troll, to thyself be—enough!" it runs.

TROLL COURTIER (*to* PEER GYNT). Well, do you fathom it?

PEER GYNT. It seem rather hazy.

THE TROLL KING. "Enough," my son—that word so fraught with meaning—must be the motto written on your buckler.

PEER GYNT (*scratching his head*). Well, but——

THE TROLL KING. It *must*, if you're to be a king here!

PEER GYNT. All right; so be it. It is not much worse than——

THE TROLL KING. Next you must learn to value rightly our simple, homely way of living. (*He beckons. Two* TROLLS *with pigs' heads, wearing white nightcaps, bring food and drink.*) Our cows give cakes and our oxen mead; no matter whether their taste is sour or sweet; the great thing to remember is that they're home-made and home-brewed.

PEER GYNT (*pushing the things away from him*). The devil take your home-brewed drink! I'll never get used to your country's habits.

THE TROLL KING. The bowl goes with it, and it is golden. Who takes the bowl gets my daughter, too.

PEER GYNT (*thoughtfully*). Of course we're told that a man should master his disposition, and in the long run perhaps the drink will taste less sour. So, here goes!

{Drinks.

THE TROLL KING. Now that was sensibly said. But you spit?

PEER GYNT. I must trust to the force of habit.

THE TROLL KING. Next, you must take off all your Christian clothing; for you must know we boast that in the Dovrë all's mountain-made; we've nothing from the valleys except the bows of silk that deck our tail-tips.

PEER GYNT (*angrily*).   I haven't got a tail!

THE TROLL KING.   Then you shall have one. (*To one of the courtiers.*) See that my Sunday tail is fastened on him.

PEER GYNT.   No, that he shan't! Do you want to make a fool of me?

THE TROLL KING.   Don't try with tail-less rump to court my daughter.

PEER GYNT.   Making a beast of a man!

THE TROLL KING.   My son, you're wrong there; I'd only make a courtly wooer of you. And, as a mark of very highest honour, the bow you wear shall be of bright flame-colour.

PEER GYNT (*reflectively*).   We're taught, of course, that man is but a shadow; and one must pay some heed to use and wont, too. So, tie away!

THE TROLL KING.   You're coming to your senses.

TROLL COURTIER.   Just see how nicely you can wag and wave it!

PEER GYNT (*angrily*).   Now, do you mean to ask anything more of me? Do you want me to give up my Christian faith?

THE TROLL KING.   No, to keep that you are perfectly welcome. Faith is quite free and pays no duty; it's his dress and its cut that a Troll should be known by. If we're of one mind as to manners and costume you're free to believe what would give us the horrors.

PEER GYNT.   You are really, in spite of your many conditions, more reasonable than one might have expected.

THE TROLL KING.   We Trolls are better than our reputation, my son; and that is another difference between you and us. But now we have finished the serious part of the present assembly. Our ears and our eyes shall now be delighted. Let the harp-maid waken the Dovrë-harp's strings, let the dance-maiden tread the Dovrë-hall's floor. (*Music and a dance.*) What do you think of it?

PEER GYNT.   Think of it? H'm——

THE TROLL KING.   Tell me quite openly. What did you see?

PEER GYNT.   See? What I saw was impossibly ugly. A bell-cow thrumming her hoof on a gut-string, a sow in short stockings pretending to dance to it.

THE TROLL COURTIERS.   Eat him!

THE TROLL KING.   Remember his understanding is only human.

TROLL MAIDENS.   Oh, tear his eyes out and cut off his ears!

THE WOMAN IN GREEN (*weeping*).   Are we to endure it, my sister and I, when we've played and danced?

PEER GYNT.   Oho, was it you? Well, you know, at a banquet a joke is a joke—no offence was intended.

THE WOMAN IN GREEN.   Will you swear to me you were only joking?

PEER GYNT.   The dance and the music were both delightful.

THE TROLL KING.   It's a funny thing, this human nature; it clings to a man with such persistence. Suppose we fight it and it is wounded, there may be a scar, but it heals up quickly. My son-in-law's now most accommodating; he has willingly cast off his Christian breeches, willingly drunk of the mead-filled goblet, willingly tied on a tail behind him—is so willing, in fact, to do all we ask him that I certainly thought the old Adam banished for good and all; then, all of a sudden, we find him uppermost. Yes, my son, you certainly must undergo some treatment to cure this troublesome human nature.

PEER GYNT.   What will you do?

THE TROLL KING.   I'll scratch you slightly in the left eye, and then your vision will be oblique, and all you look on will seem to you to be perfection. Then I'll cut out your right-hand window——

PEER GYNT.   You're drunk!

THE TROLL KING (*laying some sharp instruments on the table*).   See, here are the glazier's tools. You must be tamed like a raging bullock; then you'll perceive that your bride is lovely, and never again will your sight deceive you with dancing sows or bell-cows thrumming——

PEER GYNT.   That's fool's talk.

THE OLDEST COURTIER.   It's the Troll King's word; he is the wise man and you the fool.

THE TROLL KING.   Just think what a lot of trouble and worry you will be rid of for good and all. Remember, too, that the eye is the source of the bitter, searing flood of tears.

PEER GYNT.   That's true; and it says in the family Bible: "If thine eye offend thee, pluck it out." But, tell me, when will my sight recover and be as it is now?

THE TROLL KING.   Never, my friend.

PEER GYNT.   Oh, really! Then I must decline with thanks.

THE TROLL KING.   But what do you mean to do?

PEER GYNT.   To leave you.

THE TROLL KING.   Softly! It's easy to get within here; but the Troll King's gate doesn't open outwards.

PEER GYNT.   You surely don't mean to detain me by force?

THE TROLL KING.   Now listen, Prince Peer, and give way to reason. You're cut out for a Troll. Why, look, already you bear yourself quite in a Troll-like fashion! And you want to become one, don't you?

PEER GYNT.   Of course. In return for a bride and a
well-founded kingdom I'm not unwilling to sacrifice
something; but all things have their natural limit. I have
taken a tail, it is true; but then I can undo the knots that
our friend has tied and take the thing off. I have shed my
breeches; they were old and patched; but that won't prevent
me from putting them on if I have a mind to. I shall probably find it just as easy to deal with your Trollish way of
living. I can easily swear that a cow's a maiden; an oath's
not a difficult thing to swallow. But to know that one never
can get one's freedom—not even to die as a human being—
to end one's days as a Troll of the mountains—never go
back, as you tell me plainly—that is a thing that I'll not
submit to.

THE TROLL KING.   Now, on my sins, I'm getting
angry; I'm not in the mood to be made a fool of. You scurvy
lout! Do you know who I am? To begin with, you made too
free with my daughter——

PEER GYNT.   That's a lie in your throat!

THE TROLL KING.   And you have to marry her.

PEER GYNT.   Do you dare accuse me of——?

THE TROLL KING.   Can you deny that she was the
object of all your desire?

PEER GYNT (whistles).   But no more than that. What
the deuce does that matter?

THE TROLL KING.   You human beings are always
the same. You are always ready to talk of your souls, but
heed nothing really save what is tangible. You think desires
are things that don't matter? Wait; your own eyes will prove
to you shortly——

PEER GYNT.   It's no use baiting your hook with lies!

THE TROLL KING.   My Peer, ere the year's out you'll
be a father.

PEER GYNT.   Unlock the doors. I'm going.

THE TROLL KING.   We'll send you the brat in a goat-skin.

PEER GYNT (*wiping the sweat from his brow*).   I wish I could wake up!

THE TROLL KING.   Shall we send to your Palace?

PEER GYNT.   Oh, send to the Parish!

THE TROLL KING.   As you like, Prince Peer; it's your affair solely. But one thing is certain—what's done can't be undone, and you will see how your offspring will grow up! Mongrels like that grow remarkably quickly——

PEER GYNT.   Oh, come, old chap, don't go at me like a bullock! Fair maiden, be reasonable! Let's come to terms. I have to confess that I'm neither a prince nor rich; and, however you take my measure, I'm sure you won't find you've made much of a bargain.

> {*The* WOMAN IN GREEN *faints and is carried out
> by the* TROLL MAIDENS.

THE TROLL KING (*looks at him for a while with a contemptuous expression, then says*): Dash him to bits on the rocks, my good children!

YOUNG TROLLS.   Dad, mayn't we first play at Owls and Eagles? Or the Wolf-Game? Or Grey Mouse and Red-Eyed Pussy?

THE TROLL KING.   Yes, but be quick. I'm angry and sleepy. Good night!

> {*Goes.*

PEER GYNT (*hunted by the* YOUNG TROLLS).   Let me go, you young devils!

> {*Tries to climb up the chimney.*

YOUNG TROLLS.   Hobgoblins! Brownies! Come, bite him!

PEER GYNT.   Ow!

{Tries to get away through the cellar-flap.

YOUNG TROLLS.   Stop all the holes up!

TROLL COURTIER.   How the youngsters enjoy it!

PEER GYNT *(fighting with a little* TROLL *who has bitten deep into his ear).*   You filth, let go!

TROLL COURTIER *(rapping* PEER GYNT *over the knuckles).*   A little respect for a king's son, you scoundrel!

PEER GYNT.   Ah! A rat hole!

{Runs towards it.

YOUNG TROLLS.   Stop up the holes, Brownie brothers!

PEER GYNT.   The old man was foul, but the young ones are worse!

YOUNG TROLLS.   Flay him!

PEER GYNT.   I wish I were small as a mouse!

YOUNG TROLLS *(swarming about him).*   Don't let him escape!

PEER GYNT.   I wish I were a louse!

YOUNG TROLLS.   Now jump on his face!

PEER GYNT *(smothered in Trolls).*   Help, mother, I'm dying!

{Church bells are heard afar off.

YOUNG TROLLS.   Bells in the Valley! The Black-frock's Cows!

{The TROLLS *disperse in a turmoil and wild shrieks. The Hall falls to pieces. Everything disappears.*

SCENE VII

SCENE.—*Pitch darkness,* PEER GYNT *is heard slashing and hitting about him with a branch of a tree.*

PEER GYNT.   Answer! Who are you?

A VOICE IN THE DARKNESS.   Myself!

PEER GYNT.   Let me pass, then!

VOICE.   Go round about, Peer! Room enough on the mountain.

> {PEER GYNT *tries to pass another way, but runs up against something.*

PEER GYNT.   Who are you?

VOICE.   Myself. Can you say as much?

PEER GYNT.   I can say what I like, and my sword can strike! Look out for yourself! I'm going to smash you! King Saul slew hundreds; Peer Gynt slays thousands! *(Hits about him wildly.)* Who are you?

VOICE.   Myself.

PEER GYNT.   That's a silly answer, and you can keep it. It tells me nothing. What are you?

VOICE.   The great Boyg.

PEER GYNT.   No, are you really? Things were black before! now some grey is showing. Out of my way, Boyg!

VOICE.   Go round about, Peer!

PEER GYNT.   No, through you! *(Hits out wildly.)* He's down! *(Tries to get on, but always runs up against something.)* Ha, ha! Are there more of you?

VOICE.   The Boyg, Peer Gynt. The one and only. The Boyg that's unwounded, the Boyg that was hurt. The Boyg that was dead and the Boyg that's alive.

PEER GYNT (*throwing away his branch*).   My weapon's bewitched; but I have my fists!

{*Strikes out in front of him.*

VOICE.   Yes, put your trust in your fists and strength! Ho, ho! Peer Gynt, they'll bring you out top!

PEER GYNT.   Backward or forward, it's just as far.— Out or in, the way's as narrow. It's there!—and there!—and all about me! I think I've got out, and I'm back in the midst of it. What's your name! Let me see you! Say what you are!

VOICE.   The Boyg.

PEER GYNT (*feeling round him*).   Neither dead, nor alive; slime and mistiness; no shape or form! It's as if one were smothered amidst any number of bears that are growling at being waked up! (*Shrieks.*) Why don't you hit out at me!

VOICE.   The Boyg's not so foolish as that.

PEER GYNT.   Oh, strike at me!

VOICE.   The Boyg doesn't strike.

PEER GYNT.   Come, fight! You *shall* fight with me!

VOICE.   The great Boyg can triumph without any fighting.

PEER GYNT.   I'd far rather it were the Brownies tormenting me! Or even as much as a one-year-old Troll! Just something to fight with—and not this blank nothingness! It's snoring now! Boyg!

VOICE.   What is it?

PEER GYNT.   Show fight, will you!

VOICE.   The great Boyg can get all he wishes by gentleness.

PEER GYNT (*biting his own hands and arms*).   Oh, for claws and teeth that would tear my flesh! I must see a drop of my own blood flow!

{A Sound is heard like the beating of wings of great birds.

BIRDS' CRIES. Is he coming, Boyg?

VOICE. Yes, foot by foot.

BIRDS' CRIES. Sisters afar off, fly to meet us!

PEER GYNT. If you mean to save me, girl, be quick! Don't hang your head and look down blushing. Your prayer-book! Hit him straight in the eye with it!

BIRDS' CRIES. He's failing!

VOICE. He's ours.

BIRDS' CRIES. Come, sisters, quickly!

PEER GYNT. An hour of torture such as this is too dear a price to pay for life.

{Sinks down.

BIRDS' CRIES. Boyg, he is down! Boyg, seize him! Seize him!

{Church bells and the singing of psalms are heard in the distance.

VOICE *(with a gasp, as the Boyg gradually dwindles away to nothing).* He was too strong. There were women behind him.

SCENE VIII

SCENE.—*On the hillside outside a hut on* AASE'S *mountain pasture. It is sunrise. The door of the hut is barred. Everything is empty and still.* PEER GYNT *lies asleep by the hut. Presently he wakes and looks around him with listless and heavy eyes.*

PEER GYNT *(spitting).* I'd give the world for a pick-led herring! *(He spits again; then he sees* HELGA *approaching, carrying a basket of food.)* You here, youngster? What do you want?

HELGA.   It was Solveig——

PEER GYNT *(springing up).*   Where is she?

HELGA.   Behind the hut.

SOLVEIG *(from behind the hut).*   If you come any nearer, I'll run away!

PEER GYNT *(standing still).*   Perhaps you're afraid I shall carry you off?

SOLVEIG.   For shame!

PEER GYNT.   Do you know where I was last night? The Troll King's daughter is hunting me down.

SOLVEIG.   'Twas well done, then, that we rang the bells.

PEER GYNT.   Oh, Peer Gynt's not quite the lad to get caught—What's that you say?

HELGA *(crying).*   She's running away. *(Runs after Solveig.)* Wait for me!

PEER GYNT *(gripping her by the arm).*   See what I've got in my pocket! A fine silver button! And you shall have it if you speak up for me!

HELGA.   Oh, let me go!

PEER GYNT.   Take it, then.

HELGA.   Oh, let me go!—and my basket!

PEER GYNT.   You had better look out if you don't——!

HELGA.   Oh, you frighten me!

PEER GYNT *(quietly, as he lets her go).*   No; all I meant was: don't let her forget me!

*{*HELGA *runs off.*

Act III

Scene I

SCENE.—*The depths of a pine-wood. It is a grey autumn day, and snow is falling.* PEER GYNT *is in his shirtsleeves, felling timber. He has just tackled a tall tree with crooked branches.*

PEER GYNT.   Oh, yes, you're tough, my ancient friend, but that won't help you; you're coming down! *(Sets to work again.)* I know you're wearing a coat of mail; but I'll slash through, were it never so strong. Yes, you may shake your crooked arms; I daresay you're both fierce and angry, but all the same you shall bow to me———! *(Suddenly breaks off sullenly.)* What lies! It's only an ancient tree. What lies! I'm fighting no mail-clad foe; it's only a fir with its bark all cracked. It's toilsome work, this felling timber; but the devil's own job when all the time one's dreams get mixed up with one's working. All that must stop———this daytime dreaming and always being in the clouds. My lad, remember that you're an outlaw! Your only shelter's in this forest. *(Works again hurriedly for a while.)* An outlaw, yes. You have no mother to bring you food and spread your table. If you want to eat, you must help yourself; get what you can from the woods and the stream, forage for sticks if you want a fire, look to yourself for everything. If you need clothes, you must skin a deer; if you want a wall to put round your house,

you must break the stones; if you want to build, you must
fell the timber and shoulder it and carry it to the spot you've
chosen. *(He lets his axe fall and stares in front of him.)* I'll build
a beauty! Up on the roof I'll have a tower and weather-vane,
and on the gable-end I'll carve a lovely mermaid. Vane and
locks shall be of brass, and window-panes shall shine so
bright that from afar people shall wonder what it is that
they see gleaming in the sun. *(Laughs bitterly.)* Damned lies!
Why, there I go again! Remember that you're an outlaw,
boy! *(Sets to work feverishly.)* A well-thatched hut is quite
enough to keep out both the frost and rain. *(Looks up at the
tree.)* It's giving way. One more stroke! There! He's down
and fallen all his length, and all the undergrowth is quivering. *(Sets to work to lop off the branches, all at once he stops and
listens, with uplifted axe.)* There's someone coming! Ingrid's
father—— Trying to catch me treacherously! *(Hides behind
a tree and peeps out.)* A boy! Just one. And he looks frightened.
He's glancing round him. What is that he's hiding underneath his jacket? A sickle. Now he stands and looks——
He lays his hand upon a log—— What now? Why does he
brace himself——? Ugh! He has chopped a finger off! And
now he's bleeding like a pig—— And now he runs off with
his hand wrapped in a clout. *(Comes forward.)* He must be
mad! Chopped it right off!—a precious finger! And did it,
too, as if he meant it. Oho, I see! If one's not anxious to
serve His Gracious Majesty that is the only way. So that's
it! They would have called him for the army, but he, I see,
would be exempted. Still, to cut off——? To lose for ever—
—? The thought, perhaps—the wish—the will—— Those
I could understand; but really to *do* the deed! Ah, no—that
beats me!

{Shakes his head a little; then resumes his work.

Scene II

SCENE.—*A room in* AASE'S *house. Everything is in disorder. The clothes-chest is standing open; clothes lie scattered about; a cat is lying on the bed.* AASE *and* KARI *are trying to put things in order.*

AASE (*running to one side of the room*).   Kari, tell me——

KARI.   What is it?

AASE.   Tell me—— Where is——? Where shall I find——? Oh, tell me, where is——? What am I looking for? I'm going crazy! Where's the chest key?

KARI.   It's in the keyhole.

AASE.   What's that rumbling?

KARI.   The last load going off to Hægstad.

AASE (*weeping*).   I wish they were taking me in my coffin! What we poor creatures have to suffer! God pity me! The whole house emptied! What Hægstad left, the Judge has taken. They've scarcely left me with a rag to put upon my back. It's shameful to have pronounced so hard a sentence! (*Sits down on the edge of the bed.*) The farm's gone now, and all our land. He's a hard man, but the Law was harder; no one to help me—none showed mercy—— Peer gone, and no one to advise me.

KARI.   You've got this house until you die.

AASE.   Oh, yes—the bread of charity, for me and for my cat!

KARI.   Old mother, God help you! Peer has cost you dear.

AASE.   My Peer? I think you've lost your senses! They got their Ingrid, safe and sound. They should have rightly blamed the Devil; he is the culprit, and no other; 'twas he, the ugly beast, that tempted my poor dear boy!

KARI. Had you not better send for the priest? For all you know, things may be worse than you believe.

AASE. Send for the priest? Perhaps I'd better. (*Gets up.*) No, no—I cannot! I'm his mother; I must help the boy—it's not only my duty; I must do my best, when everyone fails me. They've left him that coat. I must get it patched. I wish I had dared to keep the bed-cover! Where are the stockings?

KARI. There, with that rubbish.

AASE (*fumbling among the things*). What's this? Look here! An old casting-ladle! He used to pretend to mould buttons with this, melt them and shape them and stamp them, too. Once, when we'd company, in came the boy and begged of his father a bit of tin. "Not tin," said John, "King Christian's coin! A silver coin to melt and show that you're the son of rich John Gynt." May God forgive him, for he was drunk; and when he was drunk it was all the same, tin or gold. Ah, here are the stockings! They are all in holes; I must darn them, Kari.

KARI. They certainly need it.

AASE. When that is done, I must go to bed. I feel so bad, so wretchedly ill. (*Joyfully.*) Oh, look here, Kari! Two flannel shirts that they have forgotten!

KARI. Aye, so they have.

AASE. That's a lucky find. You might put one of them aside. Or—no, I think we'll take them both; the one he has on is so thin and worn.

KARI. But, Aase, you know that it's a sin!

AASE. Oh, yes; but you know the parson tells us that all our sins may be forgiven.

SCENE III

SCENE.—*Outside a newly built hut in the forest. Reindeer horns over the door. Deep snow everywhere. It is nightfall.* PEER GYNT *is standing fixing a heavy wooden bolt to the door.*

PEER GYNT (*laughing now and then*).   There must be a bolt, to fasten my door against the Troll-folk and men and women. There must be a bolt, to keep me safe from all the plaguy crowd of goblins. They'll come when it's dark, and I'll hear them knocking: "Open, Peer, we are quick as thoughts! Under the bed, on the hearth in the ashes, you'll hear us creeping and crawling about; we'll fly down the chimney like fiery dragons. Hee-hee! Do you think your nails and planks can save you from plaguy goblin-thoughts?"

    {SOLVEIG *comes over the snow on skis; she has a shawl over her head and a bundle in her hand.*

SOLVEIG.   God bless your work. You must not reject me. I had your message, and you must take me.

PEER GYNT.   Solveig! It can't be——! Yes, it is! And not afraid to come so near me!

SOLVEIG.   I had your message from little Helga, and others I had from the winds and the silence. There was one in all that your mother told me, and others that came to me in my dreams. The dreary nights and the empty days brought me the message that I must come. All light had gone from my life down yonder; I had neither the heart to laugh nor to weep. I could not tell what was in your mind; I could only tell what I needs must do.

PEER GYNT.   But your father?

SOLVEIG.   I've no one on God's wide earth that I can call father or mother now; I've left them for ever.

PEER GYNT.   Solveig, my dear—— To come to me?

SOLVEIG.   Yes, to you alone; you must be all to me—
friend and comfort. *(In tears.)* The worst was leaving my
little sister; and worse than that, to leave my father; and
worst of all to leave her who carried me at her breast; no,
God forgive me, the worst indeed was the bitter sorrow that
I must part from all my dear ones!

PEER GYNT.   And do you know the heavy sentence
the law pronounced? They've taken from me everything that
I had or might have.

SOLVEIG.   'Twas not for what you had or might have
I give up what was dearest to me.

PEER GYNT.   And do you know that if I venture
beyond this forest I am forfeit if any man can lay hand on
me?

SOLVEIG.   When I asked my way as I came hither,
they questioned me—where was I going? "I'm going home":
that was my answer.

PEER GYNT.   Ah, then I need no bolts to guard
me, no locks against the powers of evil! My hunter's hut
is consecrated if you deign enter it and live there. Dear,
let me look at you! Not too near you—— I'd only look
at you! How lovely, how pure you are! Let my arms lift
you! How slim and light you are, my Solveig! I'd carry
you for ever, dearest, and never weary! I'll not soil you;
I'll hold your warm and lovely body at arms' length from
me! Ah, my Solveig, can I believe I've made you love me?
Both night and day 'tis what I've longed for. See, I have
built this little dwelling—— It shall come down; it's
cramped and ugly——

SOLVEIG.   Little or big, I'm happy here. Here one can
breathe, in the buffeting wind. Down yonder 'twas sultry; I
felt hemmed in; it was partly that, that drove me away. But

here, where one hears the fir-trees soughing—— Such song
and silence!—I feel at home.

PEER GYNT.   But, dear, are you sure? It means for
ever!

SOLVEIG.   There's no way back on the road I have
trodden.

PEER GYNT.   You're mine, then! Go in! I would see
you within! Go in! I will fetch some wood for a fire, to warm
you snugly and flicker brightly; you shall sit soft and never
shiver. (*He unbars the door, and* SOLVEIG *goes in. He stands silent
for a moment, then laughs aloud for joy and leaps into the air.*) My
princess! Now she is found and won! Now my palace shall
spring into being!

> {*Seizes his axe and crosses over towards the trees. At the
> same moment an elderly woman in a tattered green gown
> advances out of the wood; an ugly child with a flagon
> in his hand limps after her, holding on to her skirt.*

THE WOMAN.   Good evening, Peer Light-Foot!

PEER GYNT.   What is it? Who are you?

THE WOMAN.   Old friends, Peer Gynt! My hut is
quite near here. We're neighbours.

PEER GYNT.   Indeed? I was not aware of it.

THE WOMAN.   As your hut grew up, so mine grew
beside it.

PEER GYNT (*trying to get away*).   I'm in a great hurry.

THE WOMAN.   You always were that; but, trudging
along, in the end I come up with you.

PEER GYNT.   Old dame, you're mistaken!

THE WOMAN.   I know I was once; that day when
you made me such wonderful promises.

PEER GYNT.   I made you promises? Why, what the
devil——?

THE WOMAN.   Do you mean you've forgotten the

night when you drank at my father's? Do you mean you've forgotten——

PEER GYNT.   I mean I've forgotten what never took place to remember! What nonsense is this? And when last did we meet?

THE WOMAN.   The last time we met was the first time we met. *(To the child.)* Give your father a drink; I think he is thirsty.

PEER GYNT.   His father? You're drunk! Do you mean that this urchin——?

THE WOMAN.   You're not going to say that you can't recognize him? Have you eyes? Can't you see that he's lame in the shanks as you're lame in your mind?

PEER GYNT.   Do you mean to pretend——?

THE WOMAN.   You can't wriggle out of it!

PEER GYNT.   That long-legged brat——?

THE WOMAN.   He has grown very fast.

PEER GYNT.   Why, you ugly old hag, do you dare to assert that this——?

THE WOMAN.   Listen, Peer Gynt; you're as coarse as a bullock. *(Weeps.)* Oh, how can I help it if I'm not as fair as I was when you tempted me out on the hill-side up there in the mountains? And when in the autumn my travail came on me, I'd only the Devil to act as a midwife; so it isn't surprising I lost all my beauty. But if you would see me as fair as before, you've only to turn out that girl that's in there, out of your house and your mind and your sight; do that, dearest lad, and my ill-looks will vanish!

PEER GYNT.   Get away, you old witch!

THE WOMAN.   You shall see if I will!

PEER GYNT.   I'll break your head for you!

THE WOMAN.   Try, if you dare! You'll find me, Peer, a hard nut to crack! Every day I shall be back again, peeping at doors and spying on both of you. When you and your girl are sitting together, and you are inclined for cuddling and fondling, you'll find me beside you, claiming my share of it. She and I will share you—turn about. Good-bye, dear boy. If you like the prospect, then wed her tomorrow!

PEER GYNT.   You devil's nightmare!

THE WOMAN.   But I had forgotten! You've got to look after your little son—this graceful urchin! Come on, little imp, will you go to your father?

THE BOY (*spitting at* PEER).   If I had an axe, I'd split you in two with it! Just wait!

THE WOMAN (*kissing the* BOY). What a head he's got on his shoulders! When you've grown up you'll be just like your father!

PEER GYNT (*stamping his foot*).   I wish you——

THE WOMAN.   As far off as now we are near you?

PEER GYNT (*clinching his fists*).   And all this comes——

THE WOMAN.   Just of thoughts and desires! Hard luck for you, Peer!

PEER GYNT.   It's hardest for her—for Solveig—my loveliest, purest treasure!

THE WOMAN.   Oh, yes; the innocent always suffer— as the Devil said when his mother thrashed him because his father had come home drunk!

> {*She moves off into the wood with the* BOY, *who throws the flagon behind him.*

PEER GYNT (*after a long silence*).   "Round about," said the Boyg; that's how I must go.—My palace has tumbled about my ears! She was so near me; and now there has risen a wall between us, and all in a moment my joy is gone and everything's ugly. "Round about"—ah, yes; there's no straight road that leads through this from me to her. No straight road? All the same, there might be. If I remember aright, the Bible says something somewhere about repentance—but I've no Bible, and I've forgotten the most of it, and in this forest there's not a thing that will give me guidance. Repent? It might take years to do it before I found the way. And, meanwhile, a life that's empty, ugly, dreary; and in the end from shreds and fragments to try and patch the thing together? One can patch up a broken fiddle, but not a watch-spring. If one tramples on growing things they're spoiled for ever.—But, surely, the old witch was lying! I can put all those ugly doings out of my sight! But— can I put them out of my mind? I shall be haunted by lurking memories—of Ingrid—of those three girls upon the hillside. Will they come, too, and jeer and threaten, and beg of me to hold them closely or lift them tenderly at arms' length? It's no use! Were my arms as long as fir-trees' stems or pine-trees' branches, I should be holding *her* too near to set her down again unsullied. I must find some way round about, without a thought of gain or loss; some way to free me from such thoughts and shut them from my mind for ever. *(Takes a few steps towards the hut, then stops.)* But—go in now? Disgraced and soiled? With all these Troll-folk at my heels? Speak, and yet not tell all? Confess, and still be hiding something from her? *(Throws away his axe.)* No, no—to go and meet her now, such as I am, were sacrilege.

*(*SOLVEIG *appears at the door of the hut.*

SOLVEIG. Are you coming, dear?

PEER GYNT *(below his breath).* "Go round about"!

SOLVEIG. What do you say?

PEER GYNT. Dear, you must wait. It's dark, and I've a heavy load.

SOLVEIG.   I'll come and help you bear the load.

PEER GYNT.   No, do not come! Stay where you are! I'll bear the whole of it.

SOLVEIG.   But, dear, don't be too long.

PEER GYNT.   Be patient, child; whether the time is long or short, you must just wait.

SOLVEIG (*nodding to him*).   Yes, I will wait.

> {PEER GYNT *goes off along the forest path.* SOLVEIG *remains standing at the half-open door.*

SCENE IV

SCENE.—AASE'S *house. It is evening. A log fire is burning on the hearth and lights up the room. A cat is lying on a chair at the foot of a bed on which* AASE *is lying, fumbling restlessly with the sheets.*

AASE.   Ah me, is my son never coming? The nights are so weary and long. I've no one to take him a message, and so much to say to him now, my time's running short— oh, how quickly! To think that the end should be this! If only I'd known, I would never have said a hard word to the boy!

> {PEER GYNT *comes in.*

PEER GYNT.   Good evening!

AASE.   My boy! Oh, God bless you! My dearest, at last you have come! But how have you dared to come hither? Your life is in danger, you know.

PEER GYNT.   My life?—oh, my life doesn't matter. I had to come down to you now.

AASE. And Kari!—she said that you wouldn't! Ah, now I can leave you in peace.

PEER GYNT. Leave me? Why, what are you saying? And where do you think you can go?

AASE. Ah, Peer, it's the end that's approaching; I haven't much longer to live.

PEER GYNT *(turning away abruptly and walking across the room).* I was running away from my sorrows and thought at least here I'd be free——! Are you cold? Are your hands and your feet cold?

AASE. Yes, Peer; you'll be done with me soon. When my eyes lose their light you must close them—but tenderly, carefully, Peer. And then you must get me a coffin and see that it's handsome and fine. Ah, no, I forgot——

PEER GYNT. Do be quiet! Time enough for all that by-and-by.

AASE. Yes, yes. *(Looks uneasily round the room.)* Do you see what a little they've left me? It's all one to them.

PEER GYNT *(with a grimace).* There you go! *(Harshly.)* Yes, I know I am guilty. But what do you think is the good of raking it up to remind me?

AASE. No! It was the drink was to blame. That damnable drink that destroyed you, my boy; for you know you were drunk and didn't know what you were doing. Besides—that wild ride on the buck!—I'm sure it was not to be wondered if you were not right in your head.

PEER GYNT. Never mind all that nonsense and rubbish; never mind about anything now. Let's put off serious thinking till later—another day. *(Sits down on the edge of the bed.)* Now, mother, let's have a gossip and talk of all sorts of things, except what's ugly and horrid and hurts—let's forget all that. Bless me! Why, there's old pussy! To think that he's still alive!

AASE.   At night he seems so uneasy; and we all know what that means!

PEER GYNT (*turning away*).   What is the news in the district?

AASE (*smiling*).   They do say that hereabouts there's a girl that longs for the mountains——

PEER GYNT (*hastily*).   Mads Moen—is he content?

AASE.   They say that she will not listen to the old folks' prayers and tears. You ought to go and see her; maybe you could find a way——

PEER GYNT.   And what's become of the blacksmith?

AASE.   Oh, bother the dirty smith! I'd so much rather tell you her name—that girl's, you know——

PEER GYNT.   No, we're going to have a gossip and talk of all sorts of things, except what's ugly and horrid and hurts—let's forget all that. Shall I fetch you a drink? Are you thirsty? Can you stretch in that little bed? Let me look—why, this is surely the bed I had as a boy! Do you remember your sitting beside my bed at night smoothing the bed-spread over and singing me rhymes and songs?

AASE.   Yes, and we played at sleighing, when your father had gone away—the bed-spread was our apron, and the floor an ice-bound fjord.

PEER GYNT.   Yes, but do you remember the finest bit of it all—our pair of prancing horses?

AASE.   Why, yes—of course I do. 'Twas Kari's cat we borrowed and put up on a stool.

PEER GYNT.   To Soria-Moria Castle, that's westward of the moon and eastward of the sunrise, o'er hill and dale we flew. A stick that we found in the cupboard made you a splendid whip.

AASE.   I sat up like the driver——

PEER GYNT.   Yes, and you shook the reins; and

turned round as we galloped, to ask if I were cold. God bless you, you old scolder! You were a dear to me—— Why do you groan?

AASE.   It's my back, Peer; it's sore from lying here.

PEER GYNT.   Stretch up and I'll support you. There—now you're lying snug.

AASE (uneasily).   I want to get away, Peer.

PEER GYNT.   To get away?

AASE.   Ah, yes—it's what I'm always longing.

PEER GYNT.   What senseless talk is that? See, let me smooth the bed-clothes and then sit on the bed,—now, we will make the time fly with singing rhymes and songs.

AASE.   No, let me have my prayer-book; my mind is ill at ease.

PEER GYNT.   In Soria-Moria Castle they're having a splendid feast. Rest back upon the cushions; I'll drive you quickly there——

AASE.   But, dear, am I invited?

PEER GYNT.   Of course—and I am, too. (He throws a cord round the back of the chair on which the cat is lying, takes a stick in his hand and sits down on the foot of the bed.) Gee up! Get on with you, Blackie! Mother, you're sure you're not cold? Aha! Now we shall be moving, when Granë kicks up his heels!

AASE.   But, Peer—I hear something ringing——

PEER GYNT.   It's the glittering sleigh-bells, dear.

AASE.   They sound so strange and hollow!

PEER GYNT.   We're driving over a fjord.

AASE.   I'm frightened! What is it, that sighing and moaning so wild and drear?

PEER GYNT.   It's only the firs on the hillside whispering. Just sit still.

AASE.   I seem to see lights in the distance. What is it that's glistening there?

PEER GYNT.   It's the window and gates of the Castle. Can you hear the dancers?

AASE.   Yes.

PEER GYNT.   And outside stands Saint Peter asking you to come in.

AASE.   Does he greet me?

PEER GYNT.   Yes, with honour, and offers you sweetest wine.

AASE.   Wine! Does he offer cakes, too?

PEER GYNT.   A plateful of them, yes! And our parson's wife preparing your coffee and your dessert.

AASE.   What! Shall I really meet her?

PEER GYNT.   As soon and as oft as you please.

AASE.   You're driving your poor old mother to a splendid party, Peer!

PEER GYNT (*smacking his whip*).   Gee up! Get on with you, Blackie!

AASE.   Are you sure that you know the way?

PEER GYNT (*smacking his whip again*).   I can see the road.

AASE.   But the journey makes me feel ill and tired.

PEER GYNT.   I can see the Castle before me; the drive will soon be done.

AASE.   I'll lie back with my eyes shut and trust to you, my boy!

PEER GYNT.   Now show your paces, Granë! The Castle is all agog; the folk all swarm to the gateway; Peer Gynt and his mother arrive! Why, what's that, Mister Saint Peter? You won't let my mother in? You must look far, I can tell you, to find a worthier soul. Of myself I will say nothing; I can turn back to the gate. I'll take pot-luck, if you'll have

me; if not, it's all one to me. Like the Devil in the pulpit,
I've told a heap of lies and have called my dear old mother
a silly old hen, I know, because she cackled and scolded; but
things must be different here. You must respect and revere
her, sincerely and honestly; you'll not get anyone better from
our parts nowadays.—Oho! Here's God the father! Saint Peter, you'll catch it now! *(Speaks in a deep voice.)* "Just stop
that bullying, will you! Mother Aase is welcome here!"
(Laughs aloud and turns to his mother.) I knew how 'twould be!
Saint Peter is singing small enough now! *(His voice takes on
an anxious tone.)* Why do you stare so, mother? Have you lost
your senses, dear? *(Goes to the head of the bed.)* You mustn't
lie and stare so——! Speak, mother; it's I, your boy! *(Feels
her forehead and hands cautiously; then throws the cord away on to
the chair and says in a low voice):* So it's that!—You may rest
now, Granë; our journey's over and done. *(Shuts her eyes and
bends over her.)* Thanks, dear, for all you gave me, thrashings
and kisses alike! And now it's for you to thank me——
(Presses his cheek against her lips.) There—that was the driver's
fee.

*{*KARI *comes in.*

KARI.   What? Peer! Then her deepest sorrow and
grieving will be forgot! Good Lord, how sound she is sleeping! Or is she——?

PEER GYNT.   Hush, she is dead.

*{*KARI *weeps by* AASE'S *body.* PEER GYNT *walks to
and fro in the room; at last he stops by the bedside.*

PEER GYNT.   See that she's decently buried. I must
try to escape from here.

KARI.   Where shall you go?

PEER GYNT.   To the sea-coast.

KARI.   So far! Aye, and farther still.

*{*Goes out.*

Act IV

Scene I

SCENE.—*A grove of palm-trees on the south-west coast of Morocco. A dining-table is spread under an awning; rush matting underfoot. Farther back in the grove hammocks are hanging. A steam yacht, flying the Norwegian and American flags, is flying off the shore. A jolly-boat is drawn up on the beach. It is nearly sundown.* PEER GYNT, *now a good-looking middle-aged man, dressed in a neat travelling-suit, with a pair of gold-mounted eyeglasses dangling on his breast, is presiding at table as host to* MR. COTTON, MONSIEUR BALLON, HERR VON EBER-KOPF, AND HERR TRUMPETERSTRAALE. *The party have just finished a meal.* PEER GYNT *is passing the wine.*

PEER GYNT.   Drink, gentlemen! If man is meant for pleasure, let him take his pleasure. The past's the past—what's done is done—so we are taught. What may I give you?

HERR TRUMPETERSTRAALE.   As host, dear brother Gynt, you're splendid!

PEER GYNT.   The credit's just as much my purse's, my cook's and steward's——

MR. COTTON.   Very well, then here's a health to all the four!

MONSIEUR BALLON.   Monsieur, your taste—your

ton—is such as nowadays one seldom meets with amongst men living *en garçon*—a certain *je ne sais quoi*——

HERR VON EBERKOPF.   Quite so; a breath, a gleam of introspection—world-citizenship's inspiration; a glance that pierces clouds, that's free from any narrow prejudices; a glimpse of higher criticism; a simple nature coupled with a life's experience and thereby uplifted to the highest power. I think that's what you meant—eh, Monsieur?

MONSIEUR BALLON.   Yes, very possibly. In French it doesn't sound quite so impressive.

HERR VON EBERKOPF.   Of course not. French is somewhat cramped. But if we want to trace the source of this phenomenon——

PEER GYNT.   That's easy; it's just because I've never married. Why, gentlemen, the thing's as clear as daylight. What's a man's first duty? The answer's brief: To be himself—to take good care of all that touches himself and what is his. But how can he do this if his existence is that of a pack-camel laden with someone else's weal and woe?

HERR VON EBERKOPF.   But I dare say you've had to fight for this self-centred concentration?

PEER GYNT.   Oh, yes, I've had to fight for it, but I have always won the honours; though once I very nearly fell into a trap, for all my cunning. I was a wild, good-looking spark and let my roving fancy capture a girl who was of royal blood——

MONSIEUR BALLON.   Of royal blood?

PEER GYNT (*carelessly*).   Or very nearly. You know——

HERR TRUMPETERSTRAALE (*thumping on the table*).   These damned aristocrats!

PEER GYNT (*shrugging his shoulders*).   These bogus

Highnesses, whose pride is to keep off from their escutcheon the slightest speck of what's plebeian.

MR. COTTON.   And so it came to nothing, then?

MONSIEUR BALLON.   The family opposed the match?

PEER GYNT.   Quite the reverse!

MONSIEUR BALLON.   Ah!

PEER GYNT *(discreetly)*.   Well, you see, things took a turn which made them think that it was high time we were married. But, to be candid, the affair from first to last was most distasteful. In certain things I'm very dainty, and also like my independence; and when her father came and hinted that he would make it a condition that I should change my name and status and lose my own nobility—with lots of similar conditions I could not stomach or accept—I gracefully retired from it, refused the father's ultimatum and gave my youthful bride her congé. *(Drums on the table with his fingers and says with a pious air.)*   Ah, yes, there is a Hand that guides us, and we poor men can trust to that. It's very comforting to know it.

MONSIEUR BALLON.   So the affair went by the board?

PEER GYNT.   No, it took on another aspect. Outsiders meddled in the game and raised an unexpected pother. The youngsters of the family were much the worst. I had to battle with seven of them all at once. I never shall forget that time, though I emerged from it the victor. Some blood was split; but still that blood sealed my certificate of valour and proved what I remarked just now—that there's a Hand that guides us wisely.

HERR VON EBERKOPF.   You have an outlook upon life that proves you a philosopher. For, while an ordinary thinker sees every detail separately and never grasps the whole completely, your vision covers all together. You have a universal standard to measure life with. Your perceptions, like rays of sunlight, emanating from a great central contemplation, pierce every fallacy.—And yet you say you had no education?

PEER GYNT.   I am, as I've already told you, a self-taught man in every way. I've never learnt methodically, but I have thought and speculated and read a bit on every subject. I was not young when I began; and so, of course, it wasn't easy to plough the field of knowledge up and do the thing at all completely. I've learnt my history in scraps; for more than that I've had no leisure. And since, when evil days assail, a man needs certain things to trust in, I fitfully absorbed religion; I found that it assimilated much easier if taken that way. No use to glut one's self with reading, but to select what may be useful——

MR. COTTON.   Ah, now, that's practical!

PEER GYNT.   Dear friends, just think what my career has been. What was I when I first went westwards? Quite penniless and empty-handed. I had to work hard for my food——No easy job, believe me, often; but life, my friends, is always sweet, and death, as we all know, is bitter. Well! Luck, you see, did not desert me, and good old Fate was always kindly. Things moved, and I was always careful, and so things went from good to better; and, ten years after that, they called me the Crœsus of the Charlestown traders; my name was known in every port and luck pursued me with my shipping——

MR. COTTON.   What was your trade?

PEER GYNT.   I trafficked most in negro slaves for Carolina and idols that were sent to China.

MONSIEUR BALLON.   Oh, fie, for shame!

HERR TRUMPETERSTRAALE.   Friend Gynt, how could you?

PEER GYNT.   You think my enterprise was passing beyond the bounds of what was lawful? I felt the same thing very keenly; I found it hateful in the end. But, once begun, you may believe me 'twas difficult enough to end it. In any case, so big a business affected others by the thousand; to break it off too suddenly would have, of course, been most disastrous. I never like to break things off; but all the same, I must admit I've always fully been alive to what you'd call the consequences; and, when I've overstepped the bounds, it's always made me feel uneasy. Besides, I wasn't growing younger. By that time I was nearly fifty, and by degrees my hair was greying; and, though my health was always perfect, thoughts such as this cropped up to plague me; "who knows how short the time may be before the Great Assize is summoned and sheep from goats are separated?" What could I do? To cease my trade with China was impossible. I found a way. I opened up a second traffic to those waters; and, though each spring I sent to China shiploads of idols, every autumn I sent out Missionaries furnished with everything that could be needful to work conversion—stockings, rum, Bibles and rice——

MR. COTTON.   All at a profit?

PEER GYNT.   Oh, well, of course.—The plan worked well. For every idol sold out yonder there was a duly baptized coolie, so one thing neutralized the other. We kept the Missionaries busy, because they had to counteract the idols that we were exporting.

MR. COTTON.   But what about the negro traffic?

PEER GYNT.   Why, there my morals triumphed also. I felt the trade was scarcely suited to one whose years were fast increasing; you never know when death may claim you. And then there were the thousand pitfalls dug by our philanthropic friends, besides the chance of being caught and daily risks from wind and weather. By taking thought I found a way. "You'll have to reef your sails, friend Peter, and see"—so I said to myself—"how you can best retrieve your error!" I bought land in a southern state and held back my last load of niggers (which was of first-class quality) and settled them on the plantation. They throve apace, grew fat and sleek, and they, as well as I, were happy. Yes, without bragging I may say I treated them like any father—— And the result was handsome profit. I built them schools, so as to set a standard of morality to be maintained, and saw to it that it was kept well up to mark. And then, to make the change complete, out of the business I retired, and sold, with livestock, as it stood, the whole plantation. When I left, to all alike, both young and old, a gratis gift of grog was issued, and every nigger got a skinful. The widows, as an extra gift, were given snuff. And so I hope—unless the Word is merely froth which says one's deeds are surely good if they are not as surely evil—that all my errors are forgot, and that perhaps in greater measure than in most people's case, my deeds will more than balance out my sins.

HERR VON EBERKOPF (*clinking glasses with him*). How edifying 'tis to hear a scheme of life worked out so deftly, freed from the fog of theories and undisturbed by outer clamour!

PEER GYNT (*who during the foregoing conversation has been applying steadily to the bottle*).   We northern men are famous hands at planning a campaign! The secret of life's success is very simple—merely to keep one's ear shut tight to the insidious advances of a pernicious reptile.

MR. COTTON.   Aye, but what's the reptile, my dear friend?

PEER GYNT.   A small one, always tempting men to take irrevocable steps. (*Drinks again.*) A man can venture without fear and keep his courage, if he's careful not to get definitely caught in any of life's cunning pitfalls—if he looks forward and beyond the present moment and its chances, and always carefully preserves a bridge behind him to retire on. That theory has held me up and always coloured all my conduct—a theory I inherited and learnt at home from early childhood.

MONSIEUR BALLON.   You're a Norwegian, I believe?

PEER GYNT.   By birth, yes; but by disposition I am a citizen of the world. For the good fortune I've enjoyed, I have to thank America; my well-stocked library I owe to Germany's advanced young thinkers; from France I get my taste in dress, my manners, and whatever turn I have for subtleness of mind; England has taught me industry and care for my own interests; the Jews have taught me how to wait; from Italy I've caught a dash of taste for *dolce far niente;* and once, when in a sorry fix, I reached the goal of my desire by trusting to good Swedish steel.

HERR TRUMPETERSTRAALE *(lifting his glass).*   Ah, Swedish steel——!

HERR VON EBERKOPF.   Yes, first and foremost we offer homage to the man who is a swordsman.

{They clink glasses and drink with PEER GYNT *who is beginning to get heated with wine.*

MR. COTTON.   All you've said is excellent; but now, sir, pray tell us what you propose to do with all your wealth.

PEER GYNT *(smiling).*   Do with it, eh?

ALL *(drawing nearer to him).*   Yes, let us hear!

PEER GYNT.   Well, first of all, to travel; and that's why, you see, I took you all on board my yacht as company. I had a mind to have a choir to worship at my Altar of the Golden Calf——

HERR VON EBERKOPF.   How witty!

MR. COTTON.   Yes, but no one sails for the mere pleasure of a journey. You have an object, without doubt; what is it?

PEER GYNT.   To be Emperor.

ALL.   What!

PEER GYNT (*nodding his head*).   To be Emperor.

ALL.   But where?

PEER GYNT.   Of the whole world.

MONSIEUR BALLON.   But how, my friend——?

PEER GYNT.   Just simply by the power of gold! It's not a new idea at all; it has inspired my every effort. In boyish dreams I used to travel over the sea upon a cloud; I tried to soar to fancied grandeurs and then dropped down on to all-fours; but to its goal my mind was constant. Somewhere—I can't remember where—it says that if a man shall win the whole wide world, but lose *himself,* all that he gains is only like a wreath upon an empty skull. That's what it says—or something like it—and, trust me, it is pretty true.

HERR VON EBERKOPF.   But what, then, is the Gyntian Self?

PEER GYNT.   The world which lies within my brain; which makes me *me* and no one else—no more than God can be the Devil.

HERR TRUMPETERSTRAALE.   Now I can see at what you're driving!

MONSIEUR BALLON.   Sublime philosopher!

HERR VON EBERKOPF.   Great poet!

PEER GYNT (*with growing exaltation*).   The Gyntian Self!—An army, that, of wishes, appetites, desires! The Gyntian Self! It is a sea of fancies, claims and aspirations; in fact, it's all that swells within my breast and makes it come about that I am I and live as such. But, just as our Good

Lord has need of earthly mould to be earth's God, so I have need of lots of gold if I'm to be an Emperor.

MONSIEUR BALLON.   But you are rich!

PEER GYNT.   Not rich enough. Enough, perhaps, for me to pose for two or three days as a princeling in some such place as Lippe-Detmold; but I must be *myself*—complete—A Gynt fit for the universe—Sir Peter Gynt from head to heels!

MONSIEUR BALLON *(in transports)*.   To purchase all the loveliest things the world can offer!

HERR VON EBERKOPF.   All the bins of century-old Johannisberger!

HERR TRUMPETERSTRAALE.   The armoury of Charles the Twelfth!

MR. COTTON.   But, before all, to seize the chance of profitable business.

PEER GYNT.   Well, I've found a way to get them all, and that is why we're anchored here! To-night our course will be to northward. The newspapers I've just received have brought me some important news. *(Rises and lifts his glass.)*   It shows that fortune always favours those who have confidence to grasp it——

ALL.   Well? Tell us——!

PEER GYNT.   Greece is in an uproar.

ALL. *(springing to their feet)*.   What, have the Greeks——?

PEER GYNT.   They have revolted.

ALL.   Hurrah!

PEER GYNT.   And Turkey's in a hole.

MONSIEUR BALLON.   To Greece! The way to glory's open! I'll help them with my sword of France!

HERR VON EBERKOPF.   I with my voice—but at a distance!

MR. COTTON.   I'll get a contract to supply them!

HERR TRUMPETERSTRAALE.   Let us away! I'll find at Bender Charles the Twelfth's famous spur-buckles!

MONSIEUR BALLON (*falling on* PEER GYNT'S *neck*).   Forgive me, friend, if for a moment I had misjudged you!

HERR VON EBERKOPF (*grasping* PEER GYNT *by the hand*). I'm a fool! I almost took you for a scoundrel!

MR. COTTON.   That's much too strong—say, rather, for a simpleton——

HERR TRUMPETERSTRAALE (*embracing* PEER GYNT). And I, dear friend, had put you down as an example of the worst type of Yankee rascal! Forgive me!

HERR VON EBERKOPF.   We were all mistaken——

PEER GYNT.   What do you mean?

HERR VON EBERKOPF.   We now can glimpse the banners of the Gyntian army of wishes, appetites, desires——!

MONSIEUR BALLON (*admiringly*).   That's what you meant by "being a Gynt"!

HERR VON EBERKOPF (*in the same tone*).   A Gynt that's worthy of all honour!

PEER GYNT.   But tell me——?

MONSIEUR BALLON.   Don't you understand?

PEER GYNT.   I'm hanged if I can take your meaning.

MONSIEUR BALLON.   Why, aren't you going to help the Greeks with money and with ships?

PEER GYNT (*whistling*).   No, thank you! I'm going to help the stronger side and lend my money to the Turks.

MONSIEUR BALLON.   Impossible!

HERR VON EBERKOPF.   That's very funny!—But you, of course, must have your joke!

*{*PEER GYNT *is silent for a moment, then leans on a chair and assumes an air of importance.*

PEER GYNT.   Gentlemen, we had better part before the last remains of friendship dissolve like wreaths of smoke. The man who hasn't anything may lightly take any chances; those whose all is no more than the scrap of earth they stand on, are the fittest far for sacrifice and cannon-fodder. But when a man's well off, as I am, he risks a greater stake than they. Pray go to Greece. I'll land you there and furnish you with weapons gratis; the more you fan the flame of strife, the better it will be for me. Strike hard for Freedom and the Right! Attack the Turks and give them hell; and meet a glorious end upon a janissary's spear-point.—But, excuse me if I don't come with you. *(Slaps his pockets.)* I've money in my pockets, and I am Myself—Sir Peer Gynt.

{Puts up his umbrella and goes into the grove where the hammocks are hanging.

HERR TRUMPETERSTRAALE.   The swine!

MONSIEIR BALLON.   He has no sense of honour!

MR. COTTON.   Oh, honour—let that pass. But think what splendid profits we could make if only Greece could free herself——

MONSIEUR BALLON.   I saw myself acclaimed a victor by crowds of lovely Grecian women!

HERR TRUMPETERSTRAALE.   I felt those famous buckles safe within my Swedish grasp!

HERR VON EBERKOPF.   I saw my glorious fatherland's *Kultur* spread widely over land and sea——

MR. COTTON.   The actual loss is worst of all. Goddam!—I feel inclined to cry! I saw myself proprietor of Mount Olympus, which contains (unless what men have said is false) rich veins of copper to be worked; and the renowned

Castalian stream—its many waterfalls would yield a thousand horsepower, easily!

HERR TRUMPETERSTRAALE.   I shall go, all the same! My sword is worth more, still than Yankee gold.

MR. COTTON.   Perhaps: but, fighting in the ranks, we should be merely swamped by numbers. What profit should we get from that?

MONSIEUR BALLON.   Curse it! So near the heights of fortune—and then to be dashed down again.

MR. COTTON (*shaking his fist at the yacht*).   To think that all this nabob's gold, that he has sweated from his niggers, is in that ship!

HERR VON EBERKOPF.   An inspiration! Come on, and let us act! His empire shall come to nothing now! Hurrah!

MONSIEUR BALLON.   What will you do?

HERR VON EBERKOPF.   I'll seize his power! the crew will easily be bought. On board! I'll commandeer his yacht!

MR. COTTON.   You'll—what?

HERR VON EBERKOPF.   I mean to bag the lot.

{Goes towards the jolly-boat.

MR. COTTON.   It's clearly to my interest to share with you.

{Follows him.

HERR TRUMPETERSTRAALE.   There goes a scamp!
MONSIEUR BALLON.   A proper scoundrel! But—*enfin!*

{Follows the others.

HERR TRUMPETERSTRAALE.   Well, I suppose I may as well go with them—under protest, though!

{Follows.

Scene II

SCENE.—*Another part of the coast. Moonlight and passing clouds. Out at sea the yacht is seen steaming at full speed.* PEER GYNT *is running along the shore, now pinching himself in the arm, now staring out at sea.*

PEER GYNT. It's nightmare!—Illusion!—I soon shall wake up! It's heading to sea! And at top of its speed! It's a dream, and I'm sleeping! I'm drunk or I'm mad! *(Wrings his hands.)* It's impossible that I should perish like this! *(Tears his hair.)* It's a dream! It *must* be—it *shall* be—a dream! It's terrible! Ah, but alas it is true! My scoundrelly friends——! Oh, hear me, Good Lord! You are Wisdom and Justice—oh, punish them, Lord! *(Stretches up his arms.)* It is I—Peer Gynt! Do look after me, Lord! Take care of me, Father, or else I shall die! Make them slacken the engines—or cast off the gig! Stop the robbers! Make something go wrong with the works! Do listen! Leave other folk's matters alone! The world will look after itself while You do.—He's not listening. He is as deaf as a post! It's too much! A God that can't think what to do! *(Beckons up to the sky.)* I say! I've disposed of my negro plantation, and sent heaps of Missionaries out to Asia. Don't You think that one good turn's deserving another? Oh, help me to get on the ship——! *(A sudden glare rises into the sky from the yacht, followed by a thick cloud of smoke. A dull explosion is heard.* PEER GYNT *utters a shriek and sinks down on the sand. The smoke gradually disperses and the yacht is seen to have disappeared.* PEER GYNT *looks up, with a pale face, and says in a low voice.)* 'Twas a judgment! Sunk with all hands in a moment of time! All thanks to the chances of fortune. *(Emotionally.)* No, no! There was more than the chance of fortune in this, that I should be saved while the rest of them perish. Thanks be to Thee who hast been my protector and kept an eye on me in spite of my failings! *(Takes a deep breath.)* What a wonderful feeling of safety and comfort it gives you to know that you're specially guarded! But where shall I find meat and drink in the desert? I don't know, I'm sure. But He will understand. It *can't* be so dangerous.—— *(In a loud and insinuating voice.)* He will not suffer such a poor little sparrow as I am to perish! I must humble myself—and allow Him some time. The Lord will provide; I must not be downhearted.—— *(Springs to his feet with a cry of terror.)* Did I hear a lion? That growl in the rushes——? *(His teeth chatter.)* No, it was no lion. *(Pulls himself together.)* I'm certain it was! Those creatures, of course, know to keep at a distance; they dare not take bites at a lord of creation. They have instinct, of course; it's by instinct they feel that an elephant's not a safe thing to attack.—All the same, I will see if I can't find a tree. Ah, there I see palms and acacias waving; if I climb one of them, I'll get safety and shelter—especially if I can only remember some psalms to repeat.—— *(Climbs up a tree.)* "Lo, morning and evening are different things"—that's a verse that is often discussed and examined. *(Settles himself in the tree.)* How pleasant it is to feel that one's soul is so nobly uplifted! Thoughts that ennoble are worth more than riches. I'll trust myself to Him. He knows just how far I am able to drink of the cup of affliction. He takes a most fatherly interest in me—— *(Looks out over the sea, and whispers with a sigh):* but He's not what you'd call economical over it!

SCENE III

SCENE.—*A Moroccan camp on the edge of the desert, at night.* WARRIORS *are resting by a watch-fire.*

A SLAVE (*running in and tearing his hair*).   Gone is the Emperor's white charger!

ANOTHER SLAVE.   The Emperor's sacred garb is stolen!

A CHIEF OF THE WARRIORS (*coming in*).   A hundred strokes of the bastinado to all of you, if the thieves escape!
        {THE WARRIORS *spring on to their steeds and gallop off in all directions.*

SCENE IV

SCENE.—*A clump of palm-trees and acacias. It is dawn.* PEER GYNT, *in a tree, is trying to defend himself with a broken-off branch against a swarm of Apes.*

PEER GYNT.   I've spent an extremely uncomfortable night. (*Hits about him.*) Is that them again? The infernal creatures! They're throwing down fruit. No, it's something else. Apes are the most disgusting beasts! It is written that one must watch and fight; but I can't do it—I'm wearied out. (*Is disturbed again. Speaks impatiently.*) I must make an end of all this discomfort—try and get hold of one of these creatures, hang him and flay him and dress myself up from head to foot in his shaggy hide; then the others will think I am one of them.—We men are but nothing, after all, and must bow to the force of circumstances.—Another lot! Why they swarm like flies! Away with you! Shoo! They act like madmen. If only I could get a false tail—or something to make me look like a beast—what's that up there above my head? *(Looks up.)* An old one—his paws chock-full of filth! *(Crouches down nervously and keeps still for a little. The* APE *makes a movement;* PEER GYNT *tries to coax him, as one would a dog.)* Hullo, old man! Is that you up there? He's a good chap, if you speak to him kindly. *He* won't throw things down—will he? No! It's I! Good dog! We're the best of friends. Wuff, wuff! Do you hear, I can speak your language: old man and I are as good as cousins! Would he like a nice bit of sugar——? The dirty beast! He's thrown the lot all over me! Disgusting brute!—Or was it food, perhaps? Its taste was unfamiliar, certainly. But taste is mostly a thing of habit. What is it that some philosopher has said: You must just spit and trust to force of habit.—Here's the crowd of youngsters now! *(Hits about him.)* This is too much! That man, who's his Creator's image, should have to suffer.—Murder! Help! The old one's foul, but the youngsters fouler!

SCENE V

SCENE.—*A rocky spot overlooking the desert. It is early morning. On one side, a ravine with the entrance to a cave. A* THIEF *and a* RECEIVER OF STOLEN GOODS *are standing in the ravine, with the Emperor's charger and robe. The charger, richly caparisoned, is tied to a rock.* HORSEMEN *are seen in the distance.*

THIEF.   Spear-points, gleaming in the sunshine! See! see!

RECEIVER.   I hear them galloping over the sand! Woe! Woe!

THIEF (*folding his arms on his breast*).   My father thieved; his son must steal.

RECEIVER.   My father received; and so must I.

THIEF.   We must bear our lot and be ourselves.

RECEIVER (*listening*).   Footsteps in the thicket! Away! But where?

THIEF.   The cave is deep and the Prophet great!

> {*They fly, leaving the stolen goods behind them.. The* HORSEMEN *disappear in the distance.* PEER GYNT *comes in, whittling a reed.*

PEER GYNT.   Really a most enchanting morning! The beetles are busy at work in the sand; out of their shells the snails are peeping. Morning! Ah, morning's worth more than gold! It's strange what a very remarkable power there is in daylight. In its beams you feel so safe—your courage waxes—you're ready to fight wild bulls, if need be. What silence around me! These rural joys—it's strange that I never appreciated these things so much till now. To think that men live cooped up in great cities, just to be pestered and plagued by people. Look at those lizards, bustling about enjoying the air and thinking of nothing. What innocence in the life of beasts! They perform the behest of their great Creator, their character stamped indelibly on them; they are *themselves,* whether playing or fighting—themselves, as they were when He first said "Be." (*Puts on his eye-glasses.*) A toad—looking out of a piece of sandstone, only his head peeping out of his chamber. He sits, as if looking out of a window at the world; to himself he is—enough. *(Thought-fully.)* Enough? Where have I read that before? Most probably in the Great Book I read as a boy. Or perhaps it was in the Prayer-book? Or else set down in Solomon's Proverbs? Dear me—I notice, as years go on, I cannot remember times and places as once I used. *(Sits down in the shade.)* Here's a spot that's cool; I'll sit and rest my bones awhile. Ah, here are ferns—one can eat the roots. *(Tastes one.)* It's really food for beasts; but then the Book says we must subdue our nature, and, further, that pride must be abased. "Who humbleth himself, shall be exalted." *(Uneasily.)* Exalted? Of course that will happen to me—the contrary's quite unthinkable. Fate surely will help me away from here and set my feet on the road to fortune. This is but a test; if the Lord will grant me strength to endure, I'll be rescued later. *(Shakes off such thoughts, lights a cigar, stretches himself out and gazes over the desert.)* What an enormous, boundless waste!— Far off, there, I can see an ostrich.—It is hard to perceive the Almighty's purpose in all this dead and empty desert, where there is nothing that is life-giving; a burnt-up waste that profits no one, this bit of the world that's for ever sterile; a corpse that never, since it was shaped, has brought its Creator anything—not even thanks. Why was it made? Nature is ever extravagant.—Is that the sea that glitters yonder, away in the east? No—only mirage. The sea's to the west, where, like a dam, sandhills protect the desert from it. *(An idea strikes him.)* A dam! Then I might——! The hills are low. A dam! Then a cutting—a canal—and through the gap the rushing waters would fill the desert with a life-flood, and all this empty burnt-up grave become a fresh and rippling ocean! Islands would show in it where now there are oases; to the north, Atlas would fringe the shore with verdure; and

to the south, like heedless birds, white sails would skim
along, where now the caravans plod painfully; a lively breeze
would dissipate this stuffy air, and from the clouds a gentle
dew would fall. In time town after town would be estab-
lished, and grass grow round the swaying palm-trees. The
country beyond the Sahara's edge, away in the south, would
become a land of busy trade and seamen's ventures. Steam
should drive works in Tombuktu, new colonies arise in
Bornu, and the explorer should be carried safe in his waggon
through the land of Habes to the Upper Nile. Then in the
middle of my sea, on the most fertile, rich oasis, I'll settle
Norsemen—for the blood of dalesmen is the nearest thing
to that of royalty; a cross with Arab blood will do the rest.
And on a cape with sloping shore I'll build Peeropolis, the
capital! The old world's out of date; and now it is the turn
of Gyntiana, my new-born land! *(Springs up.)* I only need
some capital, and the thing is done—a golden key, and the
ocean's gate is open! A crusade 'gainst death! That grisly
miser shall disgorge the hidden treasure that he's hoarding.
There is a world-wide wish for freedom. Like Noah's donkey
in the Ark, I'll bray my message to the world; Liberty's
baptism I will pour over these prisoned shores, till they grow
lovely in their freedom!—Forward! In east or west I'll have
to seek the money for the work! My kingdom—or half my
kingdom—for a horse! *(The horse in the ravine neighs.)* A horse!
And robes! And ornaments! And weapons! *(Goes nearer.)* It's
impossible—and yet it's true!—I know I've read somewhere
that faith can move a mountain, but never thought that it
could bring a horse! I must be dreaming—— No, it is a
fact—there stands the horse! *Ab esse ad posse,* etcetera.——
(Puts on the robe and looks himself over.) Sir Peter—and Turk
from head to foot! Well, truly one can never tell what's
going to happen to one! Come up, Granë, my steed! *(Climbs*

into the saddle.) Gold stirrups, too! Great folk are known by
the steeds they ride!

{Gallops away across the desert.

SCENE VI

SCENE.—*The tent of an Arab Chieftain, on an oasis.* PEER
GYNT, *in his oriental robes, is taking his ease on a divan,
drinking coffee and smoking a long pipe.* ANITRA *and a troupe
of* GIRLS *are dancing and singing to him.*

CHORUS OF GIRLS.   The Prophet is come! The
Prophet, the Lord, the All-Wise One, to us, to us he has
come, riding over the sea of sand! The Prophet, the Lord,
the Infallible, to us, to us he has come sailing over the sea
of sand! Blow flute! Sound drum! The Prophet, the Prophet
is come!

ANITRA.   His charger is white as milk in the streams
of Paradise! Bend the knee! Bow low! His eyes are stars that
flash and yet are full of love. No earth-born eyes can meet
the flashing of those stars! Across the desert he came, decked
with gold and pearls. Where he rode it was light; behind
him all was dark, drought and the dread simoom. The
Mighty One has come! Over the desert he came, clothed in
mortal shape. Kaaba is empty now! Himself has told us so.

CHORUS OF GIRLS.   Blow flute! Sound drum! The
Prophet, the Prophet is come.

{The girls dance to soft music.

PEER GYNT.   I have read in a book, and the saying's
true, that no man's a prophet in his own country.—This

life's a deal more to my liking than that which I led as a Charlestown trader. There was something false about it all, something foreign to me and shady; I never could feel myself at home, or feel I had chosen the right profession, *Qu'allais-je faire dans cette galère,* grubbing about with business matters? I can't understand it, the more I try—it simply happened, and that is all. To climb up the world on moneybags is just like building a house on sand. If you wear rings and a watch, and so forth, people will curtsey and bow to you, take off their hats if you wear a breast-pin; but the rings and the pin are not yourself. Now a Prophet—he has a definite status; you know exactly where you're standing, if a man salutes you, it's for *yourself,* and not because of your pounds and shillings. You are what you are without pretence. Owing nothing to chance or accident, independent of patents or concessions. A Prophet—yes, that's the life for me. And it happened so unexpectedly—simply from riding across the desert and coming upon these children of nature. The Prophet had come; it was clear to them. But indeed it was not my design to deceive them—an official reply from a Prophet is one thing, and a lie quite another; in any case, too, I can always retire from my present position. I'm in no way bound; so it's not so bad. It's all, so to speak, like a private arrangement. I can go as I came; my steed's standing ready; in short, I am master of the situation.

ANITRA *(at the door of the tent).* Prophet and Master!

PEER GYNT. What is it, my slave?

ANITRA. At the door of the tent stand sons of the desert, craving to look on the face of the Prophet——

PEER GYNT. Stop! You can tell them they must keep their distance; I will receive their petitions at a distance. Tell them no man may set his foot within here! Menfolk, my child, are but a set of scoundrels—they are, in fact,

a filthy lot of rascals. You, my Anitra, cannot well imagine
with what barefaced impertinence they cheat one—h'm!—I
should say, how grievously they sin. Now, no more of that!
Come, dance for me, my children! I would forget these
thoughts that make me angry.

THE GIRLS (*as they dance*).   The Prophet is good! His
heart is distressed for the sins that the sons of earth have
committed. The Prophet is kind! All praise to his kindness
which leads such poor sinners to Paradise!

PEER GYNT (*whose eyes have followed* ANITRA *through the
dance*).   Her legs flit about like nimble drumsticks! She's
really a tasty morsel, the baggage! It's true her figure's pronounced in some ways—not quite in accord with the stan-
dards of beauty; but what is beauty? A mere convention, a
currency coined for a special purpose. And it's just these
extravagances that tickle a palate that's sated with what is
normal. In marriage there's always something wanting; she's
either too fat or else too scraggy, annoyingly young or alarm-
ingly ancient; and if she's between the two, she's insipid.—
Her feet, it is true, might well be cleaner, also her arms—
especially that one. But, after all, that's nothing to matter;
one might rather call it a qualification.—Anitra, come here!

ANITRA.   Thy slave, my Master!

PEER GYNT.   You attract me, child! The Prophet is
moved. If you don't believe me, I'll prove it to you—I'll
make you a Houri in Paradise!

ANITRA.   Impossible, Master!

PEER GYNT.   You don't believe me? As I am alive,
I'm in real earnest!

ANITRA.   But I've no soul!

PEER GYNT.   Then you shall have one!

ANITRA.   How shall I, Master?

PEER GYNT.   That's my affair. I shall look after your

education. No soul? It's true you are pretty stupid; I've noticed that fact with some regret; but there's room enough in you for a soul. Come here! Let me measure your head. Oh, yes, there's plenty of room, as I knew there was. True enough, you'll never be anything much; a great soul will be quite beyond you. But, pshaw! it really doesn't matter; you'll have enough to prevent your feeling ashamed of it——

ANITRA. My Lord is kind——

PEER GYNT. You're hesitating? What is the matter?

ANITRA. I'd rather have——

PEER GYNT. Speak out, at once!

ANITRA. I don't care so much about having a soul; I'd rather have——

PEER GYNT. What?

ANITRA (*pointing to his turban*). That lovely opal!

PEER GYNT (*in raptures, as he hands her the jewel*). Anitra, you're one of Eve's true daughters! Your charm attracts me—for I am a man; and, as a noted writer puts it: *"Das ewig weibliche zeihet uns an."*

SCENE VII

SCENE.—*A grove of palm-trees outside* ANITRA'S *tent. The moon is shining.* PEER GYNT, *with an Arabian lute in his hands, is sitting under a tree. His beard and hair have been trimmed, which makes him look considerably younger.*

PEER GYNT (*plays and sings*).

> I locked the gate of Paradise
> And took away the key.

My bark afar the north wind bore,
While lovely women on the shore
Were weeping there for me.

Southward I sailed the salty depths
Before the die was cast;
    Where palms were waving proud
      and free
    Around an inlet of the sea,
I burned my ship at last.

A desert-ship I mounted then—
A four-legged ship, I trow—
    To bear me o'er the desert dark.
    I am a bird of passage! Hark!
I'm twittering on a bough!

Anitra, thou art like the wine
Of palm-trees, sparkling clear!
    Angora-goats'-milk cheese is good,
    But it's not half so sweet a food
As thou, Anitra dear!

(Slings the lute over his shoulder and approaches the tent.)
All is silent! Now I wonder if she heard my little song? Is
she there behind the curtain, peeping out with nothing on?
What's that sound? It's like a bottle someone is uncork-
ing!—There! There again I heard it—Is it sighs of love?—
a lover's song?—No, it's clearly someone snoring. Lovely
sound! Anitra sleeps! Nightingales, desist from singing! You
shall suffer if you dare with your silly cluck and gurgle.—
Oh, well, after all—sing on! Every nightingale's a songster,

just as I am one myself; with their notes, like me, they
capture tender, delicate young hearts. Night's cool hours
are meant for singing; singing is our common sphere;
singing is the art of being *us*—Peer Gynt and nightingale.
And to hear Anitra sleeping is the topmost bliss of love;
it's like lifting up a goblet to the lips, but drinking
naught.—Oh, but here she comes! Well, really, after all
that is the best.

ANITRA *(at her tent door)*.   Did I hear my Master calling?

PEER GYNT.   Yes, my dear, the Prophet called. I was
wakened by a hubbub; cats were fighting all around——

ANITRA.   Ah, they were not fighting, Master. It was
something worse than that.

PEER GYNT.   What was it?

ANITRA.   Oh, spare me!

PEER GYNT.   Tell me!

ANITRA.   I am blushing!

PEER GYNT *(going close to her)*.   Do you mean the
emotion I was feeling when you had my opal, dear?

ANITRA *(horrified)*.   Don't compare yourself, great
Master, to an old disgusting cat!

PEER GYNT.   Child—considered just as lovers,
there's perhaps not much to choose 'twixt a tom-cat and a
Prophet.

ANITRA.   Honeyed jests, great Master, fall from your
lips.

PEER GYNT.   My little friend, you, like other girls,
pass judgment solely by a great man's looks, I am really very
playful—especially when *tête-à-tête*. My position makes it
needful for me to put on a mask of most serious behaviour;
I'm constrained by daily duties and the nature of the business relative to my great office, to assume a weighty manner,

and at times may seem to others too prophetically abrupt;
but 'tis all upon the surface.——Away with all that bosh! In
private I am Peer—that's who I am. Come, now, I will drop
the Prophet; you shall know my very self! *(Sits down under a
tree and draws* ANITRA *closer to him.)* Come, Anitra, let us
dally underneath this waving palm! You shall smile and I
shall whisper nothings in your ear; and then we'll reverse
the parts we're playing, your sweet lips shall whisper love
in my ear while I sit smiling!

ANITRA *(lying at his feet).*   All you say is sweet as
music, though I don't quite understand. Tell me, Master,
can your daughter get a soul by listening?

PEER GYNT.   Presently you shall be dowered with
the light of life—a soul; when upon the rosy portals of the
dawn we see in gold "I am daybreak" clearly written,——then
it will be time enough to begin your education. But for me
to play schoolmaster and to waste this lovely night trying
to collect together weatherbeaten bits of lore, would be stupid altogether, even if I wanted to. And, besides, considered
rightly, souls are not the chiefest things in our lives; it's
hearts that matter.

ANITRA.   Speak on, Master! When you speak, it's
like opals flashing fire.

PEER GYNT.   Too much cleverness is folly; and the
fruit of cowardice pushed too far, is cruelty. Truth, if it's
exaggerated, is no more than wisdom's self turned hind-
foremost.——Yes, my child, you may take my word for it,
there are people in the world gorged with soul but dull of
vision. I once knew a chap like that; he seemed brighter
than his fellows; yet he let resounding phrases which he did
not understand quite mislead him from his business.——Look
around this fair oasis, at the desert; if my turban I took off
and fluttered gently once or twice, the mighty ocean at my

bidding would invade it, filling up its every corner. But I'd be a silly cuckoo if I set about creating seas and continents. Do you know, my child, what life is?

ANITRA.   No, instruct me.

PEER GYNT.   Life means passing safe and dry-shod down the rushing stream of time. Manly strength is what is needed to be what I am, my dear. Age makes eagles lose their feathers, makes old fogies' footsteps fail, sets an old crone's teeth decaying, gives an old man withered hands,— and they all get withered souls. Give me youth! I mean as Sultan, ardent and vigorous, to rule—not the realms of Gyntiana with their palm-trees and their vines—but the realm of fresh young beauty that lies in a maiden's thoughts. So you see, my child, the reason why I graciously was pleased to bestow my love upon you; why I chose your little heart, so to speak, to be the empire that shall be my caliphate. None but I shall know your longings; in the empire of my love I must reign supreme, unquestioned! For you must be mine alone. I shall be your gentle gaoler, binding you with gold and gems. If we part, life will be empty—or, at any rate, for you! Not a fibre of your being, not an instinct of your will, but shall know me as their master—you shall be so filled with me. And your raven locks—your beauty—all in you that can allure—these shall be a pleasant garden for your Sultan's foot to tread. And that's why it's really lucky you've an empty little head. Souls are apt to make their owners too absorbed about themselves. And—while we're upon the topic—if you like, I'll seal the pact by bestowing on your ankle this fine bangle. That, I think, fairly meets the situation. Me—instead of soul—you'll have; otherwise, the *status quo.* (ANITRA *snores.*) What? Is she sleeping? Have my words fallen on unheeding ears? No; it shows the power lying in my words—that, like a stream, they transport her gently with them to the land of dreams. *(Gets up and puts some jewels in her lap.)* Anitra! Here are jewels! Here are more! Sleep, Anitra! Dream of Peer! Sleep, for in your sleep you've set a crown upon your Emperor's head! Peer Gynt has won a victory of personality to-night.

SCENE VIII

SCENE.—*A caravan route. The oasis is visible in the remote background.* PEER GYNT, *on his white horse, is galloping over the desert, holding* ANITRA *before him on the pommel of his saddle.*

ANITRA.   Let go! I'll bite you!

PEER GYNT.   You little rogue!

ANITRA.   What do you want to do?

PEER GYNT.   To play at love and falcon! To carry you off and do all sorts of reckless things!

ANITRA.   For shame! An old Prophet, too!

PEER GYNT.   Oh, bosh! The Prophet is not old, you goose! Do you think this looks as if he were old?

ANITRA.   Let me go! I want to go home!

PEER GYNT.   You flirt! Home! To father-in-law! That's good! We birds that have flown out of our cage dare not be seen by him again. Besides, my child, no one should stay too long in the same place; he's apt to lose as much in estimation as he can gain by making friends; and this is especially the case when he's a Prophet, or the like. His should be flying visits—seen as snatches of a song are heard.

It was time that my visit should come to an end; these sons of the desert are shifty creatures,—incense and gifts have both been lacking for some days.

ANITRA.   Yes, but *are* you a Prophet?

PEER GYNT.   I am your Emperor! *(Tries to kiss her, but she draws back.)* Oh, come! Don't be a proud little birdie, now!

ANITRA.   Give me the ring that's on your finger.

PEER GYNT.   Take the lot if you wish, dear!

ANITRA.   Your words are like life-giving music!

PEER GYNT.   What happiness 'tis to be loved like this! Let me dismount! I will lead the horse and be your slave! *(Hands her the whip and dismounts.)* See now, my pretty, my beautiful rose—here am I now, and here I'll tread the sands until I get a sunstroke and have to stop. I am young, Anitra! Remember that! You mustn't look at my deeds too closely; jokes and fun are what youth is known by! And, if you were not quite so stupid, my graceful flower, you'd understand that, since your lover is full of fun, *ergo* he's young!

ANITRA.   Yes, you are young. Have you any more rings?

PEER GYNT.   Of course I'm young! Look, I am bounding like a deer! If there was any green-stuff handy, I'd make myself a wreath! Aha! Of course I'm young! Just see me dance!

{Dances and sings.

> I am a happy little cock!
> Peck me, my little pullet!
> Houp-là! Just see me foot it!
> I am a happy little cock!

ANITRA.   You're sweating, my Prophet; I'm afraid
you will melt. Let me carry that bag that weighs down on
your belt.

PEER GYNT.   What tender concern! You shall carry
the purse; hearts that are loving have no need of gold!

{Dances and sings again.

> He is a madcap, your little Peer!
> He doesn't know what he is doing!
> And doesn't care—if he keeps going!
> He is a madcap, your little Peer!

ANITRA.   How joyful 'tis to see the Prophet dancing!

PEER GYNT.   Oh, drop that "Prophet" nonsense!
Let's put on each other's clothes! Come on! You take yours
off!

ANITRA.   Your caftan is too long, your belt too
roomy, your stockings much too small.

PEER GYNT.   *Eh bien!* Instead, inflict some pain upon
me; for 'tis sweet for loving hearts to suffer for their love!
And, when we come to where my castle stands——

ANITRA.   Your Paradise? Have we got far to ride?

PEER GYNT.   A thousand miles or so!

ANITRA.   Oh, what a way!

PEER GYNT.   Then you shall have the soul I promised you——

ANITRA.   No, thanks; I think I'll do without the
soul. But you were asking for some pain——

PEER GYNT.   Ah, yes! Something severe but brief—
a passing pang——!

ANITRA.   Anitra must obey the Prophet! So—farewell!

{Hits him smartly over the fingers with the whip and
gallops back over the desert at full speed.

PEER GYNT *(after standing for a long time as if thunder-*
struck).   Well, I am——

SCENE IX

SCENE.—*The same as the preceding, an hour later.* PEER GYNT
is taking off his Turkish dress bit by bit, deliberately and
thoughtfully. When he has finished, he takes a travelling-cap
out of his coat pocket, puts it on and stands once more in European
dress. He flings the turban far away from him.

PEER GYNT.   There lies the Turk, and here stand I!
A pagan existence is no good at all. It's lucky that I can
throw it away with the clothes, and that it's not bred in the
bone. *Qu'allais-je faire dans cette galère?* It's certainly best to
live as a Christian, avoid the temptation of sumptuous garments, fashion your life by what's lawful and moral; in fact,
be yourself—and deserve at the last a funeral oration and
wreaths on your coffin. *(Takes a few steps.)* The baggage!—
Only a little more, and I believe she'd have turned my head.
But I'll be hanged if I understand what it was in her that
so upset me. I am well out of it! If the joke had been pursued
a little farther, it would have made me ridiculous.—I have
erred, no doubt; but it's comforting to feel that my erring
was the result of the position I had assumed; it was not I,
myself, that erred. It was, as a fact, the prophetic life—
devoid of any savouring salt of active work—that caused in
me these lapses into want of taste. It's a sorry business being

a Prophet! In the course of your duties you're apt to get heedless. You're sober and dignified; all of a sudden you find you're nothing of the sort. I certainly gave proof of it by paying homage to that goose, still, all the same—— *(Bursts out laughing.)* Just think of it! Spending the time in wanton dancing! Trying to stem the stream of life by fooling like that!—sweet music, caresses, sighs—and in the end be plucked like any silly hen! Prophetically wild behaviour!—Plucked!—To my shame I've been plucked badly! Still, I've a little left in hand,—some in America, and some safe in my pocket; so I'm not quite on the rocks. And, after all, a moderate amount of wealth is best. I am no longer tied by horses, coachmen and the like; I've neither carriages nor luggage to give me trouble. In a word, I'm master of the situation.—Which way shall I choose? Many are open. It's in such choice that wisdom counts. My business life is a finished chapter; my love affairs, discarded garments; and I have no mind to retrace my steps. "Forward or back it's just as far; out or in, it's just as narrow"—as I think it says in some clever book. I must find some new, some ennobling task; an object that's worth my pains and money. Suppose I wrote, without concealment, the story of my life—a book to serve as a guide and an example to others after me? Or, wait——! I've lots of time at my command—suppose I become a travelling scholar, making a study of bygone ages? That, I believe, is the thing for me! I'd always a fancy for history, and lately I've improved my knowledge. I'll trace the story of mankind! Float like a feather upon the stream of history; and live again, as in a dream, the days of old; see the fierce fights the heroes waged—but from a vantage-point that's safe, that of an onlooker; see how thinkers were slaughtered, martyrs bled; how kingdoms rose and kingdoms fell; watch epochs of world-history grow from their birth; and, in a word, skim all the cream of history.—I must try and get hold of a book of Becker's and go chronologically about it. It's true that my previous knowledge is sketchy, and history's rather an intricate matter,—but what is the odds! It frequently happens that very unusual methods of starting lead to the most original outcome.—To see one's goal and drive towards it, steeling one's heart, is most uplifting! *(With restrained emotion.)* Breaking through every bond that hinders, sundering ties of home and friendship, bidding adieu to love's soft promptings, to solve the mystery of truth! *(Wipes a tear from his eye.) That* is the test of a real enquirer! It makes me happy beyond measure to feel I have solved the great enigma of my destiny. I've only, now, to hold my course through thick and thin! I think I may be well forgiven if I feel proud, and call Peer Gynt a Man, and Manhood's Emperor! The Past shall be a lock to which I have the key; I will desert the sordid paths of modern life. The Present is not worth a shoe-lace. The ways of men are empty, faithless; their minds are dull, their deeds are futile—*(Shrugs his shoulders.)* And women—well their name is frailty! *(Moves on.)*

SCENE X

SCENE. —*Outside a hut in a forest in the far north of Norway. It is a summer's day. The door, which stands open, is furnished with a massive wooden bolt; above the door a pair of reindeer horns is fixed. A herd of goats are feeding by the wall.* SOLVEIG, *now a fair and handsome middle-aged woman, is sitting spinning in the sunshine.*

SOLVEIG *(looks down the path and sings).*

It may not be till winter's past,
And spring and summer—the whole long year;
But I know that you will come at last,
And I shall wait, for I promised you, dear.

> *{Calls to her goats, then resumes her spinning and singing.*

God guard you, dear, where'er you be!
If in Heaven, God have you in His care!
I shall wait till you come back to me;
If you're waiting above, I shall meet you there!

SCENE XI

SCENE.—*In Egypt, at the foot of the statue of Memnon, at dawn. PEER GYNT comes walking along, stops and looks around him.*

PEER GYNT.   I think that this place will do for a start.—Now, for a change, I'm an Egyptian; but Egyptian always upon the basis of the Gyntian Self. I'll wander later into Assyria. I'll stop short of going back to the Creation, for that would only lead to danger. I'll skirt the edges of Bible history. No doubt I'll discover certain traces that will confirm it; but to go minutely into it is not according to my plan of action. *(Sits down on a stone.)* I'll rest awhile and wait with patience until I've heard the Statue singing its customary morning song; and, after I have had my breakfast, I'll climb the Pyramid, and then, if I have time I'll look inside it. Then to the Red Sea, where perhaps I shall discover King Potiphar's grave. Then I will be an Asiatic; in Babylon I'll seek the famous Hanging Gardens and Concubines—the fairest products, that's to say, of civilization. Then a leap, and I'll be at the walls of Troy; and then the sea-route is direct to beautiful old Athens. There, I shall examine, stone by stone, the pass Leonidas defended; I'll make myself familiar with all the best philosophies; find out the gaol where Socrates laid down his life as sacrifice—but, stop a minute, I forgot——! Greece is at war, so for the present I must put Hellenism aside. *(Looks at his watch.)* What a ridiculous time the sun takes in rising! My time's precious. Well, then,—from Troy—that's where I'd got to—*(Gets up and listens.)* I wonder what that curious murmur——?

{The sun rises.

The Memnon Statue (singing).
From the demi-god's ashes arise new-born
    Singing birds.
    Zeus, the all-knowing,
    Shaped them for conflict.
    Owl of Wisdom,
    Where sleep my birds?
You must die if you read not
    The Riddle of the Song!

PEER GYNT.   I really do believe I heard sounds from the Statue! That would be the music of the past. I heard the rise and fall of the Statue's voice. I'll note that down for consideration at experts' hands. *(Makes a note in his pocket-*

book.) "The Statue sang. I heard the sounds quite plainly, but could not completely understand the words. I have, of course, no doubt the whole thing was hallucination. Otherwise, I have not observed anything of importance so far."

{He moves on.

SCENE XII

SCENE.—*Near the village of Gizeh, by the great Sphinx carved out of the rocks. In the distance are seen the spires and minarets of Cairo.* PEER GYNT *arrives; he examines the Sphinx carefully, sometimes through his eye-glass, sometimes through the hollow of his hand.*

PEER GYNT.   Now where in the world have I met before something I only half remember that this ugly thing reminds me of? For met it I have—either north or south. Was it a man? And, in that case, who? The Memnon Statue reminded me of the Troll King of our fairy tales, sitting like that, all stiff and rigid, resting his rump on a piece of rock; but this remarkable mongrel here, this monster, half lion and half woman—have I known it, too, in a fairy tale? Or have I some real recollection of it? A fairy tale?—No, I know the chap! It's the Boyg, if you please, whose skull I cracked—I meant to say that I dreamt I did, for I was lying ill of a fever. *(Goes nearer to the Sphinx.)* The selfsame eyes, the selfsame lips! Not quite so sluggish—a bit more cunning—but in the main points just the same. Well, Boyg, old fellow, you're like a lion, seen from behind and in the daylight! Are you still full of riddles? We'll try and see;

we'll see if you answer as you did before. (*Calls to the Sphinx.*) Hi, Boyg! Who are you?

VOICE (*from behind the Sphinx*).   *Ach, Sfinx, wer bist du?*

PEER GYNT.   What's that? An echo in German? Astounding!

VOICE.   *Wer bist du?*

PEER GYNT.   It's got a perfect accent! The observation's new, and my own. (*Makes a note in his book.*) "Echo in German—with Berlin accent."

{BEGRIFFENFELDT *comes from behind the Sphinx.*

BEGRIFFENFELDT.   A man!

PEER GYNT.   Oh—it was *he* that was talking. (*Makes a further note.*) "Came later to another conclusion."

BEGRIFFENFELDT (*with signs of great excitement*).   Excuse me, sir——! A vital question——! What was it brought you here to-day?

PEER GYNT.   A visit. I'm greeting a friend of my youth.

BEGRIFFENFELDT.   The Sphinx?

PEER GYNT.   Yes, I knew him in days gone by.

BEGRIFFENFELDT.   Splendid!—And after the night I've spent! My forehead is throbbing as if it would burst!— You know him, sir? Then speak! What is he? Can you tell me that?

PEER GYNT.   What is he? Yes, I can tell you that. He is *himself*.

BEGRIFFENFELDT (*with a start*).   Ha! Like a flash I see the answer to life's enigma!—Is it certain that he's himself?

PEER GYNT.   Yes; at least, he said so.

BEGRIFFENFELDT.   Himself! The great awakening's come! (*Takes off his hat.*) Your name, sir?

PEER GYNT.   I am called Peer Gynt.

BEGRIFFENFELDT *(with an air of quiet amazement).* Peer Gynt! Allegorical! What one expected. Peer Gynt? That means: the Great Unknown—the Messiah that was announced to me——

PEER GYNT. No—really? And you came here to find him——?

BEGRIFFENFELDT. Peer Gynt! Profound! Enigmatic! Incisive! Each word is full of deepest teaching! What are you?

PEER GYNT *(modestly).* I have always tried to be myself. And, for the rest, my passport——

BEGRIFFENFELDT. Enigmatic, too! All an enigma! *(Grasps him by the hand.)* Come to Cairo! Come! I have found the Emperor of Exegesis!

PEER GYNT. Emperor?

BEGRIFFENFELDT. Come!

PEER GYNT. Am I really known——?

BEGRIFFENFELDT *(dragging him away with him).* The Emperor of Exegesis—based on Self!

SCENE XIII

SCENE.—*In a lunatic asylum at Cairo. A big courtyard surrounded by high walls and buildings with barred windows. Iron cages on the ground level. Three of the* KEEPERS *are in the courtyard. A fourth comes in.*

FOURTH KEEPER. I say, Schafmann—where's the Director?

ANOTHER KEEPER.   He went out this morning, long before dawn.

FOURTH KEEPER.   I'm afraid something's happened that has upset him, because in the night——

ANOTHER.   Hush! Here he comes!

{BEGRIFFENFELDT shows PEER GYNT in, locks the gate and puts the key in his pocket.

PEER GYNT *(aside).*   He is a remarkably learned man; almost all that he says is beyond understanding. *(Looks round him.)* So this, then, is your Savants' Club?

BEGRIFFENFELDT.   Yes, here you'll find them, bag and baggage—the coterie of seventy professors of Exegesis. Lately a hundred and three new ones joined them.—*(Calls to the KEEPERS.)* Mikkel, Schlingelberg, Schafmann, Fuchs— into the cages with you! Quick!

THE KEEPERS.   We!

BEGRIFFENFELDT.   Yes—who else? Get on! get on! As the world's topsy-turvy, we must follow suit! *(Shuts them up in the cage.)* The mighty Peer has come to us to-day; so you can join the others.—I will say no more.

{Locks the cage and throws the key into a well.

PEER GYNT.   But why—my dear Director——?

BEGRIFFENFELDT.   Don't call me that! I *was* Director until—— Sir, can you keep a secret? I must unburden myself——

PEER GYNT.   What is it?

BEGRIFFENFELDT.   Promise me that you will not tremble.

PEER GYNT.   I will try not to.

BEGRIFFENFELDT *(takes him into a corner and whispers).*   Absolute reason expired at eleven o'clock last night!

PEER GYNT.   God help us——!

BEGRIFFENFELDT.   Yes, it's a great disaster. In *my* position, too, you see, it's doubly disagreeable; because this place, until it happened, was known as a lunatic asylum.

PEER GYNT.   A lunatic asylum!

BEGRIFFENFELDT.   Ah, not *now*, you understand!

PEER GYNT *(aside, growing pale)*.   I see exactly how it is; this fellow is mad—and not a soul suspects it.

{Moves away.

BEGRIFFENFELDT *(following him)*.   I hope you have really understood me? To say it's dead is not accurate. It has left itself—got out of its skin like my friend Baron Munchausen's fox.

PEER GYNT *(trying to get away)*.   Excuse me——

BEGRIFFENFELDT *(holding on to him)*.   No, it was like an eel, not a fox. A nail right through its eye—and there it was, squirming on the wall——

PEER GYNT.   How on earth am I to save myself?

BEGRIFFENFELDT.   Just one slit round the neck— and pop! Out of its pelt it came!

PEER GYNT.   Quite mad!

BEGRIFFENFELDT.   And now the fact is evident that this same exit-from-itself entails a revolution in all the world. All persons who up to that time were known as mad at eleven o'clock last night became normal; this, in conformity with Reason in its newest phase. And, if you consider the matter farther, it's clear that from the selfsame hour our so-called wise men all went mad.

PEER GYNT.   Speaking of time, my time is precious——

BEGRIFFENFELDT.   Your time? You've jogged my memory! *(Opens a door and calls out.)* Come out! The appointed time has come! Reason is dead. Long live Peer Gynt!

PEER GYNT.   No, my dear friend——!

{The mad folk come one after another into the courtyard.

BEGRIFFENFELDT.   Good morning to you! Come out and greet the dawn of freedom! Your Emperor's here!

PEER GYNT.   Their Emperor?

BEGRIFFENFELDT.   Certainly!

PEER GYNT.   It's too great an honour—far more than——

BEGRIFFENFELDT.   No false modesty at such a time as this!

PEER GYNT.   At least give me some respite!—I'm not fit for such a task; I'm quite dumbfounded!

BEGRIFFENFELDT.   The man who guessed the Sphinx's riddle! Who is himself!

PEER GYNT.   That's just my trouble. I am myself in every way! but here, so far as I can see, everyone gets outside themselves.

BEGRIFFENFELDT.   Outside themselves? Oh, no, you're wrong. It's here that men are most themselves—themselves and nothing but themselves—sailing with out-spread sails of self. Each shuts himself in a cask of self, the cask stopped with a bung of self and seasoned in a well of self. None has a tear for others' woes or cares what any other thinks. We are ourselves in thought and voice—ourselves up to the very limit; and, consequently, if we want an Emperor, it's very clear that you're the man.

PEER GYNT.   I wish to goodness——!

BEGRIFFENFELDT.   Don't be downhearted; everything that's new, at first seems strange to one. "One's self"—well, as a specimen, I'll choose the first that comes to hand. *(To a gloomy figure that is passing.)* Good morning, Huhu! Still, my lad, looking the picture of misery?

HUHU *(a Language-Reformer from Malabar)*. What can I

do, when generation after generation dies lacking an interpreter? *(To* PEER GYNT.*)* You're a stranger; will you listen?

PEER GYNT *(bowing).*   By all means.

HUHU.   Then pay attention.—Away in the East, like a bridal crown, lie the shores of Malabar. Portuguese and Hollanders try to civilize the place, where there still survive a lot of original Malabari. These good folk have muddled up their language and now rule supreme in that land. But, long ago, that same countryside was ruled by Orang-outangs. The woods were all theirs; and they could fight, growl and snarl to hearts' content—live, in fact, as Nature made them; they could screech without permission and were lords of all the country. Then there came this horde of strangers and disturbed the primal language that was spoken in the forests. Now four hundred years have passed—that means many generations—and so long a time as that, as one knows, can easily stamp out aborigines. The forest cries have long been dumb, not a growl is ever heard; if we want to speak our minds, we must have recourse to words. It applies to all alike—Portuguese and Hollanders, Hybrid races, Malabari—all are equally affected. I have tried my best to fight for our real forest-tongue; tried to bring its corpse to life; upheld people's right to screech, screeched myself and pointed out the necessity of screeching in our folk-songs. But my efforts met with no result whatever.—Now I think you understand what my grievance is. I thank you for your courtesy in listening. If you think you can advise me what to do, I beg you'll tell me!

PEER GYNT *(aside).*   They say that when you are in Rome you should do as the Romans do. *(Aloud.)* My friend, if I remember rightly, there are forests in Morocco where there are Orang-outangs that have neither songs nor teacher;

and their language much resembles that of Malabar; if you were, like many other statesmen, to expatriate yourself for the good of these same people, it would be a noble action and a fine example also.

HUHU.   Let me thank you, sir, for listening; I will follow your advice. (*With an impressive gesture.*) In the east they flout their singer! The west has its Orang-outangs!

{*Goes out.*

BEGRIFFENFELDT.   Now, surely you'll say that *he's* himself! He's full of himself and nothing else; himself in every word he says—himself when he's beside himself. Come here! I want to show you another, who's been no less conformable to Reason since last night's occurrence. (*To a* FELLAH *who is carrying about a Mummy on his back.*) King Apis, how goes it, my noble sir?

FELLAH (*fiercely, to* PEER GYNT).   Am I King Apis?

PEER GYNT (*getting behind* BEGRIFFENFELDT).   I'm afraid I'm not quite qualified to say; but I should think, if I may judge from what your voice suggests to me——

FELLAH.   Now you are lying, too!

BEGRIFFENFELDT.   Your Highness must kindly deign to let us have an explanation.

FELLAH.   Well, I will. (*Turns to* PEER GYNT.) You see this man I'm carrying? King Apis was his name. They call him now a Mummy; and, what is more, he's dead. He built up all the Pyramids, and carved the mighty Sphinx and fought—so the Director says—with Turks on every side. And therefore the Egyptians worshipped him as a God and set up in their temples his statue as a bull. But *I* am that King Apis—it's just as clear as day; if you don't understand it, I'll make you very soon. King Apis was out a-hunting, and got down from his horse and stepped aside for a moment in my grandfather's field. The soil King Apis fertilized has nourished *me* with corn; and, if more proof is needed, I have invisible horns. Then don't you think it's damnable that I can't get my due? By my birth I am King Apis, but only a Fellah here. If you think you can advise me, tell me, without delay, what I'm to do to make myself like Apis, the great king.

PEER GYNT. Your Highness must build Pyramids and carve a mighty Sphinx, and fight—as the Director says—with Turks on every side.

FELLAH. Yes, that's a likely story! A Fellah! A hungry louse! It's all I can do to keep my hut clear of the rats and mice. Come, think of something better, to make me great and safe, and also make me look like King Apis that's on my back.

PEER GYNT. Suppose your Highness hanged yourself, and then, deep in the ground, within a coffin's sheltering walls, behaved like one that's dead——

FELLAH. I'll do it! Let me have a rope! To the gallows with my head! I'll not be quite like him at first, but time will alter that.

{*Goes away and makes preparations to hang himself.*

BEGRIFFENFELDT. A great personality that, my friend—a man with method——

PEER GYNT. Yes, so I see.—But he really *is* hanging himself! God help us! I feel quite sick—and my brain is turning!

BEGRIFFENFELDT. A transitional stage; it won't last long.

PEER GYNT. Transition? To what? I really must go——

BEGRIFFENFELDT (*holding him back*). Are you mad?

PEER GYNT. Not yet! Mad? God forbid!

{Amidst an uproar, Hussein, *a Minister of State, pushes his way through the other lunatics.*

Hussein.   They tell me an Emperor's come to-day. *(To* Peer Gynt.*)* Is it you?

Peer Gynt *(desperately).*   They've settled that it is!

Hussein.   Good.—Here are papers that need an answer.

Peer Gynt *(tearing his hair).*   Aha! Go on! The more the merrier!

Hussein.   Perhaps you will honour me with a dip? *(Bows low.)* I am a pen.

Peer Gynt *(bowing still lower).*   And I am merely a trumpery imperial parchment.

Hussein.   My history, sir, is briefly this: they think me a sand-box, and not a pen.

Peer Gynt.   And mine, Sir Pen, succinctly told: I'm a paper that's never been written on.

Hussein.   They never will understand what I'm meant for; they all want to use me to sprinkle sand!

Peer Gynt.   I was a book with silver clasps, when I belonged to a woman once. Madness or wisdom is merely a misprint.

Hussein.   But, think—how wretched to be a pen that never has tasted the edge of a knife!

Peer Gynt *(leaping into the air).*   Think what it is to be a reindeer that's always jumping down from a height and never reaching solid ground!

Hussein.   A knife! I am blunt; I need repairing! The world will perish if I'm not mended!

Peer Gynt.   That would be sad when, like all that He made, our Heavenly Father admired it so much.

Begriffenfeldt.   Here's a knife!

HUSSEIN *(grasping it).* Ah, how I shall lick up the ink! How lovely to cut one's self!

{Cuts his throat.

BEGRIFFENFELDT *(moving to one side).* Don't splash me!

PEER GYNT *(with growing terror).* Hold him!

HUSSEIN. Yes, hold me! That's the word! Hold! Hold the Pen! Is the paper there——? *(Falls.)* I'm worn out. A postscript—don't forget it: He was a pen in the hands of others.

PEER GYNT. What shall I——? What am I? Oh, Thou—keep hold! I am what Thou wilt—a Turk, a Sinner, a Troll; only help me! Something has burst within me! *(Shrieks.)* I cannot remember Thy name—help me, Thou— Guardian of all madmen!

{Sinks down in a swoon. BEGRIFFENFELDT, *holding a straw crown in his hand, leaps on to* PEER GYNT *and sits astride of him.*

BEGRIFFENFELDT. See how he sits enthroned in the mud!—He's out of himself! Let us crown him now! *(Puts the crown on* PEER GYNT'S *head and shouts:)* Long live the Emperor of Self!

SCHAFMANN *(in the cage).* Es lebe hoch der grosse Peer!

ACT V

SCENE I

SCENE.—*On board a ship in the North Sea, off the coast of Norway. Sunset and a threatening sky.* PEER GYNT, *now a vigorous old man with grey hair and beard, is on the poop. His clothes, which are somewhat the worse for wear, are half sailor-like; he wears a pilot-jacket and sea-boots. He looks weatherbeaten, and his expression has hardened. The* CAPTAIN *is at the wheel with the* HELMSMAN. *The crew is forward.* PEER GYNT *is leaning his arms on the gunwale and gazing at the land.*

PEER GYNT.   There's Hallingskarven in winter dress; he shows up well in the evening light. And there's his brother Jöklen behind, still wearing his ice-green glacier cap; and, like a lady dressed in white, lies Folgefond behind them both.—Don't try any follies, my ancient friends! Stay where you are—you are made of stone.

CAPTAIN (*calling forward*).   Two men to the wheel—and hoist the light!

PEER GYNT.   It's blowing.

CAPTAIN.   Aye, we'll have a storm.

PEER GYNT.   Can one see Rondë from the sea?

CAPTAIN.   No—it lies hidden behind Faanen.

PEER GYNT.   Or Blaahö?

CAPTAIN.   No; but, from aloft, Galdhöpiggen when the weather's clear.

PEER GYNT.   Which way's Harteigen?

CAPTAIN *(pointing).*   Over there.

PEER GYNT.   Of course.

CAPTAIN.   You seem to know the country.

PEER GYNT.   I passed this way when I sailed from home; and early impressions, as they say, last longest. *(Spits over the side and continues gazing at the coast.)* It is over there—where the hillside glens are blue, in the dark and narrow valleys, and along the open fjords—that is where the people live. *(Looks at the* CAPTAIN.*)* Not many houses on this coast.

CAPTAIN.   No, they are few and far between.

PEER GYNT.   Shall we be in by morning?

CAPTAIN.   Aye, I hope so, if the night is not too bad.

PEER GYNT.   It's gathering in the west.

CAPTAIN.   It is.

PEER GYNT.   Oh, by the way, look here—remind me, when we're settling up, that I intend to make a present to the crew——

CAPTAIN.   You're very good.

PEER GYNT.   It will only be a small one. I made money, but I've lost it; Fate and I have fallen out. You know what I have got on board; well, that's the lot. The rest of it has taken wings and flown away.

CAPTAIN.   Oh, what you've got is quite enough to win respect from folk at home.

PEER GYNT.   I have no folk. There's no one waiting for this rich ugly uncle.—Well, I shall be spared some fuss at landing.

CAPTAIN.   The storm is brewing.

PEER GYNT.   Now remember, if any of you need it badly I'm not close-fisted with my money.

CAPTAIN.   That's kind. They're mostly badly off; they all have wives and families—can scarcely live upon their pay—and, if your kindness sends them home with something extra in their pockets, to-morrow's home-coming will never be forgotten.

PEER GYNT.   What's all that? Do you say they've wives and children? Married?

CAPTAIN.   Yes, married—all the lot. The poorest of them all's the Cook; his house is never free from hunger.

PEER GYNT.   Married? And someone waiting there to greet them when they come? Is that it?

CAPTAIN.   Of course, like all poor folk.

PEER GYNT.   Supposing it's evening when they come—what then?

CAPTAIN.   Then I expect that something tasty will have been got for the occasion——

PEER GYNT.   A lamp upon the table?

CAPTAIN.   Aye, and maybe two; a dram to drink——

PEER GYNT.   They'll sit at ease, in warmth and comfort, with children round them? And such hubbub in the room that no one hears half the other says to them, just because they are so happy?

CAPTAIN.   Very likely; and that's why it's so kind of you to promise they shall have a little present.

PEER GYNT (banging his fist on the gunwale).   No, I'm damned if they shall have it! Do you think me such a fool as to fork out for the pleasure of helping other people's children? I've worked too hard to get my money! No one's waiting for old Peer Gynt.

CAPTAIN.   Just as you please; it's your own money.

PEER GYNT.   Quite so. It's mine and no one else's. Directly you have cast your anchor I'll settle up for what I owe you for my cabin passage hither from Panama; and then I'll give you something for a dram of brandy for the crew;

but not a penny more than that. You may have leave to
knock me down if I give more!

CAPTAIN.   You'll get my receipt, and nothing else.
Now please excuse me; the storm is rising.

> *{He crosses the deck. It has become dark, and the cabin
> lamps are being lit. The sea grows rougher. Fog and
> thick clouds gather.*

PEER GYNT.   Provide for a crowd of others' chil-
drene——? Fill others' hearts with happiness and so be always in their thoughts——? There's no one wasting
thoughts on me. Lamps on their tables? I'll put them out!
I'll find some way——! I will make them drunk; not one
of these fellows shall go home sober. They shall go drunk
to their wives and children; they shall swear—bang loudly
on the table—frighten their families out of their wits! Their
wives shall scream and run out of the house, and their children, too! I'll spoil their pleasure! *(The ship rolls heavily; he
stumbles and has difficulty in holding on.)* That was a bad one!
The sea's as busy as if it were paid for what it's doing. It's
the same always, up here in the north; the sea to fight with,
fierce and angry—— *(Listens.)* What was that cry?

THE WATCH *(forward)*.   A wreck to leeward!

CAPTAIN *(amidships)*.   Starboard the helm! Keep her
close to the wind!

HELMSMAN.   Are there men on the wreck?

THE WATCH.   I can make out three.

PEER GYNT.   Lower a boat——!

CAPTAIN.   It would only capsize.

> *{Goes forward.*

PEER GYNT.   Who thinks of that? *(To the crew.)* If
you're men, you'll save them! You're surely not afraid of a
wetting?

BOATSWAIN.   It's impossible in such a sea as this.

PEER GYNT.   They're calling again! The wind is raging.—Cook, won't you try? Come on! I'll pay you——

COOK.   Not if you gave me twenty guineas.

PEER GYNT.   You dogs! You cowards! Don't you know that these are men that have wives and children who are waiting——?

BOATSWAIN.   Patience will do them good.

CAPTAIN.   Keep her stern to the breakers!

HELMSMAN.   The wreck's gone under.

PEER GYNT.   Was that sudden silence——?

BOATSWAIN.   If they are married, as you suggest, then the world's the richer by three newly-created widows.

{The storm increases in violence. PEER GYNT *goes aft.*

PEER GYNT.   There's no more Faith among men any longer—no more Christianity worth the name; there's little that's good in their words or their deeds, and they pay no heed to the Powers Above. In a storm like to-night's, one may very well be afraid of God; these brutes should cower and remember that, as the saying goes, it's risky to play with elephants,—and then they defy Him openly! *I'm* guiltless enough; if it comes to judgment, I can prove that I made an offer to pay them. But what do I get in return for that? I know they say that your head lies easy if your conscience is clear. That may be true on *terra firma;* but on the sea, where an honest man's quite the exception, I don't consider it worth a rush. At sea you never can be yourself; you simply sink or swim with the others; should the hour of vengeance chance to strike for the Cook and the Boatswain, I most likely should be swept along to perdition with them: there's no respect for individuals,—you're nothing more than one of the crowd. My mistake has been that I've been too meek and get the blame for all that has happened. If I were younger, I do believe I'd change my tune and play the boss. There's time for it yet! It shall get abroad that Peer has come overseas a winner! By hook or crook I'll get back the farm; I'll build on it—it shall look like a castle. But not a soul shall come into my house! They shall stand at the door and twiddle their caps, they shall beg—I'll let them do *that* with pleasure—but I'll not give them a single farthing. If I've had to smart from the lash of fortune, they'll find out that I can hit back again———

> {A STRANGER *is seen standing beside* PEER GYNT *in the gloom, bowing politely to him.*

STRANGER. Good evening!

PEER GYNT. Good evening! What———? Who are you?

STRANGER. Your fellow-passenger, at your service.

PEER GYNT. Indeed? I thought I was the only one.

STRANGER. A wrong impression, corrected now.

PEER GYNT. But it's very strange I have never seen you until this evening———

STRANGER. I don't go out in daytime.

PEER GYNT. Perhaps you are not well? You're as white as a sheet———

STRANGER. I'm quite well, thank you.

PEER GYNT. What a storm!

STRANGER. Yes, what a blessing, man!

PEER GYNT. A blessing?

STRANGER. The waves are mountains high. It makes one's mouth water to think of the wrecks that there will be tonight!—of the corpses that will be washed ashore.

PEER GYNT. God forbid!

STRANGER. Have you ever seen a man that has been strangled—or hanged—or drowned?

PEER GYNT.   What on earth do you mean?

STRANGER.   There's a grin on their faces; but the grin is ghastly, and for the most part they've bitten their tongues.

PEER GYNT.   Do go away!

STRANGER.   Only one question! Suppose, for instance, that the ship should run aground to-night and sink——

PEER GYNT.   Then do you think there's danger?

STRANGER.   I really don't know what to answer. Suppose I'm saved and you get drowned——

PEER GYNT.   Oh, bosh——!

STRANGER.   Well, it's just possible. With one foot in the grave, a man inclines to charitable thoughts——

PEER GYNT (*putting his hand in his pocket*).   I see, it's money that you want!

STRANGER.   No; but if you would be so kind as to present me with your corpse——?

PEER GYNT.   This is too much!

STRANGER.   Merely your corpse! It's for a scientific purpose——

PEER GYNT.   Get out!

STRANGER.   But, my dear friend, consider—the thing would be to your advantage! I'd have you opened and laid bare. It really is the seat of dreaming that I am seeking; but, besides, I'd have you thoroughly examined——

PEER GYNT.   Get out!

STRANGER.   But, sir—a mere drowned corpse!

PEER GYNT.   Blasphemous man! You encourage the storm! What folly! In all this wind and rain and heavy seas and every sign that some fatality may happen—here are you asking for something worse!

STRANGER.   I see that you're not disposed, for the

moment, to carry the matter farther. But time so very often will alter things. *(Bows politely.)* We shall meet when you're sinking, if not before; then, perhaps, you'll be in a better humour.

{Goes into the cabin.

PEER GYNT.   Unpleasant fellows, these men of science! Freethinkers, too—— *(To the* BOATSWAIN *who is passing.)* A word, my friend! Who is that lunatic passenger?

BOATSWAIN.   I did not know we had any but you.

PEER GYNT.   No other? Why, this gets worse and worse. *(To a* SAILOR *who comes out of the cabin.)* Who went into the cabin just now?

SAILOR.   The ship's dog, sir!

{Passes on.

THE WATCH *(calling out).*   Land close ahead!

PEER GYNT.   My trunk! My box! Bring them up on deck!

BOATSWAIN.   We have something else to think about now.

PEER GYNT.   Captain, I wasn't serious in what I said! I was only joking! Of course I'm going to help the Cook——!

CAPTAIN.   The jib has gone!

MATE.   There went the foresail!

BOATSWAIN *(calling from forward).*   Breakers ahead!

CAPTAIN.   She'll go to pieces!

{The ship strikes. Noise and confusion.

SCENE II

SCENE.—*Off the coast, amongst rocks and breakers. The ship is sinking. Through the mist, glimpses are caught of a boat with two men in it. A breaking wave fills it; it capsizes; a scream is heard, then all is still for a while. Soon afterwards the boat comes into sight, floating keel uppermost.* PEER GYNT *comes to the surface near the boat.*

PEER GYNT.   Help! Help! A boat!—Help! I shall sink! God save me—as the Bible says!

> {*Clings tight to the keel of the boat. The* COOK *comes to the surface on the other side of the boat.*

COOK.   Oh, God—for my dear children's sake be pitiful! Let me be saved!

> {*Holds on to the keel.*

PEER GYNT.   Let go!

COOK.   Let go!

PEER GYNT.   I'll push you off!

COOK.   I'll push *you* off!

PEER GYNT.   I'll kick you off! Let go your hold! It won't bear two!

COOK.   I know. Get off!

PEER GYNT.   Get off yourself!

COOK.   Not likely!

> {*They fight. The* COOK *gets one hand hurt, but clings fast to the boat with the other hand.*

PEER GYNT.   Take your hand away!

COOK.   Be kind! Be merciful!—Just think of my young children there at home!

PEER GYNT.   I have more need to live than you, for I have got no children yet.

COOK. Let go! You've had your life; I'm young!

PEER GYNT. Be quick and sink; you're much too heavy.

COOK. Have mercy! For God's sake let go! There's no one that will mourn for you——*(Shrieks and slips down.)* I'm drowning!

PEER GYNT *(catching hold of the* COOK'S *hair).* No, I've got you tight by your back hair; repeat "Our Father"!

COOK. I can't remember—all seems dark——

PEER GYNT. Say what is most essential! Quick!

COOK. "Give us this day"——

PEER GYNT. Oh, skip all that; you have got all that you will need.

COOK. "Give us this day"——

PEER GYNT. The same old song! It's easy seen you were a cook——

{His grip gives way.

COOK *(sinking).* "Give us this day our"——

{Goes under.

PEER GYNT. Amen, lad! You were yourself up to the end. *(Swings himself up on to the keel of the boat.)* Where there is life there's always hope——

{The STRANGER *is seen in the water, catching hold of the boat.*

STRANGER. Good morning!

PEER GYNT. Eh!

STRANGER. I heard a cry; it's funny I should find you here. Well? Do you see I spoke the truth?

PEER GYNT. Let go! There's barely room for one!

STRANGER. I'll swim quite well with my left leg. I'll float if only I insert my finger-tip into this crack. But what about your corpse?

PEER GYNT. Be quiet!

STRANGER.   The rest is absolutely done for———

PEER GYNT.   Do hold your tongue!

STRANGER.   Just as you wish.

{Silence.

PEER GYNT.   Well?

STRANGER.   I am silent.

PEER GYNT.   Devil's tricks!—What are you doing?

STRANGER.   I am waiting.

PEER GYNT *(tearing his hair).*   I shall go mad! What are you?

STRANGER *(nodding to him).*   Friendly!

PEER GYNT.   Go on! What more?

STRANGER.   What do you think? Don't you know anyone that's like me?

PEER GYNT.   I know the Devil———

STRANGER *(lowering his voice).*   Is he wont to light us on the darkest paths of life when we're beset by fear?

PEER GYNT.   Oh! So it seems, on explanation, that you're a messenger of the light?

STRANGER.   Friend, have you known—say, twice a year—what terror really means?

PEER GYNT.   Of course. One is afraid when danger threatens; but your words are ambiguous———

STRANGER.   Well, have you ever, even once, triumphed as the result of terror?

PEER GYNT *(looking at him).*   If you have come to guide my steps, 'twas stupid not to come before. It's not much good to choose the time when I'm most likely to be drowned.

STRANGER.   And would your triumph be more likely if you sat snugly by your fire?

PEER GYNT.   Perhaps not; but your talk was foolish. How could you think it would affect me?

STRANGER.   Where I come from, they think a smile worth quite as much as any pathos.

PEER GYNT.   There is a time for everything. Things which a publican may do are most disgraceful in a bishop.

STRANGER.   The souls of those bygone days whose ashes rest in funeral urns aren't always in a solemn humour.

PEER GYNT.   Leave me, you bugbear! Get away! I won't die! I must get to land!

STRANGER.   As far as that goes, make your mind quite easy; no one ever dies until he's seen the fifth act through.

{Disappears.

PEER GYNT.   Ah, it slipped out of him at last;—he was a wretched Moralist.

SCENE III

SCENE.—*A churchyard high up in the mountains. A funeral is going on. The* PRIEST *and the* MOURNERS *are just finishing the last verse of a hymn.* PEER GYNT *is passing on the road and stops at the churchyard gate.*

PEER GYNT.   Here's another man going the way of all flesh. Well, God be praised that it isn't me!

{Goes into the churchyard.

PRIEST.   Now that his soul has gone to meet its God, and this poor dust waits like an empty husk,—let us, dear friends, in a few words recall the dead man's journey on this earth of ours. He wasn't rich, nor was he very clever; his voice was weak, his bearings scarcely manly; he had no strength of mind, nor much decision; nor in his own home did he seem the master. His manner when he came to church was such as if he felt he must request permission to take his seat among the congregation. Of Gudbrandsdal he was, you know, a native, and he was scarce a boy when he came hither; and, to the last, as you no doubt have noticed, he always kept his right hand in his pocket. That same peculiarity I mention was probably the only thing that stamped his picture on our minds; that, and the shyness—the almost shame-faced diffidence—with which he bore himself when he came in amongst us. But, though he was so diffident and quiet, and to the last was almost like a stranger, you know quite well, in spite of his concealment, the hand he hid had no more than four fingers.—I well remember, many years ago, during the war, one morning a Conscription was held at Lundë. Everyone was full of Norway's troubles and her doubtful future. Behind a table, I remember, sat a Captain and the Mayor, and several Sergeants; and one by one our lads came in, were measured, enrolled and duly sworn in to the army. The room was full; and outside in the courtyard was heard the noise of the young people's laughter. A name was called out, and a lad came in with face as white as snow upon the hilltops. They told him to come forward to the table. His right hand was all swathed up in a napkin; he gasped and swallowed—tried to find his voice—but seemed as if he had no words to answer the Captain's questions. Still, at last, he did; and then, with crimson face and faltering tongue that sometimes let the words out with a rush, he mumbled some tale of an accident—a reaping-hook that slipped and cut his finger clean off his hand. There was a sudden silence. Men exchanged glances; lips were curled in scorn; looks of disdain were flashed upon the lad, who stood there staring with unseeing eyes; he felt their scorn although he did not see it. And then the Captain, an old grey-haired man, stood up, and spat, and pointed to the door and said: "Begone!"—and so the lad went out. Those in the room divided to make way, so that he ran the gauntlet of them all. He reached the door and then took to his heels; ran up the hillside—through the woods and pastures, up over rocks and stones, stumbling and slipping—to where his home was, far up in the mountains. 'Twas six months after that when he came hither, bringing his mother, children and betrothed. He leased some land upon the mountain-side near to where Lomb is bounded by the moor. As soon as it was possible, he married the mother of his children; built a house; broke up the stony ground with such success that yellow grain in patches soon appeared amidst the rocks. It's true that when he went to church he kept his right hand in his pocket; but on his farm I know he worked as well with nine fingers as others with their ten.—Then, one wet spring, a flood swept all away. They saved their lives, but nothing else; and, poor and naked as he was, he set to work to clear the soil afresh; and by the autumn he'd built himself a house on safer ground. Safer? Yes, from the flood but not the mountains. For, two years later, in an avalanche all that he had was overwhelmed again. But even avalanches had no power to daunt his soul. He set to work to dig and clear the snow and save what might be left; and, ere the winter's snow had come again, he'd built his little house a third time up. Three sons he had—three fine young lads—and they must go to school, and school was far away; and so, from where the public roadway ended, he had to cut a steep and narrow path through the hard snow. And then—what did he do? The eldest boy had to climb up and scramble as best he could; and where it was too steep his father roped him to him for support. The other two he carried in his arms and on his back. And thus, year after year, he drudged; and his three sons grew to be men. Then came a time when he might surely ask for something in return from them; but they, three prosperous men in far America, had quite forgotten their Norwegian father and how he used to help them to the school. He was a man whose vision never saw farther than what lay nearest to his hand. Words which resound in other people's hearts were meaningless to him as tinkling bells; Family, Country—all that's best and brightest—was blurred and hidden by a veil of tears. But never did I know a man so humble. From that Conscription Day he carried with him the sense of guilt, which showed as plainly on him as did the blush of shame upon his cheek and his four fingers hidden in his pocket. A breaker of his country's laws? Perhaps! But there is something that outshines the law as certainly as Glittertinde's peaks stand gleaming in the sun above the clouds. He was a bad citizen, no doubt; for Church and State alike, a sterile tree; but up there on the rocky mountainside, in the small circle of his hearth and home, where his work lay, *there* I say he was great, because he was himself. 'Twas only there the metal he was made of could ring true. His life was like a melody that's played on muted strings.—And therefore, peace be with you, poor silent warrior, who fought and fell waging the little war of peasant's life! We will not seek to search the heart and reins; that's not a task for us, but for his Maker. Still, this I hope—and hope with confidence: that this man, as he stands before the Throne, is not a cripple in the eyes of God!

> {*The congregation disperses.* PEER GYNT *remains alone.*

PEER GYNT.   Well, *that's* what I call Christianity! Nothing in it to make one feel uneasy. Indeed the theme of the Priest's address—that we should all strive to be ourselves—is really extremely edifying. *(Looks into the grave.)* Was it he, I wonder, who slashed his knuckles when I was felling trees in the forest? Who knows? If I were not standing here by the grave of this congenial spirit, I might believe that it was myself that was sleeping there and was listening in dreams to praises that I deserved. It's really a beautiful Christian practice to take a kindly retrospect of the whole life of the departed. I'd readily accept a verdict from this most worthy priest.—However, I've still some time left, I expect, before the sexton comes and claims me; and, as the Scripture says: "The best is still the best"; and, in like manner: "Sufficient for the day is the evil thereof"; and, further: "Do not borrow trouble."—The Church is the only comforter. Up till now I have never given the credit to it that is its due; but now I know what good it does you to hear authority proclaim: "As you have sowed, so must you reap." We must be ourselves; in everything, both great and small, we must look after ourselves and what concerns ourselves. Though Fortune fail us we shall win respect, if our careers have been shaped in accordance with this doctrine.— And now for home! What though the way be steep and narrow—what though Fortune be still malicious—old Peer Gynt will go his own way, and remain, as always: poor but virtuous.

(Goes.

SCENE IV

SCENE.—*A hillside showing the dried-up bed of a stream, by which stands a ruined mill. The ground is torn up, and everything is in a ruinous state. Outside the mill an auction is taking place; there is a large and noisy gathering of people, and drinking is going on. PEER GYNT is sitting on a heap of rubbish near the mill.*

PEER GYNT.   Backward or forward, it's just as far; out or in, the way's as narrow. Time destroys and the stream cuts through. "Round about," said the Boyg; and we needs must, here.

A MAN IN MOURNING.   Now there's nothing left but the rubbish. *(Looks at PEER GYNT.)* Strangers, too? God save you, sir!

PEER GYNT.   Well met! This is a merry scene; is it a christening, or a wedding?

MAN IN MOURNING.   I should rather say a house-warming; the bride, poor thing, is food for worms.

PEER GYNT.   And worms are fighting for rags and scraps.

MAN IN MOURNING.   It's a finished story, and this is the end.

PEER GYNT.   Every story ends the same; I've known them all since I was a boy.

A YOUNG BOY *(holding a casting-ladle)*.   Look what a fine thing I have bought! Peer Gynt used to mould buttons with this.

ANOTHER.   I got a fine purse for a farthing!

A THIRD.   A pedlar's pack for twopence halfpenny!

PEER GYNT.   Peer Gynt? Who was he?

MAN IN MOURNING.   I only know he was brother-in-law to the bridegroom, Death, and also to the blacksmith Aslak.

A MAN IN GREY.   You're forgetting me; you must be drunk!

MAN IN MOURNING.   You're forgetting the loft-door at Hægstad.

MAN IN GREY.   So I was; but you were never dainty.

MAN IN MOURNING.   If only she doesn't play Death a trick——

MAN IN GREY.   Come on! Have a drink with your relation!

MAN IN MOURNING.   Relation be damned! Your drunken fancies——

MAN IN GREY.   Oh, nonsense! Blood is thicker than that; at least we're both Peer Gynt's relations.

{They go off together.

PEER GYNT (*aside*).   I'm meeting old friends.

A BOY (*calling after the* MAN IN MOURNING).   My poor dead mother will come after you, Aslak, if you get drinking.

PEER GYNT (*getting up*).   The Agriculturalists are wrong; it doesn't smell better the deeper you dig.

A BOY (*with a bearskin*).   Here's the Dovrë-Cat!—or at least his skin! It was he chased the Troll on Christmas Eve.

ANOTHER (*with a pair of reindeer-horns*).   Here's the fine buck on which Peer Gynt rode right along the ridge of Gendin.

A THIRD (*with a hammer, calls to the* MAN IN MOURNING).   Hi! Aslak! Do you know this hammer? Was it this you used when the Devil escaped?

A FOURTH (*showing his empty hands*).   Mads Moen, here's the invisible cloak in which Peer Gynt and Ingrid vanished.

PEER GYNT.   Some brandy, boys! I'm feeling old; I'll hold an auction of all my rubbish.

A BOY.   What have you got to sell?

PEER GYNT.   A castle; it's up at Rondë, and solidly built

BOY.   I bid one button!

PEER GYNT.   A drink with it, then; it's a sin and a shame to offer less.

ANOTHER BOY.   He's a merry old chap!

{*The crowd gathers round* PEER GYNT.

PEER GYNT.   Granë, my horse!—Who bids?

ONE OF THE CROWD.   Where is he?

PEER GYNT.   Away in the West! Near the sunset, boys! He can trot as fast as Peer Gynt could make up his lies.

VOICES.   What more have you?

PEER GYNT.   Both gold and rubbish! I bought them at a loss, and now I'll sell them at a sacrifice.

A BOY.   Put them up!

PEER GYNT.   A vision of a prayer-book! You may have it for a hook and eye.

BOY.   Deuce take your visions!

PEER GYNT.   Then—my Empire! I throw it to you; you may scramble for it!

BOY.   Does a crown go with it?

PEER GYNT.   A lovely crown of straw, and it will fit the first that puts it on.—Here's something more! An empty egg! Grey hair of a madman! The Prophet's beard!—You may have them all, if you'll only show me on the hillside a signpost marked: "This is the way"!

THE MAYOR (*who has come up*).   The way you're going on, my man, I think will lead you to the lock-up.

PEER GYNT (*with his hat in his hand*).   Very likely. But, tell me, who was Peer Gynt?

THE MAYOR.   Oh, bother——!

PEER GYNT.   Excuse me—I want to know——!

THE MAYOR.   Well,—they say, an incurable romancer.

PEER GYNT.   Romancer?

THE MAYOR.   Yes; romanced about all sorts of glorious deeds as if he had done all of them himself. Excuse me now, my friend, I'm busy——

{Goes away.

PEER GYNT.   And where's this wonderful fellow now?

AN ELDERLY MAN.   He went oversea to a foreign land and came to grief as one might have expected. It's many years now since he was hanged.

PEER GYNT.   Hanged? Dear me! I was sure of it; the late Peer Gynt was himself to the last. (*Bows.*) Good-bye. I'm much obliged to you all! (*Takes a few steps, then stops.*) You merry boys and lovely women, may I tell you a story in return?

VOICES.   Yes, if you know one!

PEER GYNT.   Certainly. (*Comes back to them. His face takes on an altered expression.*) I was in San Francisco, gold-digging, and the whole town was full of freaks; one played the fiddle with his toes, one danced fandangoes on his knees, a third, I heard, kept making verses while holes were bored right through his skull. To this freak-show the Devil came, to try his luck like so many others. His line was this: he could imitate the grunting of a pig exactly. His personality attracted although he was not recognized. The house was full and on tenterhooks of expectation. In he strode, dressed in a cape with flowing wings; *Man muss sich drappieren,* as the Germans say. But no one knew that in his cape he had a little pig concealed. And now he started his performance. The Devil pinched; the pig gave tongue. The whole was a fantasia on a pig's life, from birth to slaughter, ending up with a shriek like that which follows on the slaughterer's stroke; with which, the artist bowed and went.——Then there arose a keen discussion among the experts in the audience. The noises were both praised and censured; some found the tone of them too thin. Others declared the dying shriek was far too studied; but they all were of the same mind on one point: That the performance was, *qua* grunt, exceedingly exaggerated. You see, that's what the Devil got, because he'd made the sad mistake of reckoning without his public.

> *(Bows and goes away. An uneasy silence falls on the crowd.*

SCENE V

SCENE.——*A clearing in a great forest, on the Eve of Pentecost. In the background is seen a hut, with a pair of reindeer-horns over the door.* PEER GYNT *is on all-fours on the ground, grubbing up wild onions.*

PEER GYNT.   This is one standpoint. Where is the next? One should try all things and choose the best. I have done that; I've been a Caesar, and now I'm behaving like Nebuchadnezzar. So I might go through Bible history. This

old boy's back to mother earth. I remember the Book says:
"Dust thou art." The great thing in life is to fill your belly.
Fill it with onions? It matters little; I'll fit some cunning
traps and snares. There is a brook; I'll not go thirsty; and
all wild things shall do my bidding. And, suppose I die—
which perhaps may happen—I'll creep beneath a fallen tree;
like the bear, I'll cover myself with leaves and scratch in the
bark, in great big letters: "Here lies Peer Gynt, a decent
chap, who was Emperor of all the Beasts."—Emperor?
(Laughs to himself.) You absurd old humbug! You're not an
emperor, you're an onion! Now, my dear Peer, I'm going to
peel you, however little you may enjoy it. *(Takes an onion
and peels it, layer by layer.)* There's the untidy outer husk;
that's the shipwrecked man on the wreck of the boat; next
layer's the Passenger, thin and skinny—still smacking of
Peer Gynt a little. Next we come to the gold-digger self;
the pith of it's gone—someone's seen to that. This layer with
a hardened edge is the fur-hunter of Hudson's Bay. The next
one's like a crown. No, thank you! We'll throw it away
without further question. Here's the Antiquarian, short and
sturdy; and here is the Prophet, fresh and juicy; he stinks,
as the saying goes, of lies enough to bring water to your
eyes. This layer, effeminately curled, is the man who lived
a life of pleasure. The next looks sickly. It's streaked with
black. Black may mean missionaries or negroes. *(Pulls off
several layers together.)* There's a most surprising lot of layers!
Are we never coming to the kernel? *(Pulls all that is left to
pieces.)* There isn't one! To the innermost bit it's nothing but
layers, smaller and smaller. Nature's a joker! *(Throws the bits
away from him.)* Deuce take all thinking! If you begin that,
you may miss your footing. Well, anyway, *I* don't run that
risk as long as I'm down on all-fours here. *(Scratches the back
of his head.)* Life's an uncommonly odd contraption; it plays

an underhand game with us; if you try to catch hold of it, it eludes you, and you get what you didn't expect—or nothing. *(Goes closer to the hut, looks at it and starts.)* That hut? In the forest——! Eh? *(Rubs his eyes.)* I'm certain I must have seen that hut before. The reindeer-horns there, over the door——! A mermaid carved on the end of the gable——! That's a lie! No mermaid—just logs and nails—and the bolt that should keep out plaguy thoughts——!

{SOLVEIG'S *voice is heard from the hut.*

SOLVEIG *(singing).*

> Now all is ready for Pentecost.
> Dear lad far away, are you coming near?
> If your burden's heavy, then rest awhile;
> I shall wait, because I promised you, dear.

{PEER GYNT *rises to his feet, deathly pale and quiet.*

PEER GYNT. *One who remembered—and one who forgot; one who has kept what the other has lost. Life's serious, not a foolish jest! Ah, misery! Here* my Empire lay!

{*Runs into the wood.*

SCENE VI

SCENE.—*A moor with firs, at night. A forest fire has laid it waste. Charred tree-trunks for miles around. Patches of white mist are lying here and there over the ground.* PEER GYNT *comes running over the moor.*

PEER GYNT. Ashes, mists and dust clouds flying— fine material to build with! Stench and rottenness within

them; all a whited sepulchre. Fancies, dreams and stillborn
wisdom for a base, while lies shall serve for a staircase for
the building of a lofty pyramid. Flight from everything
that's worthy; no repentance—terror; these shall cap a building labelled: "Petruf Gyntus Caesar fecit"! *(Listens.)* What
is that sound like children's weeping?—Weeping that is half
a song? What are these that I see rolling at my feet, like
balls of thread? *(Kicks his feet about.)* Get away! You block
the path up!

THE THREADBALLS (on the ground).

> We are thoughts;
> You should have thought us;
> Little feet, to life
> You should have brought us!

PEER GYNT *(going round them).* I've only brought *one*
thought to life,—and it was wry and bandy-legged!

THE THREADBALLS.

> We should have risen
> With glorious sound;
> But here like threadballs
> We are earth-bound.

PEER GYNT *(stumbling).* Threadballs! You infernal
rascals! Are you tripping up your father?

{Runs away.

WITHERED LEAVES *(flying before the wind).*

> We are a watchword;
> You should have used us!

> Life, by your sloth,
> Has been refused us.
> By worms we're eaten
> All up and down;
> No fruit will have us
> For spreading crown.

PEER GYNT.   Still, you have not been born for nothing; lie still, and you will serve for manure.

A SIGHING IN THE AIR.

> We are songs;
> You should have sung us!
> In the depths of your heart
> Despair has wrung us!
> We lay and waited;
> You called us not.
> May your throat and voice
> With poison rot!

PEER GYNT.   Poison yourselves, you silly doggerel!
Had I any time for verse and twaddle?

> > {Goes to one side.

DEWDROPS (dropping from the branches).

> We are tears
> Which were never shed.
> The cutting ice
> Which all hearts dread
> We could have melted;
> But now its dart
> Is frozen into
> A stubborn heart.

The wound is closed;
Our power is lost.

PEER GYNT.   Thanks!—I wept at Rondesvalen and
got a thrashing on the backside!

BROKEN STRAWS.

We are deeds
You have left undone;
Strangled by doubt,
Spoiled ere begun.
At the Judgment Day
We shall be there
To tell our tale;
How will you fare?

PEER GYNT.   Rubbish! You can't condemn a man
for actions that he *hasn't* done!

AASE'S VOICE (*from afar off*).

Fi, what a driver!
Ugh! You've upset me
Into a snowdrift,
Muddied and wet me.
Peer, where's the Castle?
You've driven madly;
The whip in your hand
The Devil's used badly!

PEER GYNT.   I'd best be off while I am able. If I
have to bear the burden of the Devil's sins, I'll sink into the
ground. I find my own quite a heavy enough load.

{Runs off.

SCENE VII

SCENE.—*Another part of the moor.*

PEER GYNT (*singing*).

> A sexton! a sexton! Where are you all?
> Open your bleating mouths and sing!
> We've bands of crape tied round our hats,
> And plenty of corpses for burying!

> {The BUTTON MOULDER, *carrying his box of tools
> and a big casting-ladle, comes in by a side path.*

BUTTON MOULDER.   Well met, gaffer!

PEER GYNT.   Good evening, my friend!

BUTTON MOULDER.   You seem in a hurry. Where
are you going?

PEER GYNT.   To a funeral.

BUTTON MOULDER.   Really? My sight's not good—
excuse me—is your name by any chance Peer?

PEER GYNT.   Peer Gynt's my name.

BUTTON MOULDER.   What a piece of luck! It was
just Peer Gynt I was looking for.

PEER GYNT.   Were you? What for?

BUTTON MOULDER.   Well, as you see, I am a button
moulder; and you must be popped into my Castle-ladle.

PEER GYNT.   What for?

BUTTON MOULDER.   So as to be melted down.

PEER GYNT.   Melted?

BUTTON MOULDER.   Yes; it's clean and it's empty.
Your grave is dug and your coffin ordered; your body will

make fine food for worms; but the Master's orders bid me fetch your soul at once.

PEER GYNT.   Impossible! Like this?—without the slightest warning?

BUTTON MOULDER.   Alike for funerals and confinements the custom is to choose the day without giving the slightest warning to the chief guest of the occasion.

PEER GYNT.   Quite so. My head is going round! You are——?

BUTTON MOULDER.   You heard; a button moulder.

PEER GYNT.   I understand! A favorite child is called by lots of names.—Well, Peer, so *that's* to be the end of your journey!—Still, it's a scurvy trick to play me. I deserved something a little kinder. I'm not so bad as perhaps you think; I've done some little good in the world. At worst I might be called a bungler, but certainly not an out-and-out sinner.

BUTTON MOULDER.   But that is just the point, my man. In the highest sense you're not a sinner; so you escape the pangs of torment and come into the Casting-ladle.

PEER GYNT.   Oh, call it what you like—a ladle or the bottomless pit—it's just the same! Ginger is always hot in the mouth, whatever you may be pleased to call it. Satan, away!

BUTTON MOULDER.   You are not so rude as to think that I've a cloven hoof?

PEER GYNT.   Cloven hoof of fox's claws—whichever you like. So now pack off! Mind your own business and be off!

BUTTON MOULDER.   My friend, you're under a great delusion. We're both in a hurry; so, to save time, I'll try to explain the matter to you. You are, as you yourself have said, nothing great in the way of a sinner—scarcely a middling one, perhaps——

PEER GYNT.   Now you are talking reasonably.

BUTTON MOULDER.   Wait a bit!—I think it would be going too far to call you virtuous——

PEER GYNT.   I certainly don't lay claim to that.

BUTTON MOULDER.   Well, then, say, something betwixt and between. Sinners in the true grand style are seldom met with nowadays; that style of sin needs power of mind—it's something more than dabbling in mud.

PEER GYNT.   That's perfectly true; one should go at it with something of a Berserk's fury.

BUTTON MOULDER.   You, on the contrary, my friend, took sinning lightly.

PEER GYNT.   Just, my friend, a little mud-splashed, so to speak.

BUTTON MOULDER.   Now we're agreed. The bottomless pit is not for you who played with mud.

PEER GYNT.   Consequently, my friend, I take it that I may have your leave to go just as I came?

BUTTON MOULDER.   Oh, no, my friend—consequently you'll be melted down.

PEER GYNT.   What's this new game that you've invented while I have been abroad?

BUTTON MOULDER.   The practice is just as old as the Creation and was invented for the purpose of keeping things up to the standard. You know in metal work, for instance, it sometimes happens that a casting turns out a failure, absolutely—buttons are turned out without loops. What would you do in such a case?

PEER GYNT.   I'd throw the trash away.

BUTTON MOULDER.   Exactly. Your father had the reputation of reckless wastefulness as long as he had anything to waste. The Master, on the other hand, is economical, you see, and therefore is a man of substance. He never throws away as useless a single thing that may be dealt with as raw material.—Now, *you* were meant to be a gleaming button on the world's waistcoat, but your loop was missing; so you've got to go into the scrap-heap, to be merged into the mass.

PEER GYNT.   But do you mean that I've got to be melted down with any Tom and Dick and Harry and moulded fresh?

BUTTON MOULDER.   That's what I mean. That's what we've done to not a few, it's what they do at the mint with the money when the coin is too much worn with use.

PEER GYNT.   But it's simply disgusting niggardliness! My dear friend, won't you let me go? A loopless button—a smooth-worn coin—what are they to a man of your master's substance?

BUTTON MOULDER.   The fact of your having a soul's enough to give you a certain intrinsic value.

PEER GYNT.   No, I say! No! With tooth and nail I'll fight against it! I'd rather, far, put up with anything than that!

BUTTON MOULDER.   But what do you mean by "anything"? You must be reasonable, you know; you're not the sort that goes to heaven——

PEER GYNT.   I'm humble; I don't aim so high as that; but I'm not going to lose a single jot of what's myself. Let me be sentenced in ancient fashion; Send me to Him with the Cloven Hoof for a certain time—say, a hundred years, if the sentence must be a very severe one. That's a thing I dare say one might put up with; the torture would then be only moral, and perhaps, after all, not so very tremendous. It would be a transition, so to speak, as the fox said. If you wait, there comes deliverance and you may get back; meanwhile you hope for better days. But the other idea—to be swallowed up like a speck in a mass of strange material—this ladle business—losing all the attributes that make a Gynt—*that* fills my inmost soul with horror!

BUTTON MOULDER.   But, my dear Peer, there is no need for you to make so great a fuss about so small a thing; because you never yet have been yourself. What difference can it make to you if, when you die, you disappear?

PEER GYNT.   *I've* never been myself! Haha! You almost make me laugh. Peer Gynt anything but himself!— No, no, friend Button Moulder, you are wrong; you're judging blindly. If you searched my inmost being, you would find I'm Peer right through, and nothing else.

BUTTON MOULDER.   Impossible. Here are my orders. See, they say: "You will fetch Peer Gynt. He has defied his destiny. He is a failure, and must go straight into the Casting-ladle."

PEER GYNT.   What nonsense! It must surely mean some other Gynt. Are you quite sure that it says Peer?— not John, or Rasmus?

BUTTON MOULDER.   I melted them down long ago. Now, come along and don't waste time.

PEER GYNT.   No, that I won't! Suppose to-morrow you found that it meant someone else? That would be pleasant! My good man, you must be careful, and remember what a responsibility——

BUTTON MOULDER.   I've got my orders to protect me.

PEER GYNT.   Give me a little respite, then!

BUTTON MOULDER.   What for?

PEER GYNT.   I will find means to prove that, all my life, I've been myself; that is, of course, the point at issue.

BUTTON MOULDER.   Prove it? But how?

PEER GYNT.   With witnesses and testimonials.

BUTTON MOULDER.   I fear that you won't satisfy the Master.

PEER GYNT.   I'm quite sure that I shall! Besides, we'll talk about that when the time comes. Dear man, just let me have myself on loan for quite a little while. I will come back to you. We men are not born more than once, you know, and naturally we make a fight to keep the self with which we came into the world.—Are we agreed?

BUTTON MOULDER.   So be it. But, remember this: At the next crossroads we shall meet.

{PEER GYNT *runs off.*

SCENE VIII

SCENE.—*Another part of the moor.*

PEER GYNT (*running in*).   Time is money, as people say. If I only knew where the crossroads are—it may be near, or it may be far. The ground seems to burn my feet like fire. A witness! A witness! Where shall I find one? It's next to impossible, here in the forest. The world's a bungle! It's managed wrong, if it's necessary for a man to prove his rights that are clear as the noonday sun!

{*A bent* OLD MAN, *with a staff in his hand and a bag on his back, hobbles up to* PEER GYNT.

OLD MAN.   Kind sir, give a homeless old man a penny!

PEER GYNT.   I'm sorry—I have no change about me——

OLD MAN.   Prince Peer! Can it be that we meet at last?

PEER GYNT.   Why, who——?

OLD MAN.   He's forgotten the old man at Rondë!

PEER GYNT.   You surely are never——?

OLD MAN.   The King of the Dovrë.

PEER GYNT.   The Troll King? Really? The Troll King?—Answer!

OLD MAN.   I'm he, but in different circumstances.

PEER GYNT.   Ruined?

OLD MAN.   Aye, robbed of everything; a tramp, and as hungry as a wolf.

PEER GYNT.   Hurrah! Such witnesses as this don't grow on every tree!

OLD MAN.   Your Highness has grown grey too since last we met.

PEER GYNT.   Worry and age, dear father-in-law. Well, let's forget our private affairs; and, above all, our family squabbles. I was a foolish youth——

OLD MAN.   Yes, yes; you were young, and youth must have its fling. And it's lucky for you that you jilted your bride; you've escaped a lot of shame and bother, for afterwards she went clean to the bad——

PEER GYNT.   Dear me!

OLD MAN.   Now she may look after herself. Just think—she and Trond have gone off together.

PEER GYNT.   What Trond?

OLD MAN.   Of the Valfjeld.

PEER GYNT.   He? Aha, I robbed him of the cowherd girls.

OLD MAN.   But my grandson's grown a fine big fellow and has bouncing babies all over the country.

PEER GYNT.   Now, my dear man, I must cut you short: I am full of quite a different matter.—I'm in rather a difficult position and have to get a certificate or a testimonial from someone; and I think you'll be the very person. I can always raise the wind enough to stand you a drink——

OLD MAN.   Oh! Can I really be of assistance to Your Highness? Perhaps, if that is so, you'll give me a character in return?

PEER GYNT.   With pleasure. I'm a little short of ready money and have to be careful in every way.—Now, listen to me. Of course you remember how I came that night to woo your daughter——

OLD MAN.   Of course, Your Highness!

PEER GYNT.   Oh, drop the title! Well, you wanted to do me violence—to spoil my sight by cutting my eyeball and turn Peer Gynt into a Troll. What did I do? I strongly objected; swore I would stand on my own feet; gave up my love, and power and honours, simply and solely to be myself. I want you to swear to that in court——

OLD MAN.   I can't do that!

PEER GYNT.   What's that you're saying?

OLD MAN.   You'll surely not force me to swear a lie? Remember that you put on Troll breeches and tasted our mead——

PEER GYNT.   Yes, you tempted me. But I resolutely made up my mind that I would not give in. And *that's* the way a man shows what he's worth. A song depends on its concluding verse.

OLD MAN.   But the conclusion, Peer, was just the opposite of what you think.

PEER GYNT.   What do you mean?

OLD MAN.   You took away my motto graven on your heart.

PEER GYNT.   What motto?

OLD MAN.   That compelling word——

PEER GYNT.   Word——?

OLD MAN.   ——that distinguishes a Troll from Mankind: "Troll, to thyself be—*Enough*"!

PEER GYNT (*with a shriek*).   Enough!

OLD MAN.   And, ever since, with all the energy you have, you've lived according to that motto.

PEER GYNT.   I? I? Peer Gynt?

OLD MAN (*weeping*).   You're most ungrateful. You've lived like a Troll, but have kept it secret. The word I taught has enabled you to move in the world like a well-to-do man; and now you begin abusing me and the word to which you owe gratitude.

PEER GYNT.   *Enough!*—A mere Troll! An egoist! It must be nonsense—it can't be true!

OLD MAN (*producing a bundle of newspapers*).   Don't you suppose that we have our papers? Wait; I will show you in black and white how the *Bloksberg Post* has sung your praises; the *Heklefjeld News* has done the same ever since the winter you went abroad. Will you read them, Peer? I'll be pleased to let you. Here's an article signed: "Stallion's Hoof." Here's one: "On the National Spirit of Trolldom"; the writer shows how true it is that it doesn't depend upon horns or tails, but on having the spirit of Trollhood in one. "Our 'Enough,'" he concludes, "is what gives the stamp of Troll to Man"; and he mentions you as a striking instance.

PEER GYNT.   I—a Troll?

OLD MAN.   It seems quite clear.

PEER GYNT.   Then I might have stayed where I was

and lived in peace and comfort at Rondë! I might have saved shoe leather and spared myself much toil and trouble! Peer Gynt—a Troll! It's a pack of lies! Good-bye! Here's a penny to buy tobacco.

OLD MAN.   But, dear Prince Peer——!

PEER GYNT.   Oh, drop this nonsense! You're mad, or else you're in your dotage. Go to a hospital.

OLD MAN.   Aye, it's that I'm looking for. But, as I told you, my grandson's very influential in all this part and tells the people I don't exist except in legends. The saying goes that one's relations are always the worst; and now, alas, I feel the truth of it. It's sad to be looked on as being merely a legendary personage——

PEER GYNT.   Dear man, you're not the only one to suffer that mishap.

OLD MAN.   And then, we Trolls have nothing in the way of Charities or Savings Banks or Alms-boxes; such institutions would never be acceptable at Rondë.

PEER GYNT.   No; and there you see the work of your confounded motto—your fine "To thyself be *enough*"!

OLD MAN.   Your Highness has no need to grumble. And if, in some way or another——?

PEER GYNT.   You're on the wrong scent altogether; I'm at the end of my resources.

OLD MAN.   Impossible! Your Highness ruined?

PEER GYNT.   Cleared out. Even my princely self is now in pawn. And that's your fault, you cursed Trolls! It only shows what comes of evil company.

OLD MAN.   So there's another of my hopes destroyed!—Good-bye! I'd better try and beg my way down to the town——

PEER GYNT.   And when you're there, what will you do?

OLD MAN.　　　I'll try and go upon the stage. They're advertising for National Types in the papers.

PEER GYNT.　　　Well, good luck to you!—And give my kind regards to them! If I can only free myself, I'll go the same way, too. I'll write a farce that shall be both profound and entertaining, and its title shall be: "Sic Transit Gloria Mundi."

　　　　　　　{Runs off along the path, leaving the OLD MAN *calling after him.*

SCENE IX

SCENE.—*At crossroads.*

PEER GYNT.　　　This is the tightest corner, Peer, you've ever been in. The Trolls' "Enough" has done for you. Your ship's a wreck; you must cling to the wreckage—anything— to avoid the general rubbish heap.

BUTTON MOULDER (*at the parting of the ways*).　　　Well, Peer Gynt? And your witnesses?

PEER GYNT.　　　What, crossroads here? This is quick work.

BUTTON MOULDER.　　　I can read your face as easily as I can a book and know your thoughts.

PEER GYNT.　　　I'm tired from running—one goes astray——

BUTTON MOULDER.　　　Yes; and, besides, what does it lead to?

PEER GYNT.　　　True enough; in the woods, in this failing light——

BUTTON MOULDER. There's an old man trudging alone; shall we call him?

PEER GYNT. No, let him alone; he's a drunken scamp.

BUTTON MOULDER. But perhaps he could——

PEER GYNT. Hush! No—don't call him!

BUTTON MOULDER. Is that the way of it?

PEER GYNT. Just one question: What is it really to "be one's self"?

BUTTON MOULDER. That's a strange question for a man who just now——

PEER GYNT. Tell me what I ask you.

BUTTON MOULDER. To be one's self is to slay one's self. But as perhaps that explanation is thrown away on you, let's say: to follow out, in everything, what the Master's intention was.

PEER GYNT. But suppose a man was never told what the Master's intention was?

BUTTON MOULDER. Insight should tell him.

PEER GYNT. But our insight so often is at fault, and then we're thrown out of our stride completely.

BUTTON MOULDER. Quite so, Peer Gynt. And lack of insight gives to our friend with the Cloven Hoof his strongest weapon, let me tell you.

PEER GYNT. It's all an extremely subtle problem.— But, listen; I give up my claim to have been myself; it very likely would be too difficult to prove it. I'll not attempt to fight the point. But, as I was wandering all alone over the moor just now, I felt a sudden prick from the spur of conscience. I said to myself: "You are a sinner——"

BUTTON MOULDER. Oh, now you're back to where you started——

PEER GYNT. No, not at all; I mean a *great* one,—

not only in deed, but in thought and word. I lived a dreadful life abroad——

BUTTON MOULDER.   May be; but have you anything to show to prove it?

PEER GYNT.   Give me time; I'll find a priest and get it all in writing, properly attested.

BUTTON MOULDER.   If you can do that, it will clear things up, and you will be spared the Casting-ladle. But my orders, Peer——

PEER GYNT.   They're on very old paper; it certainly dates from a long time back, when the life I lived was loose and foolish. I posed as a Prophet and Fatalist.—Well, may I try?

BUTTON MOULDER.   But——

PEER GYNT.   Be obliging! I'm sure you have no great press of business. It's excellent air in this part of the country; they say it adds years to the people's lives. The parson at Justedal used to say: "It is seldom that anyone dies in this valley."

BUTTON MOULDER.   As far as the next crossroads—no farther.

PEER GYNT.   I must find a parson, if I have to go through fire and water to get him!

SCENE X

SCENE.— *A heathery slope. A winding path leads up to the hills.*

PEER GYNT.   You never can tell what will come in useful as Esben said of the magpie's wing. Who would have thought that one's sinfulness would, in the end, prove one's salvation? The whole affair is a ticklish business, for it's out of the frying-pan into the fire; but still there's a saying that's very true—namely, that while there's life there's hope. (*A* THIN PERSON, *dressed in a priest's cassock which is well tucked up, and carrying a bird-catcher's net over his shoulder, comes running down the hill.*) Who's that with the bird-net? It's a parson! Hurrah! I am really in luck to-day!—Good afternoon, sir! The path is rough——

THIN PERSON.   It is; but what would not one put up with to win a soul?

PEER GYNT.   Oh, then there's someone who's bound for heaven?

THIN PERSON.   Not at all; I hope he's bound for another place.

PEER GYNT.   May I walk with you a little way?

THIN PERSON.   By all means; I'm glad of company.

PEER GYNT.   Something is on my mind——

THIN PERSON.   Speak on!

PEER GYNT.   You have the look of an honest man. I have always kept my country's laws and have never been put under lock and key; still, a man misses his footing sometimes and stumbles——

THIN PERSON.   That's so, with the best of us.

PEER GYNT.   These trifles, you know——

THIN PERSON.   Only trifles?

PEER GYNT.   Yes; I have never gone in for wholesale sinning.

THIN PERSON.   Then, my dear man, don't bother me. I'm not the man you seem to think. I see you're looking at my fingers; what do you think of them?

PEER GYNT.   Your nails seem most remarkably developed.

THIN PERSON.   And now you're glancing at my feet?

PEER GYNT *(pointing)*.   Is that hoof natural?

THIN PERSON.   Of course.

PEER GYNT *(lifting his hat)*. I would have sworn you were a parson. And so I have the honour to meet——? What luck! If the front door is open, one doesn't use the servants' entrance; if one should meet the King himself, one need not seek approach through lackeys.

THIN PERSON.   Shake hands! You seem unprejudiced. My dear sir, what can I do to serve you? You must not ask me for wealth or power; I haven't such a thing to give you, however willing I might be. You wouldn't believe how bad things are with us just now; nothing goes right; souls are so scarce—just now and then a single one——

PEER GYNT.   Have people, then, improved so wonderfully?

THIN PERSON.   No, just the reverse,—deteriorated shamefully; the most of them end in the Casting-ladle.

PEER GYNT.   Ah! I've heard a little about that; it really was on that account that I approached you.

THIN PERSON.   Speak quite freely!

PEER GYNT.   Well, if it's not too much to ask, I'm very anxious to secure——

THIN PERSON.   A snug retreat, eh?

PEER GYNT.   You have guessed what I would say before I said it. You say you're not doing much business, and so perhaps my small suggestion may not irksome——

THIN PERSON.   But, my friend——

PEER GYNT.   I do not ask for much. Of course I shouldn't look for any wages, but only as far as possible to be treated as one of the family.

THIN PERSON.   A nice warm room?

PEER GYNT.   But not too warm. And, preferably, I should like an easy access, in and out, so that I could retrace my steps if opportunity should offer for something better.

THIN PERSON.   My dear friend, I really am extremely sorry, but you can't think how very often exactly similar requests are made to me by people leaving the scene of all their earthly labours.

PEER GYNT.   But when I call to mind my conduct in days gone by, it seems to me I am just suited for admittance——

THIN PERSON.   But they were trifles——

PEER GYNT.   In a sense still, now that I remember it, I did some trade in negro slaves——

THIN PERSON.   I have had folk who carried on a trade in minds and wills, but still did it half-heartedly,—and they didn't get in.

PEER GYNT.   Well—I've exported idols of Buddha out to China.

THIN PERSON.   Rubbish! We only laugh at those. I have known folk disseminating uglier idols, far—in sermons, in art and literature—and yet not getting in.

PEER GYNT.   Yes, but—look here! I've passed myself off as a Prophet!

THIN PERSON.   Abroad? That's nothing! Such escapades end mostly in the Casting-ladle. If you've no stronger claim than that, I can't admit you, however much I'd like to do it.

PEER GYNT.   Well, but—listen! I had been ship-wrecked, and was clinging fast to a boat that had been cap-sized. "A drowning man clings to a straw," the saying goes; but there's another, "Everyone for himself";—and so the fact that the ship's cook was drowned was certainly half due to me.

THIN PERSON.   It would have been more to the point if you had been responsible for stealing half a cook-maid's virtue. Begging your pardon, what's the good of all this talk of half a sin? Who do you think, in these hard times, is going to waste expensive fuel on worthless rubbish such as that? Now, don't be angry; it's your sins and not yourself I'm sneering at. Excuse my speaking out so plainly. Be wise, my friend, and give it up; resign yourself to the Casting-ladle. Suppose I gave you board and lodging, what would you gain by that? Consider—you are a reasonable man; your memory's good, it's very true; but everything you can recall, whether you judge it with your head or with your heart, is nothing more than what our Swedish friends would call "Very poor sport." There's nothing in it that's worth a tear or worth a smile, worth boasting or despairing of, noth-ing to make one hot or cold—only, perhaps, to make one angry.

PEER GYNT.   You can't tell where the shoe is pinch-ing unless you've got it on, you know.

THIN PERSON.   That's true; and—thanks to so-and-so—I only need one odd one. Still, I'm glad you mentioned shoes, because it has reminded me that I must push along. I've got to fetch a joint I hope will prove a fat one. I haven't any time to spare to stand here gossiping like this——

PEER GYNT.   And may I ask what sort of brew of sin this fellow has concocted?

THIN PERSON.   As far as I can gather, he has been persistently himself by day and night; and that is what is at the root of the whole matter.

PEER GYNT.   Himself? Does your domain include people like *that?*

THIN PERSON.   Just as it happens; the door is always left ajar. Remember that there are two ways a man can be himself; a cloth has both a right side and a wrong. You know they've lately invented in Paris a method by which they can take a portrait by means of the sun. They can either make a picture like the original, or else what is called a negative, the latter reverses the light and shade; to the casual eye it's far from pretty; but the likeness is in it, all the same, and to bring it out is all that is needed. If in the conduct of its life a soul has photographed itself so as to make a negative, they don't on that account destroy the plate; they send it on to me. I take in hand the rest of the process and proceed to effect a transformation. I steam it, dip it, burn it, clean it, with sulphur and other ingredients, till I get the likeness the plate should give,—that's to say, what is called a positive. But when, as in your case, it's half rubbed out, no sulphur or lye is of any use.

PEER GYNT.   So, then, one may come to you like soot and depart like snow?—May I ask what name is on the particular negative that you're on the point of converting now into a positive?

THIN PERSON.   Yes—Peer Gynt.

PEER GYNT.   Peer Gynt? Indeed! Is Peer Gynt himself?

THIN PERSON.   He swears he is.

PEER GYNT.   He's a truthful man.

THIN PERSON.   You know him, perhaps?

PEER GYNT.   Just as one knows so many people.

THIN PERSON.   I've not much time; where did you see him last?

PEER GYNT.   At the Cape.

THIN PERSON.   The Cape of Good Hope?

PEER GYNT.   Yes—but I think he's just on the point of leaving there.

THIN PERSON.   Then I must start for there at once. I only hope I'm in time to catch him! I've always had bad luck at the Cape—it's full of Missionaries from Stavanger.

{Goes off southwards.

PEER GYNT.   The silly creature! He's off at a run; on a wrong scent, too. He'll be disappointed. It was quite a pleasure to fool such a donkey. A nice chap, he, to give himself airs and come the superior over me! He has nothing to give himself airs about! He won't grow fat on his trade, I'll warrant; he'll lose his job if he isn't careful. H'm! *I'm* not so very secure in the saddle; I am out of the "self"-aristocracy for good and all, as it seems to me. *(A shooting-star flashes across the sky. He nods to it.)* : Peer Gynt salutes you, Brother Star! To shine,—to be quenched, and lost in the void———. *(Pulls himself together apprehensively and plunges deeper into the mist. After a short silence he calls out)* Is there no one in the universe—nor in the abyss, nor yet in heaven———? *(Retraces his steps, throws his hat on the ground and tears his hair. By degrees he grows calmer.)* So poor, so miserably poor may a soul return to the darkling mists and become as nothing. Beautiful earth, forgive me for having trodden thee all to no purpose. Beautiful sun, thy glorious rays have shone upon an empty shell—no one within to receive warmth and comfort from thee, the owner never in his house. Beautiful sun, beautiful earth, 'twas but for naught you warmed and nourished my mother. Nature is a spendthrift, and the Spirit but a greedy miser. One's life's a heavy price to pay for being born.—I will go up, up to the highest mountain-tops; I'll see the sun rise once again and gaze upon the promised land until my eyes are weary. Then the snow may fall and cover me, and on my resting-place be written as epitaph: "The Tomb of *No One!*" And—after that—well, come what may.

CHURCHFOLK *(singing on the road).*

> Oh, blessed day when the Gift of Tongues
> Descended on earth in rays of fire!
> O'er all the world creation sings
> The language of the heavenly choir!

PEER GYNT *(crouching down in terror).*   I will not look! There's nothing there but desert waste.—I am in terror of being dead long ere my death.

> {*Tries to steal into the thickets, but finds himself standing at crossroads.*

SCENE XI

SCENE.—*Crossroads.* PEER GYNT *is confronted by the Button Moulder.*

BUTTON MOULDER.   Good morning, Peer Gynt! Where's your list of sins?

PEER GYNT.   I assure you that I have shouted and whistled for all I knew!

BUTTON MOULDER.   But you found no one?

PEER GYNT. Only a travelling photographer.

BUTTON MOULDER. Well, your time is up.

PEER GYNT. Everything's up. The owl smells a rat. Do you hear him hooting?

BUTTON MOULDER. That's the matins bell——

PEER GYNT (*pointing*). What's that, that's shining?

BUTTON MOULDER. Only a light in a house.

PEER GYNT. That sound like wailing?

BUTTON MOULDER. Only a woman's song.

PEER GYNT. 'Tis there—there I shall find my list of sins!

BUTTON MOULDER (*grasping him by the arm*). Come, set your house in order.

> {*They have come out of the wood and are standing near* SOLVEIG'S *hut. Day is dawning.*

PEER GYNT. Set my house in order? That's it!—Go! Be off! Were your ladle as big as a coffin, I tell you 'twould not hold me and my list!

BUTTON MOULDER. To the third crossroads, Peer; but *then*——!

> {*Moves aside and disappears.*

PEER GYNT (*approaching the hut*). Backward or forward, it's just as far; out or in, the way's as narrow. (*Stops.*) No! Like a wild unceasing cry I seem to hear a voice that bids me go in—go back—back to my home. (*Takes a few steps, then stops again.*) "Round about," said the Boyg! (*Hears the sound of singing from the hut.*) No; this time it's straight ahead in spite of all, however narrow be the way!

> {*Runs towards the hut. At the same time* SOLVEIG *comes to the door, guiding her steps with a stick (for she is nearly blind). She is dressed for church and carries a prayer-book wrapped up in a handkerchief. She stands still, erect and gentle.*

PEER GYNT (*throwing himself down on the threshold*). Pronounce the sentence of a sinner!

SOLEVIG. 'Tis he! 'Tis he! Thanks be to God. (*Gropes for him.*)

PEER GYNT. Tell me how sinfully I have offended!

SOLVEIG. You have sinned in nothing, my own dear lad! (*Gropes for him again and finds him.*)

BUTTON MOULDER (*from behind the hut*). Where is that list of sins, Peer Gynt?

PEER GYNT. Cry out, cry out my sins aloud!

SOLVEIG. (*sitting down beside him*). You have made my life a beautiful song. Bless you for having come back to me! And blest be this morn of Pentecost!

PEER GYNT. Then I am lost!

SOLVEIG. There is One who will help.

PEER GYNT (*with a laugh*). Lost! Unless you can solve a riddle!

SOLVEIG. What is it?

PEER GYNT. What is it? You shall hear. Can you tell me where Peer Gynt has been since last we met?

SOLVEIG. Where he has been?

PEER GYNT. With the mark of destiny on his brow—the man that he was when a thought of God's created him! Can you tell me that? If not, I must go to my last home in the land of shadows.

SOLVEIG (*smiling*). That riddle's easy.

PEER GYNT. Tell me, then—where was my real self, complete and true—the Peer who bore the stamp of God upon his brow?

SOLVEIG. In my faith, in my hope and in my love.

PEER GYNT. What are you saying? It is a riddle that you are speaking now. So speaks a mother of her child.

SOLVEIG.   Ah, yes; and that is what I am; but He who grants a pardon for the sake of a mother's prayers, He is his father.

> {*A ray of light seems to flash on* PEER GYNT. *He cries out.*

PEER GYNT.   Mother and wife! You stainless woman! Oh, hide me, hide me in your love!

> {*Clings to her and buries his face in her lap. There is a long silence. The sun rises.*

SOLVEIG (*singing softly*).

Sleep, my boy, my dearest boy!
I will rock you to sleep and guard you.

The boy has sat on his mother's lap.
The two have played the livelong day.

The boy has lain on his mother's breast
The livelong day. God bless you, my sweet!

The boy has lain so close to my heart.
The livelong day. He is weary now.

Sleep, my boy, my dearest boy!
I will rock you to sleep and guard you.

> {*The* BUTTON MOULDER'S *voice is heard from behind the hut.*

BUTTON MOULDER.   At the last crossroads I shall meet you, Peer; *then* we'll see whether——! I say no more.

SOLVEIG (*singing louder in the sunshine*).   I will rock you to sleep and guard you! Sleep and dream, my dearest boy!

Hedda Gabler

(1890)

Problems of Self Realization

Characters

GEORGE TESMAN.*
HEDDA TESMAN, *his wife.*
MISS JULIANA TESMAN, *his aunt.*
MRS. ELVSTED.
JUDGE† BRACK.
EILERT LÖVBORG.
BERTA, *servant of the Tesmans.*

The scene of the action is Tesman's villa, in the west end of Christiania.

well made play
plays that posed problems
not from throne - from
kitchen stool
Romantic period
Social problem play

* Tesman, whose Christian name in the original is "Jörgen," is described as "stipendiat i kulturhistorie"—that is to say, the holder of a scholarship for purposes of research into the History of Civilisation.

† In the original "Assessor."

Act 1

~

A spacious, handsome, and tastefully furnished drawing-room, dec-
orated in dark colours. In the back, a wide doorway with cur-
tains drawn back, leading into a smaller room decorated in the
same style as the drawing-room. In the right-hand wall of the
front room, a folding door leading out to the hall. In the opposite
wall, on the left, a glass door, also with curtains drawn back.
Through the panes can be seen part of a verandah outside and
trees covered with autumn foliage. An oval table, with a cover
on it, and surrounded by chairs, stands well forward. In front,
by the wall on the right, a wide stove of dark porcelain, a high-
backed arm-chair, a cushioned foot-rest and two foot-stools. A
settee, with a small round table in front of it, fills the upper
right-hand corner. In front, on the left, a little way from the
wall, a sofa. Further back than the glass door, a piano. On
either side of the doorway at the back a whatnot with terra-
cotta and majolica ornaments. —Against the back wall of the
inner room a sofa, with a table, and one or two chairs. Over the
sofa hangs the portrait of a handsome elderly man in a General's
uniform. Over the table a hanging lamp, with an opal glass
shade. —A number of bouquets are arranged about the drawing-
room, in vases and glasses. Others lie upon the tables. The floors
in both rooms are covered with thick carpets. —Morning light.
The sun shines in through the glass door.

MISS JULIANA TESMAN, *with her bonnet on and carrying a par-*
asol, comes in from the hall, followed by BERTA, *who carries*

a bouquet wrapped in paper. MISS TESMAN *is a comely and pleasant-looking lady of about sixty-five. She is nicely but simply dressed in a grey walking costume.* BERTA *is a middle-aged woman of plain and rather countrified appearance.*

MISS TESMAN *(stops close to the door, listens and says softly).* Upon my word, I don't believe they are stirring yet!

BERTA *(also softly).* I told you so, Miss. Remember how late the steamboat got in last night. And then, when they got home!—good Lord, what a lot the young mistress had to unpack before she could get to bed.

MISS TESMAN. Well, well—let them have their sleep out. But let us see that they get a good breath of the fresh morning air when they do appear.

{She goes to the glass door and throws it open.

BERTA *(beside the table, at a loss what to do with the bouquet in her hand).* I declare there isn't a bit of room left. I think I'll put it down here, Miss.

{She places it on the piano.

MISS TESMAN. So you've got a new mistress now, my dear Berta. Heaven knows it was a wrench to me to part with you.

BERTA *(on the point of weeping).* And do you think it wasn't hard for me, too, Miss? After all the blessed years I've been with you and Miss Rina.*

MISS TESMAN. We must make the best of it, Berta. There was nothing else to be done. George can't do without you, you see—he absolutely can't. He has had you to look after him ever since he was a little boy.

BERTA. Ah, but, Miss Julia, I can't help thinking

---

* Pronounced Reena.

of Miss Rina lying helpless at home there, poor thing. And with only that new girl, too! She'll never learn to take proper care of an invalid.

MISS TESMAN.   Oh, I shall manage to train her. And of course, you know, I shall take most of it upon myself. You needn't be uneasy about my poor sister, my dear Berta.

BERTA.   Well, but there's another thing, Miss. I'm so mortally afraid I shan't be able to suit the young mistress.

MISS TESMAN.   Oh well—just at first there may be one or two things——

BERTA.   Most like she'll be terrible grand in her ways.

MISS TESMAN.   Well, you can't wonder at that— General Gabler's daughter! Think of the sort of life she was accustomed to in her father's time. Don't you remember how we used to see her riding down the road along with the General? In that long black habit—and with feathers in her hat?

BERTA.   Yes, indeed—I remember well enough——! But good Lord, I should never have dreamt in those days that she and Master George would make a match of it.

MISS TESMAN.   Nor I.—But, by-the-bye, Berta— while I think of it: in future you mustn't say Master George You must say Dr. Tesman.

BERTA.   Yes, the young mistress spoke of that, too— last night—the moment they set foot in the house. Is it true then, Miss?

MISS TESMAN.   Yes, indeed it is. Only think, Berta—some foreign university has made him a doctor— while he has been abroad, you understand. I hadn't heard a word about it, until he told me himself upon the pier.

BERTA.   Well, well, he's clever enough for anything,

he is. But I didn't think he'd have gone in for doctoring people, too.

MISS TESMAN.   No, no, it's not that sort of doctor he is. (*Nods significantly.*) But let me tell you, we may have to call him something still grander before long.

BERTA.   You don't say so! What can that be, Miss?

MISS TESMAN (*smiling*).   H'm—wouldn't you like to know! (*With emotion.*) Ah, dear, dear—if my poor brother could only look up from his grave now and see what his little boy has grown into! (*Looks around.*) But bless me, Berta—why have you done this? Taken the chintz covers off all the furniture?

BERTA.   The mistress told me to. She can't abide covers on the chairs, she says.

MISS TESMAN.   Are they going to make this their everyday sitting-room then?

BERTA.   Yes, that's what I understood—from the mistress. Master George—the doctor—he said nothing.

> {GEORGE TESMAN *comes from the right into the inner room, humming to himself, and carrying an unstrapped empty portmanteau. He is a middle-sized, young-looking man of thirty-three, rather stout, with a round, open, cheerful face, fair hair and beard. He wears spectacles and is somewhat carelessly dressed in comfortable indoor clothes.*

MISS TESMAN.   Good morning, good morning, George.

TESMAN (*in the doorway between the rooms*). Aunt Julia! Dear Aunt Julia! (*Goes up to her and shakes hands warmly.*) Come all this way—so early! Eh?

MISS TESMAN.   Why, of course I had to come and see how you were getting on.

TESMAN.　　In spite of your having had no proper night's rest?

MISS TESMAN.　　Oh, that make no difference to me.

TESMAN.　　Well, I suppose you got home all right from the pier? Eh?

MISS TESMAN.　　Yes, quite safely, thank goodness. Judge Brack was good enough to see me right to my door.

TESMAN.　　We were so sorry we couldn't give you a seat in the carriage. But you saw what a pile of boxes Hedda had to bring with her.

MISS TESMAN.　　Yes, she had certainly plenty of boxes.

BERTA (to TESMAN).　　Shall I go in and see if there's anything I can do for the mistress?

TESMAN.　　No, thank you, Berta—you needn't. She said she would ring if she wanted anything.

BERTA (going towards the right).　　Very well.

TESMAN.　　But look here—take this portmanteau with you.

BERTA (taking it).　　I'll put it in the attic.

{She goes out by the hall door.

TESMAN.　　Fancy, Auntie—I had the whole of that portmanteau chock full of copies of documents. You wouldn't believe how much I have picked up from all the archives I have been examining—curious old details that no one has had any idea of——

MISS TESMAN.　　Yes, you don't seem to have wasted your time on your wedding trip, George.

TESMAN.　　No, that I haven't. But do take off your bonnet, Auntie. Look here! Let me untie the strings—eh?

MISS TESMAN (while he does so).　　Well, well—this is just as if you were still at home with us.

TESMAN (with the bonnet in his hand, looks at it from all

sides).   Why, what a gorgeous bonnet you've been investing in!

MISS TESMAN.   I bought it on Hedda's account.

TESMAN.   On Hedda's account? Eh?

MISS TESMAN.   Yes, so that Hedda needn't be ashamed of me if we happened to go out together.

TESMAN (*patting her cheek*).   You always think of everything, Aunt Julia. (*Lays the bonnet on a chair beside the table.*) And now, look here—suppose we sit comfortably on the sofa and have a little chat, till Hedda comes.

> {*They seat themselves. She places her parasol in the corner of the sofa.*

MISS TESMAN (*takes both his hands and looks at him*).   What a delight it is to have you again, as large as life, before my very eyes, George! My George—my poor brother's own boy!

TESMAN.   And it's a delight for me, too, to see you again, Aunt Julia! You, who have been father and mother in one to me.

MISS TESMAN.   Oh, yes, I know you will always keep a place in your heart for your old aunts.

TESMAN.   And what about Aunt Rina? No improvement—eh?

MISS TESMAN.   Oh, no—we can scarcely look for any improvement in her case, poor thing. There she lies, helpless, as she has lain for all these years. But heaven grant I may not lose her yet awhile! For if I did, I don't know what I should make of my life, George—especially now that I haven't you to look after any more.

TESMAN (*patting her back*).   There, there, there——!

MISS TESMAN (*suddenly changing her tone*).   And to think that here are you a married man, George!—And that you should be the one to carry off Hedda Gabler—the beautiful Hedda Gabler! Only think of it—she, that was so beset with admirers!

TESMAN (*hums a little and smiles complacently*). Yes, I fancy I have several good friends about town who would like to stand in my shoes—eh?

MISS TESMAN. And then this fine long wedding-tour you have had! More than five—nearly six months——

TESMAN. Well, for me it has been a sort of tour of research as well. I have had to do so much grubbing among old records—and to read no end of books, too, Auntie.

MISS TESMAN. Oh, yes, I suppose so. (*More confidentially, and lowering her voice a little.*) But listen now, George— have you nothing—nothing special to tell me?

TESMAN. As to our journey?

MISS TESMAN. Yes.

TESMAN. No, I don't know of anything except what I have told you in my letters. I had a doctor's degree conferred on me—but that I told you yesterday.

MISS TESMAN. Yes, yes, you did. But what I mean is—haven't you any—any—expectations——?

TESMAN. Expectations?

MISS TESMAN. Why, you know, George—I'm your old auntie!

TESMAN. Why, of course I have expectations.

MISS TESMAN. Ah!

TESMAN. I have every expectation of being a professor one of these days.

MISS TESMAN. Oh, yes, a professor——

TESMAN. Indeed, I may say I am certain of it. But my dear Auntie—you know all about that already!

MISS TESMAN (*laughing to herself*). Yes, of course I

do. You are quite right there. *(Changing the subject.)* But we were talking about your journey. It must have cost a great deal of money, George?

TESMAN.   Well, you see—my handsome travelling-scholarship went a good way.

MISS TESMAN.   But I can't understand how you can have made it go far enough for two.

TESMAN.   No, that's not so easy to understand—eh?

MISS TESMAN.   And especially travelling with a lady—they tell me that makes it ever so much more expensive.

TESMAN.   Yes, of course—it makes it a little more expensive. But Hedda had to have this trip, Auntie! She really had to. Nothing else would have done.

MISS TESMAN.   No, no, I suppose not. A wedding-tour seems to be quite indispensable nowadays.—But tell me now—have you gone thoroughly over the house yet?

TESMAN.   Yes, you may be sure I have. I have been afoot ever since daylight.

MISS TESMAN.   And what do you think of it all?

TESMAN   I'm delighted! Quite delighted! Only I can't think what we are to do with the two empty rooms between this inner parlour and Hedda's bedroom.

MISS TESMAN *(laughing)*.   Oh, my dear George, I daresay you may find some use for them—in the course of time.

TESMAN.   Why of course you are quite right, Aunt Julia! You mean as my library increases—eh?

MISS TESMAN.   Yes, quite so, my dear boy. It was your library I was thinking of.

TESMAN.   I am specially pleased on Hedda's account. Often and often, before we were engaged, she said that she would never care to live anywhere but in Secretary Falk's villa.*

MISS TESMAN.   Yes, it was lucky that this very house should come into the market, just after you had started.

TESMAN.   Yes, Aunt Julia, the luck was on our side, wasn't it—eh?

MISS TESMAN.   But the expense, my dear George! You will find it very expensive, all this.

TESMAN (*looks at her, a little cast down*).   Yes, I suppose I shall, Aunt!

MISS TESMAN.   Oh, frightfully!

TESMAN.   How much do you think? In round numbers?—Eh?

MISS TESMAN.   Oh, I can't even guess until all the accounts come in.

TESMAN.   Well, fortunately, Judge Brack has secured the most favorable terms for me,—so he said in a letter to Hedda.

MISS TESMAN.   Yes, don't be uneasy, my dear boy.—Besides, I have given security for the furniture and all the carpets.

TESMAN.   Security? You? My dear Aunt Julia—what sort of security could you give?

MISS TESMAN.   I have given a mortgage on our annuity.

TESMAN (*jumps up*).   What! On your—and Aunt Rina's annuity!

MISS TESMAN.   Yes, I knew of no other plan, you see.

TESMAN (*placing himself before her*).   Have you gone out of your senses, Auntie! Your annuity—it's all that you and Aunt Rina have to live upon.

---

*   In the original, "Statsradinde Falks villa"—showing that it had belonged to the widow of a cabinet minister.

Miss Tesman.   Well, well, don't get so excited about it. It's only a matter of form you know——Judge Brack assured me of that. It was he that was kind enough to arrange the whole affair for me. A mere matter of form, he said.

Tesman.   Yes, that may be all very well. But nevertheless——

Miss Tesman.   You will have your own salary to depend upon now. And, good heavens, even if we did have to pay up a little——! To eke things out a bit at the start——! Why, it would be nothing but a pleasure to us.

Tesman.   Oh, Auntie—will you never be tired of making sacrifices for me!

Miss Tesman (*rises and lays her hands on his shoulders*).   Have I any other happiness in this world except to smooth your way for you, my dear boy? You, who have had neither father nor mother to depend on. And now we have reached the goal, George! Things have looked black enough for us, sometimes; but, thank heaven, now you have nothing to fear.

Tesman.   Yes, it is really marvellous how everything has turned out for the best.

Miss Tesman.   And the people who opposed you—who wanted to bar the way for you—now you have them at your feet. They have fallen, George. Your most dangerous rival—his fall was the worst.—And now he has to lie on the bed he has made for himself—poor misguided creature.

Tesman.   Have you heard anything of Eilert? Since I went away, I mean.

Miss Tesman.   Only that he is said to have published a new book.

Tesman.   What! Eilert Lövborg! Recently—eh?

Miss Tesman.   Yes, so they say. Heaven knows

whether it can be worth anything! Ah, when your new book appears—that will be another story, George! What is it to be about?

TESMAN.	It will deal with the domestic industries of Brabant during the Middle Ages.

MISS TESMAN.	Fancy—to be able to write on such a subject as that!

TESMAN.	However, it may be some time before the book is ready. I have all these collections to arrange first, you see.

MISS TESMAN.	Yes, collecting and arranging—no one can beat you at that. There you are my poor brother's own son.

TESMAN.	I am looking forward eagerly to setting to work at it; especially now that I have my own delightful home to work in.

MISS TESMAN.	And, most of all, now that you have got the wife of your heart, my dear George.

TESMAN (*embracing her*).	Oh, yes, yes, Aunt Julia. Hedda—she is the best part of it all! (*Looks towards the doorway.*) I believe I hear her coming—eh?

> {HEDDA *enters from the left through the inner room. She is a woman of nine-and-twenty. Her face and figure show refinement and distinction. Her complexion is pale and opaque. Her steel-grey eyes express a cold, unruffled repose. Her hair is of an agreeable medium brown, but not particularly abundant. She is dressed in a tasteful, somewhat loose-fitting morning gown.*

MISS TESMAN (*going to meet* HEDDA).	Good morning, my dear Hedda! Good morning, and a hearty welcome.

HEDDA (*holds out her hand*).	Good morning, dear Miss Tesman! So early a call! That is kind of you.

MISS TESMAN (*with some embarrassment*).   Well—has the bride slept well in her new home?

HEDDA.   Oh, yes, thanks. Passably.

TESMAN (*laughing*).   Passably! Come, that's good, Hedda! You were sleeping like a stone when I got up.

HEDDA.   Fortunately. Of course one has always to accustom one's self to new surroundings, Miss Tesman— little by little. (*Looking towards the left.*) Oh—there the servant has gone and opened the verandah door and let in a whole flood of sunshine.

MISS TESMAN (*going towards the door*).   Well, then, we will shut it.

HEDDA.   No, no, not that! Tesman, please draw the curtains. That will give a softer light.

TESMAN (*at the door*).   All right—all right. There now, Hedda, now you have both shade and fresh air.

HEDDA.   Yes, fresh air we certainly must have, with all these stacks of flowers—— But—won't you sit down, Miss Tesman?

MISS TESMAN.   No, thank you. Now that I have seen that everything is all right here—thank heaven!—I must be getting home again. My sister is lying longing for me, poor thing.

TESMAN.   Give her my very best love, Auntie; and say I shall look in and see her later in the day.

MISS TESMAN.   Yes, yes, I'll be sure to tell her. But by-the-bye, George—(*feeling in her dress pocket*)—I had almost forgotten—I have something for you here.

TESMAN.   What is it, Auntie? Eh?

MISS TESMAN (*produces a flat parcel wrapped in newspaper and hands it to him*).   Look here, my dear boy.

TESMAN (*opening the parcel*).   Well, I declare!—Have

you really saved them for me, Aunt Julia! Hedda! isn't this touching—eh?

HEDDA (*beside the whatnot on the right*).　　Well, what is it?

TESMAN.　　My old morning-shoes! My slippers.

HEDDA.　　Indeed. I remember you often spoke of them while we were abroad.

TESMAN.　　Yes, I missed them terribly. (*Goes up to her.*) Now you shall see them, Hedda!

HEDDA (*going towards the stove*).　　Thanks, I really don't care about it.

TESMAN (*following her*).　　Only think—ill as she was, Aunt Rina embroidered these for me. Oh, you can't think how many associations cling to them.

HEDDA (*at the table*).　　Scarcely for me.

MISS TESMAN.　　Of course not for Hedda, George.

TESMAN.　　Well, but now that she belongs to the family, I thought——

HEDDA (*interrupting*).　　We shall never get on with this servant, Tesman.

MISS TESMAN.　　Not get on with Berta?

TESMAN.　　Why, dear, what puts that in your head? Eh?

HEDDA (*pointing*).　　Look there! She has left her old bonnet lying about on a chair.

TESMAN (*in consternation, drops the slippers on the floor*).　　Why, Hedda——

HEDDA.　　Just fancy, if any one should come in and see it!

TESMAN.　　But Hedda—that's Aunt Julia's bonnet.

HEDDA.　　Is it!

MISS TESMAN (*taking up the bonnet*).　　Yes, indeed it's mine. And what's more, it's not old, Madam Hedda.

HEDDA.   I really did not look closely at it, Miss Tesman.

MISS TESMAN. *(trying on the bonnet).*   Let me tell you it's the first time I have worn it—the very first time.

TESMAN.   And a very nice bonnet it is, too—quite a beauty!

MISS TESMAN.   Oh, it's no such great things, George. *(Looks around her.)* My parasol——? Ah, here. *(Takes it.)* For this is mine, too—*(mutters)*—not Berta's.

TESMAN.   A new bonnet and a new parasol! Only think, Hedda!

HEDDA.   Very handsome indeed.

TESMAN.   Yes, isn't it? Eh? But Auntie, take a good look at Hedda before you go! See how handsome she is!

MISS TESMAN.   Oh, my dear boy, there's nothing new in that. Hedda was always lovely.

{She nods and goes towards the right.

TESMAN *(following).*   Yes, but have you noticed what splendid condition she is in? How she has filled out on the journey?

HEDDA *(crossing the room).*   Oh, do be quiet——!

MISS TESMAN *(who has stopped and turned).*   Filled out?

TESMAN.   Of course you don't notice it so much now that she has that dress on. But I, who can see——

HEDDA *(at the glass door, impatiently).*   Oh, you can't see anything.

TESMAN.   It must be the mountain air in the Tyrol——

HEDDA *(curtly, interrupting).*   I am exactly as I was when I started.

TESMAN.   So you insist; but I'm quite certain you are not. Don't you agree with me, Auntie?

MISS TESMAN *(who has been gazing at her with folded hands).*   Hedda is lovely—lovely—lovely. *(Goes up to her, takes her head between both hands, draws it downwards and kisses her hair).* God bless and preserve Hedda Tesman——for George's sake.

HEDDA *(gently freeing herself).*   Oh——! Let me go.

MISS TESMAN *(in quiet emotion).*   I shall not let a day pass without coming to see you.

TESMAN.   No, you won't, will you, Auntie? Eh?

MISS TESMAN.   Good-bye—good-bye!

> {She goes out by the hall door. TESMAN *accompanies her. The door remains half open.* TESMAN *can be heard repeating his message to* AUNT RINA *and his thanks for the slippers.*
>
> {In the meantime, HEDDA *walks about the room, raising her arms and clenching her hands as if in desperation. Then she flings back the curtains from the glass door and stands there looking out.*
>
> {Presently TESMAN *returns and closes the door behind him.*

TESMAN *(picks up the slippers from the floor).*   What are you looking at, Hedda?

HEDDA *(once more calm and mistress of herself).*   I am only looking at the leaves. They are so yellow—so withered.

TESMAN *(wraps up the slippers and lays them on the table).*   Well you see, we are well into September now.

HEDDA *(again restless).*   Yes, to think of it!—Already in—in September.

TESMAN.   Don't you think Aunt Julia's manner was strange, dear? Almost solemn? Can you imagine what was the matter with her? Eh?

HEDDA.   I scarcely know her, you see. Is she not often like that?

TESMAN.   No, not as she was today.

HEDDA (*leaving the glass door*).   Do you think she was annoyed about the bonnet?

TESMAN.   Oh, scarcely at all. Perhaps a little, just at the moment——

HEDDA.   But what an idea, to pitch her bonnet about in the drawing-room! No one does that sort of thing.

TESMAN.   Well, you may be sure Aunt Julia won't do it again.

HEDDA.   In any case, I shall manage to make my peace with her.

TESMAN.   Yes, my dear, good Hedda, if you only would.

HEDDA.   When you call this afternoon, you might invite her to spend the evening here.

TESMAN.   Yes, that I will. And there's one thing more you could do that would delight her heart.

HEDDA.   What is it?

TESMAN.   If you could only prevail on yourself to say *du** to her. For my sake, Hedda? Eh?

HEDDA.   No, no, Tesman—you really mustn't ask that of me. I have told you so already. I shall try to call her "Aunt"; and you must be satisfied with that.

TESMAN.   Well, well. Only I think now that you belong to the family, you——

HEDDA.   H'm—I can't in the least see why——

{She goes up towards the middle doorway.

TESMAN (*after a pause*).   Is there anything the matter with you, Hedda? Eh?

HEDDA.   I'm only looking at my old piano. It doesn't go at all well with all the other things.

---

*   Du-thou; Tesman means, "If you could persuade to yourself to tutoyer her."

TESMAN. The first time I draw my salary, we'll see about exchanging it.

HEDDA. No, no—no exchanging. I don't want to part with it. Suppose we put it there in the inner room and then get another here in its place. When it's convenient, I mean.

TESMAN (*a little taken aback*). Yes—of course we could do that.

HEDDA (*takes up the bouquet from the piano*). These flowers were not here last night when we arrived.

TESMAN. Aunt Julia must have brought them for you.

HEDDA (*examining the bouquet*). A visiting-card. (*Takes it out and reads:*) "Shall return later in the day." Can you guess whose card it is?

TESMAN. No. Whose? Eh?

HEDDA. The name is "Mrs. Elvsted."

TESMAN. Is it really? Sheriff Elvsted's wife? Miss Rysing that was.

HEDDA. Exactly. The girl with the irritating hair, that she was always showing off. An old flame of yours I've been told.

TESMAN (*laughing*). Oh, that didn't last long; and it was before I knew you, Hedda. But fancy her being in town!

HEDDA. It's odd that she should call upon us. I have scarcely seen her since we left school.

TESMAN. I haven't seen her either for—heaven knows how long. I wonder how she can endure to live in such an out-of-the-way hole—eh?

HEDDA (*after a moment's thought says suddenly*). Tell me, Tesman—isn't it somewhere near there that he—that—Eilert Lövborg is living?

TESMAN. Yes, he is somewhere in that part of the country.

*{*BERTA *enters by the hall door.*

BERTA. That lady, ma'am, that brought some flowers a little while ago, is here again. *(Pointing.)* The flowers you have in your hand, ma'am.

HEDDA. Ah, is she? Well, please show her in.

*{*BERTA *opens the door for* MRS. ELVSTED *and goes out herself.*—MRS. ELVSTED *is a woman of fragile figure, with pretty, soft features. Her eyes are light blue, large, round, and somewhat prominent, with a startled, inquiring expression. Her hair is remarkably light, almost flaxen, and unusually abundant and wavy. She is a couple of years younger that* HEDDA. *She wears a dark visiting dress, tasteful, but not quite in the latest fashion.*

HEDDA *(receives her warmly).* How do you do, my dear Mrs. Elvsted? It's delightful to see you again.

MRS. ELVSTED *(nervously, struggling for self-control).* Yes, it's a very long time since we met.

TESMAN *(gives her his hand).* And we, too—eh?

HEDDA. Thanks for your lovely flowers——

MRS. ELVSTED. Oh, not at all—— I would have come straight here yesterday afternoon; but I heard that you were away——

TESMAN. Have you just come to town? Eh?

MRS. ELVSTED. I arrived yesterday, about midday. Oh, I was quite in despair when I heard that you were not at home.

HEDDA. In despair! How so?

TESMAN. Why, my dear Mrs. Rysing—I mean Mrs. Elvsted——

HEDDA. I hope that you are not in any trouble?

MRS. ELVSTED.   Yes, I am. And I don't know another living creature here that I can turn to.

HEDDA (*laying the bouquet on the table*).   Come—let us sit here on the sofa——

MRS. ELVSTED.   Oh, I am too restless to sit down.

HEDDA.   Oh no, you're not. Come here.

> {*She draws* MRS. ELVSTED *down upon the sofa and sits at her side.*

TESMAN.   Well? What is it, Mrs. Elvsted?

HEDDA.   Has anything particular happened to you at home?

MRS. ELVSTED.   Yes—and no. Oh—I am so anxious you should not misunderstand me——

HEDDA.   Then your best plan is to tell us the whole story, Mrs. Elvsted.

TESMAN.   I suppose that's what you have come for—eh?

MRS. ELVSTED.   Yes, yes—of course it is. Well, then, I must tell you—if you don't already know—that Eilert Lövborg is in town, too.

HEDDA.   Lövborg——!

TESMAN.   What! Has Eilert Lövborg come back? Fancy that, Hedda!

HEDDA.   Well, well—I hear it.

MRS. ELVSTED.   He has been here a week already. Just fancy—a whole week! In this terrible town, alone! With so many temptations on all sides.

HEDDA.   But my dear Mrs. Elvsted—how does he concern you so much?

MRS. ELVSTED (*looks at her with a startled air and says rapidly*).   He was the children's tutor.

HEDDA.   Your children's?

MRS. ELVSTED.   My husband's. I have none.

HEDDA.   Your step-children's, then?

MRS. ELVSTED.   Yes.

TESMAN (*somewhat hesitatingly*).   Then was he—I don't know how to express it—was he—regular enough in his habits to be fit for the post? Eh?

MRS. ELVSTED.   For the last two years his conduct has been irreproachable.

TESMAN.   Has it indeed? Fancy that, Hedda!

HEDDA.   I hear it.

MRS. ELVSTED.   Perfectly irreproachable, I assure you! In every respect. But all the same—now that I know he is here—in this great town—and with a large sum of money in his hands—I can't help being in mortal fear for him.

TESMAN.   Why did he not remain where he was? With you and your husband? Eh?

MRS. ELVSTED.   After his book was published he was too restless and unsettled to remain with us.

TESMAN.   Yes, by-the-bye, Aunt Julia told me he had published a new book.

MRS. ELVSTED.   Yes, a big book, dealing with the march of civilisation—in broad outline, as it were. It came out about a fortnight ago. And since it has sold so well, and been so much read—and made such a sensation——

TESMAN.   Has it indeed? It must be something he has had lying by since his better days.

MRS. ELVSTED.   Long ago, you mean?

TESMAN.   Yes.

MRS. ELVSTED.   No, he has written it all since he has been with us—within the last year.

TESMAN.   Isn't that good news, Hedda? Think of that.

MRS. ELVSTED.   Ah, yes, if only it would last!

HEDDA.   Have you seen him here in town?

MRS. ELVSTED.   No, not yet. I have had the greatest difficulty in finding out his address. But this morning I discovered it at last.

HEDDA *(looks searchingly at her).*   Do you know, it seems to me a little odd of your husband—h'm——

MRS. ELVSTED *(starting nervously).*   Of my husband! What?

HEDDA.   That he should send you to town on such an errand—that he does not come himself and look after his friend.

MRS. ELVSTED.   Oh, no, no—my husband has no time. And besides, I—I had some shopping to do.

HEDDA *(with a slight smile).*   Ah, that is a different matter.

MRS. ELVSTED *(rising quickly and uneasily).*   And now I beg and implore you, Mr. Tesman—receive Eilert Lövborg kindly if he comes to you! And that he is sure to do. You see, you were such great friends in the old days. And then you are interested in the same studies—the same branch of science—so far as I can understand.

TESMAN.   We used to be, at any rate.

MRS. ELVSTED.   That is why I beg so earnestly that you—you, too—will keep a sharp eye upon him. Oh, you will promise me that, Mr. Tesman—won't you?

TESMAN.   With the greatest of pleasure, Mrs. Rys-ing——

HEDDA.   Elvsted.

TESMAN.   I assure you I shall do all I possibly can for Eilert. You may rely upon me.

MRS. ELVSTED.   Oh, how very, very kind of you! *(Presses his hands.)* Thanks, thanks, thanks! *(Frightened.)* You see, my husband is so very fond of him!

HEDDA (*rising*).   You ought to write to him, Tesman. Perhaps he may not care to come to you of his own accord.

TESMAN.   Well, perhaps it would be the right thing to do, Hedda? Eh?

HEDDA.   And the sooner the better. Why not at once?

MRS. ELVSTED (*imploringly*).   Oh, if you only would!

TESMAN.   I'll write this moment. Have you his address, Mrs.—Mrs. Elvsted.

MRS. ELVSTED.   Yes. (*Takes a slip of paper from her pocket and hands it to him.*)   Here it is.

TESMAN.   Good, good. Then I'll go in—— (*Looks about him.*) By-the-bye,—my slippers? Oh, here.

{Takes the packet and is about to go.

HEDDA.   Be sure you write him a cordial, friendly letter. And a good long one, too.

TESMAN.   Yes, I will.

MRS. ELVSTED.   But please, please don't say a word to show that I have suggested it.

TESMAN.   No, how could you think I would? Eh?

{He goes out to the right, through the inner room.

HEDDA (*goes up to* MRS. ELVSTED, *smiles and says in a low voice*).   There! We have killed two birds with one stone.

MRS. ELVSTED.   What do you mean?

HEDDA.   Could you not see that I wanted him to go?

MRS. ELVSTED.   Yes, to write the letter——

HEDDA.   And that I might speak to you alone.

MRS. ELVSTED (*confused*).   About the same thing?

HEDDA.   Precisely.

MRS. ELVSTED (*apprehensively*).   But there is nothing more, Mrs. Tesman! Absolutely nothing!

HEDDA.   Oh, yes, but there is. There is a great deal more—I can see that. Sit here—and we'll have a cosy, confidential chat.

> {*She forces* MRS. ELVSTED *to sit in the easy-chair beside the stove and seats herself on one of the footstools.*

MRS. ELVSTED (*anxiously, looking at her watch*).   But, my dear Mrs. Tesman—I was really on the point of going.

HEDDA.   Oh, you can't be in such a hurry.—Well? Now tell me something about your life at home.

MRS. ELVSTED.   Oh, that is just what I care least to speak about.

HEDDA.   But to me, dear——? Why, weren't we school-fellows?

MRS. ELVSTED.   Yes, but you were in the class above me. Oh, how dreadfully afraid of you I was then!

HEDDA.   Afraid of me?

MRS. ELVSTED.   Yes, dreadfully. For when we met on the stairs you used always to pull my hair.

HEDDA.   Did I, really?

MRS. ELVSTED.   Yes, and once you said you would burn it off my head.

HEDDA.   Oh, that was all nonsense, of course.

MRS. ELVSTED.   Yes, but I was so silly in those days.— And since then, too—we have drifted so far—far apart from each other. Our circles have been so entirely different.

HEDDA.   Well, then, we must try to drift together again. Now listen! At school we said *du* to each other; and we called each other by our Christian names——

MRS. ELVSTED.   No, I am sure you must be mistaken.

HEDDA.   No, not at all! I can remember quite distinctly. so now we are going to renew our old friendship. *(Draws the footstool closer to* MRS. ELVSTED.*)* There now! *(Kisses her cheek.)* You must say *du* to me and call me Hedda.

MRS. ELVSTED *(presses and pats her hands)*. Oh, how good and kind you are! I am not used to such kindness.

HEDDA.   There, there, there! And I shall say *du* to you, as in the old days, and call you my dear Thora.

MRS. ELVSTED.   My name is Thea.*

HEDDA.   Why, of course! I meant Thea. *(Looks at her compassionately.)* So you are not accustomed to goodness and kindness, Thea? Not in your own home?

MRS. ELVSTED.   Oh, if I only had a home! But I haven't any; I have never had a home.

HEDDA *(looks at her for a moment)*.   I almost suspected as much.

MRS. ELVSTED *(gazing helplessly before her)*.   Yes— yes—yes.

HEDDA.   I don't quite remember—was it not as housekeeper that you first went to Mr. Elvsted's?

MRS. ELVSTED.   I really went as governess. But his wife—his late wife—was an invalid,—and rarely left her room. So I had to look after the housekeeping as well.

HEDDA.   And then—at last—you became mistress of the house.

MRS. ELVSTED *(sadly)*.   Yes, I did.

HEDDA.   Let me see—about how long ago was that?

MRS. ELVSTED.   My marriage?

HEDDA.   Yes.

MRS. ELVSTED.   Five years ago.

HEDDA.   To be sure; it must be that.

MRS. ELVSTED.   Oh, those five years——! Or at all

---

*   Pronounce *Tora* and *Taya*.

events the last two or three of them! Oh, if you* could only imagine——

HEDDA (*giving her a little slap on the hand*).   De? Fie, Thea!

MRS. ELVSTED.   Yes, yes, I will try—— Well, if— you could only imagine and understand——

HEDDA (*lightly*).   Eilert Lövborg has been in your neighbourhood about three years, hasn't he?

MRS. ELVSTED (*looks at her doubtfully*). Eilert Lövborg? Yes—he has.

HEDDA.   Had you known him before, in town here?

MRS. ELVSTED.   Scarcely at all. I mean—I knew him by name of course.

HEDDA.   But you saw a good deal of him in the country?

MRS. ELVSTED.   Yes, he came to us every day. You see, he gave the children lessons; for in the long run I couldn't manage it myself.

HEDDA.   No, that's clear.—And your husband——? I suppose he is often away from home?

MRS. ELVSTED.   Yes. Being sheriff, you know, he has to travel about a good deal in his district.

HEDDA (*leaning against the arm of the chair*).   Thea—my poor, sweet Thea—now you must tell me everything—ex- actly as it stands.

MRS. ELVSTED.   Well, then, you must question me.

HEDDA.   What sort of man is your husband, Thea? I mean—you know—in everyday life. Is he kind to you?

MRS. ELVSTED (*evasively*).   I am sure he means well in everything.

HEDDA.   I should think he must be altogether too

---

*   Mrs. Elvsted here uses the formal pronoun *De,* whereupon Heda rebukes her. In her next speech Mrs. Elvsted says *du.*

old for you. There is at least twenty years' difference between you, is there not?

MRS. ELVSTED *(irritably).* Yes, that is true, too. Everything about him is repellent to me! We have not a thought in common. We have no single point of sympathy—he and I.

HEDDA. But is he not fond of you all the same? In his own way?

MRS. ELVSTED. Oh, I really don't know. I think he regards me simply as a useful property. And then it doesn't cost much to keep me. I am not expensive.

HEDDA. That is stupid of you.

MRS. ELVSTED *(shakes her head).* It cannot be otherwise—not with him. I don't think he really cares for any one but himself—and perhaps a little for the children.

HEDDA. And for Eilert Lövborg, Thea.

MRS. ELVSTED *(looking at her).* For Eilert Lövborg? What puts that into your head?

HEDDA. Well, my dear—I should say, when he sends you after him all the way to town—— *(Smiling almost imperceptibly.)* And besides, you said so yourself, to Tesman.

MRS. ELVSTED *(with a little nervous twitch).* Did I? Yes, I suppose I did. *(Vehemently, but not loudly.)* No—I may just as well make a clean breast of it at once! For it must all come out in any case.

HEDDA. Why, my dear Thea——?

MRS. ELVSTED. Well, to make a long story short: My husband did not know that I was coming.

HEDDA. What! Your husband didn't know it!

MRS. ELVSTED. No, of course not. For that matter, he was away from home himself—he was travelling. Oh, I could bear it no longer, Hedda! I couldn't indeed—so utterly alone as I should have been in future.

HEDDA. Well? And then?

MRS. ELVSTED. So I put together some of my things—what I needed most—as quietly as possible. And then I left the house.

HEDDA. Without a word?

MRS. ELVSTED. Yes—and took the train straight to town.

HEDDA. Why, my dear, good Thea—to think of you daring to do it!

MRS. ELVSTED. *(rises and moves about the room).* What else could I possibly do?

HEDDA. But what do you think your husband will say when you go home again?

MRS. ELVSTED. *(at the table, looks at her).* Back to him?

HEDDA. Of course.

MRS. ELVSTED. I shall never go back to him again.

HEDDA. *(rising and going towards her).* Then you have left your home—for good and all?

MRS. ELVSTED. Yes. There was nothing else to be done.

HEDDA. But then—to take flight so openly.

MRS. ELVSTED. Oh, it's impossible to keep things of that sort secret.

HEDDA. But what do you think people will say of you, Thea?

MRS. ELVSTED. They may say what they like, for aught I care. *(Seats herself wearily and sadly on the sofa.)* I have done nothing but what I had to do.

HEDDA *(after a short silence).* And what are your plans now? What do you think of doing?

MRS. ELVSTED. I don't know yet. I only know this,

that I must live here, where Eilert Lövborg is—if I am to live at all.

HEDDA (*takes a chair from the table, seats herself beside her and strokes her hands*).   My dear Thea—how did this—this friendship—between you and Eilert Lövborg come about?

MRS. ELVSTED.   Oh, it grew up gradually. I gained a sort of influence over him.

HEDDA.   Indeed?

MRS. ELVSTED.   He gave up his old habits. Not because I asked him to, for I never dared do that. But of course he saw how repulsive they were to me; and so he dropped them.

HEDDA (*concealing an involuntary smile of scorn*). Then you have reclaimed him—as the saying goes—my little Thea.

MRS. ELVSTED.   So he says himself, at any rate. And he, on his side, has made a real human being of me—taught me to think and to understand so many things.

HEDDA.   Did he give you lessons, too, then?

MRS. ELVSTED.   No, not exactly lessons. But he talked to me—talked about such an infinity of things. And then came the lovely, happy time when I began to share in his work—when he allowed me to help him!

HEDDA.   Oh, he did, did he?

MRS. ELVSTED.   Yes! He never wrote anything without my assistance.

HEDDA.   You were two good comrades, in fact?

MRS. ELVSTED (*eagerly*).   Comrades! Yes, fancy, Hedda—that is the very word he used!—Oh, I ought to feel perfectly happy; and yet I cannot; for I don't know how long it will last.

HEDDA.   Are you no surer of him than that?

MRS. ELVSTED *(gloomily).* A woman's shadow stands between Eilert Lövborg and me.

HEDDA *(looks at her anxiously).* Who can that be?

MRS. ELVSTED. I don't know. Some one he knew in his—in his past. Some one he has never been able wholly to forget.

HEDDA. What has he told you—about this?

MRS. ELVSTED. He has only once—quite vaguely— alluded to it.

HEDDA. Well. And what did he say?

MRS. ELVSTED. He said that when they parted, she threatened to shoot him with a pistol.

HEDDA *(with cold composure).* Oh, nonsense! No one does that sort of thing here.

MRS. ELVSTED. No. And that is why I think it must have been that red-haired singing-woman whom he once——

HEDDA. Yes, very likely.

MRS. ELVSTED. For I remember they used to say of her that she carried loaded firearms.

HEDDA. Oh—then of course it must have been she.

MRS. ELVSTED *(wringing her hands).* And now just fancy, Hedda—I hear that this singing-woman—that she is in town again! Oh, I don't know what to do——

HEDDA *(glancing towards the inner room).* Hush! Here comes Tesman. *(Rises and whispers.)* Thea—all this must remain between you and me.

MRS. ELVSTED *(springing up).* Oh, yes, yes! for heaven's sake——!

    {GEORGE TESMAN, *with a letter in his hand, comes from the right through the inner room.*

TESMAN. There now—the epistle is finished.

HEDDA.   That's right. And now Mrs. Elvsted is just going. Wait a moment—I'll go with you to the garden gate.

TESMAN.   Do you think Berta could post the letter, Hedda dear?

HEDDA *(takes it).*   I will tell her to.

> {BERTA *enters from the hall.*

BERTA.   Judge Brack wishes to know if Mrs. Tesman will receive him.

HEDDA.   Yes, ask Judge Brack to come in. And look here—put this letter in the post.

BERTA *(taking the letter).*   Yes, ma'am.

> {She opens the door for JUDGE BRACK *and goes out herself.* BRACK *is a man of forty-five; thick-set, but well-built and elastic in his movements. His face is roundish with an aristocratic profile. His hair is short, still almost black, and carefully dressed. His eyes are lively and sparkling. His eyebrows thick. His moustaches are also thick, with short-cut ends. He wears a well-cut walking-suit, a little too youthful for his age. He uses an eye-glass, which he now and then lets drop.*

JUDGE BRACK *(with his hat in his hand, bowing).*   May one venture to call so early in the day?

HEDDA.   Of course one may.

TESMAN *(presses his hand).*   You are welcome at any time. *(Introducing him.)* Judge Brack—Miss Rysing——

HEDDA.   Oh——!

BRACK *(bowing).*   Ah—delighted——

HEDDA *(looks at him and laughs).*   It's nice to have a look at you by daylight, Judge!

BRACK.   Do you find me—altered?

HEDDA.   A little younger, I think.

BRACK.   Thank you so much.

TESMAN.   But what do you think of Hedda—eh? Doesn't she look flourishing? She has actually——

HEDDA.   Oh, do leave me alone. You haven't thanked Judge Brack for all the trouble he has taken——

BRACK.   Oh, nonsense—it was a pleasure to me——

HEDDA.   Yes, you are a friend indeed. But here stands Thea all impatience to be off—so *au revoir*, Judge. I shall be back again presently.

> *(Mutual salutations.* MRS. ELVSTED *and* HEDDA *go out by the hall door.*

BRACK.   Well,—is your wife tolerably satisfied——

TESMAN.   Yes, we can't thank you sufficiently. Of course she talks of a little re-arrangement here and there; and one or two things are still wanting. We shall have to buy some additional trifles.

BRACK.   Indeed!

TESMAN.   But we won't trouble you about these things. Hedda says she herself will look after what is want-ing.—Shan't we sit down? Eh?

BRACK   Thanks, for a moment. *(Seats himself beside the table.)* There is something I wanted to speak to you about, my dear Tesman.

TESMAN.   Indeed? Ah, I understand! *(Seating himself).* I suppose it's the serious part of the frolic that is coming now. Eh?

BRACK.   Oh, the money question is not so very press-ing; though, for that matter, I wish we had gone a little more economically to work.

TESMAN.   But that would never have done, you know! Think of Hedda, my dear fellow! You, who know her so well——. I couldn't possibly ask her to put up with a shabby style of living!

BRACK.   No, no—that is just the difficulty.

TESMAN.   And then—fortunately—it can't be long before I receive my appointment.

BRACK.   Well, you see—such things are often apt to hang fire for a time.

TESMAN.   Have you heard anything definite? Eh?

BRACK.   Nothing exactly definite—— *(Interrupting himself.)*   But, by-the-bye—I have one piece of news for you.

TESMAN.   Well?

BRACK.   Your old friend, Eilert Lövborg, has returned to town.

TESMAN.   I know that already.

BRACK.   Indeed! How did you learn it?

TESMAN.   From that lady who went out with Hedda.

BRACK.   Really? What was her name? I didn't quite catch it.

TESMAN.   Mrs. Elvsted.

BRACK.   Aha—Sheriff Elvsted's wife? Of course—he has been living up in their regions.

TESMAN.   And fancy—I'm delighted to hear that he is quite a reformed character!

BRACK.   So they say.

TESMAN.   And then he has published a new book—eh?

BRACK.   Yes, indeed he has.

TESMAN.   And I hear it has made some sensation!

BRACK.   Quite an unusual sensation.

TESMAN.   Fancy—isn't that good news! A man of such extraordinary talents—— I felt so grieved to think that he had gone irretrievably to ruin.

BRACK.   That was what everybody thought.

TESMAN.   But I cannot imagine what he will take to now! How in the world will he be able to make his living? Eh?

{During the last words, HEDDA *has entered by the hall door.*

HEDDA *(to* BRACK, *laughing with a touch of scorn).*   Tesman is for ever worrying about how people are to make their living.

TESMAN.   Well, you see, dear—we were talking about poor Eilert Lövborg.

HEDDA *(glancing at him rapidly).*   Oh, indeed? *(Seats herself in the arm-chair beside the stove and asks indifferently:)* What is the matter with him?

TESMAN.   Well—no doubt he has run through all his property long ago; and he can scarcely write a new book every year—eh? So I really can't see what is to become of him.

BRACK.   Perhaps I can give you some information on that point.

TESMAN.   Indeed!

BRACK.   You must remember that his relations have a good deal of influence.

TESMAN.   Oh, his relations, unfortunately, have entirely washed their hands of him.

BRACK.   At one time they called him the hope of the family.

TESMAN.   At one time, yes! But he has put an end to all that.

HEDDA.   Who knows? *(With a slight smile.)*   I hear they have reclaimed him up at Sheriff Elvsted's——

BRACK.   And then this book that he has published——

TESMAN.   Well, well, I hope to goodness they may

find something for him to do. I have just written to him. I asked him to come and see us this evening, Hedda dear.

BRACK.   But, my dear fellow, you are booked for my bachelors' party this evening. You promised on the pier last night.

HEDDA.   Had you forgotten, Tesman?

TESMAN.   Yes, I had utterly forgotten.

BRACK.   But it doesn't matter, for you may be sure he won't come.

TESMAN.   What makes you think that? Eh?

BRACK *(with a little hesitation, rising and resting his hands on the back of his chair)*.   My dear Tesman—and you, too, Mrs. Tesman—I think I ought not to keep you in the dark about something that—that——

TESMAN.   That concerns Eilert——?

BRACK.   Both you and him.

TESMAN.   Well, my dear Judge, out with it.

BRACK.   You must be prepared to find your appointment deferred longer than you desired or expected.

TESMAN *(jumping up uneasily)*.   Is there some hitch about it? Eh?

BRACK.   The nomination may perhaps be made conditional on the result of a competition——

TESMAN.   Competition! Think of that, Hedda!

HEDDA *(leans farther back in the chair)*.   Aha—aah!

TESMAN.   But who can my competitor be? Surely not——?

BRACK.   Yes, precisely—Eilert Lövborg.

TESMAN *(clasping his hands)*.   No, no—it's quite inconceivable! Quite impossible! Eh?

BRACK.   H'm—that is what it may come to, all the same.

TESMAN.   Well, but, Judge Brack—it would show

the most incredible lack of consideration for me. *(Gesticulates with his arms.)* For—just think—I'm a married man! We have married on the strength of these prospects, Hedda and I; and run deep into debt; and borrowed money from Aunt Julia, too. Good heavens, they had as good as promised me the appointment. Eh?

BRACK.   Well, well, well—no doubt you will get it in the end; only after a contest.

HEDDA *(immovable in her arm-chair)*.   Fancy, Tesman, there will be a sort of sporting interest in that.

TESMAN.   Why, my dearest Hedda, how can you be so indifferent about it.

HEDDA *(as before)*.   I am not at all indifferent. I am most eager to see who wins.

BRACK.   In any case, Mrs. Tesman, it is best that you should know how matters stand. I mean—before you set about the little purchases I hear you are threatening.

HEDDA.   This can make no difference.

BRACK.   Indeed! Then I have no more to say. Good-bye! *(To* TESMAN*)*. I shall look in on my way back from my afternoon walk and take you home with me.

TESMAN.   Oh, yes, yes—your news has quite upset me.

HEDDA *(reclining, holds out her hand)*.   Good-bye, Judge; and be sure you call in the afternoon.

BRACK.   Many thanks. Good-bye, good-bye!

TESMAN *(accompanying him to the door)*.   Good-bye, my dear Judge! You must really excuse me——

                    {JUDGE BRACK *goes out by the hall door.*

TESMAN *(crosses the room)*.   Oh, Hedda—one should never rush into adventures. Eh?

HEDDA *(looks at him, smiling)*.   Do you do that?

TESMAN. Yes, dear—there is no denying—it was adventurous to go and marry and set up house upon mere expectations.

HEDDA. Perhaps you are right there.

TESMAN. Well—at all events, we have our delightful home, Hedda! Fancy, the home we both dreamed of—the home we were in love with, I may almost say. Eh?

HEDDA (*rising slowly and wearily*). It was part of our compact that we were to go into society—to keep open house.

TESMAN. Yes, if you only knew how I had been looking forward to it! Fancy—to see you as hostess—in a select circle! Eh? Well, well, well—for the present we shall have to get on without society, Hedda—only to invite Aunt Julia now and then.—Oh, I intended you to lead such an utterly different life, dear——!

HEDDA. Of course I cannot have my man in livery just yet.

TESMAN. Oh, no, unfortunately. It would be out of the question for us to keep a footman, you know.

HEDDA. And the saddle-horse I was to have had——

TESMAN (*aghast*). The saddle-horse!

HEDDA. ——I suppose I must not think of that now.

TESMAN. Good heavens, no!—that's as clear as daylight.

HEDDA (*goes up the room*). Well, I shall have one thing at least to kill time with in the meanwhile.

TESMAN (*beaming*). Oh, thank heaven for that! What is it, Hedda? Eh?

HEDDA (*in the middle doorway, looks at him with covert scorn*). My pistols, George.

TESMAN (*in alarm*).   Your pistols!

HEDDA (*with cold eyes*).   General Gabler's pistols. .

{*She goes out through the inner room, to the left.*

TESMAN (*rushes up to the middle doorway and calls after her:*)   No, for heaven's sake, Hedda darling—don't touch those dangerous things! For my sake, Hedda! Eh?

Act II

~

The room at the TESMANS' *as in the first Act, except that the piano
has been removed, and an elegant little writing-table with book-
shelves put in its place. A smaller table stands near the sofa on
the left. Most of the bouquets have been taken away.* MRS. ELV-
STED'S *bouquet is upon the large table in front. — It is afternoon.*
HEDDA, *dressed to receive callers, is alone in the room. She stands
by the open glass door, loading a revolver. The fellow to it lies
in an open pistol-case on the writing-table.*

HEDDA (*looks down the garden, and calls:*)   So you are here
again, Judge!

BRACK (*is heard calling from a distance*).   As you see,
Mrs. Tesman!

HEDDA (*raises the pistol and points*).   Now I'll shoot
you, Judge Brack!

BRACK (*calling unseen*).   No, no, no! Don't stand aim-
ing at me!

HEDDA.   This is what comes of sneaking in by the
back way.*

{*She fires.*

BRACK (*nearer*).   Are you out of your senses——!

HEDDA.   Dear me—did I happen to hit you?

BRACK (*still outside*).   I wish you would let these
pranks alone!

---

*   "Bagveje" means both "back ways" and "underhand courses."

HEDDA.   Come in then, Judge.

         {JUDGE BRACK, *dressed as though for a men's party,
enters by the glass door. He carries a light overcoat over
his arm.*

BRACK.   What the deuce—haven't you tired of that
sport yet? What are you shooting at?

HEDDA.   Oh, I am only firing in the air.

BRACK (*gently takes the pistol out of her hand*).   Allow
me, madam! (*Looks at it.*) Ah—I know this pistol well! (*Looks
around.*) Where is the case? Ah, here it is. (*Lays the pistol in
it and shuts it.*) Now we won't play at that game any more
to-day.

HEDDA.   Then what in heaven's name would you
have me do with myself?

BRACK.   Have you had no visitors?

HEDDA (*closing the glass door*).   Not one. I suppose all
our set are still out of town.

BRACK.   And is Tesman not at home either?

HEDDA (*at the writing-table, putting the pistol-case in a
drawer which she shuts*).   No. He rushed off to his aunt's
directly after lunch; he didn't expect you so early.

BRACK.   H'm—how stupid of me not to have
thought of that!

HEDDA (*turning her head to look at him*).   Why stupid?

BRACK.   Because if I had thought of it I should have
come a little—earlier.

HEDDA (*crossing the room*).   Then you would have
found no one to receive you; for I have been in my room
changing my dress ever since lunch.

BRACK.   And is there no sort of little chink that we
could hold a parley through?

HEDDA.   You have forgotten to arrange one.

BRACK.   That was another piece of stupidity.

HEDDA.   Well, we must just settle down here—and
wait. Tesman is not likely to be back for some time yet.

BRACK.   Never mind; I shall not be impatient.

> {HEDDA *seats herself in the corner of the sofa.* BRACK
> *lays his overcoat over the back of the nearest chair and
> sits down, but keeps his hat in his hand. A short silence.
> They look at each other.*

HEDDA.   Well?

BRACK (*in the same tone*).   Well?

HEDDA.   I spoke first.

BRACK (*bending a little forward*).   Come, let us have a
cosy little chat, Mrs. Hedda.*

HEDDA (*leaning further back in the sofa*).   Does it not
seem like a whole eternity since our last talk? Of course I
don't count those few words yesterday evening and this
morning.

BRACK.   You mean since our last confidential talk?
Our last *tête-à-tête?*

HEDDA.   Well, yes—since you put it so.

BRACK.   Not a day has passed but I have wished that
you were home again.

HEDDA.   And I have done nothing but wish the same
thing.

BRACK.   You? Really, Mrs. Hedda? And I thought
you had been enjoying your tour so much!

HEDDA.   Oh, yes, you may be sure of that!

BRACK.   But Tesman's letters spoke of nothing but
happiness.

HEDDA.   Oh, Tesman! You see, he thinks nothing so

---

*   As this form of address is contrary to English usage, and as the
note of familiarity would be lacking in "Mrs. Tesman," Brack may, in stage
representation, say "Miss Hedda," thus ignoring her marriage and reverting
to the form of address no doubt customary between them of old.

delightful as grubbing in libraries and making copies of old parchments, or whatever you call them.

BRACK *(with a spice of malice).*   Well, that is his vo-cation in life—or part of it, at any rate.

HEDDA.   Yes, of course; and no doubt when it's your vocation—— But *I!* Oh, my dear Mr. Brack, how mortally bored I have been.

BRACK *(sympathetically).*   Do you really say so? In downright earnest?

HEDDA.   Yes, you can surely understand it——! To go for six whole months without meeting a soul that knew anything of our circle, or could talk about the things we are interested in.

BRACK.   Yes, yes—I too should feel that a depriva-tion.

HEDDA.   And then, what I found most intolerable of all——

BRACK.   Well?

HEDDA.   ——was being everlastingly in the com-pany of—one and the same person——

BRACK *(with a nod of assent).*   Morning, noon, and night, yes—at all possible times and seasons.

HEDDA.   I said "everlastingly."

BRACK.   Just so. But I should have thought, with our excellent Tesman, one could——

HEDDA.   Tesman is—a specialist, my dear Judge.

BRACK.   Undeniably.

HEDDA.   And specialists are not at all amusing to travel with. Not in the long run at any rate.

BRACK.   Not even—the specialist one happens to love?

HEDDA.   Faugh—don't use that sickening word!

BRACK *(taken aback).*   What do you say, Mrs. Hedda?

HEDDA (*half laughing, half irritated*).   You should just try it! To hear of nothing but the history of civilisation, morning, noon, and night——

BRACK.   Everlastingly.

HEDDA.   Yes, yes, yes! And then all this about the domestic industry of the middle ages——! That's the most disgusting part of it!

BRACK (*looks searchingly at her*).   But tell me—in that case, how am I to understand your——? H'm——

HEDDA.   My accepting George Tesman, you mean?

BRACK.   Well, let us put it so.

HEDDA.   Good heavens, do you see anything so wonderful in that?

BRACK.   Yes and no—Mrs. Hedda.

HEDDA.   I had positively danced myself tired, my dear Judge. My day was done—— (*With a slight shudder.*) Oh, no—I won't say that; nor think it either!

BRACK.   You have assuredly no reason to.

HEDDA.   Oh, reasons—— (*Watching him closely.*) And George Tesman—after all, you must admit that he is correctness itself.

BRACK.   His correctness and respectability are beyond all question.

HEDDA.   And I don't see anything absolutely ridiculous about him.—Do you?

BRACK.   Ridiculous? N—no—I shouldn't exactly say so——

HEDDA.   Well—and his powers of research, at all events, are untiring.—I see no reason why he should not one day come to the front, after all.

BRACK (*looks at her hesitatingly*).   I thought that you, like every one else, expected him to attain the highest distinction.

HEDDA (*with an expression of fatigue*).   Yes, so I did.— And then, since he was bent, at all hazards, on being allowed to provide for me—I really don't know why I should not have accepted his offer?

BRACK.   No—if you look at it in that light——

HEDDA.   It was more than my other adorers were prepared to do for me, my dear Judge.

BRACK (*laughing*).   Well, I can't answer for all the rest; but as for myself, you know quite well that I have always entertained a—a certain respect for the marriage tie—for marriage as an institution, Mrs. Hedda.

HEDDA (*jestingly*).   Oh, I assure you I have never cherished any hopes with respect to you.

BRACK.   All I require is a pleasant and intimate interior where I can make myself useful in every way and am free to come and go as—as a trusted friend——

HEDDA.   Of the master of the house, do you mean?

BRACK (*bowing*).   Frankly—of the mistress first of all; but of course of the master, too, in the second place. Such a triangular friendship—if I may call it so—is really a great convenience for all parties, let me tell you.

HEDDA.   Yes, I have many a time longed for some one to make a third on our travels. Oh—those railway-carriage *tête-à-têtes*——!

BRACK.   Fortunately your wedding journey is over now.

HEDDA (*shaking her head*).   Not by a long—long way. I have only arrived at a station on the line.

BRACK.   Well, then the passengers jump out and move about a little, Mrs. Hedda.

HEDDA.   I never jump out.

BRACK.   Really?

HEDDA.   No—because there is always some one standing by to——

BRACK *(laughing).*   To look at your ankles, do you mean.

HEDDA.   Precisely.

BRACK.   Well but, dear me——

HEDDA *(with a gesture of repulsion).*   I won't have it. I would rather keep my seat where I happen to be—and continue the *tête-à-tête.*

BRACK.   But suppose a third person were to jump in and join the couple.

HEDDA.   Ah—that is quite another matter!

BRACK.   A trusted, sympathetic friend——

HEDDA.   ——with a fund of conversation on all sorts of lively topics——

BRACK.   ——and not the least bit of a specialist!

HEDDA *(with an audible sigh).*   Yes, that would be a relief indeed.

BRACK *(hears the front door open and glances in that direction).*   The triangle is completed.

HEDDA *(half aloud).*   And on goes the train.

{GEORGE TESMAN, *in a grey walking-suit, with a soft felt hat, enters from the hall. He has a number of unbound books under his arm and in his pockets.*

TESMAN *(goes up to the table beside the corner settee).*   Ouf—what a load for a warm day—all these books. *(Lays them on the table.)* I'm positively perspiring, Hedda. Hallo—are you there already, my dear Judge? Eh? Berta didn't tell me.

BRACK *(rising).*   I came in through the garden.

HEDDA.   What books have you got there?

TESMAN *(stands looking them through).*   Some new books on my special subjects—quite indispensable to me.

HEDDA.   Your special subjects?

BRACK.   Yes, books on his special subjects, Mrs. Tes-man.

*{*BRACK *and* HEDDA *exchange a confidential smile.*

HEDDA.   Do you need still more books on your spe-cial subjects?

TESMAN.   Yes, my dear Hedda, one can never have too many of them. Of course one must keep up with all that is written and published.

HEDDA.   Yes, I suppose one must.

TESMAN *(searching among his books).*   And look here—I have got hold of Eilert Lövborg's new book, too. *(Offering it to her.)* Perhaps you would like to glance through it, Hedda? Eh?

HEDDA.   No, thank you. Or rather—afterwards per-haps.

TESMAN.   I looked into it a little on the way home.

BRACK.   Well, what do you think of it—as a spe-cialist?

TESMAN.   I think it shows quite remarkable sound-ness of judgment. He never wrote like that before. *(Putting the books together.)* Now I shall take all these into my study. I'm longing to cut the leaves——! And then I must change my clothes. *(To* BRACK.*)* I suppose we needn't start just yet? Eh?

BRACK.   Oh, dear no—there is not the slightest hurry.

TESMAN.   Well, then, I will take my time. *(Is going with his books, but stops in the doorway and turns.)* By-the-bye, Hedda—Aunt Julia is not coming this evening.

HEDDA.   Not coming? Is it that affair of the bonnet that keeps her away?

TESMAN.   Oh, not at all. How could you think such

a thing of Aunt Julia? Just fancy———! The fact is, Aunt Rina is very ill.

HEDDA.   She always is.

TESMAN.   Yes, but to-day she is much worse than usual, poor dear.

HEDDA.   Oh, then it's only natural that her sister should remain with her. I must bear my disappointment.

TESMAN.   And you can't imagine, dear, how delighted Aunt Julia seemed to be—because you had come home looking so flourishing!

HEDDA (*half aloud, rising*).   Oh, those everlasting aunts!

TESMAN.   What?

HEDDA (*going to the glass door*).   Nothing.

TESMAN.   Oh, all right.

{He goes through the inner room, out to the right.

BRACK.   What bonnet were you talking about?

HEDDA.   Oh, it was a little episode with Miss Tesman this morning. She had laid down her bonnet on the chair there—(*looks at him and smiles.*)—And I pretended to think it was the servant's.

BRACK (*shaking his head*).   Now my dear Mrs. Hedda, how could you do such a thing? To that excellent old lady, too!

HEDDA (*nervously crossing the room*).   Well, you see— these impulses come over me all of a sudden; and I cannot resist them. (*Throws herself down in the easy-chair by the stove.*) Oh, I don't know how to explain it.

BRACK (*behind the easy-chair*).   You are not really happy—that is at the bottom of it.

HEDDA (*looking straight before her*).   I know of no reason why I should be—happy. Perhaps you can give me one?

BRACK.		Well—amongst other things, because you have got exactly the home you had set your heart on.

HEDDA (*looks up at him and laughs*).		Do you too believe in that legend?

BRACK.		Is there nothing in it, then?

HEDDA.		Oh, yes, there is something in it.

BRACK.		Well?

HEDDA.		There is this in it, that I made use of Tesman to see me home from evening parties last summer——

BRACK.		I, unfortunately, had to go quite a different way.

HEDDA.		That's true. I know you were going a different way last summer.

BRACK (*laughing*).		Oh fie, Mrs. Hedda! Well, then—you and Tesman——?

HEDDA.		Well, we happened to pass here one evening; Tesman, poor fellow, was writhing in the agony of having to find conversation; so I took pity on the learned man——

BRACK (*smiles doubtfully*).		You took pity? H'm——

HEDDA.		Yes, I really did. And so—to help him out of his torment—I happened to say, in pure thoughtlessness, that I should like to live in this villa.

BRACK.		No more than that?

HEDDA.		Not that evening.

BRACK.		But afterwards?

HEDDA.		Yes, my thoughtlessness had consequences, my dear Judge.

BRACK.		Unfortunately, that too often happens, Mrs. Hedda.

HEDDA.		Thanks! So you see it was this enthusiasm for Secretary's Falk's villa that first constituted a bond of sympathy between George Tesman and me. From that came our engagement and our marriage, and our wedding journey, and all the rest of it. Well, well, my dear Judge—as you make your bed so you must lie, I could almost say.

BRACK.   This is exquisite! And you really cared not a rap about it all the time?

HEDDA.   No, heaven knows I didn't.

BRACK.   But now? Now that we have made it so home-like for you?

HEDDA.   Uh—the rooms all seem to smell of lavender and dried rose-leaves.—But perhaps it's Aunt Julia that has brought that scent with her.

BRACK *(laughing)*.   No, I think it must be a legacy from the late Mrs. Secretary Falk.

HEDDA.   Yes, there is an odour of mortality about it. It reminds me of a bouquet—the day after the ball. *(Clasps her hands behind her head, leans back in her chair and looks at him.)* Oh, my dear Judge—you cannot imagine how horribly I shall bore myself here.

BRACK.   Why should not you, too, find some sort of vocation in life, Mrs. Hedda?

HEDDA.   A vocation—that should attract me?

BRACK.   If possible, of course.

HEDDA.   Heaven knows what sort of vocation that could be. I often wonder whether—— *(Breaking off.)* But that would never do either.

BRACK.   Who can tell? Let me hear what it is.

HEDDA.   Whether I might not get Tesman to go into politics, I mean.

BRACK *(laughing)*.   Tesman? No, really now, political life is not the thing for him—not at all in his line.

HEDDA.   No, I daresay not.—But if I could get him into it all the same?

BRACK.   Why—what satisfaction could you find in

that? If he is not fitted for that sort of thing, why should you want to drive him into it?

HEDDA.   Because I am bored, I tell you! *(After a pause.)* So you think it quite out of the question that Tesman should ever get into the ministry?

BRACK.   H'm—you see, my dear Mrs. Hedda—to get into the ministry, he would have to be a tolerably rich man.

HEDDA *(rising impatiently).*   Yes, there we have it! It is this genteel poverty I have managed to drop into——! *(Crosses the room.)* That is what makes life so pitiable! So utterly ludicrous!—For that's what it is.

BRACK.   Now *I* should say the fault lay elsewhere.

HEDDA.   Where, then?

BRACK.   You have never gone through any really stimulating experience.

HEDDA.   Anything serious, you mean?.

BRACK.   Yes, you may call it so. But now you may perhaps have one in store.

HEDDA *(tossing her head).*   Oh, you're thinking of the annoyances about this wretched professorship! But that must be Tesman's own affair. I assure you I shall not waste a thought upon it.

BRACK.   No, no, I daresay not. But suppose now that what people call—in elegant language—a solemn responsibility were to come upon you? *(Smiling.)* A new responsibility, Mrs. Hedda?

HEDDA *(angrily).*   Be quiet! Nothing of that sort will ever happen!

BRACK *(warily).*   We will speak of this again a year hence—at the very outside.

HEDDA *(curtly).*   I have no turn for anything of the sort, Judge Brack. No responsibilities for me!

BRACK. Are you so unlike the generality of women as to have no turn for duties which——?

HEDDA (*beside the glass door*). Oh, be quiet, I tell you!—I often think there is only one thing in the world I have any turn for.

BRACK (*drawing near to her*). And what is that, if I may ask?

HEDDA (*stands looking out*). Boring myself to death. Now you know it. (*Turns, looks towards the inner room and laughs.*) Yes, as I thought! Here comes the Professor.

BRACK (*softly, in a tone of warning*). Come, come, come, Mrs. Hedda!

{GEORGE TESMAN, *dressed for the party, with his gloves and hat in his hand, enters from the right through the inner room.*

TESMAN. Hedda, has no message come from Eilert Lövborg? Eh?

HEDDA. No.

TESMAN. Then you'll see he'll be here presently.

BRACK. Do you really think he will come?

TESMAN. Yes, I am almost sure of it. For what you were telling us this morning must have been a mere floating rumour.

BRACK. You think so?

TESMAN. At any rate, Aunt Julia said she did not believe for a moment that he would ever stand in my way again. Fancy that!

BRACK. Well, then, that's all right.

TESMAN (*placing his hat and gloves on a chair on the right*). Yes, but you must really let me wait for him as long as possible.

BRACK. We have plenty of time yet. None of my guests will arrive before seven or half-past.

TESMAN.   Then meanwhile we can keep Hedda company and see what happens. Eh?

HEDDA (*placing* BRACK'S *hat and overcoat upon the corner settee*).   And at the worst Mr. Lövborg can remain here with me.

BRACK (*offering to take his things*).   Oh, allow me, Mrs. Tesman!—What do you mean by "At the worst"?

HEDDA.   If he won't go with you and Tesman.

TESMAN (*looks dubiously at her*).   But, Hedda dear— do you think it would quite do for him to remain with you? Eh? Remember, Aunt Julia can't come.

HEDDA.   No, but Mrs. Elvsted is coming. We three can have a cup of tea together.

TESMAN.   Oh, yes, that will be all right.

BRACK (*smiling*).   And that would perhaps be the safest plan for him.

HEDDA.   Why so?

BRACK.   Well, you know, Mrs. Tesman, how you used to gird at my little bachelor parties. You declared they were adapted only for men of the strictest principles.

HEDDA.   But no doubt Mr. Lövborg's principles are strict enough now. A converted sinner——

{BERTA *appears at the hall door.*

BERTA.   There's a gentleman asking if you are at home, ma'am——

HEDDA.   Well, show him in.

TESMAN (*softly*).   I'm sure it is he! Fancy that!

{EILERT LÖVBORG *enters from the hall. He is slim and lean; of the same age as* TESMAN, *but looks older and somewhat worn-out. His hair and beard are of a blackish brown, his face long and pale, but with patches of colour on the cheek-bones. He is dressed in a well-cut black visiting suit, quite new. He has dark gloves and a silk hat. He stops near the door and makes a rapid bow, seeming somewhat embarrassed.*

TESMAN *(goes up to him and shakes him warmly by the hand).* Well, my dear Eilert—so at last we meet again!

EILERT LÖVBORG *(speaks in a subdued voice).* Thanks for your letter, Tesman. *(Approaching* HEDDA.*)* Will you, too, shake hands with me, Mrs. Tesman?

HEDDA *(taking his hand).* I am glad to see you, Mr. Lövborg. *(With a motion of her hand.)* I don't know whether you two gentlemen——?

LÖVBORG *(bowing slightly).* Judge Brack, I think.

BRACK *(doing likewise).* Oh, yes,—in the old days——

TESMAN *(to* LÖVBORG, *with his hands on his shoulders).* And now you must make yourself entirely at home, Eilert! Mustn't he, Hedda?—For I hear you are going to settle in town again? Eh?

LÖVBORG. Yes, I am.

TESMAN. Quite right, quite right. Let me tell you, I have got hold of your new book; but I haven't had time to read it yet.

LÖVBORG. You may spare yourself the trouble.

TESMAN. Why so?

LÖVBORG. Because there is very little in it.

TESMAN. Just fancy—how can you say so?

BRACK. But it has been very much praised, I hear.

LÖVBORG. That was what I wanted; so I put nothing into the book but what every one would agree with.

BRACK. Very wise of you.

TESMAN. Well but, my dear Eilert——!

LÖVBORG. For now I mean to win myself a position again—to make a fresh start.

TESMAN (*a little embarrassed*).   Ah, that is what you wish to do? Eh?

LÖVBORG (*smiling, lays down his hat and draws a packet, wrapped in paper, from his coat pocket*).   But when this one appears, George Tesman, you will have to read it. For this is the real book—the book I have put my true self into.

TESMAN.   Indeed? And what is it?

LÖVBORG.   It is the continuation.

TESMAN.   The continuation? Of what?

LÖVBORG.   Of the book.

TESMAN.   Of the new book?

LÖVBORG.   Of course.

TESMAN.   Why, my dear Eilert—does it not come down to our own days?

LÖVBORG.   Yes, it does; and this one deals with the future.

TESMAN.   With the future! But, good heavens, we know nothing of the future!

LÖVBORG.   No; but there is a thing or two to be said about it all the same. (*Opens the packet.*)   Look here——

TESMAN.   Why, that's not your hand writing.

LÖVBORG.   I dictated it. (*Turning over the pages.*) It falls into two sections. The first deals with the civilising forces of the future. And here is the second—(*running through the pages towards the end*)—forecasting the probable line of development.

TESMAN.   How odd now! I should never have thought of writing anything of that sort.

HEDDA (*at the glass door, drumming on the pane*). H'm—I daresay not.

LÖVBORG (*replacing the manuscript in its paper and laying the packet on the table*).   I brought it, thinking I might read you a little of it this evening.

TESMAN.   That was very good of you, Eilert. But this evening——? (*Looking at* BRACK.) I don't quite see how we can manage it——

LÖVBORG.   Well, then, some other time. There is no hurry.

BRACK.   I must tell you, Mr. Lövborg—there is a little gathering at my house this evening—mainly in honour of Tesman, you know——

LÖVBORG (*looking for his hat*).   Oh—then I won't detain you——

BRACK.   No, but listen—will you not do me the favour of joining us?

LÖVBORG (*curtly and decidedly*).   No, I can't—thank you very much.

BRACK.   Oh, nonsense—do! We shall be quite a select little circle. And I assure you we shall have a "lively time," as Mrs. Hed—as Mrs. Tesman says.

LÖVBORG.   I have no doubt of it. But nevertheless——

BRACK.   And then you might bring your manuscript with you and read it to Tesman at my house. I could give you a room to yourselves.

TESMAN.   Yes, think of that, Eilert,—why shouldn't you? Eh?

HEDDA (*interposing*).   But, Tesman, if Mr. Lövborg would really rather not! I am sure Mr. Lövborg is much more inclined to remain here and have supper with me.

LÖVBORG (*looking at her*).   With you, Mrs. Tesman?

HEDDA.   And with Mrs. Elvsted.

LÖVBORG.   Ah—— (*Lightly.*) I saw her for a moment this morning.

HEDDA.   Did you? Well, she is coming this evening.

So you see you are almost bound to remain, Mr. Lövborg, or she will have no one to see her home.

LÖVBORG.   That's true. Many thanks, Mrs. Tesman—in that case I will remain.

HEDDA.   Then I have one or two orders to give the servant——

> {She goes to the hall door and rings. BERTA enters.
> HEDDA talks to her in a whisper and points towards
> the inner room. BERTA nods and goes out again.

TESMAN (at the same time, to Lövborg).   Tell me, Eilert—is it this new subject—the future—that you are going to lecture about?

LÖVBORG.   Yes.

TESMAN.   They told me at the bookseller's that you are going to deliver a course of lectures this autumn.

LÖVBORG.   That is my intention. I hope you won't take it ill, Tesman.

TESMAN.   Oh, no, not in the least! But——?

LÖVBORG.   I can quite understand that it must be disagreeable to you.

TESMAN (cast down).   Oh, I can't expect you, out of consideration for me, to——

LÖVBORG.   But I shall wait till you have received your appointment.

TESMAN.   Will you wait? Yes, but—yes, but—are you not going to compete with me? Eh?

LÖVBORG.   No; it is only the moral victory I care for.

TESMAN.   Why, bless me—then Aunt Julia was right after all! Oh, yes—I knew it! Hedda! Just fancy—Eilert Lövborg is not going to stand in our way!

HEDDA (curtly).   Our way? Pray leave me out of the question.

> {She goes up towards the inner room, where BERTA is

placing a tray with decanters and glasses on the table.
HEDDA *nods approval and comes forward again.*
BERTA *goes out.*

TESMAN *(at the same time).* And you, Judge Brack—
what do you say to this? Eh?

BRACK. Well, I say that a moral victory—h'm—
may be all very fine——

TESMAN. Yes, certainly. But all the same——

HEDDA *(looking at* TESMAN *with a cold smile).* You stand
there looking as if you were thunderstruck——

TESMAN. Yes—so I am—I almost think——

BRACK. Don't you see, Mrs. Tesman, a thunder-
storm has just passed over?

HEDDA *(pointing towards the inner room).* Will you not
take a glass of cold punch, gentlemen?

BRACK *(looking at his watch).* A stirrup-cup? Yes, it
wouldn't come amiss.

TESMAN. A capital idea, Hedda! Just the thing!
Now that the weight has been taken off my mind——

HEDDA. Will you not join them, Mr. Lövborg?

LÖVBORG *(with a gesture of refusal).* No, thank you.
Nothing for me.

BRACK. Why, bless me—cold punch is surely not
poison.

LÖVBORG. Perhaps not for every one.

HEDDA. I will keep Mr. Lövborg company in the
meantime.

TESMAN. Yes, yes, Hedda dear, do.

{He and BRACK *go into the inner room, seat themselves,*
drink punch, smoke cigarettes and carry on a lively
conversation during what follows. EILERT LÖVBORG
remains standing beside the stove. HEDDA *goes to the*
writing-table.

HEDDA (*raising her voice a little*).   Do you care to look at some photographs, Mr. Lövborg? You know Tesman and I made a tour in the Tyrol on our way home?

> {*She takes up an album, and places it on the table beside the sofa, in the further corner of which she seats herself.* EILERT LÖVBORG *approaches, stops and looks at her. Then he takes a chair and seats himself to her left, with his back towards the inner room.*

HEDDA (*opening the album*).   Do you see this range of mountains, Mr. Lövborg? It's the Ortler group. Tesman has written the name underneath. Here it is: "The Ortler group near Meran."

LÖVBORG (*who has never taken his eyes off her, says softly and slowly:*)   Hedda—Gabler!

HEDDA (*glancing hastily at him*).   Ah! Hush!

LÖVBORG (*repeats softly*).   Hedda Gabler!

HEDDA (*looking at the album*).   That was my name in the old days—when we two knew each other.

LÖVBORG.   And I must teach myself never to say Hedda Gabler again—never, as long as I live.

HEDDA (*still turning over the pages*).   Yes, you must. And I think you ought to practise in time. The sooner the better, I should say.

LÖVBORG (*in a tone of indignation*).   Hedda Gabler married? And married to—George Tesman!

HEDDA.   Yes—so the world goes.

LÖVBORG.   Oh, Hedda, Hedda—how could you* throw yourself away!

HEDDA (*looks sharply at him*).   What? I can't allow this!

LÖVBORG.   What do you mean?

---

*   He uses the familiar *du*.

{TESMAN *comes into the room and goes towards the sofa.*

HEDDA *(hears him coming and says in an indifferent tone).* And this is a view from the Val d'Ampezzo, Mr. Lövborg. Just look at these peaks! *(Looks affectionately up at* TESMAN.*)* What's the name of these curious peaks, dear?

TESMAN. Let me see. Oh, those are the Dolomites.

HEDDA. Yes, that's it!—Those are the Dolomites, Mr. Lövborg.

TESMAN. Hedda dear,—I only wanted to ask whether I shouldn't bring you a little punch after all? For yourself, at any rate—eh?

HEDDA. Yes, do, please; and perhaps a few biscuits.

TESMAN. No cigarettes?

HEDDA. No.

TESMAN. Very well.

{*He goes into the inner room and out to the right.* BRACK *sits in the inner room and keeps an eye from time to time on* HEDDA *and* LÖVBORG.

LÖVBORG *(softly, as before).* Answer me, Hedda—how could you go and do this?

HEDDA *(apparently absorbed in the album).* If you continue to say *du* to me I won't talk to you.

LÖVBORG. May I not say *du* when we are alone?

HEDDA. No. You may think it; but you mustn't say it.

LÖVBORG. Ah, I understand. It is an offence against George Tesman, whom you*—love.

HEDDA *(glances at him and smiles).* Love? What an idea!

LÖVBORG. You don't love him then!

---

* From this point onward Lövborg uses the formal *De.*

HEDDA.   But I won't hear of any sort of unfaithfulness! Remember that.

LÖVBORG.   Hedda—answer me one thing——

HEDDA.   Hush!

{TESMAN enters with a small tray from the inner room.

TESMAN.   Here you are! Isn't this tempting?

{He puts the tray on the table.

HEDDA.   Why do you bring it yourself?

TESMAN *(filling the glasses).*   Because I think it's such fun to wait upon you, Hedda.

HEDDA.   But you have poured out two glasses. Mr. Lövborg said he wouldn't have any——

TESMAN.   No, but Mrs. Elvsted will soon be here, won't she?

HEDDA.   Yes, by-the-bye—Mrs. Elvsted——

TESMAN.   Had you forgotten her? Eh?

HEDDA.   We were so absorbed in these photographs. *(Shows him a picture.)* Do you remember this little village?

TESMAN.   Oh, it's that one just below the Brenner Pass. It was there we passed the night——

HEDDA.   ——and met that lively party of tourists.

TESMAN.   Yes, that was the place. Fancy—if we could only have had you with us, Eilert! Eh?

{He returns to the inner room and sits beside BRACK.

LÖVBORG.   Answer me this one thing, Hedda——

HEDDA.   Well?

LÖVBORG.   Was there no love in your friendship for me either? Not a spark—not a tinge of love in it?

HEDDA.   I wonder if there was? To me it seems as though we were two good comrades—two thoroughly intimate friends. *(Smilingly.)* You especially were frankness itself.

LÖVBORG.   It was you that made me so.

HEDDA.   As I look back upon it all, I think there

was really something beautiful, something fascinating—something daring—in—in that secret intimacy—that comradeship which no living creature so much as dreamed of.

LÖVBORG. Yes, yes, Hedda! Was there not?—When I used to come to your father's in the afternoon—and the General sat over at the window reading his papers—with his back towards us——

HEDDA. And we two on the corner sofa——

LÖVBORG. Always with the same illustrated paper before us——

HEDDA. For want of an album, yes.

LÖVBORG. Yes, Hedda, and when I made my confessions to you—told you about myself, things that at that time no one else knew! There I would sit and tell you of my escapades—my days and nights of devilment. Oh, Hedda—what was the power in you that forced me to confess these things?

HEDDA. Do you think it was any power in me?

LÖVBORG. How else can I explain it? And all those—those roundabout questions you used to put to me——

HEDDA. Which you understood so particularly well——

LÖVBORG. How could you sit and question me like that? Question me quite frankly——

HEDDA. In roundabout terms, please observe.

LÖVBORG. Yes, but frankly nevertheless. Cross-question me about—all that sort of thing?

HEDDA. And how could you answer, Mr. Lövborg?

LÖVBORG. Yes, that is just what I can't understand—in looking back upon it. But tell me now, Hedda—was there not love at the bottom of our friendship? On your side, did you not feel as though you might purge my stains away—if I made you my confessor? Was it not so?

HEDDA.   No, not quite.

LÖVBORG.   What was your motive, then?

HEDDA.   Do you think it quite incomprehensible that a young girl—when it can be done—without any one knowing——

LÖVBORG.   Well?

HEDDA.   ——should be glad to have a peep, now and then, into a world which——

LÖVBORG.   Which——?

HEDDA.   ——which she is forbidden to know anything about?

LÖVBORG.   So that was it?

HEDDA.   Partly. Partly—I almost think.

LÖVBORG.   Comradeship in the thirst for life. But why should not that, at any rate, have continued?

HEDDA.   The fault was yours.

LÖVBORG.   It was you that broke with me.

HEDDA.   Yes, when our friendship threatened to develop into something more serious. Shame upon you, Eilert Lövborg! How could you think of wronging your—your frank comrade?

LÖVBORG (*clenching his hands*).   Oh, why did you not carry out your threat? Why did you not shoot me down?

HEDDA.   Because I have such a dread of scandal.

LÖVBORG.   Yes, Hedda, you are a coward at heart.

HEDDA.   A terrible coward. (*Changing her tone.*) But it was a lucky thing for you. And now you have found ample consolation at the Elvsteds'.

LÖVBORG.   I know what Thea has confided to you.

HEDDA.   And perhaps you have confided to her something about us?

LÖVBORG.   Not a word. She is too stupid to understand anything of that sort.

HEDDA.   Stupid?

LÖVBORG.   She is stupid about matters of that sort.

HEDDA.   And I am cowardly. *(Bends over towards him, without looking him in the face, and says more softly:)* But now I will confide something to you.

LÖVBORG *(eagerly).*   Well?

HEDDA.   The fact that I dared not shoot you down——

LÖVBORG.   Yes!

HEDDA.   ——that was not my arrant cowardice—— that evening.

LÖVBORG *(looks at her a moment, understands and whispers passionately).*   Oh, Hedda! Hedda Gabler! Now I begin to see a hidden reason beneath our comradeship! You* and I——! After all, then, it was your craving for life——

HEDDA *(softly, with a sharp glance).*   Take care! Believe nothing of the sort!

> *{Twilight has begun to fall. The hall door is opened from without by* BERTA.

HEDDA. *(Closes the album with a bang and calls smilingly:)*   Ah, at last! My darling Thea,—come along!

> *{*MRS. ELVSTED *enters from the hall. She is in evening dress. The door is closed behind her.*

HEDDA *(on the sofa, stretches out her arms towards her).*   My sweet Thea—you can't think how I have been longing for you!

> *{*MRS. ELVSTED, *in passing, exchanges slight salutations with the gentlemen in the inner room, then goes up to the table and gives* HEDDA *her hand.* EILERT LÖVBORG *has risen. He and* MRS. ELVSTED *greet each other with a silent nod.*

* In this speech he once more says *du*. Hedda addresses him throughout as *De*.

MRS. ELVSTED.   Ought I to go in and talk to your husband for a moment?

HEDDA.   Oh, not at all. Leave those two alone. They will soon be going.

MRS. ELVSTED.   Are they going out?

HEDDA.   Yes, to a supper-party.

MRS. ELVSTED (*quickly, to* LÖVBORG).   Not you?

LÖVBORG.   No.

HEDDA.   Mr. Lövborg remains with us.

MRS. ELVSTED (*takes a chair and is about to seat herself at his side*).   Oh, how nice it is here!

HEDDA.   No, thank you, my little Thea! Not there! You'll be good enough to come over here to me. I will sit between you.

MRS. ELVSTED.   Yes, just as you please.

> {*She goes round the table and seats herself on the sofa on* HEDDA'S *right.* LÖVBORG *re-seats himself on his chair.*

LÖVBORG (*after a short pause, to* HEDDA).   Is not she lovely to look at?

HEDDA (*lightly stroking her hair*).   Only to look at?

LÖVBORG.   Yes. For we two—she and I—we are two real comrades. We have absolute faith in each other; so we can sit and talk with perfect frankness——

HEDDA.   Not round about, Mr. Lövborg?

LÖVBORG.   Well——

MRS. ELVSTED (*softly clinging close to* HEDDA).   Oh, how happy I am, Hedda; For, only think, he says I have inspired him, too.

HEDDA (*looks at her with a smile*).   Ah! Does he say that, dear?

LÖVBORG.   And then she is so brave, Mrs. Tesman!

MRS. ELVSTED.   Good heavens—am I brave?

LÖVBORG. Exceedingly—where your comrade is concerned.

HEDDA. Ah yes—courage! If one only had that!

LÖVBORG. What then? What do you mean?

HEDDA. Then life would perhaps be liveable, after all. (*With a sudden change of tone.*) But now, my dearest Thea, you really must have a glass of cold punch.

MRS. ELVSTED. No, thanks—I never take anything of that kind.

HEDDA. Well, then, you, Mr. Lövborg.

LÖVBORG. Nor I, thank you.

MRS. ELVSTED. No, he doesn't either.

HEDDA (*looks fixedly at him*). But if I say you shall?

LÖVBORG. It would be no use.

HEDDA (*laughing*). Then I, poor creature, have no sort of power over you?

LÖVBORG. Not in that respect.

HEDDA. But seriously, I think you ought to—for your own sake.

MRS. ELVSTED. Why, Hedda——!

LÖVBORG. How so?

HEDDA. Or rather on account of other people.

LÖVBORG. Indeed?

HEDDA. Otherwise people might be apt to suspect that—in your heart of hearts—you did not feel quite secure—quite confident in yourself.

MRS. ELVSTED (*softly*). Oh, please, Hedda——.

LÖVBORG. People may suspect what they like—for the present.

MRS. ELVSTED (*joyfully*). Yes, let them!

HEDDA. I saw it plainly in Judge Brack's face a moment ago.

LÖVBORG. What did you see?

HEDDA.   His contemptuous smile, when you dared not go with them into the inner room.

LÖVBORG.   Dared not? Of course I preferred to stop here and talk to you.

MRS. ELVSTED.   What could be more natural, Hedda?

HEDDA.   But the Judge could not guess that. And I saw, too, the way he smiled and glanced at Tesman when you dared not accept his invitation to this wretched little supper-party of his.

LÖVBORG.   Dared not! Do you say I dared not?

HEDDA.   *I* don't say so. But that was how Judge Brack understood it.

LÖVBORG.   Well, let him.

HEDDA.   Then you are not going with them?

LÖVBORG.   I will stay here with you and Thea.

MRS. ELVSTED.   Yes, Hedda—how can you doubt that?

HEDDA (*smiles and nods approvingly to* LÖVBORG). Firm as a rock! Faithful to your principles, now and for ever! Ah, that is how a man should be! (*Turns to* MRS. ELVSTED *and caresses her.*) Well, now, what did I tell you, when you came to us this morning in such a state of distraction——

LÖVBORG (*surprised*).   Distraction!

MRS. ELVSTED (*terrified*).   Hedda—oh Hedda——!

HEDDA.   You can see for yourself; You haven't the slightest reason to be in such mortal terror——(*Interrupting herself.*) There! Now we can all three enjoy ourselves!

LÖVBORG (*who has given a start*).   Ah—what is all this, Mrs. Tesman?

MRS. ELVSTED.   Oh, my God, Hedda! What are you saying? What are you doing?

HEDDA.   Don't get excited! That horrid Judge Brack is sitting watching you.

LÖVBORG.   So she was in mortal terror! On my account!

MRS. ELVSTED (*softly and piteously*).   Oh, Hedda—now you have ruined everything!

LÖVBORG (*looks fixedly at her for a moment. His face is distorted*).   So that was my comrade's frank confidence in me?

MRS. ELVSTED (*imploringly*).   Oh, my dearest friend—only let me tell you——

LÖVBORG (*takes one of the glasses of punch, raises it to his lips and says in a low, husky voice*).   Your health, Thea!

{*He empties the glass, puts it down and takes the second.*

MRS. ELVSTED (*softly*).   Oh, Hedda, Hedda—how could you do this?

HEDDA.   *I* do it? *I?* Are you crazy?

LÖVBORG.   Here's to your health, too, Mrs. Tesman. Thanks for the truth. Hurrah for the truth!

{*He empties the glass and is about to re-fill it.*

HEDDA (*lays her hand on his arm*).   Come, come—no more for the present. Remember you are going out to supper.

MRS. ELVSTED.   No, no, no!

HEDDA.   Hush! They are sitting watching you.

LÖVBORG (*putting down the glass*).   Now, Thea—tell me the truth——

MRS. ELVSTED.   Yes.

LÖVBORG.   Did your husband know that you had come after me?

MRS. ELVSTED (*wringing her hands*).   Oh, Hedda—do you hear what he is asking?

LÖVBORG.   Was it arranged between you and him

that you were to come to town and look after me? Perhaps it was the Sheriff himself that urged you to come? Aha, my dear—no doubt he wanted my help in his office! Or was it at the card-table that he missed me?

MRS. ELVSTED (*softly, in agony*). Oh, Lövborg, Lövborg——!

LÖVBORG (*seizes a glass and is on the point of filling it*). Here's a glass for the old Sheriff, too!

HEDDA (*preventing him*). No more just now. Remember you have to read your manuscript to Tesman.

LÖVBORG (*calmly, putting down the glass*). It was stupid of me all this, Thea—to take it in this way, I mean. Don't be angry with me, my dear, dear comrade. You shall see—both you and the others—that if I was fallen once—now I have risen again! Thanks to you, Thea.

MRS. ELVSTED (*radiant with joy*). Oh, heaven be praised——!

> {BRACK *has in the meantime looked at his watch. He and* TESMAN *rise and come into the drawing-room.*

BRACK (*takes his hat and overcoat*). Well, Mrs. Tesman, our time has come.

HEDDA. I suppose it has.

LÖVBORG (*rising*). Mine, too, Judge Brack.

MRS. ELVSTED (*softly and imploringly*). Oh, Lövborg, don't do it!

HEDDA (*pinching her arm*). They can hear you!

MRS. ELVSTED (*with a suppressed shriek*). Ow!

LÖVBORG (*to* BRACK). You were good enough to invite me.

BRACK. Well, are you coming after all?

LÖVBORG. Yes, many thanks.

BRACK. I'm delighted——

LÖVBORG (*to* TESMAN, *putting the parcel of MS. in his*

pocket). I should like to show you one or two things before I send it to the printers.

TESMAN. Fancy—that will be delightful. But, Hedda dear, how is Mrs. Elvsted to get home? Eh?

HEDDA. Oh, that can be managed somehow.

LÖVBORG *(looking towards the ladies).* Mrs. Elvsted? Of course, I'll come again and fetch her. *(Approaching.)* At ten or thereabouts, Mrs. Tesman? Will that do?

HEDDA. Certainly. That will do capitally.

TESMAN. Well, then, that's all right. But you must not expect me so early, Hedda.

HEDDA. —Oh, you may stop as long—as long as ever you please.

MRS. ELVSTED *(trying to conceal her anxiety).* Well, then, Mr. Lövborg—I shall remain here until you come.

LÖVBORG *(with his hat in his hand).* Pray do, Mrs. Elvsted.

BRACK. And now off goes the excursion train, gentlemen! I hope we shall have a lively time, as a certain fair lady puts it.

HEDDA. Ah, if only the fair lady could be present unseen——!

BRACK. Why unseen?

HEDDA. In order to hear a little of your liveliness at first hand, Judge Brack.

BRACK *(laughing).* I should not advise the fair lady to try it.

TESMAN *(also laughing).* Come, you're a nice one Hedda! Fancy that!

BRACK. Well, good-bye, ladies.

LÖVBORG *(bowing).* About ten o'clock, then.

[BRACK, LÖVBORG *and* TESMAN *go out by the hall door. At the same time,* BERTA *enters from the inner room with a lighted lamp, which she places on the dining-room table; she goes out by the way she came.*

MRS. ELVSTED *(who has risen and is wandering restlessly about the room).* Hedda—Hedda—what will come of all this?

HEDDA. At ten o'clock—he will be here. I can see him already—with vine-leaves in his hair—flushed and fearless——

MRS. ELVSTED. Oh, I hope he may.

HEDDA. And then, you see—then he will have regained control over himself. Then he will be a free man for all his days.

MRS. ELVSTED. Oh, God!—if he would only come as you see him now!

HEDDA. He will come as I see him—so, and not otherwise! *(Rises and approaches* THEA.*)* You may doubt him as long as you please; *I* believe in him. And now we will try——

MRS. ELVSTED. You have some hidden motive in this, Hedda!

HEDDA. Yes, I have. I want for once in my life to have power to mould a human destiny.

MRS. ELVSTED. Have you not the power?

HEDDA. I have not—and have never had it.

MRS. ELVSTED. Not your husband's?

HEDDA. Do you think that is worth the trouble? Oh, if you could only understand how poor I am. And fate has made you so rich! *(Clasps her passionately in her arms.)* I think I must burn your hair off, after all.

MRS. ELVSTED. Let me go! Let me go! I am afraid of you, Hedda!

BERTA *(in the middle doorway).* Tea is laid in the dining-room, ma'am.

HEDDA.   Very well. We are coming.

MRS. ELVSTED.   No, no, no! I would rather go home alone! At once!

HEDDA.   Nonsense! First you shall have a cup of tea, you little stupid. And then—at ten o'clock—Eilert Lövborg will be here—with vine-leaves in his hair.

> {She drags MRS. ELVSTED almost by force towards
> the middle doorway.

Act III

The room at the TESMANS'. *The curtains are drawn over the middle doorway, and also over the glass door. The lamp, half turned down, and with a shade over it, is burning on the table. In the stove, the door of which stands open, there has been a fire, which is now nearly burnt out.*

MRS. ELVSTED, *wrapped in a large shawl, and with her feet upon a foot-rest, sits close to the stove, sunk back in the arm-chair.* HEDDA, *fully dressed, lies sleeping upon the sofa, with a sofa-blanket over her.*

MRS. ELVSTED (*after a pause, suddenly sits up in her chair and listens eagerly. Then she sinks back again wearily, moaning to herself*).   Not yet!—Oh, God—oh, God—not yet!

{BERTA *slips cautiously in by the hall door. She has a letter in her hand.*

MRS. ELVSTED (*turns and whispers eagerly*).   Well—has any one come?

BERTA (*softly*).   Yes, a girl has brought this letter.

MRS. ELVSTED (*quickly, holding out her hand*).   A letter! Give it to me!

BERTA.   No, it's for Dr. Tesman, ma'am.

MRS. ELVSTED.   Oh, indeed.

BERTA.   It was Miss Tesman's servant that brought it. I'll lay it here on the table.

MRS. ELVSTED.   Yes, do.

BERTA *(laying down the letter).* I think I had better put out the lamp. It's smoking.

MRS. ELVSTED. Yes, put it out. It must soon be daylight now.

BERTA *(putting out the lamp).* It is daylight already, ma'am.

MRS. ELVSTED. Yes, broad day! And no one come back yet——!

BERTA. Lord bless you, ma'am—I guessed how it would be.

MRS. ELVSTED. You guessed?

BERTA. Yes, when I saw that a certain person had come back to town—and that he went off with them. For we've heard enough about that gentleman before now.

MRS. ELVSTED. Don't speak so loud. You will waken Mrs. Tesman.

BERTA *(looks towards the sofa and sighs).* No, no—let her sleep, poor thing. Shan't I put some wood on the fire?

MRS. ELVSTED. Thanks, not for me.

BERTA. Oh, very well.

{She goes softly out by the hall door.

HEDDA *(is awakened by the shutting of the door and looks up).* What's that——?

MRS. ELVSTED. It was only the servant——

HEDDA *(looking about her).* Oh, we're here——! Yes, now I remember. *(Sits erect upon the sofa, stretches her self and rubs her eyes.)* What o'clock is it, Thea?

MRS. ELVSTED *(looks at her watch).* It's past seven.

HEDDA. When did Tesman come home?

MRS. ELVSTED. He has not come.

HEDDA. Not come home yet?

MRS. ELVSTED *(rising).* No one has come.

HEDDA.   Think of our watching and waiting here till four in the morning——

MRS. ELVSTED *(wringing her hands)*.   And how I watched and waited for him!

HEDDA *(yawns and says with her hand before her mouth)*.   Well, well—we might have spared ourselves the trouble.

MRS. ELVSTED.   Did you get a little sleep?

HEDDA.   Oh, yes; I believe I have slept pretty well. Have you not?

MRS. ELVSTED.   Not for a moment. I couldn't, Hedda!—not to save my life.

HEDDA *(rises and goes towards her)*.   There, there, there! There's nothing to be so alarmed about. I understand quite well what has happened.

MRS. ELVSTED.   Well, what do you think? Won't you tell me?

HEDDA.   Why, of course it has been a very late affair at Judge Brack's——

MRS. ELVSTED.   Yes, yes, that is clear enough. But all the same——

HEDDA.   And then, you see, Tesman hasn't cared to come home and ring us up in the middle of the night. *(Laughing.)* Perhaps he wasn't inclined to show himself either—immediately after a jollification.

MRS. ELVSTED.   But in that case—where can he have gone?

HEDDA.   Of course he has gone to his aunts' and slept there. They have his old room ready for him.

MRS. ELVSTED.   No, he can't be with them; for a letter has just come for him from Miss Tesman. There it lies.

HEDDA.   Indeed? *(Looks at the address.)* Why, yes, it's

addressed in Aunt Julia's own hand. Well, then, he has remained at Judge Brack's. And as for Eilert Lövborg—he is sitting, with vine-leaves in his hair, reading his manuscript.

MRS. ELVSTED.   Oh Hedda, you are just saying things you don't believe a bit.

HEDDA.   You really are a little blockhead, Thea.

MRS. ELVSTED.   Oh, yes, I suppose I am.

HEDDA.   And how mortally tired you look.

MRS. ELVSTED.   Yes, I am mortally tired.

HEDDA.   Well, then, you must do as I tell you. You must go into my room and lie down for a little while.

MRS. ELVSTED.   Oh, no, no—I shouldn't be able to sleep.

HEDDA.   I am sure you would.

MRS. ELVSTED.   Well, but your husband is certain to come soon now; and then I want to know at once——

HEDDA.   I shall take care to let you know when he comes.

MRS. ELVSTED.   Do you promise me, Hedda?

HEDDA.   Yes, rely upon me. Just you go in and have a sleep in the meantime.

MRS. ELVSTED.   Thanks; then I'll try to.

{She goes off through the inner room.

{HEDDA goes up to the glass door and draws back the curtains. The broad daylight streams into the room. Then she takes a little hand-glass from the writing-table, looks at herself in it and arranges her hair. Next she goes to the hall door and presses the bell-button.

{BERTA presently appears at the hall door.

BERTA.   Did you want anything, ma'am?

HEDDA.   Yes; you must put some more wood in the stove. I am shivering.

BERTA.   Bless me—I'll make up the fire at once. *(She*

rakes the embers together and lays a piece of wood upon them; then stops and listens.) That was a ring at the front door, ma'am.

HEDDA.   Then go to the door. I will look after the fire.

BERTA.   It'll soon burn up.

> *{She goes out by the hall door.*
> *{*HEDDA *kneels on the foot-rest and lays some more pieces of wood in the stove.*
> *{After a short pause,* GEORGE TESMAN *enters from the hall. He looks tired and rather serious. He steals on tiptoe towards the middle doorway and is about to slip through the curtains.*

HEDDA *(at the stove, without looking up).*   Good morning.

TESMAN *(turns).*   Hedda! *(Approaching her.)* Good heavens—are you up so early? Eh?

HEDDA.   Yes, I am up very early this morning.

TESMAN.   And I never doubted you were still sound asleep! Fancy that, Hedda!

HEDDA.   Don't speak so loud. Mrs. Elvsted is resting in my room.

TESMAN.   Has Mrs. Elvsted been here all night?

HEDDA.   Yes, since no one came to fetch her.

TESMAN.   Ah, to be sure.

HEDDA *(closes the door of the stove and rises).*   Well, did you enjoy yourselves at Judge Brack's?

TESMAN.   Have you been anxious about me? Eh?

HEDDA.   No, I should never think of being anxious. But I asked if you had enjoyed yourself.

TESMAN.   Oh, yes,—for once in a way. Especially the beginning of the evening; for then Eilert read me part of his book. We arrived more than an hour too early—fancy that!

And Brack had all sorts of arrangements to make—so Eilert read to me.

HEDDA (*seating herself by the table on the right*).   Well? Tell me, then—

TESMAN (*sitting on a footstool near the stove*).   Oh Hedda, you can't conceive what a book that is going to be! I believe it is one of the most remarkable things that have ever been written. Fancy that!

HEDDA.   Yes, yes; I don't care about that——

TESMAN.   I must make a confession to you, Hedda. When he had finished reading—a horrid feeling came over me.

HEDDA.   A horrid feeling?

TESMAN.   I felt jealous of Eilert for having had it in him to write such a book. Only think, Hedda!

HEDDA.   Yes, yes, I am thinking!

TESMAN.   And then how pitiful to think that he— with all his gifts—should be irreclaimable, after all.

HEDDA.   I suppose you mean that he has more courage than the rest?

TESMAN.   No, not at all—I mean that he is incapable of taking his pleasures in moderation.

HEDDA.   And what came of it all—in the end?

TESMAN.   Well, to tell the truth, I think it might best be described as an orgie, Hedda.

HEDDA.   Had he vine-leaves in his hair?

TESMAN.   Vine-leaves? No, I saw nothing of the sort. But he made a long, rambling speech in honour of the woman who had inspired him in his work—that was the phrase he used.

HEDDA.   Did he name her?

TESMAN.   No, he didn't; but I can't help thinking he meant Mrs. Elvsted. You may be sure he did.

HEDDA.   Well—where did you part from him?

TESMAN.   On the way to town. We broke up—the last of us at any rate—all together; and Brack came with us to get a breath of fresh air. And then, you see, we agreed to take Eilert home; for he had had far more than was good for him.

HEDDA.   I daresay.

TESMAN.   But now comes the strange part of it, Hedda; or, I should rather say, the melancholy part of it. I declare I am almost ashamed—on Eilert's account—to tell you——

HEDDA.   Oh, go on——

TESMAN.   Well, as we were getting near town, you see, I happened to drop a little behind the others. Only for a minute or two—fancy that!

HEDDA.   Yes, yes, yes, but——?

TESMAN.   And then, as I hurried after them—what do you think I found by the wayside? Eh?

HEDDA.   Oh, how should I know!

TESMAN.   You mustn't speak of it to a soul, Hedda! Do you hear! Promise me, for Eilert's sake. (*Draws a parcel, wrapped in paper, from his coat pocket.*) Fancy, dear—I found this.

HEDDA.   Is not that the parcel he had with him yesterday?

TESMAN.   Yes, it is the whole of his precious, irreplaceable manuscript! And he had gone and lost it and knew nothing about it. Only fancy, Hedda! So deplorably——

HEDDA.   But why did you not give him back the parcel at once?

TESMAN.   I didn't dare to—in the state he was then in——

HEDDA. Did you tell any of the others that you had found it?

TESMAN. Oh, far from it! You can surely understand that, for Eilert's sake, I wouldn't do that.

HEDDA. So no one knows that Eilert Lövborg's manuscript is in your possession?

TESMAN. No. And no one must know it.

HEDDA. Then what did you say to him afterwards?

TESMAN. I didn't talk to him again at all; for when we got in among the streets, he and two or three of the others gave us the slip and disappeared. Fancy that!

HEDDA. Indeed! They must have taken him home then.

TESMAN. Yes, so it would appear. And Brack, too, left us.

HEDDA. And what have you been doing with yourself since?

TESMAN. Well, I and some of the others went home with one of the party, a jolly fellow, and took our morning coffee with him; or perhaps I should rather call it our night coffee—eh? But now, when I have rested a little, and given Eilert, poor fellow, time to have his sleep out, I must take this back to him.

HEDDA (holds out her hand for the packet). No—don't give it to him! Not in such a hurry, I mean. Let me read it first.

TESMAN. No, my dearest Hedda, I mustn't, I really mustn't.

HEDDA. You must not?

TESMAN. No—for you can imagine what a state of despair he will be in when he awakens and misses the manuscript. He has no copy of it, you must know! He told me so.

HEDDA. *(looking searchingly at him).*   Can such a thing not be reproduced? Written over again?

TESMAN.   No, I don't think that would be possible. For the inspiration, you see——

HEDDA.   Yes, yes—I suppose it depends on that. *(Lightly.)* But, by-the-bye—here is a letter for you.

TESMAN.   Fancy——!

HEDDA. *(handing it to him).*   It came early this morning.

TESMAN.   It's from Aunt Julia! What can it be? *(He lays the packet on the other footstool, opens the letter, runs his eye through it and jumps up.)* Oh, Hedda—she says that poor Aunt Rina is dying!

HEDDA.   Well, we were prepared for that.

TESMAN.   And that if I want to see her again, I must make haste. I'll run in to them at once.

HEDDA. *(suppressing a smile).*   Will you run?

TESMAN.   Oh, dearest Hedda—if you could only make up your mind to come with me! Just think!

HEDDA *(rises and says wearily, repelling the idea).*   No, no, don't ask me. I will not look upon sickness and death. I loathe all sorts of ugliness.

TESMAN.   Well, well, then——! *(Bustling around.)* My hat—— My overcoat——? Oh, in the hall—— I do hope I mayn't come too late, Hedda! Eh?

HEDDA.   Oh, if you run——

                                        {BERTA *appears at the hall door.*

BERTA.   Judge Brack is at the door and wishes to know if he may come in.

TESMAN.   At this time! No, I can't possibly see him.

HEDDA.   But I can. *(To* BERTA.*)* Ask Judge Brack to come in.

*{*BERTA *goes out.*

HEDDA *(quickly, whispering).* The parcel, Tesman!

{She snatches it up from the stool.

TESMAN. Yes, give it to me!

HEDDA. No, no, I will keep it till you come back.

{She goes to the writing-table and places it in the book-case. TESMAN *stands in a flurry of haste and cannot get his gloves on.*

*{*JUDGE BRACK *enters from the hall.*

HEDDA *(nodding to him).* You are an early bird, I must say.

BRACK. Yes, don't you think so? *(To* TESMAN.) Are you on the move, too?

TESMAN. Yes, I must rush off to my aunts'. Fancy— the invalid one is lying at death's door, poor creature.

BRACK. Dear me, is she indeed? Then on no account let me detain you. At such a critical moment——

TESMAN. Yes, I must really rush—— Good-bye! Good-bye!

{He hastens out by the hall door.

HEDDA *(approaching).* You seem to have made a par-ticularly lively night of it at your rooms, Judge Brack.

BRACK. I assure you I have not had my clothes off, Mrs. Hedda.

HEDDA. Not you, either?

BRACK. No, as you may see. But what has Tesman been telling you of the night's adventures?

HEDDA. Oh, some tiresome story. Only that they went and had coffee somewhere or other.

BRACK. I have heard about that coffee-party already. Eilert Lövborg was not with them, I fancy?

HEDDA. No, they had taken him home before that.

BRACK.   Tesman, too?

HEDDA.   No, but some of the others, he said.

BRACK *(smiling)*.   George Tesman is really an ingenuous creature, Mrs. Hedda.

HEDDA.   Yes, heaven knows he is. Then is there something behind all this?

BRACK.   Yes, perhaps there may be.

HEDDA.   Well, then, sit down, my dear Judge, and tell your story in comfort.

> {*She seats herself to the left of the table.* BRACK *sits near her, at the long side of the table.*

HEDDA.   Now then?

BRACK.   I had special reasons for keeping track of my guests—or rather of some of my guests—last night.

HEDDA.   Of Eilert Lövborg among the rest, perhaps?

BRACK.   Frankly, yes.

HEDDA.   Now you make me really curious——

BRACK.   Do you know where he and one or two of the others finished the night, Mrs. Hedda?

HEDDA.   If it is not quite unmentionable, tell me.

BRACK.   Oh, no, it's not at all unmentionable. Well, they put in an appearance at a particularly animated soirée.

HEDDA.   Of the lively kind?

BRACK.   Of the very liveliest——

HEDDA.   Tell me more of this, Judge Brack——

BRACK.   Lövborg, as well as the others, had been invited in advance. I knew all about it. But he had declined the invitation; for now, as you know, he has become a new man.

HEDDA.   Up at the Elvsteds', yes. But he went after all, then?

BRACK.   Well, you see, Mrs. Hedda—unhappily the spirit moved him at my rooms last evening——

HEDDA.   Yes, I hear he found inspiration.

BRACK.   Pretty violent inspiration. Well, I fancy that altered his purpose; for we men folk are, unfortunately, not always so firm in our principles as we ought to be.

HEDDA.   Oh, I am sure you are an exception, Judge Brack. But as to Lövborg——?

BRACK.   To make a long story short—he landed at last in Mademoiselle Diana's rooms.

HEDDA.   Mademoiselle Diana's?

BRACK.   It was Mademoiselle Diana that was giving the soirée, to a select circle of her admirers and her lady friends.

HEDDA.   Is she a red-haired woman?

BRACK.   Precisely.

HEDDA.   A sort of a—singer?

BRACK.   Oh, yes—in her leisure moments. And moreover a mighty huntress—of men—Mrs. Hedda. You have no doubt heard of her. Eilert Lövborg was one of her most enthusiastic protectors—in the days of his glory.

HEDDA.   And how did all this end?

BRACK.   Far from amicably, it appears. After a most tender meeting, they seem to have come to blows——

HEDDA.   Lövborg and she?

BRACK.   Yes. He accused her or her friends of having robbed him. He declared that his pocket-book had disappeared—and other things as well. In short, he seems to have made a furious disturbance.

HEDDA.   And what came of it all?

BRACK.   It came to a general scrimmage, in which the ladies as well as the gentlemen took part. Fortunately the police at last appeared on the scene.

HEDDA.   The police, too?

BRACK.   Yes. I fancy it will prove a costly frolic for Eilert Lövborg, crazy being that he is.

HEDDA.   How so?

BRACK.   He seems to have made a violent resistance—to have hit one of the constables on the head and torn the coat off his back. So they had to march him off to the police-station with the rest.

HEDDA.   How have you learnt all this?

BRACK.   From the police themselves.

HEDDA (*gazing straight before her*).   So that is what happened. Then he had no vine-leaves in his hair.

BRACK.   Vine-leaves, Mrs. Hedda?

HEDDA (*changing her tone*).   But tell me now, Judge—what is your real reason for tracking out Eilert Lövborg's movements so carefully?

BRACK.   In the first place, it could not be entirely indifferent to me if it should appear in the police-court that he came straight from my house.

HEDDA.   Will the matter come into court, then?

BRACK.   Of course. However, I should scarcely have troubled so much about that. But I thought that, as a friend of the family, it was my duty to supply you and Tesman with a full account of his nocturnal exploits.

HEDDA.   Why so, Judge Brack?

BRACK.   Why, because I have a shrewd suspicion that he intends to use you as a sort of blind.

HEDDA.   Oh, how can you think such a thing!

BRACK.   Good heavens, Mrs. Hedda—we have eyes in our head. Mark my words! This Mrs. Elvsted will be in no hurry to leave town again.

HEDDA.   Well, even if there should be anything between them, I suppose there are plenty of other places where they could meet.

BRACK.   Not a single home. Henceforth, as before every respectable house will be closed against Eilert Lövborg.

HEDDA.   And so ought mine to be, you mean?

BRACK.   Yes. I confess it would be more than painful to me if this personage were to be made free of your house. How superfluous, how intrusive, he would be, if he were to force his way into——

HEDDA.   ——into the triangle?

BRACK.   Precisely. It would simply mean that I should find myself homeless.

HEDDA *(looks at him with a smile)*.   So you want to be the one cock in the basket*——that is your aim.

BRACK *(nods slowly and lowers his voice)*.   Yes, that is my aim. And for that I will fight—with every weapon I can command.

HEDDA *(her smile vanishing)*.   I see you are a dangerous person—when it comes to the point.

BRACK.   Do you think so?

HEDDA.   I am beginning to think so. And I am exceedingly glad to think—that you have no sort of hold over me.

BRACK *(laughing equivocally)*.   Well, well, Mrs. Hedda—perhaps you are right there. If I had, who knows what I might be capable of?

HEDDA.   Come, come now, Judge Brack! That sounds almost like a threat.

BRACK *(rising)*.   Oh, not at all! The triangle, you know, ought, if possible, to be spontaneously constructed.

HEDDA.   There I agree with you.

BRACK.   Well, now I have said all I had to say; and I had better be getting back to town. Good-bye, Mrs. Hedda.

*   "Eneste hane i kurven"—a proverbial saying.

{He goes towards the glass door.

HEDDA *(rising).*   Are you going through the garden?

BRACK.   Yes, it's a short cut for me.

HEDDA.   And then it is a back way, too.

BRACK.   Quite so. I have no objection to back ways. They may be piquant enough at times.

HEDDA.   When there is ball practice going on, you mean?

BRACK *(in the doorway, laughing to her).*   Oh, people don't shoot their tame poultry, I fancy.

HEDDA *(also laughing).*   Oh, no, when there is only one cock in the basket——

> *{They exchange laughing nods of farewell. He goes. She closes the door behind him.*
>
> *{*HEDDA, *who has become quite serious, stands for a moment looking out. Presently she goes and peeps through the curtain over the middle doorway. Then she goes to the writing-table, takes* LÖVBORG'S *packet out of the bookcase and is on the point of looking through its contents.* BERTA *is heard speaking loudly in the hall.* HEDDA *turns and listens. Then she hastily locks up the packet in the drawer and lays the key on the ink-stand.*
>
> *{*EILERT LÖVBORG, *with his greatcoat on and his hat in his hand, tears open the hall door. He looks somewhat confused and irritated.*

LÖVBORG *(looking towards the hall).*   And I tell you I must and will come in! There!

> *{He closes the door, turns, sees* HEDDA, *at once regains his self-control and bows.*

HEDDA *(at the writing-table).*   Well, Mr. Lövborg, this is rather a late hour to call for Thea.

LÖVBORG.   You mean rather an early hour to call on you. Pray pardon me.

HEDDA.   How do you know that she is still here?

LÖVBORG.   They told me at her lodgings that she had been out all night.

HEDDA (*going to the oval table*).   Did you notice anything about the people of the house when they said that?

LÖVBORG (*looks inquiringly at her*).   Notice anything about them?

HEDDA.   I mean, did they seem to think it odd?

LÖVBORG (*suddenly understanding*).   Oh, yes, of course! I am dragging her down with me! However, I didn't notice anything.——I suppose Tesman is not up yet?

HEDDA.   No—I think not——

LÖVBORG.   When did he come home?

HEDDA.   Very late.

LÖVBORG.   Did he tell you anything?

HEDDA.   Yes, I gathered that you had had an exceedingly jolly evening at Judge Brack's.

LÖVBORG.   Nothing more?

HEDDA.   I don't think so. However, I was so dreadfully sleepy——

{MRS. ELVSTED *enters through the curtains of the middle doorway.*

MRS. ELVSTED (*going towards him*).   Ah, Lövborg! At last——!

LÖVBORG.   Yes, at last. And too late!

MRS. ELVSTED (*looks anxiously at him*).   What is too late?

LÖVBORG.   Everything is too late now. It is all over with me.

MRS. ELVSTED.   Oh, no, no—don't say that!

LÖVBORG.　　　You will say the same when you hear——

MRS. ELVSTED.　　　I won't hear anything!

HEDDA.　　　Perhaps you would prefer to talk to her alone! If so, I will leave you.

LÖVBORG.　　　No, stay—you, too. I beg you to stay.

MRS. ELVSTED.　　　Yes, but I won't hear anything, I tell you.

LÖVBORG.　　　It is not last night's adventures that I want to talk about.

MRS. ELVSTED.　　　What is it then——?

LÖVBORG.　　　I want to say that now our ways must part.

MRS. ELVSTED.　　　Part!

HEDDA (*involuntarily*).　　　I knew it!

LÖVBORG.　　　You can be of no more service to me, Thea.

MRS. ELVSTED.　　　How can you stand there and say that! No more service to you! Am I not to help you now, as before? Are we not to go on working together?

LÖVBORG.　　　Henceforward I shall do no work.

MRS. ELVSTED (*despairingly*).　　　Then what am I to do with my life?

LÖVBORG.　　　You must try to live your life as if you had never known me.

MRS. ELVSTED.　　　But you know I cannot do that!

LÖVBORG.　　　Try if you cannot, Thea. You must go home again——

MRS. ELVSTED (*in vehement protest*).　　　Never in this world! Where you are, there will I be also! I will not let myself be driven away like this! I will remain here! I will be with you when the book appears.

HEDDA (*half aloud, in suspense*).　　　Ah, yes—the book!

LÖVBORG (*looks at her*).   My book and Thea's; for that is what it is.

MRS. ELVSTED.   Yes, I feel that it is. And that is why I have a right to be with you when it appears! I will see with my own eyes how respect and honour pour in upon you afresh. And the happiness—the happiness—oh, I must share it with you!

LÖVBORG.   Thea—our book will never appear.

HEDDA.   Ah!

MRS. ELVSTED.   Never appear!

LÖVBORG.   Can never appear.

MRS. ELVSTED (*in agonised foreboding*).   Lövborg—what have you done with the manuscript?

HEDDA (*looks anxiously at him*).   Yes, the manuscript——?

MRS. ELVSTED.   Where is it?

LÖVBORG.   Oh, Thea—don't ask me about it!

MRS. ELVSTED.   Yes, yes, I will know. I demand to be told at once.

LÖVBORG.   The manuscript—— Well, then—I have torn the manuscript into a thousand pieces.

MRS. ELVSTED (*shrieks*).   Oh, no, no——!

HEDDA (*involuntarily*).   But that's not——

LÖVBORG (*looks at her*).   Not true, you think?

HEDDA (*collecting herself*).   Oh, well, of course—since you say so. But it sounded so improbable——

LÖVBORG.   It is true, all the same.

MRS. ELVSTED (*wringing her hands*).   Oh, God—oh, God, Hedda—torn his own work to pieces!

LÖVBORG.   I have torn my own life to pieces. So why should I not tear my life-work, too——?

MRS. ELVSTED.   And you did this last night?

LÖVBORG.   Yes, I tell you! Tore it into a thousand pieces and scattered them on the fiord—far out. There there is cool sea-water, at any rate—let them drift upon it—drift with the current and the wind. And then presently they will sink—deeper and deeper—as I shall, Thea.

MRS. ELVSTED.   Do you know, Lövborg, that what you have done with the book—I shall think of it to my dying day as though you had killed a little child.

LÖVBORG.   Yes, you are right. It is a sort of child-murder.

MRS. ELVSTED.   How could you, then——! Did not the child belong to me, too?

HEDDA (almost inaudibly).   Ah, the child——

MRS. ELVSTED (breathing heavily).   It is all over, then. Well, well, now I will go, Hedda.

HEDDA.   But you are not going away from town?

MRS. ELVSTED.   Oh, I don't know what I shall do. I see nothing but darkness before me.

{She goes out by the hall door.

HEDDA (stands waiting for a moment).   So you are not going to see her home, Mr. Lövborg?

LÖVBORG.   I? Through the streets? Would you have people see her walking with me?

HEDDA.   Of course I don't know what else may have happened last night. But is it so utterly irretrievable?

LÖVBORG.   It will not end with last night—I know that perfectly well. And the thing is that now I have no taste for that sort of life either. I won't begin it anew. She has broken my courage and my power of braving life out.

HEDDA (looking straight before her).   So that pretty lit-tle fool has had her fingers in a man's destiny. (Looks at him.)   But all the same, how could you treat her so heart-lessly.

LÖVBORG.   Oh, don't say that it was heartless!

HEDDA.   To go and destroy what has filled her whole soul for months and years! You do not call that heartless!

LÖVBORG.   To you I can tell the truth, Hedda.

HEDDA.   The truth?

LÖVBORG.   First promise me—give me your word—that what I now confide to you Thea shall never know.

HEDDA.   I give you my word.

LÖVBORG.   Good. Then let me tell you that what I said just now was untrue.

HEDDA.   About the manuscript?

LÖVBORG.   Yes. I have not torn it to pieces—nor thrown it into the fiord.

HEDDA.   No, n—— But—where is it then?

LÖVBORG.   I have destroyed it none the less—utterly destroyed it, Hedda!

HEDDA.   I don't understand.

LÖVBORG.   Thea said that what I had done seemed to her like a child-murder.

HEDDA.   Yes, so she said.

LÖVBORG.   But to kill this child—that is not the worst thing a father can do to it.

HEDDA.   Not the worst?

LÖVBORG.   No. I wanted to spare Thea from hearing the worst?

HEDDA.   Then what is the worst?

LÖVBORG.   Suppose now, Hedda, that a man—in the small hours of the morning—came home to his child's mother after a night of riot and debauchery, and said: "Listen—I have been here and there—in this place and in that. And I have taken our child with me—to this place and to that. And I have lost the child—utterly lost it. The devil knows into what hands it may have fallen—who may have had their clutches on it."

HEDDA.   Well—but when all is said and done, you know—this was only a book—

LÖVBORG.   Thea's pure soul was in that book.

HEDDA.   Yes, so I understand.

LÖVBORG.   And you can understand, too, that for her and me together no future is possible.

HEDDA.   What path do you mean to take, then?

LÖVBORG.   None. I will only try to make an end of it all—the sooner the better

HEDDA *(a step nearer him).*   Eilert Lövborg—listen to me.——Will you not try to—to do it beautifully?

LÖVBORG.   Beautifully? *(Smiling.)* With vine-leaves in my hair, as you used to dream in the old days——?

HEDDA.   No, no. I have lost my faith in the vine-leaves. But beautifully nevertheless! For once in a way!—Good-bye! You must go now—and do not come here any more.

LÖVBORG.   Good-bye, Mrs. Tesman. And give George Tesman my love.

{He is on the point of going.

HEDDA.   No, wait! I must give you a memento to take with you.

{She goes to the writing-table and opens the drawer and the pistol-case; then returns to LÖVBORG *with one of the pistols.*

LÖVBORG *(looks at her).*   This? Is this the memento?

HEDDA *(nodding slowly).*   Do you recognise it? It was aimed at you once.

LÖVBORG.   You should have used it then.

HEDDA.   Take it—and do you use it now.

LÖVBORG *(puts the pistol in his breast-pocket).*   Thanks!

HEDDA.   And beautifully, Eilert Lövborg. Promise me that!

LÖVBORG.   Good-bye, Hedda Gabler.

{He goes out by the hall door.

*{*HEDDA *listens for a moment at the door. Then she goes up to the writing-table, takes out the packet of manuscript, peeps under the cover, draws a few of the sheets half out and looks at them. Next she goes over and seats herself in the arm-chair beside the stove, with the packet in her lap. Presently she opens the stove door and then the packet.*

HEDDA (*throws one of the quires into the fire and whispers to herself*).   Now I am burning your child, Thea!——Burning it, curly-locks! (*Throwing one or two more quires into the stove.*) Your child and Eilert Lövborg's. (*Throws the rest in.*) I am burning——I am burning your child.

Act IV

The same rooms at the TESMANS'. *It is evening. The drawing-room is in darkness. The back room is lighted by the hanging lamp over the table. The curtains over the glass door are drawn close.*

HEDDA, *dressed in black, walks to and fro in the dark room. Then she goes into the back room and disappears for a moment to the left. She is heard to strike a few chords on the piano. Presently she comes in sight again and returns to the drawing-room.*

BERTA *enters from the right, through the inner room, with a lighted lamp, which she places on the table in front of the corner settee in the drawing-room. Her eyes are red with weeping, and she has black ribbons in her cap. She goes quietly and circumspectly out to the right.*

HEDDA *goes up to the glass door, lifts the curtain a little aside and looks out into the darkness.*

Shortly afterwards, MISS TESMAN, *in mourning, with a bonnet and veil on, comes in from the hall.* HEDDA *goes towards her and holds out her hand.*

MISS TESMAN. Yes, Hedda, here I am, in mourning and forlorn; for now my poor sister has at last found peace.

HEDDA. I have heard the news already, as you see. Tesman sent me a card.

MISS TESMAN. Yes, he promised me he would. But nevertheless I thought that to Hedda—here in the house of life—I ought myself to bring the tidings of death.

HEDDA.   That was very kind of you.

MISS TESMAN.   Ah, Rina ought not to have left us just now. This is not the time for Hedda's house to be a house of mourning.

HEDDA (*changing the subject*).   She died quite peacefully, did she not, Miss Tesman?

MISS TESMAN.   Oh, her end was so calm, so beautiful. And then she had the unspeakable happiness of seeing George once more—and bidding him good-bye.—Has he come home yet?

HEDDA.   No. He wrote that he might be detained. But won't you sit down?

MISS TESMAN.   No thank you, my dear, dear Hedda. I should like to, but I have so much to do. I must prepare my dear one for her rest as well as I can. She shall go to her grave looking her best.

HEDDA.   Can I not help you in any way?

MISS TESMAN.   Oh, you must not think of it! Hedda Tesman must have no hand in such mournful work. Nor let her thoughts dwell on it either—not at this time.

HEDDA.   One is not always mistress of one's thoughts——

MISS TESMAN (*continuing*).   Ah, yes, it is the way of the world. At home we shall be sewing a shroud; and here there will soon be sewing, too, I suppose—but of another sort, thank God!

{GEORGE TESMAN *enters by the hall door.*

HEDDA.   Ah, you have come at last!

TESMAN.   You here, Aunt Julia? With Hedda? Fancy that!

MISS TESMAN.   I was just going, my dear boy. Well, have you done all you promised?

TESMAN.   No; I'm really afraid I have forgotten half of it. I must come to you again to-morrow. To-day my brain is all in a whirl. I can't keep my thoughts together.

MISS TESMAN.   Why, my dear George, you mustn't take it in this way.

TESMAN.   Mustn't——? How do you mean?

MISS TESMAN.   Even in your sorrow you must rejoice, as I do—rejoice that she is at rest.

TESMAN.   Oh, yes, yes—you are thinking of Aunt Rina.

HEDDA.   You will feel lonely now, Miss Tesman.

MISS TESMAN.   Just at first, yes. But that will not last very long, I hope. I daresay I shall soon find an occupant for poor Rina's little room.

TESMAN.   Indeed? Who do you think will take it? Eh?

MISS TESMAN.   Oh, there's always some poor invalid or other in want of nursing, unfortunately.

HEDDA.   Would you really take such a burden upon you again?

MISS TESMAN.   A burden! Heaven forgive you, child—it has been no burden to me.

HEDDA.   But suppose you had a total stranger on your hands——

MISS TESMAN.   Oh, one soon makes friends with sick folk; and it's such an absolute necessity for me to have some one to live for. Well, heaven be praised, there may soon be something in this house, too, to keep an old aunt busy.

HEDDA.   Oh, don't trouble about anything here.

TESMAN.   Yes, just fancy what a nice time we three might have together, if——?

HEDDA.   If——?

TESMAN (*uneasily*).   Oh, nothing. It will all come right. Let us hope so—eh?

MISS TESMAN.   Well, well, I daresay you two want to talk to each other. (*Smiling.*) And perhaps Hedda may have something to tell you, too, George. Good-bye! I must go home to Rina. (*Turning at the door.*) How strange it is to think that now Rina is with me and with my poor brother as well!

TESMAN.   Yes, fancy that, Aunt Julia! Eh?

[MISS TESMAN *goes out by the hall door.*

HEDDA (*follows* TESMAN *coldly and searchingly with her eyes*).   I almost believe your Aunt Rina's death affects you more than it does your Aunt Julia.

TESMAN.   Oh, it's not that alone. It's Eilert I am so terribly uneasy about.

HEDDA (*quickly*).   Is there anything new about him?

TESMAN.   I looked in at his rooms this afternoon, intending to tell him the manuscript was in safe keeping.

HEDDA.   Well, did you not find him?

TESMAN.   No. He wasn't at home. But afterwards I met Mrs. Elvsted, and she told me that he had been here early this morning.

HEDDA.   Yes, directly after you had gone.

TESMAN.   And he said that he had torn his manuscript to pieces—eh?

HEDDA.   Yes, so he declared.

TESMAN.   Why, good heavens, he must have been completely out of his mind! And I suppose you thought it best not to give it back to him, Hedda?

HEDDA.   No, he did not get it.

TESMAN.   But of course you told him that we had it?

HEDDA.   No. *(Quickly.)*   Did you tell Mrs. Elvsted?

TESMAN.   No; I thought I had better not. But you ought to have told him. Fancy, if, in desperation, he should go and do himself some injury! Let me have the manuscript, Hedda! I will take it to him at once. Where is it?

HEDDA *(cold and immovable, leaning on the arm-chair).*   I have not got it.

TESMAN.   Have not got it? What in the world do you mean?

HEDDA.   I have burnt it—every line of it.

TESMAN *(with a violent movement of terror).*   Burnt! Burnt Eilert's manuscript!

HEDDA.   Don't scream so. The servant might hear you.

TESMAN.   Burnt! Why, good God——! No, no, no! It's impossible!

HEDDA.   It is so, nevertheless.

TESMAN.   Do you know what you have done, Hedda? It's unlawful appropriation of lost property. Fancy that! Just ask Judge Brack, and he'll tell you what it is.

HEDDA.   I advise you not to speak of it—either to Judge Brack, or to any one else.

TESMAN.   But how could you do anything so unheard-of? What put it into your head? What possessed you? Answer me that—eh?

HEDDA *(suppressing an almost imperceptible smile).*   I did it for your sake, George.

TESMAN.   For my sake!

HEDDA.   This morning, when you told me about what he had read to you——

TESMAN.   Yes, yes—what then?

HEDDA.   You acknowledged that you envied him his work.

TESMAN.   Oh, of course I didn't mean that literally.

HEDDA.   No matter—I could not bear the idea that any one should throw you into the shade.

TESMAN *(in an outburst of mingled doubt and joy).*   Hedda! Oh, is this true? But—but—I never knew you to show your love like that before. Fancy that!

HEDDA.   Well, I may as well tell you that—just at this time—— *(Impatiently, breaking off.)* No, no; you can ask Aunt Julia. She will tell you, fast enough.

TESMAN.   Oh, I almost think I understand you, Hedda! *(Clasps his hands together.)* Great heavens! do you really mean it! Eh?

HEDDA.   Don't shout so. The servant might hear.

TESMAN *(laughing in irrepressible glee).*   The servant! Why, how absurd you are, Hedda. It's only my old Berta! Why, I'll tell Berta myself.

HEDDA *(clenching her hands together in desperation).*   Oh, it is killing me,—it is killing me, all this!

TESMAN.   What is, Hedda? Eh?

HEDDA *(coldly, controlling herself).*   All this—absurdity—George.

TESMAN.   Absurdity! Do you see anything absurd in my being overjoyed at the news! But after all—perhaps I had better not say anything to Berta.

HEDDA.   Oh—why not that, too?

TESMAN.   No, no, not yet! But I must certainly tell Aunt Julia. And then that you have begun to call me George, too! Fancy that! Oh, Aunt Julia will be so happy—so happy!

HEDDA.   When she hears that I have burnt Eilert Lövborg's manuscript—for your sake?

TESMAN.　　No, by-the-bye—that affair of the manuscript—of course nobody must know about that. But that you love me so much,* Hedda—Aunt Julia must really share my joy in that! I wonder, now, whether this sort of thing is usual in young wives? Eh?

HEDDA.　　I think you had better ask Aunt Julia that question too.

TESMAN.　　I will indeed, some time or other. (*Looks uneasy and downcast again.*) And yet the manuscript—the manuscript! Good God! it is terrible to think what will become of poor Eilert now.

　　　　　{MRS. ELVSTED, *dressed as in the first Act, with hat and cloak, enters by the hall door.*

MRS. ELVSTED (*greets them hurriedly and says in evident agitation*).　　Oh, dear Hedda, forgive my coming again.

HEDDA.　　What is the matter with you, Thea?

TESMAN.　　Something about Eilert Lövborg again—eh?

MRS. ELVSTED.　　Yes! I am dreadfully afraid some misfortune has happened to him.

HEDDA (*seizes her arm*).　　Ah.—do you think so?

TESMAN.　　Why, good Lord—what makes you think that, Mrs. Elvsted?

MRS. ELVSTED.　　I heard them talking of him at my boarding-house—just as I came in. Oh, the most incredible rumours are afloat about him to-day.

TESMAN.　　Yes, fancy, so I heard, too! And I can bear witness that he went straight home to bed last night. Fancy that!

HEDDA.　　Well, what did they say at the boarding-house?

*　　Literally, "That you burn for me."

MRS. ELVSTED. Oh, I couldn't make out anything clearly. Either they knew nothing definite, or else—— They stopped talking when they saw me; and I did not dare to ask.

TESMAN (*moving about uneasily*). We must hope—we must hope that you misunderstood them, Mrs. Elvsted.

MRS. ELVSTED. No, no; I am sure it was of him they were talking. And I heard something about the hospital or——

TESMAN. The hospital?

HEDDA. No—surely that cannot be!

MRS. ELVSTED. Oh, I was in such mortal terror! I went to his lodgings and asked for him there.

HEDDA. You could make up your mind to that, Thea!

MRS. ELVSTED. What else could I do? I really could bear the suspense no longer.

TESMAN. But you didn't find him either—eh?

MRS. ELVSTED. No. And the people knew nothing about him. He hadn't been home since yesterday afternoon, they said.

TESMAN. Yesterday! Fancy, how could they say that?

MRS. ELVSTED. Oh, I am sure something terrible must have happened to him.

TESMAN. Hedda dear—how would it be if I were to go and make inquiries——?

HEDDA. No, no—don't you mix yourself up in this affair.

{JUDGE BRACK, *with his hat in his hand, enters by the hall door, which* BERTA *opens and closes behind him. He looks grave and bows in silence.*

TESMAN. Oh, is that you, my dear Judge? Eh?

BRACK.   Yes. It was imperative I should see you this evening.

TESMAN.   I can see you have heard the news about Aunt Rina?

BRACK.   Yes, that among other things.

TESMAN.   Isn't it sad——eh?

BRACK.   Well, my dear Tesman, that depends on how you look at it.

TESMAN (*looks doubtfully at him*).   Has anything else happened?

BRACK.   Yes.

HEDDA (*in suspense*).   Anything sad, Judge Brack?

BRACK.   That, too, depends on how you look at it, Mrs. Tesman.

MRS. ELVSTED (*unable to restrain her anxiety*).   Oh! it is something about Eilert Lövborg!

BRACK (*with a glance at her*).   What makes you think that, Madam? Perhaps you have already heard something——?

MRS. ELVSTED (*in confusion*).   No, nothing at all, but——

TESMAN.   Oh, for heaven's sake, tell us!

BRACK (*shrugging his shoulders*).   Well, I regret to say Eilert Lövborg has been taken to the hospital. He is lying at the point of death.

MRS. ELVSTED (*shrieks*).   Oh, God! Oh, God——!

TESMAN.   To the hospital! And at the point of death.

HEDDA (*involuntarily*).   So soon then——

MRS. ELVSTED (*wailing*).   And we parted in anger, Hedda!

HEDDA (*whispers*).   Thea——Thea——be careful!

MRS. ELVSTED (*not heeding her*).   I must go to him! I must see him alive!

BRACK. It is useless, Madam. No one will be admitted.

MRS. ELVSTED. Oh, at least tell me what has happened to him? What is it?

TESMAN. You don't mean to say that he has himself—— Eh?

HEDDA. Yes, I am sure he has.

TESMAN. Hedda, how can you——?

BRACK (*keeping his eyes fixed upon her*). Unfortunately, you have guessed quite correctly, Mrs. Tesman.

MRS. ELVSTED. Oh, how horrible!

TESMAN. Himself, then! Fancy that!

HEDDA. Shot himself!

BRACK. Rightly guessed again, Mrs. Tesman.

MRS. ELVSTED (*with an effort at self-control*). When did it happen, Mr. Brack?

BRACK. This afternoon—between three and four.

TESMAN. But, good Lord, where did he do it? Eh?

BRACK (*with some hesitation*). Where? Well—I suppose at his lodgings.

MRS. ELVSTED. No, that cannot be; for I was there between six and seven.

BRACK. Well, then, somewhere else. I don't know exactly. I only know that he was found——. He had shot himself—in the breast.

MRS. ELVSTED. Oh, how terrible! That he should die like that!

HEDDA (*to Brack*). Was it in the breast?

BRACK. Yes—as I told you.

HEDDA. Not in the temple?

BRACK. In the breast, Mrs. Tesman.

HEDDA. Well, well—the breast is a good place, too.

BRACK. How do you mean, Mrs. Tesman?

HEDDA (*evasively*).   Oh, nothing—nothing.

TESMAN.   And the wound is dangerous, you say—eh?

BRACK.   Absolutely mortal. The end has probably come by this time.

MRS. ELVSTED.   Yes, yes, I feel it. The end! The end! Oh, Hedda——!

TESMAN.   But tell me, how have you learnt all this?

BRACK (*curtly*).   Through one of the police. A man I had some business with.

HEDDA (*in a clear voice*).   At last a deed worth doing!

TESMAN (*terrified*).   Good heavens, Hedda! what are you saying?

HEDDA.   I say there is beauty in this.

BRACK.   H'm, Mrs. Tesman——

TESMAN.   Beauty! Fancy that!

MRS. ELVSTED.   Oh, Hedda, how can you talk of beauty in such an act!

HEDDA.   Eilert Lövborg has himself made up his account with life. He has had the courage to do—the one right thing.

MRS. ELVSTED.   No, you must never think that was how it happened! It must have been in delirium that he did it.

TESMAN.   In despair!

HEDDA.   That he did not. I am certain of that.

MRS. ELVSTED.   Yes, yes! In delirium! Just as when he tore up our manuscript.

BRACK (*starting*).   The manuscript? Has he torn that up?

MRS. ELVSTED.   Yes, last night.

TESMAN (*whispers softly*).   Oh, Hedda, we shall never get over this.

BRACK.   H'm, very extraordinary.

TESMAN (*moving about the room*).   To think of Eilert going out of the world in this way! And not leaving behind him the book that would have immortalised his name——

MRS. ELVSTED.   Oh, if only it could be put together again!

TESMAN.   Yes, if it only could! I don't know what I would not give——

MRS. ELVSTED.   Perhaps it can, Mr. Tesman.

TESMAN.   What do you mean?

MRS. ELVSTED (*searches in the pocket of her dress*).   Look here. I have kept all the loose notes he used to dictate from.

HEDDA (*a step forward*).   Ah——!

TESMAN.   You have kept them, Mrs. Elvsted! Eh?

MRS. ELVSTED.   Yes, I have them here. I put them in my pocket when I left home. Here they still are——

TESMAN.   Oh, do let me see them!

MRS. ELVSTED (*hands him a bundle of papers*).   But they are in such disorder—all mixed up.

TESMAN.   Fancy, if we could make something out of them, after all! Perhaps if we two put our heads together——

MRS. ELVSTED.   Oh, yes, at least let us try——

TESMAN.   We will manage it! We must! I will dedicate my life to this task.

HEDDA.   You, George? Your life?

TESMAN.   Yes, or rather all the time I can spare. My own collections must wait in the meantime. Hedda—you understand, eh? I owe this to Eilert's memory.

HEDDA.   Perhaps.

TESMAN.   And so, my dear Mrs. Elvsted, we will give our whole minds to it. There is no use in brooding over what can't be undone—eh? We must try to control our grief as much as possible, and——

MRS. ELVSTED.   Yes, yes, Mr. Tesman, I will do the best I can.

TESMAN.   Well, then, come here. I can't rest until we have looked through the notes. Where shall we sit? Here? No, in there, in the back room. Excuse me, my dear Judge. Come with me, Mrs. Elvsted.

MRS. ELVSTED.   Oh, if only it were possible!

> {TESMAN *and* MRS. ELVSTED *go into the back room.*
> *She takes off her hat and cloak. They both sit at the*
> *table under the hanging lamp and are soon deep in an*
> *eager examination of the papers.* HEDDA *crosses to the*
> *stove and sits in the arm-chair. Presently* BRACK *goes*
> *up to her.*

HEDDA (*in a low voice*).   Oh, what a sense of freedom it gives one, this act of Eilert Lövborg's.

BRACK.   Freedom, Mrs. Hedda? Well, of course, it is a release for him——

HEDDA.   I mean for me. It gives me a sense of freedom to know that a deed of deliberate courage is still possible in this world,—a deed of spontaneous beauty.

BRACK (*smiling*).   H'm—my dear Mrs. Hedda——

HEDDA.   Oh, I know what you are going to say. For you are a kind of specialist, too, like—you know!

BRACK (*looking hard at her*).   Eilert Lövborg was more to you than perhaps you are willing to admit to yourself. Am I wrong?

HEDDA.   I don't answer such questions. I only know that Eilert Lövborg has had the courage to live his life after his own fashion. And then—the last great act, with its beauty! Ah! that he should have the will and the strength to turn away from the banquet of life—so early.

BRACK.   I am sorry, Mrs. Hedda,—but I fear I must dispel an amiable illusion.

HEDDA.   Illusion?

BRACK.   Which could not have lasted long in any case.

HEDDA.   What do you mean?

BRACK.   Eilert Lövborg did not shoot himself—voluntarily.

HEDDA.   Not voluntarily?

BRACK.   No. The thing did not happen exactly as I told it.

HEDDA (*in suspense*).   Have you concealed something? What is it?

BRACK.   For poor Mrs. Elvsted's sake I idealised the facts a little.

HEDDA.   What are the facts?

BRACK.   First, that he is already dead.

HEDDA.   At the hospital?

BRACK.   Yes—without regaining consciousness.

HEDDA.   What more have you concealed?

BRACK.   This—the event did not happen at his lodgings.

HEDDA.   Oh, that can make no difference.

BRACK.   Perhaps it may. For I must tell you—Eilert Lövborg was found shot in—in Mademoiselle Diana's boudoir.

HEDDA (*makes a motion as if to rise, but sinks back again*).   That is impossible, Judge Brack! He cannot have been there again to-day.

BRACK.   He was there this afternoon. He went there, he said, to demand the return of something which they had taken from him. Talked wildly about a lost child——

HEDDA.   Ah—so that was why——

BRACK.   I thought probably he meant his manuscript! but now I hear he destroyed that himself. So I suppose it must have been his pocket-book.

HEDDA.   Yes, no doubt. And there—there he was found?

BRACK.   Yes, there. With a pistol in his breast-pocket, discharged. The ball had lodged in a vital part.

HEDDA.   In the breast—yes.

BRACK.   No—in the bowels.

HEDDA (*looks up at him with an expression of loathing*).   That, too! Oh, what curse is it that makes everything I touch turn ludicrous and mean?

BRACK.   There is one point more, Mrs. Hedda—another disagreeable feature in the affair.

HEDDA.   And what is that?

BRACK.   The pistol he carried——

HEDDA (*breathless*).   Well? What of it?

BRACK.   He must have stolen it.

HEDDA (*leaps up*).   Stolen it! That is not true! He did not steal it!

BRACK.   No other explanation is possible. He must have stolen it—— Hush!

     {TESMAN *and* MRS. ELVSTED *have risen from the table in the back room and come into the drawing room.*

TESMAN (*with the papers in both his hands*).   Hedda dear, it is almost impossible to see under that lamp. Think of that!

HEDDA.   Yes, I am thinking.

TESMAN.   Would you mind our sitting at your writing-table—eh?

HEDDA.   If you like. (*Quickly.*) No, wait! Let me clear it first!

TESMAN.   Oh, you needn't trouble, Hedda. There is plenty of room.

HEDDA.   No, no, let me clear it, I say! I will take these things in and put them on the piano. There!

{She has drawn out an object, covered with sheet music, from under the bookcase, places several other pieces of music upon it and carries the whole into the inner room, to the left. TESMAN *lays the scraps of paper on the writing-table and moves the lamp there from the corner table. He and* MRS. ELVSTED *sit down and proceed with their work.* HEDDA *returns.*

HEDDA *(behind* MRS. ELVSTED'S *chair, gently ruffling her hair).*   Well, my sweet Thea,—how goes it with Eilert Lövborg's monument?

MRS. ELVSTED *(looks dispiritedly up at her).*   Oh, it will be terribly hard to put in order.

TESMAN.   We must manage it. I am determined. And arranging other people's papers is just the work for me.

*{*HEDDA *goes over to the stove and seats herself on one of the footstools.* BRACK *stands over her, leaning on the armchair.*

HEDDA *(whispers).*   What did you say about the pistol?

BRACK *(softly).*   That he must have stolen it.

HEDDA.   Why stolen it?

BRACK.   Because every other explanation ought to be impossible, Mrs. Hedda.

HEDDA.   Indeed?

BRACK *(glances at her).*   Of course Eilert Lövborg was here this morning. Was he not?

HEDDA.   Yes.

BRACK.   Were you alone with him?

HEDDA.   Part of the time.

BRACK.   Did you not leave the room whilst he was here?

HEDDA.   No.

BRACK.   Try to recollect. Were you not out of the room a moment?

HEDDA.   Yes, perhaps just a moment—out in the hall.

BRACK.   And where was your pistol-case during that time?

HEDDA.   I had it locked up in——

BRACK.   Well, Mrs. Hedda?

HEDDA.   The case stood there on the writing-table.

BRACK.   Have you looked since, to see whether both the pistols are there?

HEDDA.   No.

BRACK.   Well, you need not. I saw the pistol found in Lövborg's pocket, and I knew it at once as the one I had seen yesterday—and before, too.

HEDDA.   Have you it with you?

BRACK.   No; the police have it.

HEDDA.   What will the police do with it?

BRACK.   Search till they find the owner.

HEDDA.   Do you think they will succeed?

BRACK (*bends over her and whispers*).   No, Hedda Gabler—not so long as I say nothing.

HEDDA (*looks frightened at him*).   And if you do not say nothing,—what then?

BRACK (*shrugs his shoulders*).   There is always the possibility that the pistol was stolen.

HEDDA (*firmly*).   Death rather than that.

BRACK (*smiling*).   People say such things—but they don't do them.

HEDDA (*without replying*).   And supposing the pistol was not stolen, and the owner is discovered? What then?

BRACK.   Well, Hedda—then comes the scandal.

HEDDA.   The scandal!

BRACK.   Yes, the scandal—of which you are mortally afraid. You will, of course, be brought before the court—both you and Mademoiselle Diana. She will have to explain how the thing happened—whether it was an accidental shot or murder. Did the pistol go off as he was trying to take it out of his pocket, to threaten her with? Or did she tear the pistol out of his hand, shoot him and push it back into his pocket? That would be quite like her; for she is an able-bodied young person, this same Mademoiselle Diana.

HEDDA.   But *I* have nothing to do with all this repulsive business.

BRACK.   No. But you will have to answer the question: Why did you give Eilert Lövborg the pistol? And what conclusions will people draw from the fact that you did give it to him?

HEDDA (*lets her head sink*).   That is true. I did not think of that.

BRACK.   Well, fortunately, there is no danger, so long as I say nothing.

HEDDA (*looks up at him*).   So I am in your power, Judge Brack. You have me at your beck and call, from this time forward.

BRACK (*whispers softly*).   Dearest Hedda—believe me—I shall not abuse my advantage.

HEDDA.   I am in your power none the less. Subject to your will and your demands. A slave, a slave then! (*Rises impetuously.*) No, I cannot endure the thought of that! Never!

BRACK (*looks half-mockingly at her*).   People generally get used to the inevitable.

HEDDA (*returns his look*).   Yes, perhaps. (*She crosses to the writing-table. Suppressing an involuntary smile, she imitates* TESMAN'S *intonations.*) Well? Are you getting on, George? Eh?

TESMAN.   Heaven knows, dear. In any case it will be the work of months.

HEDDA (*as before*).   Fancy that! (*Passes her hands softly through* MRS. ELVSTED'S *hair.*) Doesn't it seem strange to you, Thea? Here are you sitting with Tesman—just as you used to sit with Eilert Lövborg?

MRS. ELVSTED.   Ah, if I could only inspire your husband in the same way.

HEDDA.   Oh, that will come, too—in time.

TESMAN.   Yes, do you know, Hedda—I really think I begin to feel something of the sort. But won't you go and sit with Brack again?

HEDDA.   Is there nothing I can do to help you two?

TESMAN.   No, nothing in the world. (*Turning his head.*) I trust to you to keep Hedda company, my dear Brack.

BRACK (*with a glance at* HEDDA).   With the very greatest of pleasure.

HEDDA.   Thanks. But I am tired this evening. I will go in and lie down a little on the sofa.

TESMAN.   Yes, do dear—eh?

> (HEDDA *goes into the back room and draws the curtains. A short pause. Suddenly she is heard playing a wild dance on the piano.*

MRS. ELVSTED (*starts from her chair*).   Oh—what is that?

TESMAN (*runs to the doorway*).   Why, my dearest Hedda—don't play dance music to-night! Just think of Aunt Rina! And of Eilert, too!

HEDDA (*puts her head out between the curtains*).   And of

Aunt Julia. And of all the rest of them.——After this, I will be quiet.

{*Closes the curtains again.*

TESMAN (*at the writing-table*).   It's not good for her to see us at this distressing work. I'll tell you what, Mrs. Elvsted,——you shall take the empty room at Aunt Julia's, and then I will come over in the evenings, and we can sit and work there—eh?

HEDDA (*in the inner room*).   I hear what you are saying, Tesman. But how am *I* to get through the evenings out here?

TESMAN (*turning over the papers*).   Oh, I daresay Judge Brack will be so kind as to look in now and then, even though I am out.

BRACK (*in the armchair, calls out gaily*).   Every blessed evening, with all the pleasure in life, Mrs. Tesman! We shall get on capitally together, we two!

HEDDA (*speaking loud and clear*).   Yes, don't you flatter yourself we will, Judge Brack? Now that you are the one cock in the basket——

{*A shot is heard within.* TESMAN, MRS. ELVSTED *and* BRACK *leap to their feet.*

TESMAN.   Oh, now she is playing with those pistols again.

{*He throws back the curtains and runs in, followed by* MRS. ELVSTED. HEDDA *lies stretched on the sofa, lifeless. Confusion and cries.* BERTA *enters in alarm from the right.*

TESMAN (*shrieks to* BRACK).   Shot herself! Shot herself in the temple! Fancy that!

BRACK (*half-fainting in the armchair*).   Good God!—people don't do such things.

The Master
Builder

~

(1892)

Characters

HALVARD SOLNESS, *Master Builder.*

ALINE SOLNESS, *his wife.*

DOCTOR HERDAL, *physician.*

KNUT BROVIK, *formerly an architect, now in*
   SOLNESS'S *employment.*

RAGNER BROVIK, *his son, draughtsman.*

KAIA FOSLI, *his niece, book-keeper.*

MISS HILDA WANGEL.

Some Ladies.

A Crowd in the street.

The action passes in and about SOLNESS'S *house.*

Act I

A plainly furnished work-room in the house of HALVARD SOLNESS. *Folding doors on the left lead out to the hall. On the right is the door leading to the inner rooms of the house. At the back is an open door into the draughtsmen's office. In front, on the left, a desk with books, papers and writing materials. Further back than the folding-door, a stove. In the right-hand corner, a sofa, a table and one or two chairs. On the table a water-bottle and glass. A smaller table, with a rocking-chair and arm-chair, in front on the right. Lighted lamps, with shades, on the table in the draughtsmen's office, on the table in the corner and on the desk.*

In the draughtsmen's office sit KNUT BROVIK *and his son* RAGNAR, *occupied with plans and calculations. At the desk in the outer office stands* KAIA FOSLI, *writing in the ledger.* KNUT BROVIK *is a spare old man with white hair and beard. He wears a rather threadbare but well-brushed black coat, spectacles and a somewhat discoloured white neckcloth.* RAGNAR BROVIK *is a well-dressed, light-haired man in his thirties, with a slight stoop.* KAIA FOSLI *is a slightly built girl, a little over twenty, carefully dressed and delicate-looking. She has a green shade over her eyes. ——All three go on working for some time in silence.*

KNUT BROVIK (*rises suddenly, as if in distress, from the table; breathes heavily and laboriously as he comes forward into the doorway*).   No, I can't bear it much longer!

KAIA (*going up to him*).   You are feeling very ill this evening, are you not, uncle?

BROVIK. Oh, I seem to get worse every day.

RAGNAR (*has risen and advances*).   You ought to go home, father. Try to get a little sleep——

BROVIK (*impatiently*).   Go to bed, I suppose? Would you have me stifled outright?

KAIA.   Then take a little walk.

RAGNAR.   Yes, do. I will come with you.

BROVIK (*with warmth*).   I will not go till he comes! I am determined to have it out this evening with——(*in a tone of suppressed bitterness*)—with him—with the chief.

KAIA (*anxiously*).   Oh no, uncle—do wait awhile before doing that.

RAGNAR. Yes, better wait, father!

BROVIK (*draws his breath laboriously*).   Ha—ha——! I haven't much time for waiting.

KAIA (*listening*).   Hush! I hear him on the stairs.

> {*All three go back to their work. A short silence.*
> {*HALVARD SOLNESS comes in through the hall door. He is a man no longer young, but healthy and vigorous, with close-cut curly hair, dark moustache and dark thick eyebrows. He wears a greyish-green buttoned jacket with an upstanding collar and broad lapels. On his head he wears a soft grey felt hat, and he has one or two light portfolios under his arm.*

SOLNESS (*near the door, points towards the draughtsmen's office, and asks in a whisper:*)   Are they gone?

KAIA (*softly, shaking her head*).   No.

> {*She takes the shade off her eyes. SOLNESS crosses the room, throws his hat on a chair, places the portfolios on the table by the sofa and approaches the desk again.*

KAIA *goes on writing without intermission, but seems
nervous and uneasy.*

SOLNESS *(aloud).*   What is that you are entering,
Miss Fosli?

KAIA *(starts).*   Oh, it is only something that——

SOLNESS.   Let me look at it, Miss Fosli. *(Bends over
her, pretends to be looking into the ledger, and whispers:)* Kaia!

KAIA *(softly, still writing).*   Well?

SOLNESS.   Why do you always take that shade off
when I come?

KAIA *(as before).*   I look so ugly with it on.

SOLNESS *(smiling).*   Then you don't like to look ugly,
Kaia?

KAIA *(half glancing up at him).*   Not for all the world.
Not in your eyes.

SOLNESS *(stroking her hair gently).*   Poor, poor little
Kaia——

KAIA *(bending her head).*   Hush—they can hear you.

{SOLNESS *strolls across the room to the right, turns
and pauses at the door of the draughtsmen's office.*

SOLNESS.   Has any one been here for me?

RAGNAR *(rising).*   Yes, the young couple who want
a villa built, out at Lövstrand.

SOLNESS *(growling).*   Oh, those two! They must wait.
I am not quite clear about the plans yet.

RAGNAR *(advancing, with some hesitation).*   They were
very anxious to have the drawings at once.

SOLNESS *(as before).*   Yes, of course—so they all are.

BROVIK *(looks up).*   They say they are longing so to
get into a house of their own.

SOLNESS.   Yes, yes—we know all that! And so they
are content to take whatever is offered them. They get a—
a roof over their heads—an address—but nothing to call a

home. No thank you! In that case, let them apply to somebody else. Tell them that, the next time they call.

BROVIK (*pushes his glasses up on to his forehead and looks in astonishment at him.*)   To somebody else? Are you prepared to give up the commission?

SOLNESS (*impatiently*).   Yes, yes, yes, devil take it! If that is to be the way of it———. Rather that, than build away at random. (*Vehemently.*) Besides, I know very little about these people as yet.

BROVIK.   The people are safe enough. Ragnar knows them. He is a friend of the family. Perfectly safe people.

SOLNESS.   Oh, safe—safe enough! That is not at all what I mean. Good Lord—don't you understand me either? (*Angrily.*) I won't have anything to do with these strangers. They may apply to whom they please, so far as I am concerned.

BROVIK (*rising*).   Do you really mean that?

SOLNESS (*sulkily*).   Yes I do,—For once in a way.

> {*He comes forward.*
> {BROVIK *exchanges a glance with* RAGNER, *who makes a warning gesture. Then* BROVIK *comes into the front room.*

BROVIK.   May I have a few words with you?

SOLNESS.   Certainly.

BROVIK (*to* KAIA). Just go in there for a moment, Kaia.

KAIA (*uneasily*).   Oh, but uncle———

BROVIK.   Do as I say, child. And shut the door after you.

> {KAIA *goes reluctantly into the draughtsmen's office, glances anxiously and imploringly at* SOLNESS, *and shuts the door.*

BROVIK (*lowering his voice a little*).   I don't want the poor children to know how ill I am.

SOLNESS.   Yes, you have been looking very poorly of late.

BROVIK.   It will soon be all over with me. My strength is ebbing—from day to day.

SOLNESS.   Won't you sit down?

BROVIK.   Thanks—may I?

SOLNESS *(placing the arm-chair more conveniently).*   Here—take this chair.—And now?

BROVIK *(has seated himself with difficulty).*   Well, you see, it's about Ragnar. That is what weighs most upon me. What is to become of him?

SOLNESS. Of course your son will stay with me as long as ever he likes.

BROVIK. But that is just what he does not like. He feels that he cannot stay here any longer.

SOLNESS. Why, I should say he was very well off here. But if he wants more money, I should not mind——

BROVIK. No, no! It is not that. *(Impatiently.)*   But sooner or later he, too, must have a chance of doing something on his own account.

SOLNESS *(without looking at him).*   Do you think that Ragnar has quite talent enough to stand alone?

BROVIK. No, that is just the heartbreaking part of it— I have begun to have my doubts about the boy. For you have never said so much as—as one encouraging word about him. And yet I cannot but think there must be something in him—he can't be without talent.

SOLNESS. Well, but he has learnt nothing—nothing thoroughly, I mean. Except, of course, to draw.

BROVIK *(looks at him with covert hatred and says hoarsely).*   You had learned little enough of the business when you were in my employment. But that did not prevent you from setting to work—*(breathing with difficulty)*—and pushing your way up and taking the wind out of my sails—mine, and so many other people's.

SOLNESS. Yes, you see—circumstances favoured me.

BROVIK. You are right there. Everything favoured you. But then how can you have the heart to let me go to my grave—without having seen what Ragnar is fit for? And of course I am anxious to see them married, too—before I go.

SOLNESS (*sharply*).   Is it she who wishes it?

BROVIK. Not Kaia so much as Ragnar—he talks about it every day. (*Appealingly.*) You must—you must help him to get some independent work now! I must see something that the lad has done. Do you hear?

SOLNESS (*peevishly*).   Hang it, man, you can't expect me to drag commissions down from the moon for him!

BROVIK.   He has the chance of a capital commission at this very moment. A big bit of work.

SOLNESS (*uneasily, startled*).   Has he?

BROVIK.   If you would give your consent.

SOLNESS.   What sort of work do you mean?

BROVIK (*with some hesitation*).   He can have the building of that villa out at Lövstrand.

SOLNESS. That! Why, I am going to build that myself.

BROVIK.   Oh, you don't much care about doing it.

SOLNESS (*flaring up*).   Don't care! I? Who dares to say that?

BROVIK.   You said so yourself just now.

SOLNESS.   Oh, never mind what I say.—Would they give Ragnar the building of that villa?

BROVIK.   Yes. You see, he knows the family. And then—just for the fun of the thing—he has made drawings and estimates and so forth——

SOLNESS. Are they pleased with the drawings? The people who will have to live in the house?

BROVIK. Yes. If you would only look through them and approve of them.

SOLNESS. Then they would let Ragnar build their home for them?

BROVIK. They were immensely pleased with his idea. They thought it exceedingly original, they said.

SOLNESS. Oho! Original! Not the old-fashioned stuff that *I* am in the habit of turning out!

BROVIK. It seemed to them different.

SOLNESS (*with suppressed irritation*).   So it was to see Ragnar that they came here—whilst I was out!

BROVIK. They came to call upon you—and at the same time to ask whether you would mind retiring——

SOLNESS (*angrily*).   Retire? I?

BROVIK. In case you thought that Ragnar's drawings——

SOLNESS. I? Retire in favour of your son!

BROVIK. Retire from the agreement, they meant.

SOLNESS. Oh, it comes to the same thing. (*Laughs angrily.*)   So that is it, is it? Halvard Solness is to see about retiring now! To make room for younger men! For the very youngest, perhaps! He must make room! Room! Room!

BROVIK. Why, good heavens! there is surely room for more than one single man——

SOLNESS. Oh, there's not so very much room to spare either. But, be that as it may—I will never retire! I will never give way to anybody! Never of my own free will. Never in this world will I do that!

BROVIK (*rises with difficulty*).   Then I am to pass out of life without any certainty? Without a gleam of happiness? Without any faith or trust in Ragnar? Without having seen a single piece of work of his doing? Is that to be the way of it?

SOLNESS (*turns half aside and mutters*).   H'm—don't ask more just now.

BROVIK.   I must have an answer to this one question. Am I to pass out of life in such utter poverty?

SOLNESS (*seems to struggle with himself; finally he says, in a low but firm voice:*)   You must pass out of life as best you can.

BROVIK.   Then be it so.

{*He goes up the room.*

SOLNESS (*following him, half in desperation*).   Don't you understand that I cannot help it? I am what I am, and I cannot change my nature!

BROVIK.   No, no; I suppose you can't. (*Reels and supports himself against the sofa-table.*)   May I have a glass of water?

SOLNESS.   By all means.

{*Fills a glass and hands it to him.*

BROVIK.   Thanks.

{*Drinks and puts the glass down again.*

{SOLNESS *goes up and opens the door of the draughtsmen's office.*

SOLNESS.   Ragnar—you must come and take your father home.

{RAGNAR *rises quickly. He and* KAIA *come into the work-room.*

RAGNAR.   What is the matter, father?

BROVIK.   Give me your arm. Now let us go.

RAGNAR.   Very well. You had better put your things on, too, Kaia.

SOLNESS.   Miss Fosli must stay—just for a moment. There is a letter I want written.

BROVIK (*looks at* SOLNESS).   Good night. Sleep well—if you can.

SOLNESS.　　Good night.

*{*BROVIK *and* RAGNAR *go out by the hall door.* KAIA *goes to the desk.* SOLNESS *stands with bent head, to the right, by the armchair.*

KAIA *(dubiously).*　　Is there any letter——?

SOLNESS *(curtly).*　　No, of course not. *(Looks sternly at her.)* Kaia!

KAIA *(anxiously, in a low voice).*　　Yes!

SOLNESS *(points imperatively to a spot on the floor).*　　Come here! At once!

KAIA *(hesitatingly).*　　Yes.

SOLNESS *(as before).*　　Nearer!

KAIA *(obeying).*　　What do you want with me?

SOLNESS *(looks at her for a while).*　　Is it you I have to thank for all this?

KAIA.　　No, no, don't think that!

SOLNESS.　　But confess now—you want to get married!

KAIA *(softly).*　　Ragnar and I have been engaged for four or five years, and so——

SOLNESS.　　And so you think it time there were an end to it. Is not that so?

KAIA.　　Ragnar and Uncle say I must. So I suppose I shall have to give in.

SOLNESS *(more gently).*　　Kaia, don't you really care a little bit for Ragnar, too?

KAIA.　　I cared very much for Ragnar once—before I came here to you.

SOLNESS.　　But you don't now? Not in the least?

KAIA *(passionately, clasping her hands and holding them out towards him).*　　Oh, you know very well there is only one person I care for now! One, and one only, in all the world! I shall never care for any one else.

SOLNESS.   Yes, you say that. And yet you go away from me—leave me alone here with everything on my hands.

KAIA.   But could I not stay with you, even if Rag-nar——?

SOLNESS (*repudiating the idea*).   No, no, that is quite impossible. If Ragnar leaves me and starts work on his own account, then of course he will need you himself.

KAIA (*wringing her hands.*)   Oh, I feel as if I could not be separated from you! It's quite, quite impossible!

SOLNESS.   Then be sure you get those foolish notions out of Ragnar's head. Marry him as much as you please—(*alters his tone.*)—I mean—don't let him throw up his good situation with me. For then I can keep you, too, my dear Kaia.

KAIA.   Oh yes, how lovely that would be, if it could only be managed!

SOLNESS (*clasps her head with his two hands and whispers*).   For I cannot get on without you, you see. I must have you with me every single day.

KAIA (*in nervous exaltation*).   My God! My God!

SOLNESS (*kisses her hair*).   Kaia—Kaia!

KAIA (*sinks down before him*).   Oh, how good you are to me! How unspeakably good you are!

SOLNESS (*vehemently*).   Get up! For goodness' sake get up! I think I hear some one!

> {He helps her to rise. She staggers over to the desk.
> {MRS. SOLNESS *enters by the door on the right. She looks thin and wasted with grief, but shows traces of bygone beauty. Blonde ringlets. Dressed with good taste, wholly in black. Speaks somewhat slowly and in a plaintive voice.*

MRS. SOLNESS (*in the doorway*).   Halvard!

SOLNESS (*turns*).   Oh, are you there, my dear——?

MRS. SOLNESS (*with a glance at* KAIA).　　I am afraid I am disturbing you.

SOLNESS.　　Not in the least. Miss Fosli has only a short letter to write.

MRS. SOLNESS.　　Yes, so I see.

SOLNESS.　　What do you want with me, Aline?

MRS. SOLNESS. I merely wanted to tell you that Dr. Herdal is in the drawing-room. Won't you come and see him, Halvard?

SOLNESS (*looks suspiciously at her*).　　H'm—is the doctor so very anxious to talk to me?

MRS. SOLNESS.　　Well, not exactly anxious. He really came to see me; but he would like to say how-do-you-do to you at the same time.

SOLNESS (*laughs to himself*).　　Yes, I daresay. Well, you must ask him to wait a little.

MRS. SOLNESS.　　Then you will come in presently?

SOLNESS.　　Perhaps I will. Presently, presently, dear. In a little while.

MRS. SOLNESS (*glancing again at* KAIA).　　Well, now, don't forget, Halvard.

　　　　　　　　　{*Withdraws and closes the door behind her.*

KAIA (*softly*).　　Oh dear, oh dear—I am sure Mrs. Solness thinks ill of me in some way!

SOLNESS.　　Oh, not in the least. Not more than usual, at any rate. But all the same, you had better go now, Kaia.

KAIA.　　Yes, yes, now I must go.

SOLNESS (*severely*).　　And mind you get that matter settled for me. Do you hear?

KAIA.　　Oh, if it only depended on me——

SOLNESS　　I will have it settled, I say! And to-morrow too—not a day later!

KAIA (*terrified*).   If there's nothing else for it, I am quite willing to break off the engagement.

SOLNESS (*angrily*).   Break it off? Are you mad? Would you think of breaking it off?

KAIA (*distracted*).   Yes, if necessary. For I must—I must stay here with you! I can't leave you! That is utterly—utterly impossible!

SOLNESS (*with a sudden outburst*).   But deuce take it—how about Ragnar then! It's Ragnar that I——

KAIA (*looks at him with terrified eyes*).   It is chiefly on Ragnar's account, that—that you——

SOLNESS (*collecting himself*).   No, no, of course not! You don't understand me either. (*Gently and softly.*)   Of course it is you I want to keep—you above everything, Kaia. But for that very reason, you must prevent Ragnar, too, from throwing up his situation. There, there,—now go home.

KAIA.   Yes, yes—good-night, then.

SOLNESS.   Good-night. (*As she is going.*) Oh, stop a moment! Are Ragnar's drawings in there?

KAIA.   I did not see him take them with him.

SOLNESS.   Then just go and find them for me. I might perhaps glance over them, after all.

KAIA (*happy*).   Oh yes, please do!

SOLNESS.   For your sake, Kaia dear. Now, let me have them at once, please.

> {KAIA *hurries into the draughtsmen's office, searches anxiously in the table-drawer, finds a portfolio and brings it with her.*

KAIA.   Here are all the drawings.

SOLNESS.   Good. Put them down there on the table.

KAIA (*putting down the portfolio*).   Good-night, then. (*Beseechingly.*) And please, please think kindly of me.

SOLNESS.   Oh, that I always do. Good-night, my dear little Kaia. *(Glances to the right.)* Go, go now!

> {MRS. SOLNESS *and* DR. HERDAL *enter by the door on the right. He is a stoutish, elderly man, with a round, good-humoured face, clean shaven, with thin, light hair, and gold spectacles.*

MRS. SOLNESS *(still in the doorway).*   Halvard, I cannot keep the doctor any longer.

SOLNESS.   Well then, come in here.

MRS. SOLNESS (to KAIA, *who is turning down the desk-lamp).*   Have you finished the letter already, Miss Fosli?

KAIA *(in confusion).*   The letter——?

SOLNESS.   Yes, it was quite a short one.

MRS. SOLNESS.   It must have been very short.

SOLNESS.   You may go now, Miss Fosli. And please come in good time to-morrow morning.

KAIA.   I will be sure to. Good-night, Mrs. Solness.

> {She goes out by the hall door.

MRS. SOLNESS.   She must be quite an acquisition to you, Halvard, this Miss Fosli.

SOLNESS.   Yes, indeed. She is useful in all sorts of ways.

MRS. SOLNESS.   So it seems.

DR. HERDAL.   Is she good at book-keeping too?

SOLNESS.   Well—of course she has had a good deal of practice during these two years. And then she is so nice and willing to do whatever one asks of her.

MRS. SOLNESS.   Yes, that must be very delightful——

SOLNESS.   It is. Especially when one is not too much accustomed to that sort of thing.

MRS. SOLNESS *(in a tone of gentle remonstrance).*   Can you say that, Halvard?

SOLNESS. Oh, no, no, my dear Aline; I beg your pardon.

MRS. SOLNESS. There's no occasion.—Well then, doctor, you will come back later on and have a cup of tea with us?

DR. HERDAL. I have only that one patient to see and then I'll come back.

MRS. SOLNESS. Thank you.

{She goes out by the door on the right.

SOLNESS. Are you in a hurry, doctor?

DR. HERDAL. No, not at all.

SOLNESS. May I have a little chat with you?

DR. HERDAL. With the greatest of pleasure.

SOLNESS. Then let us sit down. *(He motions the doctor to take the rocking-chair and sits down himself in the armchair. Looks searchingly at him.)* Tell me—did you notice anything odd about Aline?

DR. HERDAL. Do you mean just now, when she was here?

SOLNESS. Yes, in her manner to me. Did you notice anything?

DR. HERDAL *(smiling)*. Well, I admit—one couldn't well avoid noticing that your wife—h'm——

SOLNESS. Well?

DR. HERDAL. ——that your wife is not particularly fond of this Miss Fosli.

SOLNESS. Is that all? I have noticed that myself.

DR. HERDAL. And I must say I am scarcely surprised at it.

SOLNESS. At what?

DR. HERDAL. That she should not exactly approve of your seeing so much of another woman, all day and every day.

SOLNESS. No, no, I suppose you are right there— and Aline too. But it's impossible to make any change.

DR. HERDAL.   Could you not engage a clerk?

SOLNESS.   The first man that came to hand? No, thank you—that would never do for me.

DR. HERDAL.   But now, if your wife——? Suppose, with her delicate health, all this tries her too much?

SOLNESS.   Even than—I might almost say—it can make no difference. I must keep Kaia Fosli. No one else could fill her place.

DR. HERDAL.   No one else?

SOLNESS. *(curtly).*   No, no one.

DR. HERDAL *(drawing his chair closer).*   Now listen to me, my dear Mr. Solness. May I ask you a question, quite between ourselves?

SOLNESS.   By all means.

DR. HERDAL.   Women, you see—in certain matters, they have a deucedly keen intuition——

SOLNESS.   They have, indeed. There is not the least doubt of that. But——?

DR. HERDAL.   Well, tell me now—if your wife can't endure this Kaia Fosli——?

SOLNESS.   Well, what then?

DR. HERDAL.   ——may she not have just—just the least little bit of reason for this instinctive dislike?

SOLNESS *(looks at him and rises).*   Oho!

DR. HERDAL.   Now don't be offended—but hasn't she?

SOLNESS *(with curt decision).*   No.

DR. HERDAL.   No reason of any sort?

SOLNESS.   No other reason than her own suspicious nature.

DR. HERDAL.   I know you have known a good many women in your time.

SOLNESS.   Yes, I have.

DR. HERDAL.   And have been a good deal taken with some of them, too.

SOLNESS.   Oh, yes, I don't deny it.

DR. HERDAL.   But as regards Miss Fosli, then? There is nothing of that sort in the case?

SOLNESS.   No; nothing at all—on my side.

DR. HERDAL.   But on her side?

SOLNESS.   I don't think you have any right to ask that question, doctor.

DR. HERDAL.   Well, you know, we were discussing your wife's intuition.

SOLNESS.   So we were. And for that matter—(*lowers his voice*)—Aline's intuition, as you call it—in a certain sense, it has not been so far astray.

DR. HERDAL.   Aha! there we have it!

SOLNESS (*sits down*).   Doctor Herdal—I am going to tell you a strange story—if you care to listen to it.

DR. HERDAL.   I like listening to strange stories.

SOLNESS.   Very well then. I daresay you recollect that I took Knut Brovik and his son into my employment—after the old man's business had gone to the dogs.

DR. HERDAL.   Yes, so I have understood.

SOLNESS.   You see, they really are clever fellows, these two. Each of them has talent in his own way. But then the son took it into his head to get engaged; and the next thing, of course, was that he wanted to get married—and begin to build on his own account. That is the way with all these young people.

DR. HERDAL (*laughing*).   Yes, they have a bad habit of wanting to marry.

SOLNESS.   Just so. But of course that did not suit my

plans; for I needed Ragnar myself—and the old man, too. He is , exceedingly good at calculating bearing-strains and cubic contents—and all that sort of devilry, you know.

DR. HERDAL.   Oh, yes, no doubt that's indispensable.

SOLNESS.   Yes, it is. But Ragnar was absolutely bent on setting to work for himself. He would hear of nothing else.

DR. HERDAL.   But he has stayed with you all the same.

SOLNESS.   Yes, I'll tell you how that came about. One day this girl, Kaia Fosli, came to see them on some errand or other. She had never been here before. And when I saw how utterly infatuated they were with each other, the thought occurred to me: if I could only get her into the office here, then perhaps Ragnar, too, would stay where he is.

DR. HERDAL.   That was not at all a bad idea.

SOLNESS.   Yes, but at the time I did not breathe a word of what was in my mind. I merely stood and looked at her—and kept on wishing intently that I could have her here. Then I talked to her a little, in a friendly way—about one thing and another. And then she went away.

DR. HERDAL.   Well?

SOLNESS.   Well, then, next day, pretty late in the evening, when old Brovik and Ragnar had gone home, she came here again and behaved as if I had made an arrangement with her.

DR. HERDAL.   An arrangement? What about?

SOLNESS.   About the very thing my mind had been fixed on. But I hadn't said one single word about it.

DR. HERDAL.   That was most extraordinary.

SOLNESS.   Yes, was it not? And now she wanted to

know what she was to do here—whether she could begin the very next morning, and so forth.

DR. HERDAL.   Don't you think she did it in order to be with her sweetheart?

SOLNESS.   That was what occurred to me at first. But no, that was not it. She seemed to drift quite away from him—when once she had come here to me.

DR. HERDAL.   She drifted over to you, then?

SOLNESS.   Yes, entirely. If I happen to look at her when her back is turned, I can tell that she feels it. She quivers and trembles the moment I come near her. What do you think of that?

DR. HERDAL.   H'm—that's not very hard to explain.

SOLNESS.   Well, but what about the other thing? That she believed I had said to her what I had only wished and willed—silently—inwardly—to myself? What do you say to that? Can you explain that, Dr. Herdal?

DR. HERDAL.   No, I won't undertake to do that.

SOLNESS.   I felt sure you would not; and so I have never cared to talk about it till now. But it's a cursed nuisance to me in the long run, you understand. Here I have to go on day after day pretending——. And it's a shame to treat her so, too, poor girl. (*Vehemently.*) But I cannot do anything else. For if she runs away from me—then Ragnar will be off too.

DR. HERDAL.   And you have not told your wife the rights of the story?

SOLNESS.   No.

DR. HERDAL.   Then why on earth don't you?

SOLNESS. (*looks fixedly at him, and says in a low voice:*) Because I seem to find a sort of—of salutary self-torture in allowing Aline to do me an injustice.

DR. HERDAL (*shakes his head*).   I don't in the least understand what you mean.

SOLNESS.   Well, you see—it is like paying off a little bit of a huge, immeasurable debt——

DR. HERDAL.   To your wife?

SOLNESS.   Yes; and that always helps to relieve one's mind a little. One can breathe more freely for a while, you understand.

DR. HERDAL.   No, goodness knows, I don't understand at all——

SOLNESS (*breaking off, rises again*).   Well, well, well— then we won't talk any more about it. (*He saunters across the room, returns and stops beside the table. Looks at the doctor with a sly smile.*) I suppose you think you have drawn me out nicely now, doctor?

DR. HERDAL (*with some irritation*).   Drawn you out? Again I have not the faintest notion what you mean, Mr. Solness.

SOLNESS.   Oh come, out with it; I have seen it quite clearly, you know.

DR. HERDAL.   What have you seen?

SOLNESS (*in a low voice, slowly*).   That you have been quietly keeping an eye upon me.

DR. HERDAL.   That *I* have! And why in all the world should I do that?

SOLNESS.   Because you think that I—— (*Passionately.*) Well, devil take it—you think the same of me as Aline does.

DR. HERDAL.   And what does she think about you?

SOLNESS (*having recovered his self-control*).   She has begun to think that I am—that I am—ill.

DR. HERDAL   Ill! You! She has never hinted such a thing to me. Why, what can she think is the matter with you?

SOLNESS (*leans over the back of the chair and whispers*).   Aline had made up her mind that I am mad. That is what she thinks.

DR. HERDAL (*rising*).   Why, my dear good fellow——!

SOLNESS.   Yes, on my soul she does! I tell you it is so. And she has got you to think the same! Oh, I can assure you, doctor, I see it in your face as clearly as possible. You don't take me in so easily, I can tell you.

DR. HERDAL (*looks at him in amazement*).   Never, Mr. Solness—never has such a thought entered my mind.

SOLNESS (*with an incredulous smile*).   Really? Has it not?

DR. HERDAL.   No, never! Nor your wife's mind either, I am convinced. I could almost swear to that.

SOLNESS.   Well, I wouldn't advise you to. For, in a certain sense, you see, perhaps—perhaps she is not so far wrong in thinking something of the kind.

DR. HERDAL.   Come now, I really must say——

SOLNESS (*interrupting, with a sweep of his hand*).   Well, well, my dear doctor—don't let us discuss this any further. We had better agree to differ. (*Changes to a tone of quiet amusement.*) But look here now, doctor—h'm——

DR. HERDAL.   WELL?

SOLNESS.   Since you don't believe that I am—ill—and crazy, and mad, and so forth——

DR. HERDAL.   What then?

SOLNESS.   Then I daresay you fancy that I am an extremely happy man.

DR. HERDAL.   Is that mere fancy?

SOLNESS (*laughs*).   No, no—of course not! Heaven forbid! Only think—to be Solness the master builder! Halvard Solness! What could be more delightful?

DR. HERDAL.   Yes, I must say it seems to me you have had the luck on your side to an astounding degree.

SOLNESS (*suppresses a gloomy smile*).   So I have, I can't complain on that score.

DR. HERDAL.   First of all that grim old robbers' castle was burnt down for you. And that was certainly a great piece of luck.

SOLNESS (*seriously*).   It was the home of Aline's family. Remember that.

DR. HERDAL.   Yes, it must have been a great grief to her.

SOLNESS.   She has not got over it to this day—not in all these twelve or thirteen years.

DR. HERDAL.   Ah, but what followed must have been the worst blow for her.

SOLNESS.   The one thing with the other.

DR. HERDAL.   But you—yourself—you rose upon the ruins. You began as a poor boy from a country village—and now you are at the head of your profession. Ah, yes, Mr. Solness, you have undoubtedly had the luck on your side.

SOLNESS (*looking at him with embarrassment*).   Yes, but that is just what makes me so horribly afraid.

DR. HERDAL.   Afraid? Because you have the luck on your side!

SOLNESS.   It terrifies me—terrifies me every hour of the day. For sooner or later the luck must turn, you see.

DR. HERDAL.   Oh nonsense! What should make the luck turn?

SOLNESS (*with firm assurance*).   The younger generation.

DR. HERDAL.   Pooh! The younger generation! You are not laid on the shelf yet, I should hope. Oh no—your position here is probably firmer now than it has ever been.

SOLNESS. The luck will turn. I know it—I feel the day approaching. Some one or other will take it into his head to say: Give me a chance! And then all the rest will come clamouring after him, and shake their fists at me and shout: Make room—make room—make room! Yes, just you see, doctor—presently the younger generation will come knock at my door——

DR. HERDAL (*laughing*). Well, and what if they do?

SOLNESS. What if they do? Then there's an end of Halvard Solness.

> {*There is a knock at the door on the left.*

SOLNESS (*starts*). What's that? Did you not hear something?

DR. HERDAL. Some one is knocking at the door.

SOLNESS (*loudly*). Come in.

> {HILDA WANGEL *enters by the hall door. She is of middle height, supple and delicately built. Somewhat sunburnt. Dressed in a tourist costume, with skirt caught up for walking, a sailor's collar open at the throat and a small sailor hat on her head. Knapsack on back, plaid in strap, and alpenstock.*

HILDA (*goes straight up to* SOLNESS, *her eyes sparkling with happiness*). Good evening!

SOLNESS (*looks doubtfully at her*). Good evening——

HILDA (*laughs*). I almost believe you don't recognise me!

SOLNESS. No—I must admit that—just for the moment——

DR. HERDAL (*approaching*). But I recognise you, my dear young lady——

HILDA (*pleased*). Oh, is it you that——

DR. HERDAL. Of course it is. (*To* SOLNESS.) We met

at one of the mountain stations this summer. *(To* HILDA.*)* What became of the other ladies?

HILDA Oh, they went westward.

DR. HERDAL. They didn't much like all the fun we used to have in the evenings.

HILDA. No, I believe they didn't.

DR. HERDAL. *(holds up his finger at her).* And I am afraid it can't be denied that you flirted a little with us.

HILDA. Well that was better fun than to sit there knitting stockings with all those old women.

DR. HERDAL *(laughs).* There I entirely agree with you.

SOLNESS. Have you come to town this evening?

HILDA. Yes, I have just arrived.

DR. HERDAL. Quite alone, Miss Wangel?

HILDA. Oh, yes!

SOLNESS. Wangel? Is your name Wangel?

HILDA *(looks in amused surprise at him).* Yes, of course it is.

SOLNESS. Then you must be a daughter of the district doctor up at Lysanger?

HILDA *(as before).* Yes, who else's daughter should I be?

SOLNESS. Oh, then I suppose we met up there, that summer when I was building a tower on the old church.

HILDA. *(more seriously).* Yes, of course it was then we met.

SOLNESS. Well, that is a long time ago.

HILDA *(looks hard at him).* It is exactly ten years.

SOLNESS. You must have been a mere child then, I should think.

HILDA *(carelessly).* Well, I was twelve or thirteen.

DR. HERDAL.   Is this the first time you have ever been up to town, Miss Wangel?

HILDA.   Yes, it is indeed.

SOLNESS.   And don't you know any one here?

HILDA.   Nobody but you. And of course, your wife.

SOLNESS.   So you know her, too?

HILDA.   Only a little. We spent a few days together at the sanatorium.

SOLNESS.   Ah, up there?

HILDA.   She said I might come and pay her a visit if ever I came up to town. (*Smiles.*) Not that that was necessary.

SOLNESS.   Odd that she should never have mentioned it.

> {HILDA *puts her stick down by the stove, takes off the knapsack and lays it and the plaid on the sofa.* DR. HERDAL *offers to help her.* SOLNESS *stands and gazes at her.*

HILDA (*going towards him*).   Well, now I must ask you to let me stay the night here.

SOLNESS.   I am sure there will be no difficulty about that.

HILDA.   For I have no other clothes than those I stand in, except a change of linen in my knapsack. And that has to go to the wash, for it's very dirty.

SOLNESS.   Oh, yes, that can be managed. Now I'll just let my wife know——

DR. HERDAL.   Meanwhile I will go and see my patient.

SOLNESS.   Yes, do; and come again later on.

DR. HERDAL (*playfully, with a glance at* HILDA).   Oh, that I will, you may be very certain! (*Laughs.*) So your prediction has come true, Mr. Solness!

SOLNESS.   How so?

DR. HERDAL.   The younger generation did come knocking at your door.

SOLNESS (*cheerfully*).   Yes, but in a very different way from what I meant.

DR. HERDAL.   Very different, yes. That's undeniable.

> {*He goes out by the hall door.* SOLNESS *opens the door on the right and speaks into the side room.*

SOLNESS.   Aline! Will you come in here, please. Here is a friend of yours—Miss Wangel.

MRS. SOLNESS (*appears in the doorway*).   Who do you say it is? (*Sees* HILDA.) Oh, is it you, Miss Wangel? (*Goes up to her and offers her hand.*) So you have come to town after all.

SOLNESS.   Miss Wangel has this moment arrived; and she would like to stay the night here.

MRS. SOLNESS.   Here with us? Oh yes, certainly.

SOLNESS.   Till she can get her things a little in order, you know.

MRS. SOLNESS.   I will do the best I can for you. It's no more than my duty. I suppose your trunk is coming on later?

HILDA.   I have no trunk.

MRS. SOLNESS.   Well, it will be all right, I daresay. In the meantime, you must excuse my leaving you here with my husband, until I can get a room made a little comfortable for you.

SOLNESS.   Can we not give her one of the nurseries? They are all ready as it is.

MRS. SOLNESS.   Oh, yes. There we have room and to spare. (*To* HILDA.) Sit down now, and rest a little.

> {*She goes out to the right.*
> {HILDA, *with her hands behind her back, strolls about*

the room and looks at various objects. SOLNESS *stands
in front, beside the table, also with his hands behind
his back, and follows her with his eyes.*

HILDA (*stops and looks at him*).   Have you several nurseries?

SOLNESS.   There are three nurseries in the house.

HILDA.   That's a lot. Then I suppose you have a great
many children?

SOLNESS.   No. We have no child. But now you can
be the child here, for the time being.

HILDA.   For to-night, yes. I shall not cry. I mean to
sleep as sound as a stone.

SOLNESS.   Yes, you must be very tired, I should
think.

HILDA.   Oh, no! But all the same—— It's so deli-
cious to lie and dream.

SOLNESS.   Do you dream much of nights?

HILDA.   Oh, yes! Almost always.

SOLNESS.   What do you dream about most?

HILDA.   I shan't tell you to-night. Another time,
perhaps.

> *She again strolls about the room, stops at the desk and
> turns over the books and papers a little.*

SOLNESS (*approaching*).   Are you searching for anything?

HILDA.   No, I am merely looking at all these things.
(*Turns.*) Perhaps I mustn't?

SOLNESS.   Oh, by all means.

HILDA.   Is it you that write in this great ledger?

SOLNESS.   No, it's my book-keeper.

HILDA.   Is it a woman?

SOLNESS (*smiles*).   Yes.

HILDA.   One you employ here, in your office?

SOLNESS.   Yes.

HILDA.   Is she married?

SOLNESS.   No, she is single.

HILDA.   Oh, indeed!

SOLNESS.   But I believe she is soon going to be married.

HILDA.   That's a good thing for her.

SOLNESS.   But not such a good thing for me. For then I shall have nobody to help me.

HILDA.   Can't you get hold of some one else who will do just as well?

SOLNESS.   Perhaps you would stay here and write in the ledger?

HILDA (*measures him with a glance*).   Yes, I daresay! No, thank you—nothing of that sort for me.

> {*She again strolls across the room and sits down in the rocking-chair.* SOLNESS, *too, goes to the table.*

HILDA (*continuing*).   For there must surely be plenty of other things to be done here. (*Looks smiling at him.*) Don't you think so, too?

SOLNESS.   Of course. First of all, I suppose, you want to make a round of the shops and get yourself up in the height of fashion.

HILDA (*amused*).   No, I think I shall let that alone!

SOLNESS.   Indeed.

HILDA.   For you must know I have run through all my money.

SOLNESS (*laughs*).   Neither trunk nor money, then.

HILDA.   Neither one nor the other. But never mind—it doesn't matter now.

SOLNESS.   Come now, I like you for that.

HILDA.   Only for that?

SOLNESS. For that among other things. *(Sits in the armchair.)* Is you father alive still?

HILDA. Yes, father's alive.

SOLNESS. Perhaps you are thinking of studying here?

HILDA. No, that hadn't occurred to me.

SOLNESS. But I suppose you will be staying for some time?

HILDA. That must depend upon circumstances.

{She sits awhile rocking herself and looking at him, half seriously, half with a suppressed smile. Then she takes off her hat and puts it on the table in front of her.

HILDA. Mr. Solness!

SOLNESS. Well?

HILDA. Have you a very bad memory?

SOLNESS. A bad memory? No, not that I am aware of.

HILDA. Then have you nothing to say to me about what happened up there?

SOLNESS *(in momentary surprise).* Up at Lysanger? *(Indifferently.)* Why, it was nothing much to talk about, it seems to me.

HILDA *(looks reproachfully at him).* How can you sit there and say such things?

SOLNESS. Well, then, you talk to me about it.

HILDA. When the tower was finished, we had grand doings in the town.

SOLNESS. Yes, I shall not easily forget that day.

HILDA *(smiles).* Will you not? That comes well from you.

SOLNESS. Comes well?

HILDA.   There was music in the churchyard—and many, many hundreds of people. We school-girls were dressed in white; and we all carried flags.

SOLNESS.   Ah yes, those flags—I can tell you I remember them!

HILDA.   Then you climbed right up the scaffolding, straight to the very top; and you had a great wreath with you; and you hung that wreath right away up on the weather-vane.

SOLNESS (*curtly interrupting*).   I always did that in those days. It was an old custom.

HILDA.   It was so wonderfully thrilling to stand below and look up at you. Fancy, if he should fall over! He—the master builder himself!

SOLNESS (*as if to divert her from the subject*).   Yes, yes, yes, that might very well have happened, too. For one of those white-frocked little devils,—she went on in such a way, and screamed up at me so——

HILDA (*sparkling with pleasure*).   "Hurrah for Master Builder Solness!" Yes!

SOLNESS.   ——and waved and flourished with her flag, so that I—so that it almost made me giddy to look at it.

HILDA (*in a lower voice, seriously*).   That little devil—that was *I*.

SOLNESS (*fixes his eyes steadily upon her*).   I am sure of that now. It must have been you.

HILDA (*lively again*).   Oh, it was so gloriously thrilling! I could not have believed there was a builder in the whole world that could build such a tremendously high tower. And then, that you yourself should stand at the very top of it, as large as life! And that you should not be the

least bit dizzy! It was that above everything that made one—
made one dizzy to think of.

SOLNESS.   How could you be so certain that I was
not——?

HILDA (*scouting the idea*).   No indeed! Oh, no! I knew
that instinctively. For if you had been, you could never have
stood up there and sung.

SOLNESS (*looks at her in astonishment*).   Sung? Did *I*
sing?

HILDA.   Yes, I should think you did.

SOLNESS (*shakes his head*).   I have never sung a note
in my life.

HILDA.   Yes indeed, you sang then. It sounded like
harps in the air.

SOLNESS (*thoughtfully*).   This is very strange—all
this.

HILDA (*is silent awhile, looks at him and says in a low
voice:*)   But then,—it was after that—and the real thing
happened.

SOLNESS.   The real thing?

HILDA (*sparkling with vivacity*).   Yes, I surely don't
need to remind you of that?

SOLNESS.   Oh, yes, do remind me a little of that, too.

HILDA.   Don't you remember that a great dinner was
given in your honour at the Club?

SOLNESS.   Yes, to be sure. It must have been the
same afternoon, for I left the place next morning.

HILDA.   And from the Club you were invited to
come round to our house to supper.

SOLNESS.   Quite right, Miss Wangel. It is wonderful
how all these trifles have impressed themselves on your
mind.

HILDA.   Trifles! I like that! Perhaps it was a trifle, too, that I was alone in the room when you came in?

SOLNESS.   Were you alone?

HILDA (*without answering him*).   You didn't call me a little devil then?

SOLNESS.   No, I suppose I did not.

HILDA.   You said I was lovely in my white dress, and that I looked like a little princess.

SOLNESS.   I have no doubt you did, Miss Wangel.— And besides—I was feeling so buoyant and free that day——

HILDA.   And then you said that when I grew up I should be your princess.

SOLNESS (*laughing a little*).   Dear, dear—did I say that, too?

HILDA.   Yes, you did. And when I asked how long I should have to wait, you said that you would come again in ten years—like a troll and carry me off—to Spain or some such place. And you promised you would buy me a kingdom there.

SOLNESS (*as before*).   Yes, after a good dinner one doesn't haggle about the halfpence. But did I really say all that?

HILDA (*laughs to herself*).   Yes. And you told me, too, what the kingdom was to be called.

SOLNESS.   Well, what was it?

HILDA.   It was to be called the kingdom of Orangia,* you said.

SOLNESS.   Well, that was an appetising name.

HILDA.   No, I didn't like it a bit; for it seemed as though you wanted to make game of me.

---

*   In the original "Appelsinia," "appelsin" meaning "orange."

SOLNESS.   I am sure that cannot have been my intention.

HILDA.   No, I should hope not——considering what you did next——

SOLNESS.   What in the world did I do next?

HILDA.   Well, that's the finishing touch, if you have forgotten that, too. I should have thought no one could help remembering such a thing as that.

SOLNESS.   Yes, yes, just give me a hint, and then perhaps——Well——

HILDA (*looks fixedly at him*).   You came and kissed me, Mr. Solness.

SOLNESS (*open-mouthed, rising from his chair*).   I did!

HILDA.   Yes, indeed you did. You took me in both your arms, and bent my head back and kissed me—many times.

SOLNESS.   Now really, my dear Miss Wangel——!

HILDA (*rises*).   You surely cannot mean to deny it?

SOLNESS.   Yes, I do. I deny it altogether!

HILDA (*looks scornfully at him*).   Oh, indeed!

{*She turns and goes slowly close up to the stove, where she remains standing motionless, her face averted from him, her hands behind her back. Short pause.*

SOLNESS (*goes cautiously up behind her*).   Miss Wangel——!

HILDA (*is silent and does not move*).

SOLNESS.   Don't stand there like a statue. You must have dreamt all this. (*Lays his hand on her arm.*) Now just listen——

HILDA (*makes an impatient movement with her arm*).

SOLNESS (*as a thought flashes upon him*). Or——! Wait a moment! There is something under all this, you may depend!

HILDA (*does not move*).

SOLNESS (*in a low voice, but with emphasis*).   I must have thought all that. I must have wished it—have willed it—have longed to do it. And then———. May not that be the explanation?

HILDA (*is still silent*).

SOLNESS (*impatiently*).   Oh very well, deuce take it all—then I did it, I suppose.

HILDA (*turns her head a little, but without looking at him*).   Then you admit it now?.

SOLNESS.   Yes—whatever you like.

HILDA.   You came and put your arms around me?

SOLNESS.   Oh, yes!

HILDA.   And bent my head back?

SOLNESS.   Very far back.

HILDA.   And kissed me?

SOLNESS.   Yes, I did.

HILDA.   Many times?

SOLNESS.   As many as ever you like.

HILDA (*turns quickly towards him and has once more the sparkling expression of gladness in her eyes*).   Well, you see, I got it out of you at last!

SOLNESS (*with a slight smile*).   Yes—just think of my forgetting such a thing as that.

HILDA (*again a little sulky, retreats from him*).   Oh, you have kissed so many people in your time, I suppose.

SOLNESS.   No, you mustn't think that of me. (HILDA *seats herself in the armchair.* SOLNESS *stands and leans against the rocking-chair. Looks observantly at her.*) Miss Wangel!

HILDA.   Yes!

SOLNESS.   How was it now? What came of all this—between us two?

HILDA.   Why, nothing more came of it. You know

that quite well. For then the other guests came in, and then—bah!

SOLNESS.   Quite so! The others came in. To think of my forgetting that, too!

HILDA.   Oh, you haven't really forgotten anything: you are only a little ashamed of it all. I am sure one doesn't forget things of that kind.

SOLNESS.   No, one would suppose not.

HILDA (*lively again, looks at him*).   Perhaps you have even forgotten what day it was?

SOLNESS.   What day——?

HILDA.   Yes, on what day did you hang the wreath on the tower? Well? Tell me at once!

SOLNESS.   H'm—I confess I have forgotten the particular day. I only knew it was ten years ago. Sometime in the autumn.

HILDA (*nods her head slowly several times*).   It was ten years ago—on the 19th of September.

SOLNESS.   Yes, it must have been about that time. Fancy your remembering that, too! (*Stops.*) But wait a moment——! Yes—it's the 19th of September to-day.

HILDA.   Yes, it is; and the ten years are gone. And you didn't come—as you promised me.

SOLNESS.   Promised you? Threatened, I suppose you mean?

HILDA.   I don't think there was any sort of threat in that.

SOLNESS.   Well then, a little bit of fun.

HILDA.   Was that all you wanted? To make fun of me?

SOLNESS.   Well, or to have a little joke with you. Upon my soul, I don't recollect. But it must have been something of that kind; for you were a mere child then.

HILDA.   Oh, perhaps I wasn't quite such a child either. Not such a mere chit as you imagine.

SOLNESS (*looks searchingly at her*).   Did you really and seriously expect me to come again?

HILDA (*conceals a half-teasing smile*).   Yes, indeed; I did expect that of you.

SOLNESS.   That I should come back to your home and take you away with me?

HILDA.   Just like a troll—yes.

SOLNESS.   And make a princess of you?

HILDA.   That's what you promised.

SOLNESS.   And give you a kingdom as well?

HILDA (*looks up at the ceiling*).   Why not? Of course it need not have been an actual, every-day sort of kingdom.

SOLNESS.   But something else just as good?

HILDA.   Yes, at least as good. (*Looks at him a moment.*) I thought, if you could build the highest church-towers in the world, you could surely manage to raise a kingdom of one sort or another as well.

SOLNESS (*shakes his head*).   I can't quite make you out, Miss Wangel.

HILDA.   Can you not? To me it seems all so simple.

SOLNESS.   No, I can't make up my mind whether you mean all you say, or are simply having a joke with me.

HILDA (*smiles*).   Making fun of you, perhaps? I, too?

SOLNESS.   Yes, exactly. Making fun—of both of us. (*Looks at her.*) Is it long since you found out that I was married?

HILDA.   I have known it all along. Why do you ask me that?

SOLNESS (*lightly*).   Oh, well, it just occurred to me. (*Looks earnestly at her and says in a low voice.*) What have you come for?

HILDA. I want my kingdom. The time is up.

SOLNESS (*laughs involuntarily*). What a girl you are!

HILDA (*gaily*). Out with my kingdom, Mr. Solness! (*Raps with her fingers.*) The kingdom on the table!

SOLNESS (*pushing the rocking-chair nearer and sitting down*). Now, seriously speaking—what have you come for? What do you really want to do here?

HILDA. Oh, first of all, I want to go around and look at all the things that you have built.

SOLNESS. That will give you plenty of exercise.

HILDA. Yes, I know you have built a tremendous lot.

SOLNESS. I have indeed—especially of late years.

HILDA. Many church-towers among the rest? Immensely high ones?

SOLNESS. No. I build no more church-towers now. Nor churches either.

HILDA. What do you build, then?

SOLNESS. Homes for human beings.

HILDA (*reflectively*). Couldn't you build a little—a little bit of a church-tower over these homes as well?

SOLNESS (*starting*). What do you mean by that?

HILDA. I mean—something that points—points up into the free air. With the vane at a dizzy height.

SOLNESS (*pondering a little*). Strange that you should say that—for that is just what I am most anxious to do.

HILDA (*impatiently*). Why don't you do it, then?

SOLNESS (*shakes his head*). No, the people will not have it.

HILDA. Fancy their not wanting it!

SOLNESS (*more lightly*). But now I am building a new home for myself—just opposite here.

HILDA. For yourself?

SOLNESS.   Yes. It is almost finished. And on that there is a tower.

HILDA.   A high tower?

SOLNESS.   Yes.

HILDA.   Very high?

SOLNESS.   No doubt people will say it is too high—too high for a dwelling-house.

HILDA.   I'll go out and look at that tower the first thing to-morrow morning.

SOLNESS (*sits resting his cheek on his hand and gazes at her*).   Tell me, Miss Wangel—what is your name? Your Christian name, I mean?

HILDA.   Why, Hilda, of course.

SOLNESS (*as before*).   Hilda? Indeed?

HILDA.   Don't you remember that? You called me Hilda yourself—that day when you misbehaved.

SOLNESS.   Did I really?

HILDA.   But then you said "little Hilda"; and I didn't like that.

SOLNESS.   Oh, you didn't like that, Miss Hilda?

HILDA.   No, not at such a time as that. But—"Princess Hilda"—that will sound very well, I think.

SOLNESS.   Very well indeed. Princess Hilda of—of—what was to be the name of the kingdom?

HILDA.   Pooh! I won't have anything to do with that stupid kingdom. I have set my heart upon quite a different one!

SOLNESS (*has leaned back in the chair, still gazing at her*).   Isn't it strange——? The more I think of it now, the more it seems to me as though I had gone about all these years torturing myself with—h'm——

HILDA.   With what?

SOLNESS.   With the effort to recover something—some experience, which I seemed to have forgotten. But I never had the least inkling of what it could be.

HILDA.   You should have tied a knot in your pockethandkerchief, Mr. Solness.

SOLNESS.   In that case, I should simply have had to go racking my brains to discover what the knot could mean.

HILDA.   Oh, yes, I suppose there are trolls of that kind in the world, too.

SOLNESS (*rises slowly*).   What a good thing it is that you have come to me now.

HILDA (*looks deeply into his eyes*).   Is it a good thing?

SOLNESS.   For I have been so lonely here. I have been gazing so helplessly at it all. (*In a lower voice.*) I must tell you—I have begun to be so afraid—so terribly afraid of the younger generation.

HILDA (*with a little snort of contempt*).   Pooh—is the younger generation a thing to be afraid of?

SOLNESS.   It is indeed. And that is why I have locked and barred myself in. (*Mysteriously.*) I tell you the younger generation will one day come and thunder at my door! They will break in upon me!

HILDA.   Then I should say you ought to go out and open the door to the younger generation.

SOLNESS.   Open the door?

HILDA.   Yes. Let them come in to you on friendly terms, as it were.

SOLNESS.   No, no, no! The younger generation—it means retribution, you see. It comes, as if under a new banner, heralding the turn of fortune.

HILDA (*rises, looks at him and says with a quivering twitch of her lips*).   Can I be of any use to you, Mr. Solness?

SOLNESS.   Yes, you can indeed! For you, too, come—
under a new banner, it seems to me. Youth marshalled
against youth——!

> {DR. HERDAL *comes in by the hall-door.*

DR. HERDAL.   What—you and Miss Wangel here
still?

SOLNESS.   Yes. We have had no end of things to talk
about.

HILDA.   Both old and new.

DR. HERDAL.   Have you really?

HILDA.   Oh, it has been the greatest fun. For Mr.
Solness—he has such a miraculous memory. All the least
little details he remembers instantly.

> {MRS. SOLNESS *enters by the door on the right.*

MRS. SOLNESS.   Well, Miss Wangel, your room is
quite ready for you now.

HILDA.   Oh, how kind you are to me!

SOLNESS (*to* MRS. SOLNESS).   The Nursery?

MRS. SOLNESS.   Yes, the middle one. But first let us
go in to supper.

SOLNESS (*nods to* HILDA).   Hilda shall sleep in the
nursery, she shall.

MRS. SOLNESS (*looks at him*).   Hilda?

SOLNESS.   Yes, Miss Wangel's name is Hilda. I knew
her when she was a child.

MRS. SOLNESS.   Did you really, Halvard? Well, shall
we go? Supper is on the table.

> {*She takes* DR. HERDAL'S *arm and goes out with him
> to the right.* HILDA *has meanwhile been collecting her
> travelling things.*

HILDA (*softly and rapidly to* SOLNESS).   Is it true, what
you said? Can I be of use to you?

SOLNESS (*takes the things from her*).   You are the very being I have needed most.

HILDA (*looks at him with happy, wondering eyes and clasps her hands*).   But then, great heavens——!

SOLNESS (*eagerly*).   What——?

HILDA.   Then I have my kingdom!

SOLNESS (*involuntarily*).   Hilda——!

HILDA (*again with the quivering twitch of her lips*). Almost—I was going to say.

{She goes out to the right, SOLNESS *follows her.*

Act II

A prettily furnished small drawing-room in SOLNESS'S house. In the back, a glass door leading out to the verandah and garden. The right-hand corner is cut off transversely by a large bay-window, in which are flower-stands. The left-hand corner is similarly cut off by a transverse wall, in which is a small door papered like the wall. On each side, an ordinary door. In front, on the right, a console table with a large mirror over it. Well-filled stands of plants and flowers. In front, on the left, a sofa with a table and chairs. Further back, a bookcase. Well forward in the room, before the bay window, a small table and some chairs. It is early in the day.

SOLNESS sits by the little table with RAGNAR BROVIK'S portfolio open in front of him. He is turning the drawings over and closely examining some of them. MRS. SOLNESS moves about noiselessly with a small watering-pot, attending to her flowers. She is dressed in black as before. Her hat, cloak and parasol lie on a chair near the mirror. Unobserved by her, SOLNESS now and again follows her with his eyes. Neither of them speaks.

KAIA FOSLI enters quietly by the door on the left.

SOLNESS (turns his head, and says in an off-hand tone of indifference). Well, is that you?

KAIA. I merely wished to let you know that I have come.

SOLNESS. Yes, yes, that's all right. Hasn't Ragnar come, too?

KAIA.   No, not yet. He had to wait a little while to
see the doctor. But he is coming presently to hear——

SOLNESS.   How is the old man to-day?

KAIA.   Not well. He begs you to excuse him; he is
obliged to keep his bed to-day.

SOLNESS.   Why, of course; by all means let him rest.
But now, get to work.

KAIA.   Yes. *(Pauses at the door.)* Do you wish to speak
to Ragnar when he comes?

SOLNESS.   No—I don't know that I have anything
particular to say to him.

> {KAIA *goes out again to the left.* SOLNESS *remains
> seated, turning over the drawings.*

MRS. SOLNESS *(over beside the plants).*   I wonder if he
isn't going to die now, as well?

SOLNESS *(looks up to her).*   As well as who?

MRS. SOLNESS *(without answering).*   Yes, yes—depend
upon it, Halvard, old Brovik is going to die, too. You'll see
that he will.

SOLNESS.   My dear Aline, ought you not to go out
for a little walk?

MRS. SOLNESS.   Yes, I suppose I ought to.

> {She *continues to attend to the flowers.*

SOLNESS *(bending over the drawings).*   Is she still
asleep?

MRS. SOLNESS *(looking at him).*   Is it Miss Wangel
you are sitting there thinking about?

SOLNESS *(indifferently).*   I just happened to recollect
her.

MRS. SOLNESS.   Miss Wangel was up long ago.

SOLNESS.   Oh, was she?

MRS. SOLNESS.   When I went in to see her, she was
busy putting her things in order.

{She goes in front of the mirror and slowly begins to put on her hat.

SOLNESS *(after a short pause).* So we have found a use for one of our nurseries after all, Aline.

MRS. SOLNESS. Yes, we have.

SOLNESS. That seems to me better than to have them all standing empty.

MRS. SOLNESS. That emptiness is dreadful; you are right there.

SOLNESS *(closes the portfolio, rises and approaches her).* You will find that we shall get on far better after this, Aline. Things will be more comfortable. Life will be easier—especially for you.

MRS. SOLNESS *(looks at him).* After this?

SOLNESS. Yes, believe me, Aline——

MRS. SOLNESS. Do you mean—because she has come here?

SOLNESS *(checking himself).* I mean, of course—when once we have moved into the new house.

MRS. SOLNESS *(takes her cloak).* Ah, do you think so, Halvard? Will it be better then?

SOLNESS. I can't think otherwise. And surely you think so, too?

MRS. SOLNESS. I think nothing at all about the new house.

SOLNESS *(cast down).* It's hard for me to hear you say that; for you know it is mainly for your sake that I have built it.

{He offers to help her on with her cloak.

MRS. SOLNESS *(evades him).* The fact is, you do far too much for my sake.

SOLNESS *(with a certain vehemence).* No, no, you really

mustn't say that, Aline! I cannot bear to hear you say such things!

MRS. SOLNESS.   Very well, then I won't say it, Halvard.

SOLNESS.   But I stick to what *I* said. You'll see that things will be easier for you in the new place.

MRS. SOLNESS.   O heavens—easier for me——!

SOLNESS (*eagerly*).   Yes, indeed they will! You may be quite sure of that! For you see—there will be so very, very much there that will remind you of your own home——

MRS. SOLNESS.   The home that used to be father's and mother's—and that was burnt to the ground——

SOLNESS (*in a low voice*).   Yes, yes, my poor Aline. That was a terrible blow for you.

MRS. SOLNESS (*breaking out in lamentation*).   You may build as much as ever you like, Halvard—you can never build up again a real home for me!

SOLNESS (*crosses the room*).   Well, in heaven's name, let us talk no more about it, then.

MRS. SOLNESS.   Oh, yes, Halvard, I understand you very well. You are so anxious to spare me—and to find excuses for me, too—as much as ever you can.

SOLNESS (*with astonishment in his eyes*).   *You!* Is it you—yourself, that you are talking about, Aline?

MRS. SOLNESS.   Yes, who else should it be but myself?

SOLNESS (*involuntarily to himself*).   That, too!

MRS. SOLNESS.   As for the old house, I wouldn't mind so much about that. When once misfortune was in the air—why——

SOLNESS.   Ah, you are right there. Misfortune will have its way—as the saying goes.

MRS. SOLNESS.   But it's what came of the fire—the dreadful thing that followed——! That is the thing! That, that, that!

SOLNESS (*vehemently*).   Don't think about that, Aline!

MRS. SOLNESS.   Ah, that is exactly what I cannot help thinking about. And now, I must speak about it, too; for I don't seem able to bear it any longer. And then never to be able to forgive myself——

SOLNESS (*exclaiming*).   Yourself——!

MRS. SOLNESS.   Yes, for I had duties on both sides—both towards you and towards the little ones. I ought to have hardened myself—not to have let the horror take such hold upon me—nor the grief for the burning of my old home. (*Wrings her hands.*) Oh, Halvard, if I had only had the strength!

SOLNESS (*softly, much moved, comes closer*).   Aline—you must promise me never to think these thoughts any more.—Promise me that, dear!

MRS. SOLNESS.   Oh, promise, promise! One can promise anything.

SOLNESS (*clenches his hands and crosses the room*).   Oh, but this is hopeless, hopeless! Never a ray of sunlight! Not so much as a gleam of brightness to light up our home!

SOLNESS.   This is no home, Halvard.

SOLNESS.   Oh no, you may well say that. (*Gloomily.*)And God knows whether you are not right in saying that it will be no better for us in the new house, either.

MRS. SOLNESS.   It will never be any better. Just as empty—just as desolate—there as here.

SOLNESS (*vehemently*).   Why in all the world have we built it then? Can you tell me that?

MRS. SOLNESS.   No; you must answer that question for yourself.

SOLNESS (*glances suspiciously at her*).   What do you mean by that, Aline?

MRS. SOLNESS.   What do I mean?

SOLNESS.   Yes, in the devil's name! You said it so strangely—as if you had hidden some meaning in it.

MRS. SOLNESS.   No, indeed, I assure you——

SOLNESS (*comes closer*).   Oh, come now—I know what I know. I have both my eyes and my ears about me, Aline—you may depend upon that!

MRS. SOLNESS.   Why, what are you talking about? What is it?

SOLNESS (*places himself in front of her*).   Do you mean to say you don't find a kind of lurking, hidden meaning in the most innocent word I happen to say?

MRS. SOLNESS.   I, do you say? I do that?

SOLNESS (*laughs*).   Ho-ho-ho! It's natural enough, Aline! When you have a sick man on your hands——

MRS. SOLNESS (*anxiously*).   Sick? Are you ill, Halvard?

SOLNESS (*violently*).   A half-mad man then! A crazy man! Call me what you will.

MRS. SOLNESS (*feels blindly for a chair and sits down*). Halvard—for God's sake——

SOLNESS.   But you are wrong, both you and the doctor. I am not in the state you imagine.

> {He walks up and down the room. MRS. SOLNESS
> follows him anxiously with her eyes. Finally he goes up
> to her.

SOLNESS (*calmly*).   In reality there is nothing whatever the matter with me.

MRS. SOLNESS.   No, there isn't, is there? But then what is it that troubles you so?

SOLNESS.   Why this, that I often feel ready to sink under this terrible burden of debt——

MRS. SOLNESS.   Debt, do you say? But you owe no one anything, Halvard!

SOLNESS (*softly, with emotion*).   I owe a boundless debt to you—to you—to you, Aline.

MRS. SOLNESS (*rises slowly*).   What is behind all this? You may just as well tell me at once.

SOLNESS.   But there is nothing behind it; I have never done you any wrong—not wittingly and wilfully, at any rate. And yet—and yet it seems as though a crushing debt rested upon me and weighed me down.

MRS. SOLNESS.   A debt to me?

SOLNESS.   Chiefly to you.

MRS. SOLNESS.   Then you are—ill after all, Halvard.

SOLNESS (*gloomily*).   I suppose I must be—or not far from it. (*Looks towards the door to the right, which is opened at this moment.*) Ah! now it grows lighter.

> {HILDA WANGEL *comes in. She has made some alteration in her dress and let down her skirt.*

HILDA.   Good morning, Mr. Solness!

SOLNESS (*nods*).   Slept well?

HILDA.   Quite deliciously! Like a child in a cradle. Oh—I lay and stretched myself like—like a princess!

SOLNESS (*smiles a little*).   You were thoroughly comfortable then?

HILDA.   I should think so.

SOLNESS.   And no doubt you dreamed, too.

HILDA.   Yes, I did. But that was horrid.

SOLNESS.   Was it?

HILDA.   Yes, for I dreamed I was falling over a frightfully high, sheer precipice. Do you never have that kind of dream?

SOLNESS.　Oh yes—now and then——

HILDA.　It's tremendously thrilling—when you fall and fall——

SOLNESS.　It seems to make one's blood run cold.

HILDA.　Do you draw your legs up under you while you are falling?

SOLNESS.　Yes, as high as ever I can.

HILDA.　So do I.

MRS. SOLNESS (*takes her parasol*).　I must go into town now, Halvard. (*To* HILDA.) And I'll try to get one or two things that you may require.

HILDA (*making a motion to throw her arms round her neck*).　Oh, you dear, sweet Mrs. Solness! You are really much too kind to me! Frightfully kind——

MRS. SOLNESS (*deprecatingly, freeing herself*).　Oh, not at all. It's only my duty, so I am very glad to do it.

HILDA (*offended, pouts*).　But really, I think I am quite fit to be seen in the streets—now that I've put my dress to rights. Or do you think I am not?

MRS. SOLNESS.　To tell you the truth, I think people would stare at you a little.

HILDA (*contemptuously*).　Pooh! Is that all? That only amuses me.

SOLNESS (*with suppressed ill-humour*).　Yes, but people might take it into their heads that you were mad, too, you see.

HILDA.　Mad? Are there so many mad people here in town, then?

SOLNESS (*points to his own forehead*).　Here you see one, at all events.

HILDA.　You—Mr. Solness!

MRS. SOLNESS.　Oh, don't talk like that, my dear Halvard!

SOLNESS.   Have you not noticed that yet?

HILDA.   No, I certainly have not. *(Reflects and laughs a little.)* And yet—perhaps in one single thing.

SOLNESS.   Ah, do you hear that, Aline?

MRS. SOLNESS.   What is that one single thing, Miss Wangel?

HILDA.   No, I won't say.

SOLNESS.   Oh, yes, do!

HILDA.   No, thank you—I am not so mad as that.

MRS. SOLNESS.   When you and Miss Wangel are alone, I daresay she will tell you, Halvard.

SOLNESS.   Ah—you think she will?

MRS. SOLNESS.   Oh, yes, certainly. For you have known her so well in the past. Ever since she was a child— you tell me.

> *{She goes out by the door on the left.*

HILDA *(after a little while).*   Does your wife dislike me very much?

SOLNESS.   Did you think you noticed anything of the kind?

HILDA.   Did you not notice it yourself?

SOLNESS *(evasively).*   Aline has become exceedingly shy with strangers of late years.

HILDA.   Has she really?

SOLNESS.   But if only you could get to know her thoroughly——! Ah! she is so good—so kind—so excellent a creature——

HILDA *(impatiently).*   But if she is all that—what made her say about her duty?

SOLNESS.   Her duty?

HILDA.   She said that she would go out and buy something for me, because it was her duty. Oh, I can't bear that ugly, horrid word!

SOLNESS.   Why not?

HILDA.   It sounds so cold and sharp and stinging. Duty—duty—duty. Don't you think so, too? Doesn't it seem to sting you?

SOLNESS.   H'm—haven't thought much about it.

HILDA.   Yes, it does. And if she is so good—as you say she is—why should she talk in that way?

SOLNESS.   But, good Lord, what would you have had her say, then?

HILDA.   She might have said she would do it because she had taken a tremendous fancy to me. She might have said something like that—something really warm and cordial, you understand.

SOLNESS (*looks at her*).   Is that how you would like to have it?

HILDA.   Yes, precisely. (*She wanders about the room, stops at the bookcase and looks at the books.*) What a lot of books you have.

SOLNESS.   Yes, I have got together a good many.

HILDA.   Do you read them all, too?

SOLNESS.   I used to try to. Do you read much?

HILDA.   No, never! I have given it up. For it all seems so irrelevant.

SOLNESS.   That is just my feeling.

      {HILDA *wanders about a little, stops at the small table, opens the portfolio and turns over the contents.*

HILDA.   Are all these drawings yours?

SOLNESS.   No, they are drawn by a young man whom I employ to help me.

HILDA.   Some one you have taught?

SOLNESS.   Oh, yes, no doubt he has learnt something from one, too.

HILDA (*sits down*).   Then I suppose he is very clever. (*Looks at a drawing.*) Isn't he?

SOLNESS.   Oh, he might be worse. For my purpose——

HILDA.   Oh, yes—I'm sure he is frightfully clever.

SOLNESS.   Do you think you can see that in the drawings?

HILDA.   Pooh—these scrawlings! But if he has been learning from you——

SOLNESS.   Oh, so far as that goes—there are plenty of people that have learnt from me and have come to little enough for all that.

HILDA (*looks at him and shakes her head*).   No, I can't for the life of me understand how you can be so stupid.

SOLNESS.   Stupid? Do you think I am so very stupid?

HILDA.   Yes, I do indeed. If you are content to go about here teaching all these people——

SOLNESS (*with a slight start*).   Well, and why not?

HILDA (*rises, half serious, half laughing*).   No indeed, Mr. Solness! What can be the good of that? No one but you should be allowed to build. You should stand quite alone— do it all yourself. Now you know it.

SOLNESS (*involuntarily*).   Hilda——!

HILDA.   Well!

SOLNESS.   How in the world did that come into your head?

HILDA.   Do you think I am so very far wrong, then?

SOLNESS.   No, that's not what I mean. But now I'll tell you something.

HILDA.   Well?

SOLNESS.   I keep on—incessantly—in silence and alone—brooding on that very thought.

HILDA.   Yes, that seems to me perfectly natural.

SOLNESS (*looks somewhat searchingly at her*).   Perhaps you have noticed it already?

HILDA.   No, indeed I haven't.

SOLNESS.   But just now—when you said you thought I was—off my balance? In one thing, you said——

HILDA.   Oh, I was thinking of something quite different.

SOLNESS.   What was it?

HILDA.   I am not going to tell you.

SOLNESS (*crosses the room*).   Well, well—as you please. (*Stops at the bow-window.*) Come here, and I will show you something.

HILDA (*approaching*).   What is it?

SOLNESS.   Do you see—over there in the garden——?

HILDA.   Yes?

SOLNESS (*points*).   Right above the great quarry——?

HILDA.   That new house, you mean?

SOLNESS.   The one that is being built, yes. Almost finished.

HILDA.   It seems to have a very high tower.

SOLNESS.   The scaffolding is still up.

HILDA.   Is that your new house?

SOLNESS.   Yes.

HILDA.   The house you are soon going to move into?

SOLNESS.   Yes.

HILDA (*looks at him*).   Are there nurseries in that house, too?

SOLNESS.   Three, as there are here.

HILDA.   And no child,

SOLNESS.   And there never will be one.

HILDA (*with a half-smile*).   Well, isn't it just as I said——?

SOLNESS.   That——?

HILDA.   That you are a little—a little mad after all.

SOLNESS.   Was that what you were thinking of?

HILDA.   Yes, of all the empty nurseries I slept in.

SOLNESS (*lowers his voice*).   We have had children— Aline and I.

HILDA (*looks eagerly at him*).   Have you——?

SOLNESS.   Two little boys. They were of the same age.

HILDA.   Twins, then.

SOLNESS.   Yes, twins. It's eleven or twelve years ago now.

HILDA (*cautiously*).   And so both of them——? You have lost both the twins, then?

SOLNESS (*with quiet emotion*).   We kept them only about three weeks. Or scarcely so much. (*Bursts forth.*) Oh, Hilda, I can't tell you what a good thing it is for me that you have come! For now at last I have some one I can talk to!

HILDA.   Can you not talk to—her, too?

SOLNESS.   Not about this. Not as I want to talk and must talk. (*Gloomily.*) And not about so many other things, either.

HILDA (*in a subdued voice*).   Was that all you meant when you said you needed me?

SOLNESS.   That was mainly what I meant—at all events, yesterday. For to-day I am not so sure——(*Breaking off.*) Come here and let us sit down, Hilda. Sit there on the sofa—so that you can look into the garden. (HILDA *seats herself in the corner of the sofa.* SOLNESS *brings a chair closer.*) Should you like to hear about it?

HILDA.   Yes, I shall love to sit and listen to you.

SOLNESS (*sits down*).   Then I will tell you all about it.

HILDA.   Now I can see both the garden and you, Mr. Solness. So now, tell away! Begin!

SOLNESS (*points towards the bow-window*).   Out there on the rising ground—where you see the new house——

HILDA.   Yes?

SOLNESS.   Aline and I lived there in the first years of our married life. There was an old house up there that had belonged to her mother; and we inherited it, and the whole of the great garden with it.

HILDA.   Was there a tower on that house, too?

SOLNESS.   No, nothing of the kind. From the outside it looked like a great, dark, ugly wooden box; but all the same, it was snug and comfortable enough inside.

HILDA.   Then did you pull down the ramshackle old place?

SOLNESS.   No, it burnt down.

HILDA.   The whole of it?

SOLNESS.   Yes.

HILDA.   Was that a great misfortune for you?

SOLNESS.   That depends on how you look at it. As a builder, the fire was the making of me——

HILDA.   Well, but——?

SOLNESS.   It was just after the birth of the two little boys——

HILDA.   The poor little twins, yes.

SOLNESS.   They came healthy and bonny into the world. And they were growing too—you could see the difference from day to day.

HILDA.   Little children do grow quickly at first.

SOLNESS.   It was the prettiest sight in the world to

see Aline lying with the two of them in her arms.—But then came the night of the fire——

HILDA (*excitedly*).   What happened? Do tell me! Was any one burnt?

SOLNESS.   No, not that. Every one got safe and sound out of the house——

HILDA.   Well, and what then——?

SOLNESS.   The fright had shaken Aline terribly. The alarm—the escape—the break-neck hurry——and then the ice-cold night air—for they had to be carried out just as they lay—both she and the little ones.

HILDA.   Was it too much for them?

SOLNESS.   Oh no, they stood it well enough. But Aline fell into a fever, and it affected her milk. She would insist on nursing them herself; because it was her duty, she said. And both our little boys, they—(*clenching his hands.*)—they—oh!

HILDA.   They did not get over that?

SOLNESS.   No, that they did not get over. That was how we lost them.

HILDA.   It must have been terribly hard for you.

SOLNESS.   Hard enough for me; but ten times harder for Aline. (*Clenching his hands in suppressed fury.*) Oh, that such things should be allowed to happen here in the world! (*Shortly and firmly.*) From the day I lost them, I had no heart for building churches.

HILDA.   Did you not like the church-tower in our town?

SOLNESS.   I didn't like it. I know how free and happy I felt when the tower was finished.

HILDA.   *I* know that, too.

SOLNESS.   And now I shall never—never build anything of that sort again! Neither churches nor church-towers.

HILDA (*nods slowly*).   Nothing but houses for people to live in.

SOLNESS.   Homes for human beings, Hilda.

HILDA.   But homes with high towers and pinnacles upon them.

SOLNESS.   If possible. (*Adopts a lighter tone.*) But, as I said before, that fire was the making of me—as a builder, I mean.

HILDA.   Why don't you call yourself an architect, like the others?

SOLNESS.   I have not been systematically enough taught for that. Most of what I know, I have found out for myself.

HILDA.   But you succeeded all the same.

SOLNESS.   Yes, thanks to the fire. I laid out almost the whole of the garden in villa lots; and there I was able to build after my own heart. So I came to the front with a rush.

HILDA (*looks keenly at him*).   You must surely be a very happy man, as matters stand with you.

SOLNESS (*gloomily*).   Happy? Do you say that, too—like all the rest of them?

HILDA.   Yes, I should say you must be. If you could only cease thinking about the two little children——

SOLNESS (*slowly*).   The two little children—they are not so easy to forget, Hilda.

HILDA (*somewhat uncertainly*).   Do you still feel their loss so much—after all these years?

SOLNESS (*looks fixedly at her, without replying*).   A happy man you said——

HILDA.   Well, now, are you not happy—in other respects?

SOLNESS (*continues to look at her*). When I told you all this about the fire—h'm——

HILDA. Well?

SOLNESS. Was there not one special thought that you—that you seized upon?

HILDA (*reflects in vain*). No. What thought should that be?

SOLNESS (*with subdued emphasis*). It was simply and solely by that fire that I was enabled to build homes for human beings. Cosy, comfortable, bright homes, where father and mother and the whole troop of children can live in safety and gladness, feeling what a happy thing it is to be alive in the world—and most of all to belong to each other—in great things and in small.

HILDA (*ardently*). Well, and is it not a great happiness for you to be able to build such beautiful homes?

SOLNESS. The price, Hilda! The terrible price I had to pay for the opportunity!

HILDA. But can you never get over that?

SOLNESS. No. That I might build homes for others, I had to forego—to forego for all time—the home that might have been my own. I mean a home for a troop of children—and for father and mother, too.

HILDA (*cautiously*). But need you have done that? For all time, you say?

SOLNESS (*nods slowly*). That was the price of this happiness that people talk about. (*Breathes heavily.*) This happiness—h'm—this happiness was not to be bought any cheaper, Hilda.

HILDA (*as before*). But may it not come right even yet?

SOLNESS. Never in this world—never. That is another consequence of the fire—and of Aline's illness afterwards.

HILDA *(looks at him with an indefinable expression).* And yet you build all these nurseries?

SOLNESS *(seriously).* Have you never noticed, Hilda, how the impossible—how it seems to beckon and cry aloud to one?

HILDA *(reflecting).* The impossible? *(With animation.)* Yes, indeed! Is that how you feel too?

SOLNESS. Yes, I do.

HILDA. There must be—a little of the troll in you, too.

SOLNESS. Why of the troll?

HILDA. What would you call it, then?

SOLNESS *(rises).* Well, well, perhaps you are right. *(Vehemently.)* But how can I help turning into a troll, when this is how it always goes with me in everything—in everything!

HILDA. How do you mean?

SOLNESS *(speaking low, with inward emotion).* Mark what I say to you, Hilda. All that I have succeeded in doing, building, creating—all the beauty, security, cheerful comfort—ay, and magnificence, too—*(Clenches his hands.)* Oh, is it not terrible even to think of——!

HILDA. What is so terrible?

SOLNESS. That all this I have to make up for, to pay for—not in money, but in human happiness. And not with my own happiness only, but with other people's, too. Yes, yes, do you see that, Hilda? That is the price which my position as an artist has cost me—and others. And every single day I have to look on while the price is paid for me anew. Over again, and over again—and over again for ever!

HILDA (*rises and looks steadily at him*).   Now I can see that you are thinking of—of her.

SOLNESS.   Yes, mainly of Aline. For Aline—she, too, had her vocation in life, just as much as I had mine. (*His voice quivers.*) But her vocation has had to be stunted, and crushed and shattered—in order that mine might force its way to—to a sort of great victory. For you must know that Aline—she, too, had a talent for building.

HILDA.   She! For building?

SOLNESS (*shakes his head*).   Not houses and towers, and spires—not such things as I work away at——

HILDA.   Well, but what then?

SOLNESS (*softly, with emotion*).   For building up the souls of little children, Hilda. For building up children's souls in perfect balance, and in noble and beautiful forms. For enabling them to soar up into erect and full-grown human souls. That was Aline's talent. And there it all lies now——unused and unusable for ever—of no earthly service to any one—just like the ruins left by a fire.

HILDA.   Yes, but even if this were so——?

SOLNESS.   It is so! It is so! I know it!

HILDA.   Well, but in any case it is not your fault.

SOLNESS (*fixes his eyes on her and nods slowly*).   Ah, that is the great, terrible question. That is the doubt that is gnawing me—night and day.

HILDA.   That?

SOLNESS.   Yes. Suppose the fault was mine—in a certain sense.

HILDA.   Your fault! The fire!

SOLNESS.   All of it; the whole thing. And yet, per-haps—I may not have had anything to do with it.

HILDA (*looks at him with a troubled expression*).   Oh, Mr.

Solness—if you can talk like that, I am afraid you must be—ill, after all.

SOLNESS. H'm—I don't think I shall ever be of quite sound mind on that point.

{RAGNAR BROVIK *cautiously opens the little door in the left-hand corners.* HILDA *comes forward.*

RAGNAR *(when he sees* HILDA*).* Oh. I beg pardon, Mr. Solness—

{*He makes a movement to withdraw.*

SOLNESS. No, no, don't go. Let us get it over.

RAGNAR. Oh, yes—if only we could.

SOLNESS. I hear your father is no better?

RAGNAR. Father is fast growing weaker—and therefore I beg and implore you to write a few kind words for me on one of the plans! Something for father to read before he——

SOLNESS *(vehemently).* I won't hear anything more about those drawings of yours!

RAGNAR. Have you looked at them?

SOLNESS. Yes—I have.

RAGNAR. And they are good for nothing? And *I* am good for nothing, too?

SOLNESS *(evasively).* Stay here with me, Ragnar. You shall have everything your own way. And then you can marry Kaia and live at your ease—and happily, too, who knows? Only don't think of building on your own account.

RAGNAR. Well, well, then I must go home and tell father what you say—I promised I would.—Is this what I am to tell father—before he dies?

SOLNESS *(with a groan).* Oh tell him—tell him what you will, for me. Best to say nothing at all to him! *(With a sudden outburst.)* I cannot do anything else, Ragnar!

RAGNAR.   May I have the drawings to take with me?

SOLNESS.   Yes, take them—take them by all means! They are lying there on the table.

RAGNAR (*goes to the table*).   Thanks.

HILDA (*puts her hand on the portfolio*).   No, no; leave them here.

SOLNESS.   Why?

HILDA.   Because I want to look at them, too.

SOLNESS.   But you have been—— (*To* RAGNAR). Well, leave them here, then.

RAGNAR.   Very well.

SOLNESS.   And go home at once to your father.

RAGNAR.   Yes. I suppose I must.

SOLNESS (*as if in desperation*).   Ragnar—you must not ask me to do what is beyond my power! Do you hear, Ragnar? You must not!

RAGNAR.   No, no. I beg your pardon——

> {*He bows and goes out by the corner door.* HILDA *goes over and sits down on a chair near the mirror.*

HILDA (*looks angrily at* SOLNESS).   That was a very ugly thing to do.

SOLNESS.   Do you think so, too?

HILDA.   Yes, it was horribly ugly—and hard and bad and cruel as well.

SOLNESS.   Oh, you don't understand my position.

HILDA.   No matter——. I say you ought not to be like that.

SOLNESS.   You said yourself, only just now, that no one but *I* ought to be allowed to build.

HILDA.   *I* may say such things—but you must not.

SOLNESS.   I most of all, surely, who have paid so dear for my position.

HILDA.   Oh yes—with what you call domestic comfort—and that sort of thing.

SOLNESS.   And with my peace of soul into the bargain.

HILDA *(rising).*   Peace of soul! *(With feeling.)* Yes, yes, you are right in that! Poor Mr. Solness—you fancy that——

SOLNESS *(with a quiet, chuckling laugh).*   Just sit down again, Hilda, and I'll tell you something funny.

HILDA *(sits down; with intent interest).*   Well?

SOLNESS.   It sounds such a ludicrous little thing; for, you see, the whole story turns upon nothing but a crack in a chimney.

HILDA.   No more than that?

SOLNESS.   No, not to begin with.

(He moves a chair nearer to HILDA and sits down.

HILDA *(impatiently, taps on her knee).*   Well, now for the crack in the chimney!

SOLNESS.   I had noticed the split in the flue long, long before the fire. Every time I went up into the attic, I looked to see if it was still there.

HILDA.   And it was?

SOLNESS.   Yes; for no one else knew about it.

HILDA.   And you said nothing?

SOLNESS.   Nothing.

HILDA.   And did not think of repairing the flue either?

SOLNESS.   Oh, yes, I thought about it—but never got any further. Every time I intended to set to work, it seemed just as if a hand held me back. Not to-day, I thought—to-morrow; and nothing ever came of it.

HILDA.   But why did you keep putting it off like that?

SOLNESS.   Because I was revolving something in my mind. *(Slowly, and in a low voice.)* Through that little black crack in the chimney, I might, perhaps, force my way upwards—as a builder.

HILDA (*looking straight in front of her*).   That must have
been thrilling.

SOLNESS.   Almost irresistible—quite irresistible. For
at that time it appeared to me a perfectly simple and
straightforward matter. I would have had it happen in the
wintertime—a little before midday. I was to be out driving
Aline in the sleigh. The servants at home would have made
huge fires in the stoves.

HILDA.   For, of course, it was to be bitterly cold that
day?

SOLNESS.   Rather biting, yes—and they would want
Aline to find it thoroughly snug and warm when she came
home.

HILDA.   I suppose she is very chilly by nature?

SOLNESS.   She is. And as we drove home, we were to
see the smoke.

HILDA.   Only the smoke?

SOLNESS.   The smoke first. But when we came up to
the garden gate, the whole of the old timber-box was to be
a rolling mass of flames.—That is how I wanted it to be,
you see.

HILDA.   Oh why, why could it not have happened
so!

SOLNESS.   You may well say that, Hilda.

HILDA.   Well, but now listen, Mr. Solness. Are you
perfectly certain that the fire was caused by that little crack
in the chimney?

SOLNESS.   No, on the contrary—I am perfectly certain that the crack in the chimney had nothing whatever to
do with the fire.

HILDA.   What?

SOLNESS.   It has been clearly ascertained that the fire

broke out in a clothes-cupboard—in a totally different part
of the house.

HILDA.   Then what is all this nonsense you are talking about the crack in the chimney?

SOLNESS.   May I go on talking to you a little, Hilda?

HILDA.   Yes, if you'll only talk sensibly——

SOLNESS.   I will try.

(He moves his chair nearer.

HILDA.   Out with it, then, Mr. Solness.

SOLNESS *(confidentially).*   Don't you agree with me,
Hilda, that there exist special, chosen people who have been
endowed with the power and faculty of desiring a thing,
craving for a thing, willing a thing—so persistently and
so—so inexorably—that at last it has to happen? Don't you
believe that?

HILDA *(with an indefinable expression in her eyes).*   If that
is so, we shall see, one of these days, whether *I* am one of
the chosen.

SOLNESS.   It is not one's self alone that can do such
great things. Oh, no—the helpers and the servers—they
must do their part, too, if it is to be of any good. But they
never come of themselves. One has to call upon them very
persistently—inwardly, you understand.

HILDA.   What are these helpers and servers?

SOLNESS.   Oh, we can talk about that some other
time. For the present, let us keep to this business of the fire.

HILDA.   Don't you think that fire would have happened all the same—even without your wishing for it?

SOLNESS.   If the house had been old Knut Brovik's,
it would never have burnt down so conveniently for him. I
am sure of that; for he does not know how to call for the
helpers—no, nor for the servers, either. *(Rises in unrest.)* So

you see, Hilda—it is my fault, after all, that the lives of the two little boys had to be sacrificed. And do you think it is not my fault, too, that Aline has never been the woman she should and might have been—and that she most longed to be?

HILDA.   Yes, but if it is all the work of those helpers and servers——?

SOLNESS.   Who called for the helpers and servers? It was I! And they came and obeyed my will. (*In increasing excitement.*) That is what people call having the luck on your side; but I must tell you what this sort of luck feels like! It feels like a great raw place here on my breast. And the helpers and servers keep on flaying pieces of skin off other people in order to close my sore!—But still the sore is not healed—never, never! Oh, if you knew how it can sometimes gnaw and burn.

HILDA (*looks attentively at him*).   You are ill, Mr. Solness. Very ill, I almost think.

SOLNESS.   Say mad; for that is what you mean.

HILDA.   No, I don't think there is much amiss with your intellect.

SOLNESS.   With what then? Out with it!

HILDA.   I wonder whether you were not sent into the world with a sickly conscience.

SOLNESS.   A sickly conscience? What devilry is that?

HILDA.   I mean that your conscience is feeble—too delicately built, as it were—hasn't strength to take a grip of things—to lift and bear what is heavy.

SOLNESS (*growls*).   H'm! May I ask, then, what sort of conscience one ought to have?

HILDA.   I should like your conscience to be—to be thoroughly robust.

SOLNESS. Indeed? Robust, eh? Is your own conscience robust, may I ask?

HILDA. Yes, I think it is. I have never noticed that it wasn't.

SOLNESS. It has not been put very severely to the test, I should think.

HILDA (*with a quivering of the lips*). Oh, it was no such simple matter to leave father—I am so awfully fond of him.

SOLNESS. Dear me! for a month or two——

HILDA. I think I shall never go home again.

SOLNESS. Never? Then why did you leave him?

HILDA (*half-seriously, half-banteringly*). Have you forgotten that the ten years are up?

SOLNESS. Oh nonsense. Was anything wrong at home? Eh?

HILDA (*quite seriously*). It was this impulse within me that urged and goaded me to come—and lured and drew me on, as well.

SOLNESS (*eagerly*). There we have it! There we have it, Hilda! There is a troll in you, too, as in me. For it's the troll in one, you see—it is that that calls to the powers outside us. And then you must give in—whether you will or no.

HILDA. I almost think you are right, Mr. Solness.

SOLNESS (*walks about the room*). Oh, there are devils innumerable abroad in the world, Hilda, that one never sees!

HILDA. Devils, too?

SOLNESS (*stops*). Good devils and bad devils; light-haired devils and black-haired devils. If only you could always tell whether it is the light or dark ones that have got hold of you! (*Paces about.*) Ho-ho! Then it would be simple enough.

HILDA (*follows him with her eyes*).   Or if one had a really vigorous, radiantly healthy conscience—so that one dared to do what one would.

SOLNESS (*stops beside the console table*).   I believe, now, that most people are just as puny creatures as I am in that respect.

HILDA.   I shouldn't wonder.

SOLNESS (*leaning against the table*).   In the sagas—— Have you read any of the old sagas?

HILDA.   Oh, yes! When I used to read books, I——

SOLNESS.   In the sagas you read about vikings, who sailed to foreign lands, and plundered and burned and killed men——

HILDA.   And carried off women——

SOLNESS.   ——and kept them in captivity——

HILDA.   ——took them home in their ships——

SOLNESS.   ——and behaved to them like—like the very worst of trolls.

HILDA (*looks straight before her, with a half-veiled look*).   I think that must have been thrilling.

SOLNESS (*with a short, deep laugh*).   To carry off women.

HILDA.   To be carried off.

SOLNESS (*looks at her a moment*).   Oh, indeed.

HILDA (*as if breaking the thread of the conversation*).   But what made you speak of these vikings, Mr. Solness?

SOLNESS.   Why, those fellows must have had robust consciences, if you like! When they got home again, they could eat, and drink and be as happy as children. And the women, too! They often would not leave them on any account. Can you understand that, Hilda?

HILDA.   Those women I can understand exceedingly well.

SOLNESS.   Oho! Perhaps you could do the same yourself?

HILDA.   Why not?

SOLNESS.   Live—of your own free will—with a ruffian like that?

HILDA.   If it was a ruffian I had come to love——

SOLNESS.   Could you come to love a man like that?

HILDA.   Good heavens, you know very well one can't choose whom one is going to love.

SOLNESS *(looks meditatively at her).*   Oh, no, I suppose it is the troll within one that's responsible for that.

HILDA *(half-laughing).*   And all those blessed devils, that you know so well—both the light-haired and the dark-haired ones.

SOLNESS *(quietly and warmly).*   Then I hope with all my heart that the devils will choose carefully for you, Hilda.

HILDA.   For me they have chosen already—once and for all.

SOLNESS *(looks earnestly at her).*   Hilda—you are like a wild bird of the woods.

HILDA.   Far from it. I don't hide myself away under the bushes.

SOLNESS.   No, no. There is rather something of the bird of prey in you.

HILDA.   That is nearer it—perhaps. *(Very earnestly.)* And why not a bird of prey? Why should not *I* go a-hunting—I, as well as the rest. Carry off the prey I want—if only I can get my claws into it and do with it as I will.

SOLNESS.   Hilda—do you know what you are?

HILDA.   Yes, I suppose I am a strange sort of bird.

SOLNESS.   No. You are like a dawning day. When I look at you—I seem to be looking towards the sunrise.

HILDA.   Tell me, Mr. Solness—are you certain that you have never called me to you? Inwardly, you know?

SOLNESS *(softly and slowly).*   I almost think I must have.

HILDA.   What did you want with me?

SOLNESS.   You are the younger generation, Hilda.

HILDA *(smiles).*   That younger generation that you are so afraid of?

SOLNESS *(nods slowly).*   And which, in my heart, I yearn towards so deeply.

> {HILDA *rises, goes to the little table and fetches* RAG-
> NAR BROVIK'S *portfolio.*

HILDA *(holds out the portfolio to him).*   We were talking about these drawings——

SOLNESS *(shortly, waving them away).*   Put those things away! I have seen enough of them.

HILDA.   Yes, but you have to write your approval on them.

SOLNESS.   Write my approval on them? Never!

HILDA.   But the poor old man is lying at death's door! Can't you give him and his son this pleasure before they are parted? And perhaps he might get the commission to carry them out, too.

SOLNESS.   Yes, that is just what he would get. He has made sure of that—has my fine gentleman!

HILDA.   Then, good heavens—if that is so—can't you tell the least little bit of a lie for once in a way?

SOLNESS.   A lie? *(Raging.)* Hilda—take those devil's drawings out of my sight!

HILDA *(draws the portfolio a little nearer to her-self).*   Well, well, well—don't bite me.—You talk of trolls—but I think you go on like a troll yourself. *(Looks around.)* Where do you keep your pen and ink?

SOLNESS.   There is nothing of the sort in here.

HILDA (*goes towards the door*).   But in the office where that young lady is——

SOLNESS.   Stay where you are, Hilda!—I ought to tell a lie, you say. Oh, yes, for the sake of his old father I might well do that—for in my time I have crushed him, trodden him under foot——

HILDA.   Him, too?

SOLNESS.   I needed room for myself. But this Ragnar—he must on no account be allowed to come to the front.

HILDA.   Poor fellow, there is surely no fear of that. If he has nothing in him——

SOLNESS (*comes closer, looks at her and whispers*).   If Ragnar Brovik gets his chance, he will strike me to the earth. Crush me—as I crushed his father.

HILDA.   Crush you? Has he the ability for that?

SOLNESS.   Yes, you may depend upon it he has the ability! He is the younger generation that stands ready to knock at my door—to make an end of Halvard Solness.

HILDA (*looks at him with quiet reproach*).   And yet you would bar him out. Fie, Mr. Solness!

SOLNESS.   The fight I have been fighting has cost heart's blood enough.—And I am afraid, too, that the helpers and servers will not obey me any longer.

HILDA.   Then you must go ahead without them. There is nothing else for it.

SOLNESS.   It is hopeless, Hilda. The luck is bound to turn. A little sooner or a little later. Retribution is inexorable.

HILDA (*in distress, putting her hands over her ears*).   Don't talk like that! Do you want to kill me? To take from me what is more than my life?

SOLNESS.   And what is that?

HILDA. The longing to see you great. To see you, with a wreath in your hand, high, high up upon a church-tower. (*Calm again.*) Come, out with your pencil now. You must have a pencil about you?

SOLNESS (*takes out his pocket-book*). I have one here.

HILDA (*lays the portfolio on the sofa-table*). Very well. Now let us two sit down here, Mr. Solness. (SOLNESS *seats himself at the table.* HILDA *stands behind him, leaning over the back of the chair.*) And now we will write on the drawings. We must write very, very nicely and cordially—for this horrid Ruar—or whatever his name is.

SOLNESS (*writes a few words, turns his head and looks at her*). Tell me one thing, Hilda.

HILDA. Yes!

SOLNESS.. If you have been waiting for me all these ten years——

HILDA. What then?

SOLNESS. Why have you never written to me? Then I could have answered you.

HILDA (*hastily*). No, no, no! That was just what I did not want.

SOLNESS. Why not?

HILDA. I was afraid the whole thing might fall to pieces.—But we were going to write on the drawings, Mr. Solness.

SOLNESS. So we were.

HILDA (*bends forward and looks over his shoulder while he writes*). Mind now, kindly and cordially! Oh how I hate—how I hate this Ruald——

SOLNESS (*writing*). Have you never really cared for any one, Hilda?

HILDA (*harshly*). What do you say?

SOLNESS. Have you never cared for any one?

HILDA. For any one else, I suppose you mean?

SOLNESS (*looks up at her*). For any one else, yes. Have you never? In all these ten years? Never?

HILDA. Oh, yes, now and then. When I was perfectly furious with you for not coming.

SOLNESS. Then you did take an interest in other people, too?

HILDA. A little bit—for a week or so. Good heavens, Mr. Solness, you surely know how such things come about.

SOLNESS. Hilda—what is it you have come for?

HILDA. Don't waste time talking. The poor old man might go and die in the meantime.

SOLNESS. Answer me, Hilda. What do you want of me?

HILDA. I want my kingdom.

SOLNESS. H'm——

> {He gives a rapid glance towards the door on the left and then goes on writing on the drawings. At the same moment MRS. SOLNESS enters; she has some packages in her hand.

MRS. SOLNESS. Here are a few things I have got for you, Miss Wangel. The large parcels will be sent later on.

HILDA. Oh, how very, very kind of you!

MRS. SOLNESS. Only my simple duty. Nothing more than that.

SOLNESS (*reading over what he has written*). Aline!

MRS. SOLNESS. Yes?

SOLNESS. Did you notice whether the—the book-keeper was out there?

MRS. SOLNESS. Yes, of course, she was out there.

SOLNESS (*puts the drawings in the portfolio*).   H'm——

MRS. SOLNESS.   She was standing at the desk, as she always is—when *I* go through the room.

SOLNESS (*rises*).   Then I'll give this to her and tell her that——

HILDA (*takes the portfolio from him*).   Oh, no, let me have the pleasure of doing that! (*Goes to the door, but turns.*)   What is her name?

SOLNESS.   Her name is Miss Fosli.

HILDA.   Pooh, that sounds too cold! Her Christian name, I mean?

SOLNESS.   Kaia—I believe.

HILDA (*opens the door and calls out*).   Kaia, come in here! Make haste! Mr. Solness wants to speak to you.

         {KAIA FOSLI *appears at the door.*

KAIA (*looking at him in alarm*).   Here I am——?

HILDA (*handing her the portfolio*).   See here, Kaia! You can take this home; Mr. Solness has written on them now.

KAIA.   Oh, at last!

SOLNESS.   Give them to the old man as soon as you can.

KAIA.   I will go straight home with them.

SOLNESS.   Yes, do. Now Ragnar will have a chance of building for himself.

KAIA.   Oh, may he come and thank you for all——?

SOLNESS (*harshly*).   I won't have any thanks! Tell him that from me.

KAIA.   Yes, I will——

SOLNESS.   And tell him at the same time that henceforward I do not require his services—nor yours either.

KAIA (*softly and quiveringly*).   Not mine either?

SOLNESS.   You will have other things to think of

now and to attend to; and that is a very good thing for you. Well, go home with the drawings now, Miss Fosli. At once! Do you hear?

KAIA *(as before)*.   Yes, Mr. Solness.

{She goes out.

MRS. SOLNESS.   Heavens! what deceitful eyes she has.

SOLNESS.   She? That poor little creature?

MRS. SOLNESS.   Oh——I can see what I can see, Halvard.—— Are you really dismissing them?

SOLNESS.   Yes.

MRS. SOLNESS.   Her as well?

SOLNESS.   Was not that what you wished?

MRS. SOLNESS.   But how can you get on without her——? Oh, well, no doubt you have some one else in reserve, Halvard.

HILDA *(playfully)*.   Well, I for one am not the person to stand at that desk.

SOLNESS.   Never mind, never mind——it will be all right, Aline. Now all you have to do is to think about moving into our new home——as quickly as you can. This evening we will hang up the wreath——*(Turns to Hilda.)*——right on the very pinnacle of the tower. What do you say to that, Miss Hilda?

HILDA *(looks at him with sparkling eyes)*.   It will be splendid to see you so high up once more.

SOLNESS.   Me!

MRS. SOLNESS.   For heaven's sake, Miss Wangel, don't imagine such a thing! My husband!——when he always gets so dizzy!

HILDA.   He get dizzy! No, I know quite well he does not!

MRS. SOLNESS.   Oh, yes, indeed he does.

HILDA.   But I have seen him with my own eyes right up at the top of a high church-tower!

MRS. SOLNESS.   Yes, I hear people talk of that; but it is utterly impossible——

SOLNESS (*vehemently*).   Impossible—impossible, yes! But there I stood all the same!

MRS. SOLNESS.   Oh, how can you say so, Halvard? Why, you can't even bear to go out on the second-story balcony here. You have always been like that.

SOLNESS.   You may perhaps see something different this evening.

MRS. SOLNESS (*in alarm*).   No, no, no! Please God I shall never see that. I will write at once to the doctor—and I am sure he won't let you do it.

SOLNESS.   Why, Aline——!

MRS. SOLNESS.   Oh, you know you're ill, Halvard. This proves it! Oh God—Oh God!

{*She goes hastily out to the right.*

HILDA (*looks intently at him*).   Is it so, or is it not?

SOLNESS.   That I turn dizzy?

HILDA.   That my master builder dares not—can-not—climb as high as he builds?

SOLNESS.   Is that the way you look at it?

HILDA.   Yes.

SOLNESS.   I believe there is scarcely a corner in me that is safe from you.

HILDA (*looks towards the bow-window*).   Up there, then. Right up there——

SOLNESS (*approaches her*).   You might have the top-most room in the tower, Hilda—there you might live like a princess.

HILDA (*indefinably, between earnest and jest*).   Yes, that is what you promised me.

SOLNESS.   Did I really?

HILDA.   Fie, Mr. Solness! You said I should be a princess, and that you would give me a kingdom. And then you went and——Well!

SOLNESS (*cautiously*).   Are you quite certain that this is not a dream—a fancy, that has fixed itself in your mind?

HILDA (*sharply*).   Do you mean that you did not do it?

SOLNESS.   I scarcely know myself. (*More softly.*) But now I know so much for certain, that I——

HILDA.   That you——? Say it at once!

SOLNESS.   —that I ought to have done it.

HILDA (*exclaims with animation*).   Don't tell me you can ever be dizzy!

SOLNESS.   This evening, then, we will hang up the wreath—Princess Hilda.

HILDA (*with a bitter curve of the lips*).   Over your new home, yes.

SOLNESS.   Over the new house, which will never be a home for me.

> {*He goes out through the garden door.*

HILDA (*looks straight in front of her with a far-away expression and whispers to herself. The only words audible are*)—frightfully thrilling——

Act III

~

The large, broad verandah of SOLNESS'S *dwelling-house. Part of
the house, with outer door leading to the verandah, is seen to the
left. A railing along the verandah to the right. At the back,
from the end of the verandah, a flight of steps leads down to the
garden below. Tall old trees in the garden spread their branches
over the verandah and towards the house. Far to the right, in
among the trees, a glimpse is caught of the lower part of the new
villa, with scaffolding round so much as is seen of the tower. In
the background the garden is bounded by an old wooden fence.
Outside the fence, a street with low, tumble-down cottages.*

Evening sky with sun-lit clouds.

*On the verandah, a garden bench stands along the wall of the house,
and in front of the bench a long table. On the other side of the
table, an arm-chair and some stools. All the furniture is of
wicker-work.*

MRS. SOLNESS, *wrapped in a large white crape shawl, sits resting
in the arm-chair and gazes over to the right. Shortly after,*
HILDA WANGEL *comes up the flight of steps from the garden.
She is dressed as in the last act and wears her hat. She has in
her bodice a little nosegay of small common flowers.*

MRS. SOLNESS (*turning her head a little*).　　Have you
been round the garden, Miss Wangel?

HILDA.　　Yes, I have been taking a look at it.

MRS. SOLNESS.　　And found some flowers, too, I see.

HILDA. Yes, Indeed! There are such heaps of them in among the bushes.

MRS. SOLNESS. Are there really? Still? You see I scarcely ever go there.

HILDA (*closer*). What! Don't you take a run down into the garden every day, then?

MRS. SOLNESS (*with a faint smile*). I don't "run" any-where, nowadays.

HILDA. Well, but do you not go down now and then to look at all the lovely things there?

MRS. SOLNESS. It has all become so strange to me. I am almost afraid to see it again.

HILDA. Your own garden!

MRS. SOLNESS. I don't feel that it is mine any longer.

HILDA. What do you mean———?

MRS. SOLNESS. No, no, it is not—not—not as it was in my mother's and father's time. They have taken away so much—so much of the garden, Miss Wangel. Fancy— they have parcelled it out—and built houses for strangers— people that I don't know. And they can sit and look in upon me from their windows.

HILDA (*with a bright expression*). Mrs. Solness!

MRS. SOLNESS. Yes!

HILDA. May I stay here with you a little?

MRS. SOLNESS. Yes, by all means, if you care to.

{HILDA *moves a stool close to the arm-chair and sits down.*

HILDA. Ah—here one can sit and sun oneself like a cat.

MRS. SOLNESS (*lays her hand softly on* HILDA'S *neck*). It is nice of you to be willing to sit with me. I thought you wanted to go in to my husband.

HILDA. What should I want with him?

MRS. SOLNESS. To help him, I thought.

HILDA. No, thank you. And besides, he is not in. He is over there with the workmen. But he looked so fierce that I did not care to talk to him.

MRS. SOLNESS. He is so kind and gentle in reality.

HILDA. He!

MRS. SOLNESS. You do not really know him yet, Miss Wangel.

HILDA (*looks affectionately at her*). Are you pleased at the thought of moving over to the new house?

MRS. SOLNESS. I ought to be pleased; for it is what Halvard wants——

HILDA. Oh, not just on that account, surely.

MRS. SOLNESS. Yes, yes, Miss Wangel; for it is only my duty to submit myself to him. But very often it is dreadfully difficult to force one's mind to obedience.

HILDA. Yes, that must be difficult indeed.

MRS. SOLNESS. I can tell you it is—when one has so many faults as I have——

HILDA. When one has gone through so much trouble as you have——

MRS. SOLNESS. How do you know about that?

HILDA. Your husband told me.

MRS. SOLNESS. To me he very seldom mentions these things.——Yes, I can tell you I have gone through more than enough trouble in my life, Miss Wangel.

HILDA (*looks sympathetically at her and nods slowly*). Poor Mrs. Solness. First of all there was the fire——

MRS. SOLNESS (*with a sigh*). Yes, everything that was mine was burnt.

HILDA. And then came what was worse.

MRS. SOLNESS (*looking inquiringly at her*). Worse?

HILDA. The worst of all.

MRS. SOLNESS. What do you mean?

HILDA (*softly*). You lost the two little boys.

MRS. SOLNESS. Oh, yes, the boys. But, you see, that was a thing apart. That was a dispensation of Providence; and in such things one can only bow in submission—yes, and be thankful, too.

HILDA. Then you are so?

MRS. SOLNESS. Not always, I am sorry to say. I know well enough that it is my duty—but all the same I cannot.

HILDA. No, no, I think that is only natural.

MRS. SOLNESS. And often and often I have to remind myself that it was a righteous punishment for me——

HILDA. Why?

MRS. SOLNESS. Because I had not fortitude enough in misfortune.

HILDA. But I don't see that——

MRS. SOLNESS. Oh, no, no, Miss Wangel—do not talk to me any more about the two little boys. We ought to feel nothing but joy in thinking of them; for they are so happy—so happy now. No, it is the small losses in life that cut one to the heart—the loss of all that other people look upon as almost nothing.

HILDA (*lays her arms on* MRS. SOLNESS'S *knees and looks up at her affectionately*). Dear Mrs. Solness—tell me what things you mean!

MRS. SOLNESS. As I say, only little things. All the old portraits were burnt on the walls. And all the old silk dresses were burnt, that had belonged to the family for generations and generations. And all mother's and grandmother's lace—that was burnt, too. And only think—the jewels, too! *(Sadly.)* And then all the dolls.

HILDA.   The dolls?

MRS. SOLNESS *(choking with tears).*   I had nine lovely dolls.

HILDA.   And they were burnt, too?

MRS. SOLNESS.   All of them. Oh, it was hard—so hard for me.

HILDA.   Had you put by all these dolls, then? Ever since you were little?

MRS. SOLNESS.   I had not put them by. The dolls and I had gone on living together.

HILDA.   After you were grown up?

MRS. SOLNESS.   Yes, long after that.

HILDA.   After you were married, too?

MRS. SOLNESS.   Oh, yes, indeed. So long as he did not see it——. But they were all burnt up, poor things. No one thought of saving them. Oh, it is so miserable to think of. You mustn't laugh at me, Miss Wangel.

HILDA.   I am not laughing in the least.

MRS. SOLNESS.   For you see, in a certain sense, there was life in them, too. I carried them under my heart—like little unborn children.

>   {DR. HERDAL, *with his hat in his hand, comes out through the door and observes* MRS. SOLNESS *and* HILDA.

DR. HERDAL.   Well, Mrs. Solness, so you are sitting out here catching cold?

MRS. SOLNESS.   I find it so pleasant and warm here to-day.

DR. HERDAL.   Yes, yes. But is there anything going on here? I got a note from you.

MRS. SOLNESS (*rises*).   Yes, there is something I must talk to you about.

DR, HERDAL.   Very well; then perhaps we had better go in. (*To* HILDA.) Still in your mountaineering dress, Miss Wangel?

HILDA (*gaily, rising*).   Yes—in full uniform! But to-day I am not going climbing and breaking my neck. We two will stop quietly below and look on, doctor.

DR. HERDAL.   What are we to look on at?

MRS. SOLNESS (*softly, in alarm, to* HILDA).   Hush, hush—for God's sake! He is coming. Try to get that idea out of his head. And let us be friends, Miss Wangel. Don't you think we can?

HILDA (*throws her arms impetuously round* MRS. SOLNESS'S *neck*).   Oh, if we only could!

MRS. SOLNESS (*gently disengages herself*).   There, there there! There he comes, doctor. Let me have a word with you.

DR. HERDAL.   Is it about him?

MRS. SOLNESS.   Yes, to be sure it's about him. Do come in.

> {*She and the doctor enter the house. Next moment* SOL-NESS *comes up from the garden by the flight of steps. A serious look comes over* HILDA'S *face.*

SOLNESS (*glances at the house-door, which is closed cautiously from within*).   Have you noticed, Hilda, that as soon as I come, she goes?

HILDA.   I have noticed that as soon as you come, you make her go.

SOLNESS.   Perhaps so. But I cannot help it. (*Looks observantly at her.*) Are you cold, Hilda? I think you look cold.

HILDA.   I have just come up out of a tomb.

SOLNESS.   What do you mean by that?

HILDA.   That I have got chilled through and through, Mr. Solness.

SOLNESS *(slowly).*   I believe I understand——

HILDA.   What brings you up here just now?

SOLNESS.   I caught sight of you from over there.

HILDA.   But then you must have seen her too?

SOLNESS.   I knew she would go at once if I came.

HILDA.   Is it very painful for you that she should avoid you in this way?

SOLNESS.   In one sense, it's a relief as well.

HILDA.   Not to have her before your eyes?

SOLNESS.   Yes.

HILDA.   Not to be always seeing how heavily the loss of the little boys weighs upon her?

SOLNESS.   Yes. Chiefly that.

> {HILDA *drifts across the verandah with her hands behind her back, stops at the railing and looks out over the garden.*

SOLNESS *(after a short pause).*   Did you have a long talk with her?

> {HILDA *stands motionless and does not answer.*

SOLNESS.   Had you a long talk, I asked?

> {HILDA *is silent as before.*

SOLNESS.   What was she talking about, Hilda?

> {HILDA *continues silent.*

SOLNESS.   Poor Aline! I suppose it was about the little boys.

HILDA *(a nervous shudder runs through her; then she nods hurriedly once or twice).*

SOLNESS.   She will never get over it—never in this world. *(Approaches her.)* Now you are standing there again like a statue; just as you stood last night.

HILDA (*turns and looks at him, with great serious eyes*). I am going away.

SOLNESS (*sharply*). Going away!

HILDA. Yes.

SOLNESS. But I won't allow you to!

HILDA. What am I to do here now?

SOLNESS. Simply to be here, Hilda!

HILDA (*measures him with a look*). Oh, thank you. You know it wouldn't end there.

SOLNESS (*heedlessly*). So much the better!

HILDA (*vehemently*). I cannot do any harm to one whom I know! I can't take away anything that belongs to her.

SOLNESS. Who wants you to do that?

HILDA (*continuing*). A stranger, yes! for that is quite a different thing! A person I have never set eyes on. But one that I have come into close contact with——! Oh, no! Oh, no! Ugh!

SOLNESS. Yes, but I never proposed you should.

HILDA. Oh, Mr. Solness, you know quite well what the end of it would be. And that is why I am going away.

SOLNESS. And what is to become of me when you are gone? What shall I have to live for then?—After that?

HILDA (*with the indefinable look in her eyes*). It is surely not so hard for you. You have your duties to her. Live for those duties.

SOLNESS. Too late. These powers—these—these——

HILDA. —devils——

SOLNESS. Yes, these devils! And the troll within me as well—they have drawn all the life-blood out of her. (*Laughs in desperation.*) They did it for my happiness! Yes, yes! (*Sadly.*) And now she is dead—for my sake. And I am chained alive to a dead woman. (*In wild anguish.*) I—I who cannot live without joy in life!

> {HILDA *moves round the table and seats herself on the bench, with her elbows on the table, and her head supported by her hands.*

HILDA (*sits and looks at him awhile*).   What will you build next?

SOLNESS (*shakes his head*).   I don't believe I shall build much more.

HILDA.   Not those cosy, happy homes for mother and father, and for the troop of children?

SOLNESS.   I wonder whether there will be any use for such homes in the coming time.

HILDA.   Poor Mr. Solness! And you have gone all these ten years—and staked your whole life—on that alone.

SOLNESS.   Yes, you may well say so, Hilda.

HILDA (*with an outburst*).   Oh, it all seems to me so foolish—so foolish!

SOLNESS.   All what?

HILDA.   Not to be able to grasp at your own happiness—at your own life! Merely because some one you know happens to stand in the way!

SOLNESS.   One whom you have no right to set aside.

HILDA.   I wonder whether one really has not the right! And yet, and yet——. Oh, if one could only sleep the whole thing away!

> {She lays her arms flat on the table, rests the left side of her head on her hands and shuts her eyes.*

SOLNESS (*turns the arm-chair and sits down at the table*). Had you a cosy, happy home—up there with your father, Hilda?

HILDA (*without stirring, answers as if half asleep*).   I had only a cage.

SOLNESS. And you are determined not to go back to it?

HILDA (*as before*). The wild bird never wants to go into the cage.

SOLNESS. Rather range through the free air——

HILDA (*still as before*). The bird of prey loves to range——

SOLNESS (*lets his eyes rest on her*). If only one had the viking-spirit in life——

HILDA (*in her usual voice; opens her eyes but does not move*). And the other thing? Say what that was!

SOLNESS. A robust conscience.

> {HILDA *sits erect on the bench, with animation. Her eyes have once more the sparkling expression of gladness.*

HILDA (*nods to him*). I know what you are going to build next!

SOLNESS. Then you know more than I do, Hilda.

HILDA. Yes, builders are such stupid people.

SOLNESS. What is it to be then?

HILDA (*nods again*). The castle.

SOLNESS. What castle?

HILDA. My castle, of course.

SOLNESS. Do you want a castle now?

HILDA. Don't you owe me a kingdom, I should like to know?

SOLNESS. You say I do.

HILDA. Well—you admit you owe me this kingdom. And you can't have a kingdom without a royal castle, I should think!

SOLNESS (*more and more animated*). Yes, they usually go together.

HILDA. Good! Then build it for me! This moment!

SOLNESS (*laughing*).   Must you have that on the instant, too?

HILDA.   Yes, to be sure! For the ten years are up now, and I am not going to wait any longer. So—out with the castle, Mr. Solness!

SOLNESS.   It's no light matter to owe you anything, Hilda.

HILDA.   You should have thought of that before. It is too late now. So—(*tapping the table*)—the castle on the table! It is my castle! I will have it at once!

SOLNESS (*more seriously, leans over towards her, with his arms on the table*).   What sort of castle have you imagined, Hilda?

> {*Her expression becomes more and more veiled. She seems gazing inwards at herself.*

HILDA (*slowly*).   My castle shall stand on a height—on a very great height—with a clear outlook on all sides, so that I can see far—far around.

SOLNESS.   And no doubt it is to have a high tower!

HILDA.   A tremendously high tower. And at the very top of the tower there shall be a balcony. And I will stand out upon it——

SOLNESS (*involuntarily clutches at his forehead*).   How can you like to stand at such a dizzy height——?

HILDA.   Yes, I will, right up there will I stand and look down on the other people—on those that are building churches, and homes for mother and father and the troop of children. And you may come up and look on at it, too.

SOLNESS (*in a low tone*).   Is the builder to be allowed to come up beside the princess?

HILDA.   If the builder will.

SOLNESS (*more softly*).   Then I think the builder will come.

HILDA *(nods).* The builder—he will come.

SOLNESS. But he will never be able to build any more. Poor builder!

HILDA *(animated).* Oh yes, he will! We two will set to work together. And then we will build the loveliest—the very loveliest—thing in all the world.

SOLNESS *(intently).* Hilda—tell me what that is!

HILDA *(looks smilingly at him, shakes her head a little, pouts and speaks as if to a child).* Builders—they are such very—very stupid people.

SOLNESS. Yes, no doubt they are stupid. But now tell me what it is—the loveliest thing in the world—that we two are to build together?

HILDA *(is silent a little while, then says with an indefinable expression in her eyes).* Castles in the air.

SOLNESS. Castles in the air?

HILDA *(nods).* Castles in the air, yes! Do you know what sort of thing a castle in the air is?

SOLNESS. It is the loveliest thing in the world, you say.

HILDA *(rises with vehemence and makes a gesture of repulsion with her hand).* Yes, to be sure it is! Castles in the air—they are so easy to take refuge in. And so easy to build, too—*(looks scornfully at him)*—especially for the builders who have a—a dizzy conscience.

SOLNESS *(rises).* After this day we two will build together, Hilda.

HILDA *(with a half-dubious smile).* A real castle in the air?

SOLNESS. Yes. One with a firm foundation under it.

{RAGNAR BROVIK *comes out from the house. He is carrying a large, green wreath with flowers and silk ribbons.*

HILDA (*with an outburst of pleasure*).   The wreath! Oh, that will be glorious!

SOLNESS (*in surprise*).   Have you brought the wreath, Ragnar?

RAGNAR.   I promised the foreman I would.

SOLNESS (*relieved*).   Ah, then I suppose your father is better?

RAGNAR.   No.

SOLNESS.   Was he not cheered by what I wrote?

RAGNAR.   It came too late.

SOLNESS.   Too late!

RAGNAR.   When she came with it he was unconscious. He had had a stroke.

SOLNESS.   Why, then, you must go home to him! You must attend to your father!

RAGNAR.   He does not need me any more.

SOLNESS.   But surely you ought to be with him.

RAGNAR.   She is sitting by his bed.

SOLNESS (*rather uncertainly*).   Kaia?

RAGNAR (*looking darkly at him*).   Yes—Kaia.

SOLNESS.   Go home, Ragnar—both to him and to her. Give me the wreath.

RAGNAR (*suppresses a mocking smile*).   You don't mean that you yourself——?

SOLNESS.   I will take it down to them myself. (*Takes the wreath from him.*) And now you go home; we don't require you to-day.

RAGNAR.   I know you do not require me any more; but to-day I shall remain.

SOLNESS.   Well, remain then, since you are bent upon it.

HILDA (*at the railing*).   Mr. Solness, I will stand here and look on at you.

SOLNESS. At me!

HILDA. It will be fearfully thrilling.

SOLNESS (*in a low tone*). We will talk about that presently, Hilda.

> {*He goes down the flight of steps with the wreath and away through the garden.*

HILDA (*looks after him, then turns to* RAGNAR). I think you might at least have thanked him.

RAGNAR. Thanked him? Ought I to have thanked him?

HILDA. Yes, of course you ought!

RAGNAR. I think it is rather you I ought to thank.

HILDA. How can you say such a thing?

RAGNAR (*without answering her*). But I advise you to take care, Miss Wangel! For you don't know him rightly yet.

HILDA (*ardently*). Oh, no one knows him as I do!

RAGNAR (*laughs in exasperation*). Thank him, when he has held me down year after year! When he made father disbelieve in me—made me disbelieve in myself! And all merely that he might——!

HILDA (*as if divining something*). That he might——! Tell me at once!

RAGNAR. That he might keep her with him.

HILDA (*with a start towards him*). The girl at the desk.

RAGNAR. Yes.

HILDA (*threateningly, clenching her hands*). That is not true! You are telling falsehoods about him!

RAGNAR. I would not believe it either until to-day—when she said so herself.

HILDA (*as if beside herself*). What did she say? I will know! At once! at once!

RAGNAR. She said that he had taken possession of

her mind—her whole mind—centred all her thoughts upon himself alone. She says that she can never leave him—that she will remain here, where he is——

HILDA (*with flashing eyes*).   She will not be allowed to!

RAGNAR (*as if feeling his way*).   Who will not allow her?

HILDA (*rapidly*).   He will not either!

RAGNAR.   Oh no—I understand the whole thing now. After this, she would merely be—in the way.

HILDA.   You understand nothing—since you can talk like that! No, I will tell you why he kept hold of her.

RAGNAR.   Well then, why?

HILDA.   In order to keep hold of you.

RAGNAR.   Has he told you so?

HILDA.   No, but it is so. It must be so! (*Wildly.*) I will—I will have it so!

RAGNAR.   And at the very moment when you came—he let her go.

HILDA.   It was you—you that he let go. What do you suppose he cares about strange women like her?

RAGNAR (*reflects*).   Is it possible that all this time he has been afraid of me?

HILDA.   He afraid! I would not be so conceited if I were you.

RAGNAR.   Oh, he must have seen long ago that I had something in me, too. Besides—cowardly—that is just what he is, you see.

HILDA.   He! Oh, yes, I am likely to believe that!

RAGNAR.   In a certain sense he is cowardly—he, the great master builder. He is not afraid or robbing others of their life's happiness—as he has done both for my father and for me. But when it comes to climbing up a paltry bit of scaffolding—he will do anything rather than that.

HILDA.   Oh, you should just have seen him high, high up—at the dizzy height where I once saw him.

RAGNAR.   Did you see that?

HILDA.   Yes, indeed I did. How free and great he looked as he stood and fastened the wreath to the church-vane!

RAGNAR.   I know that he ventured that, once in his life—one solitary time. It is a legend among us younger men. But no power on earth would induce him to do it again.

HILDA.   To-day he will do it again!

RAGNAR *(scornfully)*.   Yes, I daresay!

HILDA.   We shall see it!

RAGNAR.   That neither you nor I will see.

HILDA *(with uncontrollable vehemence)*.   I will see it! I will and must see it!

RAGNAR.   But he will not do it. He simply dare not do it. For you see he cannot get over this infirmity—master builder though he be.

{MRS. SOLNESS *comes from the house on to the veran-dah.*

MRS. SOLNESS *(looks around)*.   Is he not here? Where has he gone to?

RAGNAR.   Mr. Solness is down with the men.

HILDA.   He took the wreath with him.

MRS. SOLNESS *(terrified)*.   Took the wreath with him! oh, God! Oh, God! Brovik—you must go down to him! Get him to come back here!

RAGNAR.   Shall I say you want to speak to him, Mrs. Solness?

MRS. SOLNESS.   Oh, yes, do!—No, no—don't say
that *I* want anything! You can say that somebody is here,
and that he must come at once.

RAGNAR.   Good. I will do so, Mrs. Solness.

  {*He goes down the flight of steps and away through the
  garden.*

MRS. SOLNESS.   Oh, Miss Wangel, you can't think
how anxious I feel about him.

HILDA.   Is there anything in this to be so terribly
frightened about?

MRS. SOLNESS.   Oh, yes; surely you can understand.
Just think, if he were really to do it! If he should take it
into his head to climb up the scaffolding!

HILDA *(eagerly)*.   Do you think he will?

MRS. SOLNESS.   Oh, one can never tell what he
might take into his head. I am afraid there is nothing he
mightn't think of doing.

HILDA.   Aha! Perhaps you too think that he is—
well——?

MRS. SOLNESS.   Oh, I don't know what to think
about him now. The doctor has been telling me all sorts of
things; and putting it all together with several things I have
heard him say——

  {DR. HERDAL *looks out, at the door.*

DR. HERDAL.   Is he not coming soon?

MRS. SOLNESS.   Yes, I think so. I have sent for him
at any rate.

DR. HERDAL *(advancing)*.   I am afraid you will have
to go in, my dear lady——

MRS. SOLNESS.   Oh, no! Oh, no! I shall stay out here
and wait for Halvard.

DR. HERDAL.   But some ladies have just come to call
on you——

MRS. SOLNESS.   Good heavens, that too! And just at this moment!

DR. HERDAL.   They say they positively must see the ceremony.

MRS. SOLNESS.   Well, well, I suppose I must go to them after all. It is my duty.

HILDA.   Can't you ask the ladies to go away?

MRS. SOLNESS.   No, that would never do. Now that they are here, it is my duty to see them. But do you stay out here in the meantime—and receive him when he comes.

DR. HERDAL.   And try to occupy his attention as long as possible——

MRS. SOLNESS.   Yes, do, dear Miss Wangel. Keep a firm hold of him as ever you can.

HILDA.   Would it not be best for you to do that?

MRS. SOLNESS.   Yes; God knows that is my duty. But when one has duties in so many directions——

DR. HERDAL (*looks towards the garden*).   There he is coming.

MRS. SOLNESS.   And I have to go in!

DR. HERDAL (*to Hilda*).   Don't say anything about my being here.

HILDA.   Oh, no! I daresay I shall find something else to talk to Mr. Solness about.

MRS. SOLNESS.   And be sure you keep firm hold of him. I believe you can do it best.

{MRS. SOLNESS *and* DR. HERDAL *go into the house.* HILDA *remains standing on the verandah.* SOLNESS *comes from the garden, up the flight of steps.*

SOLNESS.   Somebody wants me, I hear.

HILDA.   Yes; it is I, Mr. Solness.

SOLNESS.   Oh, is it you, Hilda? I was afraid it might be Aline or the Doctor.

HILDA.   You are very easily frightened, it seems!

SOLNESS.   Do you think so?

HILDA.   Yes; people say that you are afraid to climb about——on the scaffoldings, you know.

SOLNESS.   Well, that is quite a special thing.

HILDA.   Then it is true that you are afraid to do it?

SOLNESS.   Yes, I am.

HILDA.   Afraid of falling down and killing yourself?

SOLNESS.   No, not of that.

HILDA.   Of what, then?

SOLNESS.   I am afraid of retribution, Hilda.

HILDA.   Of retribution? *(Shakes her head.)* I don't understand that.

SOLNESS.   Sit down and I will tell you something.

HILDA.   Yes, do! At once!

{*She sits on a stool by the railing and looks expectantly at him.*

SOLNESS *(throws his hat on the table).*   You know that I began by building churches.

HILDA *(nods).*   I know that well.

SOLNESS.   For, you see, I came as a boy from a pious home in the country; and so it seemed to me that this church-building was the noblest task I could set myself.

HILDA.   Yes, yes.

SOLNESS.   And I venture to say that I built those poor little churches with such honest and warm and heartfelt devotion that——that——

HILDA.   That——? Well?

SOLNESS.   Well, that I think that he ought to have been pleased with me.

HILDA.   He? What he?

SOLNESS.   He who was to have the churches, of course! He to whose honour and glory they were dedicated.

HILDA.   Oh, indeed! But are you certain, then, that—that he was not—pleased with you?

SOLNESS (*scornfully*).   He pleased with me! How can you talk so, Hilda? He who gave the troll in me leave to lord it just as it pleased. He who bade them be at hand to serve me, both day and night—all these—all these——

HILDA.   Devils——

SOLNESS.   Yes, of both kinds. Oh, no, he made me feel clearly enough that he was not pleased with me. (*Mysteriously.*) You see, that was really the reason why he made the old house burn down.

HILDA.   Was that why?

SOLNESS.   Yes, don't you understand? He wanted to give me the chance of becoming an accomplished master in my own sphere—so that I might build all the more glorious churches for him. At first I did not understand what he was driving at; but all of a sudden it flashed upon me.

HILDA.   When was that?

SOLNESS.   It was when I was building the church-tower up at Lysanger.

HILDA.   I thought so.

SOLNESS.   For you see, Hilda—up there, amidst those new surroundings, I used to go about musing and pondering within myself. Then I saw plainly why he had taken my little children from me. It was that I should have nothing else to attach myself to. No such thing as love and happiness, you understand. I was to be only a master builder—nothing else. And all my life long I was to go on building for him. (*Laughs.*) But I can tell you nothing came of that!

HILDA.   What did you do, then?

SOLNESS.   First of all, I searched and tried my own heart——

HILDA.   And then?

SOLNESS.   Then I did the impossible—I no less than he.

HILDA.   The impossible?

SOLNESS.   I had never before been able to climb up to a great, free height. But that day I did it.

HILDA *(leaping up)*.   Yes, yes, you did!

SOLNESS.   And when I stood there, high over everything, and was hanging the wreath over the vane, I said to him: Hear me now, thou Mighty One! From this day forward I will be a free builder—I, too, in my sphere—just as thou in thine. I will never more build churches for thee— only homes for human beings.

HILDA *(with great sparkling eyes)*.   That was the song that I heard through the air!

SOLNESS.   But afterwards his turn came.

HILDA.   What do you mean by that?

SOLNESS *(looks despondently at her)*.   Building homes for human beings—is not worth a rap, Hilda.

HILDA.   Do you say that now?

SOLNESS.   Yes, for now I see it. Men have no use for these homes of theirs—to be happy in. And I should not have had any use for such a home, if I had had one. *(With a quiet, bitter laugh.)* See, that is the upshot of the whole affair, however far back I look. Nothing really built; not anything sacrificed for the chance of building. Nothing, nothing! the whole is nothing.

HILDA.   Then you will never build anything more?

SOLNESS *(with animation)*.   On the contrary, I am just going to begin!

HILDA.   What, then? What will you build? Tell me at once!

SOLNESS.   I believe there is only one possible dwelling-place for human happiness—and that is what I am going to build now.

HILDA (*looks fixedly at him*).   Mr. Solness—you mean our castle?

SOLNESS.   The castles in the air—yes.

HILDA.   I am afraid you would turn dizzy before we got half-way up.

SOLNESS.   Not if I can mount hand in hand with you, Hilda.

HILDA (*with an expression of suppressed resentment*).   Only with me? Will there be no others of the party?

SOLNESS.   Who else should there be?

HILDA.   Oh—that girl—that Kaia at the desk. Poor thing—don't you want to take her with you, too?

SOLNESS.   Oho! Was it about her that Aline was talking to you?

HILDA.   Is it so—or is it not?

SOLNESS (*vehemently*).   I will not answer such a question. You must believe in me, wholly and entirely!

HILDA.   All these ten years I have believed in you so utterly—so utterly.

SOLNESS.   You must go on believing in me!

HILDA.   Then let me see you stand free and high up!

SOLNESS (*sadly*).   Oh Hilda—it is not every day that I can do that.

HILDA (*passionately*).   I will have you do it! I will have it! (*Imploringly.*) Just once more, Mr. Solness! Do the impossible once again!

SOLNESS (*stands and looks deep into her eyes*).   If I try it, Hilda, I will stand up there and talk to him as I did that time before.

HILDA (*in rising excitement*).   What will you say to him?

SOLNESS.　　　I will say to him: Hear me, Mighty Lord—thou may'st judge me as seems best to thee. But hereafter I will build nothing but the loveliest thing in the world——

HILDA (*carried away*).　　Yes—yes—yes!

SOLNESS.　　——build it together with a princess, whom I love——

HILDA.　　Yes, tell him that! Tell him that!

SOLNESS.　　Yes. And then I will say to him: Now I shall go down and throw my arms round her and kiss her——

HILDA.　　—many times! Say that!

SOLNESS.　　—many, many times, I will say.

HILDA.　　And then——?

SOLNESS.　　Then I will wave my hat—and come down to the earth—and do as I said to him.

HILDA (*with outstretched arms*).　　Now I see you again as I did when there was song in the air.

SOLNESS (*looks at her with his head bowed*).　　How have you become what you are, Hilda?

HILDA.　　How have you made me what I am?

SOLNESS (*shortly and firmly*).　　The princess shall have her castle.

HILDA (*jubilant, clapping her hands*).　　Oh, Mr. Solness——! My lovely, lovely castle. Our castle in the air!

SOLNESS.　　On a firm foundation.

> {*In the street a crowd of people has assembled, vaguely seen through the trees. Music of wind-instruments is heard far away behind the new house.*
>
> {MRS. SOLNESS, *with a fur collar round her neck,* DOCTOR HERDAL *with her white shawl on his arm, and some ladies, come out on the verandah.* RAGNAR BROVIK *comes at the same time up from the garden.*

MRS. SOLNESS (*to* RAGNAR).   Are we to have music, too?

RAGNAR.   Yes. It's the band of the Mason's Union. (*To* SOLNESS.) The foreman asked me to tell you that he is ready now to go up with the wreath.

SOLNESS (*takes his hat*).   Good. I will go down to him myself.

MRS. SOLNESS (*anxiously*).   What have you to do down there, Halvard?

SOLNESS (*curtly*).   I must be down below with the men.

MRS. SOLNESS.   Yes, down below—only down below.

SOLNESS.   That is where I always stand—on everyday occasions.

> {*He goes down the flight of steps and away through the garden.*

MRS. SOLNESS (*calls after him over the railing*).   But do beg the man to be careful when he goes up? Promise me that, Halvard!

DR. HERDAL (*to* MRS. SOLNESS).   Don't you see that I was right? He has given up all thought of that folly.

MRS. SOLNESS.   Oh, what a relief! Twice workmen have fallen, and each time they were killed on the spot. (*Turns to* HILDA.) Thank you, Miss Wangel, for having kept such a firm hold upon him. I should never have been able to manage him.

DR. HERDAL (*playfully*).   Yes, yes, Miss Wangel, you know how to keep firm hold on a man, when you give your mind to it.

> {MRS. SOLNESS *and* DR. HERDAL *go up to the ladies, who are standing nearer to the steps and looking over the garden.* HILDA *remains standing beside the*

railing in the foreground. RAGNAR *goes up to her.*

RAGNAR (*with suppressed laughter, half whispering*). Miss Wangel—do you see all those young fellows down in the street?

HILDA.   Yes.

RAGNAR.   They are my fellow-students, come to look at the master.

HILDA.   What do they want to look at him for?

RAGNAR.   They want to see how he daren't climb to the top of his own house.

HILDA.   Oh, that is what those boys want, is it?

RAGNAR (*spitefully and scornfully*).   He has kept us down so long—now we are going to see him keep quietly down below himself.

HILDA.   You will not see that—not this time.

RAGNAR (*smiles*).   Indeed! Then where shall we see him?

HILDA.   High—high up by the vane! That is where you will see him!

RAGNAR (*laughs*).   Him! Oh, yes, I daresay!

HILDA.   His will is to reach the top—so at the top you shall see him.

RAGNAR.   His will, yes; that I can easily believe. But he simply cannot do it. His head would swim round, long, long before he got half-way. He would have to crawl down again on his hands and knees.

DR. HERDAL (*points across*).   Look! There goes the foreman up the ladders.

MRS. SOLNESS.   And of course he has the wreath to carry, too. Oh, I do hope he will be careful!

RAGNAR (*stares incredulously and shouts*).   Why, but it's——

HILDA (*breaking out in jubilation*).   It is the master builder himself!

MRS. SOLNESS (*screams with terror*).   Yes, it is Halvard! Oh, my great God——! Halvard! Halvard!

DR. HERDAL.   Hush! Don't shout to him!

MRS. SOLNESS (*half beside herself*).   I must go to him! I must get him to come down again!

DR. HERDAL (*holds her*).   Don't move, any of you! Not a sound!

HILDA (*immovable, follows* SOLNESS *with her eyes*).   He climbs and climbs. Higher and higher! Higher and higher! Look! Just look!

RAGNAR (*breathless*).   He must turn now. He can't possibly help it.

HILDA.   He climbs and climbs. He will soon be at the top now.

MRS. SOLNESS.   Oh, I shall die of terror. I cannot bear to see it.

DR. HERDAL.   Then don't look up at him.

HILDA.   There he is standing on the topmost planks. Right at the top!

DR. HERDAL.   Nobody must move! Do you hear?

HILDA (*exulting, with quiet intensity*).   At last! At last! Now I see him great and free again!

RAGNAR (*almost voiceless*).   But this is im——

HILDA.   So I have seen him all through these ten years. How secure he stands! Frightfully thrilling all the same. Look at him! Now he is hanging the wreath round the vane.

RAGNAR.   I feel as if I were looking at something utterly impossible.

HILDA.   Yes, it is the impossible that he is doing

now! *(With the indefinable expression in her eyes.)* Can you see any one else up there with him?

RAGNAR.　　There is no one else.

HILDA.　　Yes, there is one he is striving with.

RAGNAR.　　You are mistaken.

HILDA.　　Then do you hear no song in the air, either?

RAGNAR.　　It must be the wind in the tree-tops.

HILDA.　　*I* hear a song—a mighty song! *(Shouts in wild jubilation and glee.)* Look, look! Now he is waving his hat! He is waving it to us down here! Oh, wave, wave back to him. For now it is finished! *(Snatches the white shawl from the Doctor, waves it and shouts up to* SOLNESS.*)* Hurrah for Master Builder Solness!

DR. HERDAL.　　Stop! Stop! For God's sake——!

> *{The ladies on the verandah wave their pocket-handkerchiefs, and the shouts of "Hurrah" are taken up in the street below. Then they are suddenly silenced, and the crowd bursts out into a shriek of horror. A human body, with planks and fragments of wood, is vaguely perceived crashing down behind the trees.*

MRS. SOLNESS AND THE LADIES *(at the same time).*　　He is falling! He is falling!

> *{MRS. SOLNESS totters, falls backwards, swooning, and is caught, amid cries and confusion, by the ladies. The crowd in the street breaks down the fence and storms into the garden. At the same time DR. HERDAL, too, rushes down thither. A short pause.*

HILDA *(stares fixedly upwards and says, as if petrified).*　　My Master Builder.

RAGNAR *(supports himself, trembling, against the railing).*　　He must be dashed to pieces—killed on the spot.

ONE OF THE LADIES *(whilst MRS. SOLNESS is carried into the house).*　　Run down for the doctor——

RAGNAR.   I can't stir a foot——

ANOTHER LADY.   Then call to some one!

RAGNAR *(tries to call out)*.   How is it? Is he alive?

A VOICE *(below in the garden)*.   Mr. Solness is dead!

OTHER VOICES *(nearer)*.   The head is all crushed.——
He fell right into the quarry.

HILDA *(turns to* RAGNAR *and says quietly)*.   I can't see
him up there now.

RAGNAR.   This is terrible. So, after all, he could not
do it.

HILDA *(as if in quiet spell-bound triumph)*.   But he
mounted right to the top. And I heard harps in the air.
(Waves her shawl in the air, and shrieks with wild intensity.)
My—my Master Builder!

Little Eyolf

~

(1894)

Characters

ALFRED ALLMERS, *landed proprietor and man of letters,*
    formerly a tutor.
MRS. RITA ALLMERS, *his wife.*
EYOLF, *their child, nine years old.*
MISS ASTA ALLMERS, *Alfred's younger half-sister.*
ENGINEER BORGHEIM.
THE RAT-WIFE.

The action takes place on ALLMERS'S *property, bordering on the
fiord, twelve or fourteen miles from Christiania.*

Act I

~

A pretty and richly-decorated garden-room, full of furniture, flowers, and plants. At the back, open glass doors, leading out to a verandah. An extensive view over the fiord. In the distance, wooded hillsides. A door in each of the side walls, the one on the right a folding door, placed far back. In front on the right, a sofa, with cushions and rugs. Beside the sofa, a small table, and chairs. In front, on the left, a larger table, with arm-chairs around it. On the table stands an open hand-bag. It is an early summer morning, with warm sunshine.

MRS. RITA ALLMERS *stands beside the table, facing towards the left, engaged in unpacking the bag. She is a handsome, rather tall, well-developed blonde, about thirty years of age, dressed in a light-coloured morning-gown.*

Shortly after, MISS ASTA ALLMERS *enters by the door on the right, wearing a light brown summer dress, with hat, jacket, and parasol. Under her arm she carries a locked portfolio of considerable size. She is slim, of middle height, with dark hair, and deep, earnest eyes. Twenty-five years old.*

ASTA. [*As she enters.*]   Good-morning, my dear Rita.

RITA. [*Turns her head, and nods to her.*]   What! is that you, Asta? Come all the way from town so early?

ASTA. [*Takes off her things, and lays them on a chair beside the door.*]   Yes, such a restless feeling came over me. I felt I m u s t come out to-day, and see how little Eyolf was getting on—and you too. [*Lays the portfolio on the table beside the sofa.*] So I took the steamer, and here I am.

RITA. [*Smiling to her.*]   And I daresay you met one or other of your friends on board? Quite by chance, of course.

ASTA. [*Quietly.*]   No, I did not meet a soul I knew. [*Sees the bag.*] Why, Rita, what have you got there?

RITA. [*Still unpacking.*]   Alfred's travelling-bag. Don't you recognise it?

ASTA. [*Joyfully, approaching her.*]   What! Has Alfred come home?

RITA.   Yes, only think—he came quite unexpectedly by the late train last night.

ASTA.   Oh, then that was what my feeling meant! It was that that drew me out here! And he hadn't written a line to let you know? Not even a post-card?

RITA.   Not a single word.

ASTA.   Did he not even telegraph?

RITA.   Yes, an hour before he arrived—quite curtly and coldly. [*Laughs.*] Don't you think that was like him, Asta?

ASTA.   Yes; he goes so quietly about everything.

RITA.   But that made it all the more delightful to have him again.

ASTA.   Yes, I am sure it would.

RITA.   A whole fortnight before I expected him!

ASTA.   And is he quite well? Not in low spirits?

RITA. [*Closes the bag with a snap, and smiles at her.*]   He looked quite transfigured as he stood in the doorway.

ASTA.   And was he not the least bit tired either?

RITA.   Oh, yes, he seemed to be tired enough—very tired, in fact. But, poor fellow, he had come on foot the greater part of the way.

ASTA.   And then perhaps the high mountain air may have been rather too keen for him.

RITA.   Oh, no; I don't think so at all. I haven't heard him cough once.

ASTA.   Ah, there you see now! It was a good thing, after all, that the doctor talked him into taking this tour.

RITA.   Yes, now that it is safely over.—But I can tell you it has been a terrible time for me, Asta. I have never cared to talk about it—and you so seldom came out to see me, too——

ASTA.   Yes, I daresay that wasn't very nice of me—but——

RITA.   Well, well, well, of course you had your school to attend to in town. [*Smiling.*] And then our road-maker friend—of course he was away too.

ASTA.   Oh, don't talk like that, Rita.

RITA.   Very well, then; we will leave the road-maker out of the question. You can't think how I have been longing for Alfred! How empty the place seemed! How desolate! Ugh, it felt as if there had been a funeral in the house!

ASTA.   Why, dear me, only six or seven weeks——

RITA.   Yes, but you must remember that Alfred has never been away from me before—never so much as twenty-four hours. Not once in all these ten years.

ASTA.   No; but that is just why I really think it was high time he should have a little outing this year. He ought to have gone for a tramp in the mountains every summer—he really ought.

RITA. [*Half smiling.*]   Oh yes, it's all very well for you to talk. If I were as—as reasonable as you, I suppose I should have let him go before—perhaps. But I positively could not, Asta! It seemed to me I should never get him back again. Surely you can understand t h a t?

ASTA.   No. But I daresay that is because I have no one to lose.

RITA. [*With a teasing smile.*]   Really? No one at all?

ASTA.   Not that I know of. [*Changing the subject.*]   But tell me, Rita, where is Alfred? Is he still asleep?

RITA.   Oh, not at all. He got up as early as ever to-day.

ASTA.   Then he can't have been so very tired after all.

RITA.   Yes, he was last night—when he arrived. But now he has had little Eyolf with him in his room for a whole hour and more.

ASTA.   Poor little white-faced boy! Has he to be for ever at his lessons again?

RITA. [*With a slight shrug.*]   Alfred will have it so, you know.

ASTA.   Yes; but I think you ought to put down your foot about it, Rita.

RITA. [*Somewhat impatiently.*]   Oh no: come now, I really cannot meddle with that. Alfred knows so much better about these things than I do. And what would you have Eyolf do? He can't run about and play, you see—like other children.

ASTA. [*With decision.*]   I will talk to Alfred about this.

RITA.   Yes, do; I wish you would.—Oh! here he is.

[ALFRED ALLMERS, *dressed in light summer clothes, enters by the door on the left, leading* EYOLF *by the hand. He is a slim, lightly-built man of about thirty-six or thirty-seven, with gentle eyes, and thin brown hair and beard. His expression is serious and thoughtful.* EYOLF *wears a suit cut like a uniform, with gold braid and gilt military buttons. He is lame, and walks*

with a crutch under his left arm. His leg is shrunken.
He is undersized, and looks delicate, but has beautiful
intelligent eyes.

ALLMERS. [*Drops* EYOLF'S *hand, goes up to* ASTA *with an*
expression of marked pleasure, and holds out both his hands to her.]
Asta! My dearest Asta! To think of your coming! To think
of my seeing you so soon!

ASTA.   I felt I must——. Welcome home again!

ALLMERS. [*Shaking her hands.*]   Thank you for coming.

RITA.   Doesn't he look well?

ASTA. [*Gazes fixedly at him.*]   Splendid! Quite splendid! His eyes are so much brighter! And I suppose you have
done a great deal of writing on your travels? [*With an outburst*
of joy.]   I shouldn't wonder if you had finished the whole
book, Alfred?

ALLMERS. [*Shrugging his shoulders.*]   The book? Oh,
the book——

ASTA.   Yes, I was sure you would find it go so easily
when once you got away.

ALLMERS.   So I thought too. But, do you know, I
didn't find it so at all. The truth is, I have not written a
line of the book.

ASTA.   Not a line?

RITA.   Oho! I wondered when I found all the paper
lying untouched in your bag.

ASTA.   But, my dear Alfred, what have you been doing all this time?

ALLMERS. [*Smiling.*]   Only thinking and thinking
and thinking.

RITA. [*Putting her arm round his neck.*]   And thinking
a little, too, of those you had left at home?

ALLMERS.   Yes, you may be sure of that. I have thought a great deal of you—every single day.

RITA. [*Taking her arm away.*]   Ah, that is all I care about.

ASTA.   But you haven't even touched the book! And yet you can look so happy and contented! That is not what you generally do—I mean when your work is going badly.

ALLMERS.   You are right there. You see, I have been such a fool hitherto. All the best that is in you goes into thinking. What you put on paper is worth very little.

ASTA. [*Exclaiming.*]   Worth very little!

RITA. [*Laughing.*]   What an absurd thing to say, Alfred.

EYOLF. [*Looks confidingly up at him.*]   Oh yes, Papa, what y o u write is worth a great deal!

ALLMERS. [*Smiling and stroking his hair.*]   Well, well, since y o u say so—— But I can tell you, some one is coming after me who will do it better.

EYOLF.   Who can that be? Oh, tell me!

ALLMERS.   Only wait—you may be sure he will come, and let us hear of him.

EYOLF.   And what will you do then?

ALLMERS. [*Seriously.*]   Then I will go to the mountains again——

RITA.   Fie, Alfred! For shame!

ALLMERS.   —up to the peaks and the great waste places.

EYOLF.   Papa, don't you think I shall soon be well enough for you to take me with you?

ALLMERS. [*With painful emotion.*]   Oh, yes, perhaps, my little boy.

EYOLF.   It would be so splendid, you know, if I could climb the mountains, like you.

ASTA. [*Changing the subject.*]   Why, how beautifully you are dressed to-day, Eyolf!

EYOLF.   Yes, don't you think so, Auntie?

ASTA.   Yes, indeed. Is it in honour of Papa that you have got your new clothes on?

EYOLF.   Yes, I asked Mama to let me. I wanted so to let Papa see me in them.

ALLMERS. [*In a low voice, to* RITA.]   You shouldn't have given him clothes like that.

RITA. [*In a low voice.*]   Oh, he has teased me so long about them—he had set his heart on them. He gave me no peace.

EYOLF.   And I forgot to tell you, Papa—Borgheim has brought me a new bow. And he has taught me how to shoot with it too.

ALLMERS.   Ah, there now—that's just the sort of thing for you, Eyolf.

EYOLF.   And next time he comes, I shall ask him to teach me to swim, too.

ALLMERS.   To swim! Oh, what makes you want to learn swimming?

EYOLF.   Well, you know, all the boys down at the beach can swim. I am the only one that can't.

ALLMERS. [*With emotion, taking him in his arms.*]   You shall learn whatever you like—everything you really want to.

EYOLF.   Then do you know what I want most of all, Papa?

ALLMERS.   No; tell me.

EYOLF.   I want most of all to be a soldier.

ALLMERS.   Oh, little Eyolf, there are many, many other things that are better than that.

EYOLF.   Ah, but when I grow big, then I shall h a v e to be a soldier. You know that, don't you?

ALLMERS. [*Clenching his hands together.*]   Well, well, well: we shall see——

ASTA. [*Seating herself at the table on the left.*]   Eyolf! Come here to me, and I will tell you something.

EYOLF. [*Goes up to her.*]   What is it, Auntie?

ASTA.   What do you think, Eyolf—I have seen the Rat-Wife.

EYOLF.   What! Seen the Rat-Wife! Oh, you're only making a fool of me!

ASTA.   No; it's quite true. I saw her yesterday.

EYOLF.   Where did you see her?

ASTA.   I saw her on the road, outside the town.

ALLMERS.   I saw her, too, somewhere up in the country.

RITA. [*Who is sitting on the sofa.*]   Perhaps it will be our turn to see her next, Eyolf.

EYOLF.   Auntie, isn't it strange that she should be called the Rat-Wife?

ASTA.   Oh, people just give her that name because she wanders round the country driving away all the rats.

ALLMERS.   I have heard that her real name is Varg.

EYOLF.   Varg! That means a wolf, doesn't it?

ALLMERS. [*Patting him on the head.*]   So you know that, do you?

EYOLF. [*Cautiously.*]   Then perhaps it may be true, after all, that she is a were-wolf at night. Do you believe that, Papa?

ALLMERS.   Oh, no; I don't believe it. Now you ought to go and play a little in the garden.

EYOLF.   Should I not take some books with me?

ALLMERS.   No, no books after this. You had better go down to the beach to the other boys.

EYOLF. [*Shyly.*]   No, Papa, I won't go down to the boys to-day.

ALLMERS.   Why not?

EYOLF.   Oh, because I have these clothes on.

ALLMERS. [*Knitting his brows.*]   Do you mean that they make fun of—of your pretty clothes?

EYOLF. [*Evasively.*]   No, they daren't—for then I would thrash them.

ALLMERS.   Aha!—then why———?

EYOLF.   You see, they are so naughty, these boys. And then they say I can never be a soldier.

ALLMERS. [*With suppressed indignation.*]   Why do they say that, do you think?

EYOLF.   I suppose they are jealous of me. For you know, Papa, they are so poor, they have to go about barefoot.

ALLMERS. [*Softly, with choking voice.*]   Oh, Rita—how it wrings my heart!

RITA. [*Soothingly, rising.*]   There, there, there!

ALLMERS. [*Threateningly.*]   But these rascals shall soon find out who is the master down at the beach!

ASTA. [*Listening.*]   There is some one knocking.

EYOLF.   Oh, I'm sure it's Borgheim!

RITA.   Come in.

{*The* RAT-WIFE *comes softly and noiselessly in by the door on the right. She is a thin little shrunken figure, old and grey-haired, with keen, piercing eyes, dressed in an old-fashioned flowered gown, with a black hood and cloak. She has in her hand a large red umbrella, and carries a black bag by a loop over her arm.*

EYOLF. [*Softly, taking hold of* ASTA'S *dress.*]   Auntie! That must surely be her!

THE RAT-WIFE. [*Curtseying at the door.*]   I humbly beg pardon—but are your worships troubled with any gnawing things in the house?

ALLMERS.   Here? No, I don't think so.

THE RAT-WIFE.   For it would be such a pleasure to me to rid your worships' house of them.

RITA.   Yes, yes; we understand. But we have nothing of the sort here.

THE RAT-WIFE.   That's very unlucky, that is; for I just happened to be on my rounds now, and goodness knows when I may be in these parts again.—Oh, how tired I am!

ALLMERS. [*Pointing to a chair.*]   Yes, you look tired.

THE RAT-WIFE.   I know one ought never to get tired of doing good to the poor little things that are hated and persecuted so cruelly. But it takes your strength out of you, it does.

RITA.   Won't you sit down and rest a little?

THE RAT-WIFE.   I thank your ladyship with all my heart. [*Seats herself on a chair between the door and the sofa.*] I have been out all night at my work.

ALLMERS.   Have you indeed?

THE RAT-WIFE.   Yes, over on the islands. [*With a chuckling laugh.*] The people sent for me, I can assure you. They didn't like it a bit; but there was nothing else to be done. They had to put a good face on it, and bite the sour apple. [*Looks at* EYOLF, *and nods.*] The sour apple, little master, the sour apple.

EYOLF. [*Involuntarily, a little timidly.*]   Why did they have to——

THE RAT-WIFE.   What?

EYOLF.   To bite it?

THE RAT-WIFE.   Why, because they couldn't keep

body and soul together on account of the rats and all the little rat-children, you see, young master.

RITA.   Ugh! Poor people! Have they so many of them?

THE RAT-WIFE.   Yes, it was all alive and swarming with them. [*Laughs with quiet glee.*] They came creepy-crawly up into the beds all night long. They plumped into the milk-cans, and they went pittering and pattering all over the floor, backwards and forwards, and up and down.

EYOLF. [*Softly, to* ASTA.]   I shall never go there, Auntie.

THE RAT-WIFE.   But then I came—I, and another along with me. And we took them with us, every one—the sweet little creatures! We made an end of every one of them.

EYOLF. [*With a shriek.*]   Papa—look! look!

RITA.   Good Heavens, Eyolf!

ALLMERS.   What's the matter?

EYOLF. [*Pointing.*]   There's something wriggling in the bag!

RITA. [*At the extreme left, shrieks.*]   Ugh! Send her away, Alfred.

THE RAT-WIFE. [*Laughing.*]   Oh, dearest lady, you needn't be frightened of such a little mannikin.

ALLMERS.   But what is the thing?

THE RAT-WIFE.   Why, it's only little Mopsëman. [*Loosening the string of the bag.*] Come up out of the dark, my own little darling friend.

> {*A little dog with a broad black snout pokes its head out of the bag.*

THE RAT-WIFE. [*Nodding and beckoning to* EYOLF.] Come along, don't be afraid, my little wounded warrior! He won't bite. Come here! Come here!

EYOLF. [*Clinging to* ASTA.] No, I dare not.

THE RAT-WIFE. Don't you think he has a gentle, lovable countenance, my young master?

EYOLF. [*Astonished, pointing.*] That thing t h e r e ?

THE RAT-WIFE. Yes, this thing here.

EYOLF. [*Almost under his breath, staring fixedly at the dog.*] I think he has the horriblest—countenance I ever saw.

THE RAT-WIFE. [*Closing the bag.*] Oh, it will come—it will come, right enough.

EYOLF. [*Involuntarily drawing nearer, at last goes right up to her, and strokes the bag.*] But he is lovely—lovely all the same.

THE RAT-WIFE. [*In a tone of caution.*] But now he is so tired and weary, poor thing. He's utterly tired out, he is. [*Looks at* ALLMERS.] For it takes the strength out of you, that sort of game, I can tell you, sir.

ALLMERS. What sort of game do you mean?

THE RAT-WIFE. The luring game.

ALLMERS. Do you mean that it is the dog that lures the rats?

THE RAT-WIFE. [*Nodding.*] Mopsëman and I—we two do it together. And it goes so smoothly—for all you can see, at any rate. I just slip a string through his collar, and then I lead him three times round the house, and play on my Pan's-pipes. When they hear that, they have got to come up from the cellars, and down from the garrets, and out of their holes, all the blessed little creatures.

EYOLF. And does he bite them to death then?

THE RAT-WIFE. Oh, not at all! No, we go down to the boat, he and I do—and then they follow after us, both the big ones and the little ratikins.

EYOLF. [*Eagerly.*] And what then—tell me!

THE RAT-WIFE.   Then we push out from the land, and I scull with one oar, and play on my Pan's pipes. And Mopsëman, he swims behind. [*With glittering eyes.*] And all the creepers and crawlers, they follow and follow us out into the deep, deep waters. Ay, for they h a v e to.

EYOLF.   Why do they h a v e to?

THE RAT-WIFE.   Just because they want not to— just because they are so deadly afraid of the water. That is why they have got to plunge into it.

EYOLF.   Are they drowned, then?

THE RAT-WIFE.   Every blessed one. [*More softly.*] And there it is all as still, and soft, and dark as their hearts can desire, the lovely little things. Down there they sleep a long, sweet sleep, with no one to hate them or persecute them any more. [*Rises.*] In the old days, I can tell you, I didn't need any Mopsëman. Then I did the luring myself— I alone.

EYOLF.   And what did you lure then?

THE RAT-WIFE.   Men. One most of all.

EYOLF. [*With eagerness.*]   Oh, who was that one? Tell me!

THE RAT-WIFE. [*Laughing.*]   It was my own sweetheart, it was, little heart-breaker!

EYOLF.   And where is he now, then?

THE RAT-WIFE. [*Harshly.*]   Down where all the rats are. [*Resuming her milder tone.*] But now I must be off and get to business again. Always on the move. [*To* RITA.] So your ladyship has no sort of use for me to-day? I could finish it all off while I am about it.

RITA.   No, thank you; I don't think we require anything.

THE RAT-WIFE.   Well, well, your sweet ladyship, you can never tell. If your ladyship should find that there is anything here that keeps nibbling and gnawing, and creeping and crawling, then just see and get hold of me and Mopsëman.—Good-bye, good-bye, a kind good-bye to you all.

> {*She goes out by the door on the right.*

EYOLF. [*Softly and triumphantly, to* ASTA.] Only thing, Auntie, now I have seen the Rat-Wife too!

> {RITA *goes out upon the verandah, and fans herself with her pocket-handkerchief. Shortly afterwards,* EYOLF *slips cautiously and unnoticed out to the right.*

ALLMERS. [*Takes up the portfolio from the table by the sofa.*] Is this your portfolio, Asta?

ASTA. Yes. I have some of the old letters in it.

ALLMERS. Ah, the family letters——

ASTA. You know you asked me to arrange them for you while you were away.

ALLMERS. [*Pats her on the head.*] And you have actually found time to do that, dear?

ASTA. Oh, yes. I have done it partly out here and partly at my own rooms in town.

ALLMERS. Thanks, dear. Did you find anything particular in them?

ASTA. [*Lightly.*] Oh, you know you always find something or other in such old papers. [*Speaking lower and seriously.*] It is the letters to mother that are in this portfolio.

ALLMERS. Those, of course, you must keep yourself.

ASTA. [*With an effort.*] No; I am determined that you shall look through them, too, Alfred. Some time—later on in life. I haven't the key of the portfolio with me just now.

ALLMERS. It doesn't matter, my dear Asta, for I shall never read your mother's letters in any case.

ASTA. [*Fixing her eyes on him.*] Then some time or

other—some quiet evening—I will tell you a little of what is in them.

ALLMERS.   Yes, that will be much better. But do you keep your mother's letters—you haven't so many mementos of her.

> {He hands ASTA the portfolio. She takes it, and lays it on the chair under her outdoor things. RITA comes into the room again.

RITA.   Ugh! I feel as if that horrible old woman had brought a sort of graveyard smell with her.

ALLMERS.   Yes, she was rather horrible.

RITA.   I felt almost sick while she was in the room.

ALLMERS.   However, I can very well understand the sort of spellbound fascination that she talked about. The loneliness of the mountain-peaks and of the great waste places has something of the same magic about it.

ASTA. [Looks attentively at him.]   What is it that has happened to you, Alfred?

ALLMERS. [Smiling.]   To me?

ASTA.   Yes, something has happened—something seems almost to have transformed you. Rita noticed it too.

RITA.   Yes, I saw it the moment you came. A change for the better, I hope, Alfred?

ALLMERS.   It o u g h t to be for the better. And it must and shall come to good.

RITA. [With an outburst.]   You have had some adventure on your journey! Don't deny it! I can see it in your face!

ALLMERS. [Shaking his head.]   No adventure in the world—outwardly at least. But——

RITA. [Eagerly.]   But——?

ALLMERS.   It is true that within me there has been something of a revolution.

RITA.   Oh Heavens——!

ALLMERS. [*Soothingly, patting her hand.*]   Only for the better, my dear Rita. You may be perfectly certain of that.

RITA. [*Seats herself on the sofa.*]   You must tell us all about it, at once—tell us everything!

ALLMERS. [*Turning to* ASTA.]   Yes, let us sit down, too, Asta. Then I will try to tell you as well as I can.

> {*He seats himself on the sofa at* RITA'S *side.* ASTA *moves a chair forward, and places herself near him.*

RITA. [*Looking at him expectantly.*]   Well——?

ALLMERS. [*Gazing straight before him.*]   When I look back over my life—and my fortunes—for the last ten or eleven years, it seems to me almost like a fairy-tale or a dream. Don't you think so too, Asta?

ASTA.   Yes, in many ways I think so.

ALLMERS. [*Continuing.*]   When I remember what we two used to be, Asta—we two poor orphan children——

RITA. [*Impatiently.*]   Oh, that is such an old, old story.

ALLMERS. [*Not listening to her.*]   And now here I am in comfort and luxury. I have been able to follow my vocation. I have been able to work and study—just as I had always longed to. [*Holds out his hands.*] And all this great—this fabulous good fortune we owe to you, my dearest Rita.

RITA. [*Half playfully, half angrily, slaps his hand.*]   Oh, I do wish you would stop talking like that.

ALLMERS.   I speak of it only as a sort of introduction.

RITA.   Then do skip the introduction!

ALLMERS.   Rita,—you must not think it was the doctor's advice that drove me up to the mountains.

ASTA.   Was it not, Alfred?

RITA.   What was it, then?

ALLMERS.   It was this: I found there was no more peace for me, there in my study.

RITA.   No peace! Why, who disturbed you?

ALLMERS. [*Shaking his head.*]   No one from without. But I felt as though I were positively abusing—or, say rather, wasting—my best powers—frittering away the time.

ASTA. [*With wide eyes.*]   When you were writing at your book?

ALLMERS. [*Nodding.*]   For I cannot think that my powers are confined to that alone. I must surely have it in me to do one or two other things as well.

RITA.   Was that what you sat there brooding over?

ALLMERS.   Yes, mainly that.

RITA.   And so that is what has made you so discontented with yourself of late; and with the rest of us as well. For you know you were discontented, Alfred.

ALLMERS. [*Gazing straight before him.*]   There I sat bent over my table, day after day, and often half the night too—writing and writing at the great thick book on "Human Responsibility." H'm!

ASTA. [*Laying her hand upon his arm.*]   But, Alfred— that book is to be your life-work.

RITA.   Yes, you have said so often enough.

ALLMERS.   I thought so. Ever since I grew up, I have thought so. [*With an affectionate expression in his eyes.*] And it was you that enabled me to devote myself to it, my dear Rita——

RITA.   Oh, nonsense!

ALLMERS. [*Smiling to her.*]   —you, with your gold, and your green forests——

RITA. [*Half laughing, half vexed.*]   If you begin all that rubbish again, I shall beat you.

ASTA. [*Looking sorrowfully at him.*]   But the book, Alfred?

ALLMERS.   It began, as it were, to drift away from

me. But I was more and more beset by the thought of the higher duties that laid their claims upon me.

RITA. [*Beaming, seizes his hand.*]   Alfred!

ALLMERS.   The thought of Eyolf, my dear Rita.

RITA. [*Disappointed, drops his hand.*]   Ah—of Eyolf!

ALLMERS.   Poor little Eyolf has taken deeper and deeper hold of me. After that unlucky fall from the table— and especially since we have been assured that the injury is incurable——

RITA. [*Insistently.*]   But you take all the care you possibly can of him, Alfred!

ALLMERS.   As a schoolmaster, yes; but not as a father. And it is a father that I want henceforth to be to Eyolf.

RITA. [*Looking at him and shaking her head.*]   I don't think I quite understand you.

ALLMERS.   I mean that I will try with all my might to make his misfortune as painless and easy to him as it can possibly be.

RITA.   Oh, but, dear—thank Heaven, I don't think he feels it so deeply.

ASTA. [*With emotion.*]   Yes, Rita, he does.

ALLMERS.   Yes, you may be sure he feels it deeply.

RITA. [*Impatiently.*]   But, Alfred, what more can you do for him?

ALLMERS.   I will try to perfect all the rich possibilities that are dawning in his childish soul. I will foster all the germs of good in his nature—make them blossom and bear fruit. [*With more and more warmth, rising.*] And I will do more than that! I will help him to bring his desires into harmony with what lies attainable before him. That is just what at present they are not. All his longings are for things that must for ever remain unattainable to him. But I will create a conscious happiness in his mind.

{He goes once or twice up and down the room. ASTA *and* RITA *follow him with their eyes.*

RITA.   You should take these things more quietly, Alfred!

ALLMERS. [*Stops beside the table on the left, and looks at them.*]   Eyolf shall carry on my life-work—if he wants to. Or he shall choose one that is altogether his own. Perhaps that would be best. At all events, I shall let mine rest as it is.

RITA. [*Rising.*]   But, Alfred dear, can you not work both for yourself and for Eyolf?

ALLMERS.   No, I cannot. It is impossible! I cannot divide myself in this matter—and therefore I efface myself. Eyolf shall be the complete man of our race. And it shall be my new life-work to make him the complete man.

ASTA. [*Has risen and now goes up to him.*]   This must have cost you a terribly hard struggle, Alfred?

ALLMERS.   Yes, it has. At home here, I should never have conquered myself, never brought myself to the point of renunciation. Never at home!

RITA.   Then that was why you went away this summer?

ALLMERS. [*With shining eyes.*]   Yes! I went up into the infinite solitudes. I saw the sunrise gleaming on the mountain peaks. I felt myself nearer the stars—I seemed almost to be in sympathy and communion with them. And then I found the strength for it.

ASTA. [*Looking sadly at him.*]   But you will never write any more of your book on "Human Responsibility"?

ALLMERS.   No, never, Asta. I tell you I cannot split up my life between two vocations. But I will act out my "human responsibility"—in my own life.

RITA. [*With a smile.*]   Do you think you can live up to such high resolves at home here?

ALLMERS. [*Taking her hand.*]   With you to help me, I can. [*Holds out the other hand.*] And with you too, Asta.

RITA. [*Drawing her hand away.*]   Ah—with both of us! So, after all, you can divide yourself.

ALLMERS.   Why, my dearest Rita——!

> {RITA *moves away from him and stands in the garden doorway. A light and rapid knock is heard at the door on the right.* ENGINEER BORGHEIM *enters quickly. He is a young man of a little over thirty. His expression is bright and cheerful, and he holds himself erect.*

BORGHEIM.   Good morning, Mrs. Allmers. [*Stops with an expression of pleasure on seeing* ALLMERS.] Why, what's this? Home again already, Mr. Allmers?

ALLMERS. [*Shaking hands with him.*]   Yes, I arrived last night.

RITA. [*Gaily.*]   His leave was up, Mr. Borgheim.

ALLMERS.   No, you know it wasn't, Rita——

RITA. [*Approaching.*]   Oh yes, but it was, though. His furlough had run out.

BORGHEIM.   I see you hold your husband well in hand, Mrs. Allmers.

RITA.   I hold to my rights. And besides, everything must have an end.

BORGHEIM.   Oh, not everything—I hope. Good morning, Miss Allmers!

ASTA. [*Holding aloof from him.*]   Good morning.

RITA. [*Looking at* BORGHEIM.]   Not everything, you say?

BORGHEIM.   Oh, I am firmly convinced that there are s o m e things in the world that will never come to an end.

RITA. I suppose you are thinking of love—and that sort of thing.

BORGHEIM. [*Warmly.*] I am thinking of all that is lovely!

RITA. And that never comes to an end. Yes, let us think of that, hope for that, all of us.

ALLMERS. [*Coming up to them.*] I suppose you will soon have finished your road-work out here?

BORGHEIM. I have finished it already—finished it yesterday. It has been a long business, but, thank Heaven, that has come to an end.

RITA. And you are beaming with joy over that?

BORGHEIM. Yes, I am indeed!

RITA. Well, I must say——

BORGHEIM. What, Mrs. Allmers?

RITA. I don't think it is particularly nice of you, Mr. Borgheim.

BORGHEIM. Indeed! Why not?

RITA. Well, I suppose we sha'n't often see you in these parts after this.

BORGHEIM. No, that is true. I hadn't thought of that.

RITA. Oh, well, I suppose you will be able to look in upon us now and then all the same.

BORGHEIM. No, unfortunately that will be out of my power for a very long time.

ALLMERS. Indeed! How so?

BORGHEIM. The fact is, I have got a big piece of new work that I must set about at once.

ALLMERS.—Have you indeed?—[*Pressing his hand.*]—I am heartily glad to hear it.

RITA. I congratulate you, Mr. Borgheim.

BORGHEIM. Hush, hush—I really ought to talk

openly of it as yet! But I can't help coming out with it! It is a great piece of road-making—up in the north—with mountain ranges to cross, and the most tremendous difficulties to overcome!—[*With an outburst of gladness.*]—Oh, what a glorious world this is—and what a joy it is to be a road-maker in it!

RITA. [*Smiling, and looking teasingly at him.*] Is it roadmaking business that has brought you out here to-day in such wild spirits?

BORGHEIM. No, not that alone. I am thinking of all the bright and hopeful prospects that are opening out before me.

RITA. Aha, then perhaps you have something still more exquisite in reserve!

BORGHEIM. [*Glancing towards* ASTA.] Who knows! When once happiness comes to us, it is apt to come like a spring flood. [*Turns to* ASTA.] Miss Allmers, would you not like to take a little walk with me? As we used to?

ASTA. [*Quickly.*] No—no, thank you. Not now. Not today.

BORGHEIM. Oh, do come! Only a little bit of a walk! I have so much I want to talk to you about before I go.

RITA. Something else, perhaps, that you must not talk openly about as yet?

BORGHEIM. H'm, that depends——

RITA. But there is nothing to prevent your whispering, you know. [*Half aside.*] Asta, you must really go with him.

ASTA. But, my dear Rita——

BORGHEIM. [*Imploringly.*] Miss Asta—remember it is to be a farewell walk—the last for many a day.

ASTA. [*Takes her hat and parasol.*]   Very well, suppose we take a stroll in the garden, then.

BORGHEIM.   Oh, thank you, thank you!

ALLMERS.   And while you are there you can see what Eyolf is doing.

BORGHEIM.   Ah, Eyolf, by the bye! Where is Eyolf to-day? I've got something for him.

ALLMERS.   He is out playing somewhere.

BORGHEIM.   Is he really! Then he has begun to play now? He used always to be sitting indoors over his books.

ALLMERS.   There is to be an end of that now. I am going to make a regular open-air boy of him.

BORGHEIM.   Ah, now, that's right! Out into the open air with him, poor little fellow! Good Lord, what can we possibly do better than play in this blessed world? For my part, I think all life is one long playtime!—Come, Miss Asta!

{BORGHEIM *and* ASTA *go out on the verandah and down through the garden.*

ALLMERS. [*Stands looking after them.*]   Rita—do you think there is anything between those two?

RITA.   I don't know what to say. I used to think there was. But Asta has grown so strange to me—so utterly incomprehensible of late.

ALLMERS.   Indeed! Has she? While I have been away?

RITA.   Yes, within the last week or two.

ALLMERS.   And you think she doesn't care very much about him now?

RITA.   Not seriously; not utterly and entirely; not unreservedly—I am sure she doesn't. [*Looks searchingly at him.*] Would it displease you if she did?

ALLMERS. It would not exactly displease me. But it would certainly be a disquieting thought——

RITA. Disquieting?

ALLMERS. Yes; you must remember that I am responsible for Asta—for her life's happiness.

RITA. Oh, come—responsible! Surely Asta has come to years of discretion? I should say she was capable of choosing for herself.

ALLMERS. Yes, we must hope so, Rita.

RITA. For my part, I don't think at all ill of Borgheim.

ALLMERS. No, dear—no more do I—quite the contrary. But all the same——

RITA. [Continuing.] And I should be very glad indeed if he and Asta were to make a match of it.

ALLMERS. [Annoyed.] Oh, why should you be?

RITA. [With increasing excitement.] Why, for then she would have to go far, far away with him! And she could never come out here to us, as she does now.

ALLMERS. [Stares at her in astonishment.] What! Can you really wish Asta to go away?

RITA. Yes, yes, Alfred!

ALLMERS. Why in all the world——?

RITA. [Throwing her arms passionately round his neck.] For then, at last, I should have you to myself alone! And yet—not even then! Not wholly to myself! [Bursts into convulsive weeping.] Oh, Alfred, Alfred—I cannot give you up!

ALLMERS. [Gently releasing himself.] My dearest Rita, do be reasonable!

RITA. I don't care a bit about being reasonable! I care only for you! Only for you in all the world! [Again throwing her arms round his neck.] For you, for you, for you!

ALLMERS.   Let me go, let me go—you are strangling me!

RITA. [*Letting him go.*]   How I wish I could! [*Looking at him with flashing eyes.*] Oh, if you knew how I have hated you——!

ALLMERS.   Hated me——!

RITA.   Yes—when you shut yourself up in your room and brooded over your work—till long, long into the night. [*Plaintively.*] So long, so late, Alfred. Oh, how I hated your work!

ALLMERS.   But now I have done with that.

RITA. [*With a cutting laugh.*]   Oh yes! Now you have given yourself up to something worse.

ALLMERS. [*Shocked.*]   Worse! Do you call our child something worse?

RITA. [*Vehemently.*]   Yes, I do. As he comes between you and me, I call him so. For the book—the book was not a living being, as the child is. [*With increasing impetuosity.*] But I won't endure it, Alfred! I will not endure it—I tell you so plainly!

ALLMERS. [*Looks steadily at her, and says in a low voice.*]   I am often almost afraid of you, Rita.

RITA. [*Gloomily.*]   I am often afraid of myself. And for that very reason you must not awake the evil in me.

ALLMERS.   Why, good Heavens, do I do that?

RITA.   Yes, you do—when you tear to shreds the holiest bonds between us

ALLMERS. [*Urgently.*]   Think what you're saying, Rita. It is your own child—our only child, that you are speaking of.

RITA.   The child is only half mine. [*With another outburst.*] But you shall be mine alone! You shall be wholly mine! That I have a right to demand of you!

ALLMERS. [*Shrugging his shoulders.*]   Oh, my dear Rita, it is of no use demanding anything. Everything must be freely given.

RITA. [*Looks anxiously at him.*]   And that you cannot do henceforth?

ALLMERS.   No, I cannot. I must divide myself between Eyolf and you.

RITA.   But if Eyolf had never been born? What then?

ALLMERS. [*Evasively.*]   Oh, that would be another matter. Then I should have only you to care for.

RITA. [*Softly, her voice quivering.*]   Then I wish he had never been born.

ALLMERS. [*Flashing out.*]   Rita! You don't know what you are saying!

RITA. [*Trembling with emotion.*]   It was in pain unspeakable that I brought him into the world. But I bore it all with joy and rapture for your sake.

ALLMERS. [*Warmly.*]   Oh, yes, I know, I know.

RITA. [*With decision.*]   But there it must end. I will live my life—together with you—wholly with you. I cannot go on being only Eyolf's mother—only his mother and nothing more. I w i l l not, I tell you! I c a n n o t! I will be all in all to you! To you, Alfred!

ALLMERS.   But that is just what you are, Rita. Through our child——

RITA.   Oh—vapid, nauseous phrases—nothing else! No, Alfred, I am not to be put off like that. I was fitted to b e c o m e the child's mother, but not to b e a mother to him. You must take me as I am, Alfred.

ALLMERS.   And yet you used to be so fond of Eyolf.

RITA.   I was so sorry for him—because you troubled yourself so little about him. You kept him reading and grinding at books. You scarcely even saw him.

ALLMERS. [*Nodding slowly.*]   No; I was blind. The time had not yet come for me——

RITA. [*Looking in his face.*]   But now, I suppose, it has come?

ALLMERS.   Yes, at last. Now I see that the highest task I can have in the world is to be a true father to Eyolf.

RITA.   And to me?—what will you be to me?

ALLMERS. [*Gently.*]   I will always go on caring for you—with calm, deep tenderness. [*He tries to take her hands.*]

RITA. [*Evading him.*]   I don't care a bit for your calm, deep tenderness. I want you utterly and entirely—and alone! Just as I had you in the first rich, beautiful days. [*Vehemently and harshly.*] Never, never will I consent to be put off with scraps and leavings, Alfred!

ALLMERS. [*In a conciliatory tone.*]   I should have thought there was happiness in plenty for all three of us, Rita.

RITA. [*Scornfully.*]   Then you are easy to please. [*Seats herself at the table on the left.*] Now listen to me.

ALLMERS. [*Approaching.*]   Well, what is it?

RITA. [*Looking up at him with a veiled glow in her eyes.*]   When I got your telegram yesterday evening——

ALLMERS.   Yes? What then?

RITA.   —then I dressed myself in white——

ALLMERS.   Yes, I noticed you were in white when I arrived.

RITA.   I had let down my hair——

ALLMERS.   Your sweet masses of hair——

RITA.   —so that it flowed down my neck and shoulders——

ALLMERS.   I saw it, I saw it. Oh, how lovely you were, Rita!

RITA.   There were rose-tinted shades over both the lamps. And we were alone, we two—the only waking beings in the whole house. And there was champagne on the table.

ALLMERS.   I did not drink any of it.

RITA. [*Looking bitterly at him.*]   No, that is true. [*Laughs harshly.*] "There stood the champagne, but you tasted it not"—as the poet says.

> {*She rises from the arm-chair, goes with an air of weariness over to the sofa, and seats herself, half reclining, upon it.*

ALLMERS. [*Crosses the room and stands before her.*]   I was so taken up with serious thoughts. I had made up my mind to talk to you of our future, Rita—and first and foremost of Eyolf.

RITA. [*Smiling.*]   And so you did——

ALLMERS.   No, I had not time to—for you began to undress.

RITA.   Yes, and meanwhile you talked about Eyolf. Don't you remember? You wanted to know all about little Eyolf's digestion.

ALLMERS. [*Looking reproachfully at her.*]   Rita!

RITA.   And then you got into your bed, and slept the sleep of the just.

ALLMERS. [*Shaking his head.*]   Rita—Rita!

RITA. [*Lying at full length and looking up at him.*] Alfred?

ALLMERS.   Yes?

RITA.   "There stood your champagne, but you tasted it not."

ALLMERS. [*Almost harshly.*]   No. I did not taste it.

> {*He goes away from her and stands in the garden doorway. RITA lies for some time motionless, with closed eyes.*

RITA. [*Suddenly springing up.*]　　But let me tell you one thing, Alfred.

ALLMERS. [*Turning in the doorway.*]　　Well?

RITA.　　You ought not to feel quite so secure as you do!

ALLMERS.　　Not secure?

RITA.　　No, you ought not to be so indifferent! Not so certain of your property in me!

ALLMERS. [*Drawing nearer.*]　　What do you mean by that?

RITA. [*With trembling lips.*]　　Never in a single thought have I been untrue to you, Alfred! Never for an instant.

ALLMERS.　　No, Rita, I know that—I, who know you so well.

RITA. [*With sparkling eyes.*]　　But if you disdain me——!

ALLMERS.　　Disdain! I don't understand what you mean!

RITA.　　Oh, you don't know all that might rise up within me, if——

ALLMERS.　　If?

RITA.　　If I should ever see that you did not care for me—that you did not love me as you used to.

ALLMERS.　　But, my dearest Rita—years bring a certain change with them—and that must one day occur even in us—as in every one else.

RITA.　　Never in me! And I will not hear of any change in you either—I could not bear it, Alfred. I want to keep you to myself alone.

ALLMERS. [*Looking at her with concern.*]　　You have a terribly jealous nature——

RITA.　　I can't make myself different from what I am.

[*Threateningly.*] If you go and divide yourself between me and any one else——

ALLMERS.   What then——?

RITA.   Then I will take my revenge on you, Alfred!

ALLMERS.   How "take your revenge"?

RITA.   I don't know how.—Oh yes, I do know, well enough!

ALLMERS.   Well?

RITA.   I will go and throw myself away——

ALLMERS.   Throw yourself away, do you say?

RITA.   Yes, that I will. I'll throw myself straight into the arms of—of the first man that comes in my way!

ALLMERS. [*Looking tenderly at her and shaking his head.*]   That you will never do—my loyal, proud, true-hearted Rita!

RITA. [*Putting her arms round his neck.*]   Oh, you don't know what I might come to be if you—if you did not love me any more.

ALLMERS.   Did not love you, Rita? How can you say such a thing!

RITA. [*Half laughing, lets him go.*]   Why should I not spread my nets for that—that road-maker man that hangs about here?

ALLMERS. [*Relieved.*]   Oh, thank goodness—you are only joking.

RITA.   Not at all. He would do as well as any one else.

ALLMERS.   Ah, but I suspect he is more or less taken up already.

RITA.   So much the better! For then I should take him away from some one else; and that is just what Eyolf has done to me.

ALLMERS.　　Can you say that our little Eyolf has done that?

RITA. [*Pointing with her forefinger.*]　　There, you see! You see! The moment you mention Eyolf's name, you grow tender and your voice quivers! [*Threateningly, clenching her hands.*] Oh, you almost tempt me to wish——

ALLMERS. [*Looking at her anxiously.*]　　What do I tempt you to wish, Rita?——

RITA. [*Vehemently, going away from him.*]　　No, no, no—I won't tell you that! Never!

ALLMERS. [*Drawing nearer to her.*]　　Rita! I implore you—for my sake and for your own—do not let yourself be tempted into evil.

> [BORGHEIM *and* ASTA *come up from the garden. They both show signs of restrained emotion. They look serious and dejected.* ASTA *remains out on the verandah.* BORGHEIM *comes into the room.*

BORGHEIM.　　So that is over—Miss Allmers and I have had our last walk together.

RITA. [*Looks at him with surprise.*]　　Ah! And there is no longer journey to follow the walk?

BORGHEIM.　　Yes, for me.

RITA.　　For you alone?

BORGHEIM.　　Yes, for me alone.

RITA. [*Glances darkly at* ALLMERS.]　　Do you hear that? [*Turns to* BORGHEIM.] I'll wager it is some one with the evil eye that has played you this trick.

BORGHEIM. [*Looks at her.*]　　The evil eye?

RITA. [*Nodding.*]　　Yes, the evil eye.

BORGHEIM.　　Do you believe in the evil eye, Mrs. Allmers?

RITA.　　Yes. I have begun to believe in the evil eye. Especially in a child's evil eye.

ALLMERS. [*Shocked, whispers.*]   Rita—how can you——?

RITA. [*Speaking low.*]   It is you that make me so wicked and hateful, Alfred.

> {*Confused cries and shrieks are heard in the distance, from the direction of the fiord.*

BORGHEIM. [*Going to the glass door.*]   What noise is that?

ASTA. [*In the doorway.*]   Look at all those people running down to the pier!

ALLMERS.   What can it be? [*Looks out for a moment.*] No doubt it's those street urchins at some mischief again.

BORGHEIM. [*Calls, leaning over the verandah railings.*]   I say, you boys down there! What's the matter?

> {*Several voices are heard answering indistinctly and confusedly.*

RITA.   What do they say?

BORGHEIM.   They say it's a child that's drowned.

ALLMERS.   A child drowned?

ASTA. [*Uneasily.*]   A little boy, they say.

ALLMERS.   Oh, they can all swim, every one of them.

RITA. [*Shrieks in terror.*]   Where is Eyolf?

ALLMERS.   Keep quiet—quiet. Eyolf is down in the garden, playing.

ASTA.   No, he wasn't in the garden.—

RITA. [*With upstretched arms.*]   Oh, if only it isn't he!

BORGHEIM. [*Listens, and calls down.*]   Whose child is it, do you say?

> {*Indistinct voices are heard. BORGHEIM and ASTA utter a suppressed cry, and rush out through the garden.*

ALLMERS. [*In an agony of dread.*]   It isn't Eyolf! It isn't Eyolf, Rita!

RITA. [*On the verandah, listening.*]   Hush! Be quiet! Let me hear what they are saying!

{RITA *rushes back with a piercing shriek, into the room.*

ALLMERS. [*Following her.*]   What did they say?

RITA. [*Sinking down beside the arm-chair on the left.*] They said: "The crutch is floating!"

ALLMERS. [*Almost paralysed.*]   No! No! No!

RITA. [*Hoarsely.*]   Eyolf! Eyolf! Oh, but they m u s t save him!

ALLMERS. [*Half distracted.*]   They must, they must! So precious a life!

{He *rushes down through the garden.*

Act II

~

A little narrow glen by the side of the fiord, on ALLMERS'S *property.
On the left, lofty old trees overarch the spot. Down the slope in
the background a brook comes leaping, and loses itself among the
stones on the margin of the wood. A path winds along by the
brook-side. To the right there are only a few single trees, between
which the fiord is visible. In front is seen the corner of a boat-
shed with a boat drawn up. Under the old trees on the left stands
a table with a bench and one or two chairs, all made of thin
birch-staves. It is a heavy, damp day, with driving mist-
wreaths.*

ALFRED ALLMERS, *dressed as before, sits on the bench, leaning his
arms on the table. His hat lies before him. He gazes absently
and immovably out over the water.*

Presently ASTA ALLMERS *comes down the wood-path. She is carrying an open umbrella.*

ASTA. [*Goes quietly and cautiously up to him.*]   You
ought not to sit down here in this gloomy weather, Alfred.

ALLMERS. [*Nods slowly without answering.*]

ASTA. [*Closing her umbrella.*]   I have been searching
for you such a long time.

ALLMERS. [*Without expression.*]   Thank you.

ASTA. [*Moves a chair and seats herself close to him.*]   Have
you been sitting here long? All the time?

ALLMERS. [*Does not answer at first. Presently he says:*]
No I cannot grasp it. It seems so utterly impossible.

ASTA. [*Laying her hand compassionately on his arm.*]   Poor Alfred!

ALLMERS. [*Gazing at her.*]   Is it really true then, Asta? Or have I gone mad? Or am I only dreaming? Oh, if it were only a dream! Just think, if I were to waken now!

ASTA.   Oh, if I could only waken you!

ALLMERS. [*Looking out over the water.*]   How pitiless the fiord looks to-day, lying so heavy and drowsy—leaden-grey—with splashes of yellow—and reflecting the rain-clouds.

ASTA. [*Imploringly.*]   Oh, Alfred, don't sit staring out over the fiord!

ALLMERS. [*Not heeding her.*]   Over the surface, yes. But in the depths—there sweeps the rushing undertow——

ASTA. [*In terror.*]   Oh, for God's sake—don't think of the depths!

ALLMERS. [*Looking gently at her.*]   I suppose you think he is lying close outside here? But he is not, Asta. You must not think that. You must remember how fiercely the current sweeps out here—straight to the open sea.

ASTA. [*Throws herself forward against the table, and, sobbing, buries her face in her hands.*]   Oh, God! Oh, God!

ALLMERS. [*Heavily.*]   So you see, little Eyolf has passed so far—far away from us now.

ASTA. [*Looks imploringly up at him.*]   Oh, Alfred, don't say such things!

ALLMERS.   Why, you can reckon it out for yourself— you that are so clever. In eight-and-twenty hours—nine-and-twenty hours—— Let me see——! Let me see——!

ASTA. [*Shrieking and stopping her ears.*]   Alfred!

ALLMERS. [*Clenching his hand firmly upon the table.*]   Can you conceive the meaning of a thing like this?

ASTA. [*Looks at him.*]   Of what?

ALLMERS.   Of this that has been done to Rita and me.

ASTA.   The meaning of it?

ALLMERS. [*Impatiently.*]   Yes, the meaning, I say. For, after all, there must be a meaning in it. Life, existence—destiny, c a n n o t be so utterly meaningless.

ASTA.   Oh, who can say anything with certainty about these things, my dear Alfred?

ALLMERS. [*Laughs bitterly.*]   No, no; I believe you are right there. Perhaps the whole thing goes simply by haphazard—taking its own course, like a drifting wreck without a rudder. I daresay that is how it is. At least, it seems very like it.

ASTA. [*Thoughtfully.*]   What if it only seems——?

ALLMERS. [*Vehemently.*]   Ah? Perhaps you can unravel the mystery for me? I certainly cannot. [*More gently.*] Here is Eyolf, just entering upon conscious life: full of such infinite possibilities—splendid possibilities perhaps: he would have filled my life with pride and gladness. And then a crazy old woman has only to come this way—and show a cur in a bag——

ASTA.   But we don't in the least know how it really happened.

ALLMERS.   Yes, we do. The boys saw her row out over the fiord. They saw Eyolf standing alone at the very end of the pier. They saw him gazing after her—and then he seemed to turn giddy. [*Quivering.*] And that was how he fell over—and disappeared.

ASTA.   Yes, yes. But all the same——

ALLMERS.   She has drawn him down into the depths—that you may be sure of, dear.

ASTA.   But, Alfred, why should she?

ALLMERS.   Yes, that is just the question! Why

should she? There is no retribution behind it all—no atonement, I mean. Eyolf never did her any harm. He never called names after her; he never threw stones at her dog. Why, he had never set eyes either on her or her dog till yesterday. So there is no retribution; the whole thing is utterly groundless and meaningless, Asta.—And yet the order of the world requires it.

ASTA.   Have you spoken to Rita of these things?

ALLMERS. [*Shakes his head.*]   I feel as if I can talk better to you about them. [*Drawing a deep breath.*] And about everything else as well.

> {ASTA *takes sewing-materials and a little paper parcel out of her pocket.* ALLMERS *sits looking on absently.*

ALLMERS.   What have you got there, Asta?

ASTA. [*Taking his hat.*]   Some black crape.

ALLMERS.   Oh, what is the use of that?

ASTA.   Rita asked me to put it on. May I?

ALLMERS.   Oh, yes; as far as I'm concerned——

> {She sews the crape on his hat.

ALLMERS. [*Sitting and looking at her.*]   Where is Rita?

ASTA.   She is walking about the garden a little, I think. Borgheim is with her.

ALLMERS. [*Slightly surprised.*]   Indeed! Is Borgheim out here to-day again?

ASTA.   Yes. He came out by the mid-day train.

ALLMERS.   I didn't expect that.

ASTA. [*Sewing.*]   He was so fond of Eyolf.

ALLMERS.   Borgheim is a faithful soul, Asta.

ASTA. [*With quiet warmth.*]   Yes, faithful he is, indeed. That is certain.

ALLMERS. [*Fixing his eyes upon her.*]   You are really fond of him?

ASTA.   Yes, I am.

ALLMERS.   And yet you cannot make up your mind to———?

ASTA. [*Interrupting.*]   Oh, my dear Alfred, don't talk of t h a t!

ALLMERS.   Yes, yes; tell me why you cannot?

ASTA.   Oh, no! Please! You really must not ask me. You see, it's so painful for me.—There now! The hat is done.

ALLMERS.   Thank you.

ASTA.   And now for the left arm.

ALLMERS.   Am I to have crape on it too?

ASTA.   Yes, that is the custom.

ALLMERS.   Well—as you please.

> *She moves close up to him and begins to sew.*

ASTA.   Keep your arm still—then I won't prick you.

ALLMERS. [*With a half-smile.*]   This is like the old days.

ASTA.   Yes, don't you think so?

ALLMERS.   When you were a little girl you used to sit just like this, mending my clothes. The first thing you ever sewed for me—that was black crape, too.

ASTA.   Was it?

ALLMERS.   Round my student's cap—at the time of father's death.

ASTA.   Could I sew then? Fancy, I have forgotten it.

ALLMERS.   Oh, you were such a little thing then.

ASTA.   Yes, I was little then.

ALLMERS.   And then, two years afterwards—when we lost your mother—then again you sewed a big crape band on my sleeve.

ASTA.   I thought it was the right thing to do.

ALLMERS. [*Patting her hand.*]   Yes, yes, it was the right thing to do, Asta. And then when we were left alone in the world, we two———. Are you done already?

ASTA. Yes. [*Putting together her sewing-materials.*] It was really a beautiful time for us, Alfred. We two alone.

ALLMERS. Yes, it was—though we had to toil so hard.

ASTA. Y o u toiled.

ALLMERS. [*With more life.*] Oh, you toiled too, in your way, I can assure you—[*smiling*]—my dear, faithful—Eyolf.

ASTA. Oh—you mustn't remind me of that stupid nonsense about the name.

ALLMERS. Well, if you had been a boy, you would have been called Eyolf.

ASTA. Yes, i f ! But when you began to go to college——. [*Smiling involuntarily.*] I wonder how you could be so childish.

ALLMERS. Was it I that was childish?

ASTA. Yes, indeed, I think it was, as I look back upon it all. You were ashamed of having no brother—only a sister.

ALLMERS. No, no, it was you, dear—y o u were ashamed.

ASTA. Oh yes, I too, perhaps—a little. And somehow or other I was sorry for you——

ALLMERS. Yes, I believe you were. And then you hunted up some of my old boy's clothes——

ASTA. Your fine Sunday clothes—yes. Do you remember the blue blouse and knickerbockers?

ALLMERS. [*His eyes dwelling upon her.*] I remember so well how you looked when you used to wear them.

ASTA. Only when we were at home, alone, though.

ALLMERS. And how serious we were, dear, and how mightily pleased with ourselves. I always called you Eyolf.

ASTA.   Oh, Alfred, I hope you have never told Rita this?

ALLMERS.   Yes, I believe I did once tell her.

ASTA.   Oh, Alfred, how could you do that?

ALLMERS.   Well, you see—one tells one's wife everything—very nearly.

ASTA.   Yes, I suppose one does.

ALLMERS. [*As if awakening, clutches at his forehead and starts up.*]   Oh, how can I sit here and——

ASTA. [*Rising, looks sorrowfully at him.*]   What is the matter?

ALLMERS.   He had almost passed away from me. He had passed quite away.

ASTA.   Eyolf!

ALLMERS.   Here I sat, living in these recollections—and he had no part in them.

ASTA.   Yes, Alfred—little Eyolf was behind it all.

ALLMERS.   No, he was not. He slipped out of my memory—out of my thoughts. I did not see him for a moment as we sat here talking. I utterly forgot him all that time.

ASTA.   But surely you must take some rest in your sorrow.

ALLMERS.   No, no, no; that is just what I will not do! I must not—I have no right—and no heart for it, either. [*Going in great excitement towards the right.*] All my thoughts must be out there, where he lies drifting in the depths!

ASTA. [*Following him and holding him back.*]   Alfred—Alfred! Don't go to the fiord.

ALLMERS.   I must go out to him! Let me go, Asta! I will take the boat.

ASTA. [*In terror.*]   Don't go to the fiord, I say!

ALLMERS. [*Yielding.*]   No, no—I will not. Only let me alone.

ASTA. [*Leading him back to the table.*]   You must rest from your thoughts, Alfred. Come here and sit down.

ALLMERS. [*Making as if to seat himself on the bench.*] Well, well—as you please.

ASTA.   No, I won't let you sit there.

ALLMERS.   Yes, let me.

ASTA.   No don't. For then you will only sit looking out—— [*Forces him down upon a chair, with his back to the right.*] There now. Now that's right. [*Seats herself upon the bench.*] And now we can talk a little again.

ALLMERS. [*Drawing a deep breath audibly.*]   It was good to deaden the sorrow and heartache for a moment.

ASTA.   You m u s t do so, Alfred.

ALLMERS.   But don't you think it is terribly weak and unfeeling of me—to be able to do so?

ASTA.   Oh, no—I am sure it is impossible to keep circling for ever round one fixed thought.

ALLMERS.   Yes, for me it is impossible. Before you came to me, here I sat, torturing myself unspeakably with this crushing, gnawing sorrow——

ASTA.   Yes?

ALLMERS.   And would you believe it, Asta——? H'm——

ASTA.   Well?

ALLMERS.   In the midst of all the agony, I found myself speculating what we should have for dinner to-day.

ASTA. [*Soothingly.*]   Well, well, if only it rests you to——

ALLMERS.   Yes, just fancy, dear—it seemed as if it did give me rest. [*Holds out his hand to her across the ta-*

ble.] How good it is, Asta, that I have you with me. I am so glad of that. Glad, glad—even in my sorrow.

ASTA. [*Looking earnestly at him.*]   You ought most of all to be glad that you have Rita.

ALLMERS.   Yes, of course I should. But Rita is no kin to me—it isn't like having a sister.

ASTA. [*Eagerly.*]   Do you say that, Alfred?

ALLMERS.   Yes, our family is a thing apart. [*Half jestingly.*] We have always had vowels for our initials. Don't you remember how often we used to speak of that? And all our relations—all equally poor. And we have all the same colour of eyes.

ASTA.   Do you think I have——?

ALLMERS.   No, you take entirely after your mother. You are not in the least like the rest of us—not even like father. But all the same——

ASTA.   All the same——?

ALLMERS.   Well, I believe that living together has, as it were, stamped us in each other's image—mentally, I mean.

ASTA. [*With warm emotion.*]   Oh, you must never say that, Alfred. It is only I that have taken my stamp from you; and it is to you that I owe everything—every g o o d thing in the world.

ALLMERS. [*Shaking his head.*]   You owe me nothing, Asta. On the contrary——

ASTA.   I owe you everything! You must never doubt that. No sacrifice has been too great for you——

ALLMERS. [*Interrupting.*]   Oh, nonsense—sacrifice! Don't talk of such a thing.—I have only loved you, Asta, ever since you were a little child. [*After a short pause.*] And then it always seemed to me that I had so much injustice to make up to you for.

ASTA. [*Astonished.*]　　Injustice? You?

ALLMERS.　　Not precisely on my own account. But——

ASTA. [*Eagerly.*]　　But——?

ALLMERS.　　On father's.

ASTA. [*Half rising from the bench.*]　　On—father's! [*Sitting down again.*] What do you mean by that, Alfred?

ALLMERS.　　Father was never really kind to you.

ASTA. [*Vehemently.*]　　Oh, don't say that!

ALLMERS.　　Yes, it is true. He did not love you—not as he ought to have.

ASTA. [*Evasively.*]　　No, perhaps not as he loved you. That was only natural.

ALLMERS. [*Continuing.*]　　And he was often hard to your mother, too—at least in the last years.

ASTA. [*Softly.*]　　Mother was so much, much younger than he—remember that.

ALLMERS.　　Do you think they were not quite suited to each other?

ASTA.　　Perhaps not.

ALLMERS.　　Yes, but still——. Father, who in other ways was so gentle and warm-hearted—so kindly towards every one——

ASTA. [*Quietly.*]　　Mother, too, was not always as she ought to have been.

ALLMERS.　　Your mother was not!

ASTA.　　Perhaps not always.

ALLMERS.　　Towards father, do you mean?

ASTA.　　Yes.

ALLMERS.　　I never noticed that.

ASTA. [*Struggling with her tears, rises.*]　　Oh, my dear Alfred—let them rest—those who are gone.

{She goes towards the right.

ALLMERS. [*Rising.*]   Yes, let them rest. [*Wringing his hands.*] But those who are gone—it is they that won't let us rest, Asta. Neither day nor night.

ASTA. [*Looks warmly at him.*]   Time will make it all seem easier, Alfred.

ALLMERS. [*Looking helplessly at her.*]   Yes, don't you think it will?—But how I am to get over these terrible first days [*Hoarsely.*]—that is what I cannot imagine.

ASTA. [*Imploringly, laying her hands on his shoulders.*]   Go up to Rita. Oh, please do——

ALLMERS. [*Vehemently, withdrawing from her.*]   No, no, no—don't talk to me of that! I cannot, I tell you. [*More calmly.*] Let me remain here, with you.

ASTA.   Well, I will not leave you.

ALLMERS. [*Seizing her hand and holding it fast.*]   Thank you for that! [*Looks out for a time over the fiord.*] Where is my little Eyolf now? [*Smiling sadly to her.*] Can you tell me that— my big, wise Eyolf? [*Shaking his head.*] No one in all the world can tell me that. I know only this one terrible thing— that he is gone from me.

ASTA. [*Looking up to the left, and withdrawing her hand.*]   Here they are coming.

{Mrs. ALLMERS and ENGINEER BORGHEIM come down by the wood-path, she leading the way. She wears a dark dress and a black veil over her head. He has an umbrella under his arm.

ALLMERS. [*Going to meet her.*]   How is it with you, Rita?

RITA. [*Passing him.*]   Oh, don't ask.

ALLMERS.   Why do you come here?

RITA.   Only to look for you. What are you doing?

ALLMERS.   Nothing. Asta came down to me.

RITA.   Yes, but before Asta came? You have been away from me all the morning.

ALLMERS.   I have been sitting here looking out over the water.

RITA.   Ugh,—how can you?

ALLMERS. [*Impatiently.*]   I like best to be alone now.

RITA. [*Moving restlessly about.*]   And then to sit still! To stay in one place!

ALLMERS.   I have nothing in the world to move for.

RITA.   I cannot bear to be anywhere long. Least of all here—with the fiord at my very feet.

ALLMERS.   It is just the nearness of the fiord——

RITA. [*To* BORGHEIM.]   Don't you think he should come back with the rest of us?

BORGHEIM. [*To* ALLMERS.]   I believe it would be better for you.

ALLMERS.   No, no; let me stay where I am.

RITA.   Then I will stay with you, Alfred.

ALLMERS.   Very well; do so, then. You remain too, Asta.

ASTA. [*Whispers to* BORGHEIM]   Let us leave them alone!

BORGHEIM. [*With a glance of comprehension.*]   Miss Allmers, shall we go a little further—along the shore? For the very last time?

ASTA. [*Taking her umbrella.*]   Yes, come. Let us go a little further.

> {ASTA *and* BORGHEIM *go out together behind the boat-shed.* ALLMERS *wanders about for a little. Then he seats himself on a stone under the trees on the left.*

RITA. [*Comes up and stands before him, her hands folded and hanging down.*]   Can you think the thought, Alfred—that we have lost Eyolf?

ALLMERS. [*Looking sadly at the ground.*]   We must accustom ourselves to think it.

RITA.   I cannot. I cannot. And then that horrible sight that will haunt me all my life long.

ALLMERS. [*Looking up.*]   What sight? What have you seen?

RITA.   I have seen nothing myself. I have only heard it told. Oh——!

ALLMERS.   You may as well tell me at once.

RITA.   I got Borgheim to go down with me to the pier——

ALLMERS.   What did you want there?

RITA.   To question the boys as to how it happened.

ALLMERS.   But we know that.

RITA.   We got to know more.

ALLMERS.   Well?

RITA.   It is not true that he disappeared all at once.

ALLMERS.   Do they say that now?

RITA.   Yes. They say they saw him lying down on the bottom. Deep down in the clear water.

ALLMERS. [*Grinding his teeth.*]   And they didn't save him!

RITA.   I suppose they could not.

ALLMERS.   They could swim—every one of them. Did they tell you how he was lying whilst they could see him?

RITA.   Yes. They said he was lying on his back. And with great, open eyes.

ALLMERS.   Open eyes. But quite still?

RITA.   Yes, quite still. And then something came and swept him away. They called it the undertow.

ALLMERS. [*Nodding slowly.*]   So that was the last they saw of him.

RITA. [*Suffocated with tears.*]   Yes.

ALLMERS. [*In a dull voice.*]   And never—never will any one see him again.

RITA. [*Wailing.*]   I shall see him day and night, as he lay down there.

ALLMERS.   With great, open eyes.

RITA. [*Shuddering.*]   Yes, with great, open eyes. I see them! I see them now!

ALLMERS. [*Rises slowly and looks with quiet menace at her.*]   Were they evil, those eyes, Rita?

RITA. [*Turning pale.*]   Evil——!

ALLMERS. [*Going close up to her.*]   Were they evil eyes that stared up? Up from the depths?

RITA. [*Shrinking from him.*]   Alfred——!

ALLMERS. [*Following her.*]   Answer me! Were they a child's evil eyes?

RITA. [*Shrieks.*]   Alfred! Alfred!

ALLMERS.   Now things have come about—just as you wished, Rita.

RITA.   I! What did *I* wish?

ALLMERS.   That Eyolf were not here.

RITA.   Never for a moment have I wished that! That Eyolf should not stand between us—that was what I wished.

ALLMERS.   Well, well—he does not stand between us any more.

RITA. [*Softly, gazing straight before her.*]   Perhaps now more than ever. [*With a sudden shudder.*] Oh, that horrible sight!

ALLMERS. [*Nods.*]   The child's evil eyes.

RITA. [*In dread, recoiling from him.*]   Let me be, Alfred! I am afraid of you. I have never seen you like this before.

ALLMERS. [*Looks harshly and coldly at her.*]   Sorrow makes us wicked and hateful.

RITA. [*Terrified, and yet defiant.*]   That is what I feel, too.

> [ALLMERS *goes towards the right and looks out over the fiord.* RITA *seats herself at the table. A short pause.*

ALLMERS. [*Turning his head towards her.*]   You never really and truly loved him—never!

RITA. [*With cold self-control.*]   Eyolf would never let me take him really and truly to my heart.

ALLMERS.   Because you did not want to.

RITA.   Oh yes, I did. I did want to. But some one stood in the way—even from the first.

ALLMERS. [*Turning right round.*]   Do you mean that *I* stood in the way?

RITA.   Oh, no—not at first.

ALLMERS. [*Coming nearer her.*]   Who, then?

RITA.   His aunt.

ALLMERS.   Asta?

RITA.   Yes. Asta stood and barred the way for me.

ALLMERS.   Can you say that, Rita?

RITA.   Yes. Asta—she took him to her heart—from the moment that happened—that miserable fall.

ALLMERS.   If she did so, she did it in love.

RITA. [*Vehemently.*]   That is just it! I cannot endure to share anything with any one! Not in love.

ALLMERS.   We two should have shared him between us in love.

RITA. [*Looking scornfully at him.*]   We? Oh, the truth is you have never had any real love for him either.

ALLMERS. [*Looks at her in astonishment.*]   I have not——!

RITA. No, you have not. At first you were so utterly taken up by that book of yours—about Responsibility.

ALLMERS. [*Forcibly.*] Yes, I was. But my very book—I sacrificed for Eyolf's sake.

RITA. Not out of love for him.

ALLMERS. Why then, do you suppose?

RITA. Because you were consumed with mistrust of yourself. Because you had begun to doubt whether you had any, great vocation to live for in the world.

ALLMERS. [*Observing her closely.*] Could you see that in me?

RITA. Oh, yes—little by little. And then you needed something new to fill up your life.—It seems *I* was not enough for you any longer.

ALLMERS. That is the law of change, Rita.

RITA. And that was why you wanted to make a prodigy of poor little Eyolf.

ALLMERS. That was not what I wanted. I wanted to make a happy human being of him.—That, and nothing more.

RITA. But not out of love for him. Look into yourself! [*With a certain shyness of expression.*] Search out all that lies under—and behind your action.

ALLMERS. [*Avoiding her eyes.*] There is something you shrink from saying.

RITA. And you too.

ALLMERS. [*Looks thoughtfully at her.*] If it is as you say, then we two have never really possessed our own child.

RITA. No. Not in perfect love.

ALLMERS. And yet we are sorrowing so bitterly for him.

RITA. [*With sarcasm.*] Yes, isn't it curious that we should grieve like this over a little stranger boy?

ALLMERS. [*With an outburst.*]   Oh, don't call him a stranger!

RITA. [*Sadly shaking her head.*]   We never won the boy, Alfred. Not I—nor you either.

ALLMERS. [*Wringing his hands.*]   And now it is too late! Too late!

RITA.   And no consolation anywhere—in anything.

ALLMERS. [*With sudden passion.*]   Y o u are the guilty one in this!

RITA. [*Rising.*]   I!

ALLMERS.   Yes, you! It was your fault that he became—what he was! It was your fault that he could not save himself when he fell into the water.

RITA. [*With a gesture of repulsion.*]   Alfred—you s h a l l not throw the blame upon me!

ALLMERS. [*More and more beside himself.*]   Yes, yes, I do! It was you that left the helpless child unwatched upon the table.

RITA.   He was lying so comfortably among the cushions, and sleeping so soundly. And you had promised to look after him.

ALLMERS.   Yes, I had. [*Lowering his voice.*] But then you came—you, you, you—and lured me to you.

RITA. [*Looking defiantly at him.*]   Oh, better own at once that you forgot the child and everything else.

ALLMERS. [*In suppressed desperation.*]   Yes, that is true. [*Lower.*] I forgot the child—in your arms!

RITA. [*Exasperated.*]   Alfred! Alfred—this is intolerable of you!

ALLMERS. [*In a low voice, clenching his fists before her face.*]   In that hour you condemned little Eyolf to death.

RITA. [*Wildly.*]   You, too! You, too—if it is as you say!

ALLMERS.   Oh yes—call me to account, too—if you will. We have sinned, both of us. And so, after all, there w a s retribution in Eyolf's death.

RITA.   Retribution?

ALLMERS. [*With more self-control.*]   Yes. Judgment upon you and me. Now, as we stand here, we have our deserts. While he lived, we let ourselves shrink away from him in secret, abject remorse. We could not bear to see i t—the thing he had to drag with him——

RITA. [*Whispers.*]   The crutch.

ALLMERS.   Yes, that. And now, what we now call sorrow and heartache—is really the gnawing of conscience, Rita. Nothing else.

RITA. [*Gazing helplessly at him.*]   I feel as if all this must end in despair—in madness for both of us. For we can never—never make it good again.

ALLMERS. [*Passing into a calmer mood.*]   I dreamed about Eyolf last night. I thought I saw him coming up from the pier. He could run like other boys. So nothing had happened to him—neither the one thing nor the other. And the torturing reality was nothing but a dream, I thought. Oh, how I thanked and blessed—— [*Checking himself.*] H'm!

RITA. [*Looking at him.*]   Whom?

ALLMERS. [*Evasively.*]   Whom——?

RITA.   Yes; whom did you thank and bless?

ALLMERS. [*Putting aside the question.*]   I was only dreaming, you know——

RITA.   One whom you yourself do not believe in?

ALLMERS.   That was how I felt, all the same. Of course, I was sleeping——

RITA. [*Reproachfully.*]   You should not have taught me to doubt, Alfred.

ALLMERS. Would it have been right of me to let you go through life with your mind full of empty fictions?

RITA. It would have been better for me; for then I should have had something to take refuge in. Now I am utterly at sea.

ALLMERS. [*Observing her closely.*] If you had the choice now——. If you could follow Eyolf to where he is——?

RITA. No, you feel it so, too, don't you, Alfred! You could not either, could you?

ALLMERS. Yes? What then?

ALLMERS. If you were fully assured that you would find him again—know him—understand him——?

RITA. Yes, yes; what then?

ALLMERS. Would you, of your own free will, take the leap over to him? Of your own free will leave everything behind you? Renounce your whole earthly life? Would you, Rita?

RITA. [*Softly.*] Now, at once?

ALLMERS. Yes; to-day. This very hour. Answer me—would you?

RITA. [*Hesitating.*] Oh, I don't know, Alfred. No! I think I should have to stay here with you, a little while.

ALLMERS. For my sake?

RITA. Yes, only for your sake.

ALLMERS. But afterwards? Would you then——? Answer!

RITA. Oh, what can I answer? I c o u l d not go away from you. Never! Never!

ALLMERS. But suppose now *I* went to Eyolf? And you had the fullest assurance that you would meet both him and me there. Then would you come over to us?

RITA. I should want to—so much! so much! But——

ALLMERS. Well?

RITA. [*Moaning softly.*]   I could not—I feel it. No, no, I never could! Not for all the glory of heaven!

ALLMERS.   Nor I.

RITA.   No, you feel it so, too, don't you, Alfred! You could not either, could you?

ALLMERS.   No. For it is here, in the life of earth, that we living beings are at home.

RITA.   Yes, here lies the kind of happiness that we can understand.

ALLMERS. [*Darkly.*]   Oh, happiness—happiness——

RITA.   You mean that happiness—that we can never find it again? [*Looks inquiringly at him.*] But if——? [*Vehemently.*] No, no; I dare not say it! Nor even think it!

ALLMERS.   Yes, say it—say it, Rita.

RITA. [*Hesitatingly.*]   Could we not try to——? Would it not be possible to forget him?

ALLMERS.   Forget Eyolf?

RITA.   Forget the anguish and remorse, I mean.

ALLMERS.   Can you wish it?

RITA.   Yes,—if it were possible. [*With an outburst.*] For this—I cannot bear this for ever! Oh, can we not think of something that will bring us forgetfulness!

ALLMERS. [*Shakes his head.*]   What could that be?

RITA.   Could we not see what travelling would do— far away from here?

ALLMERS.   From home? When you know you are never really well anywhere but here.

RITA.   Well, then, let us have crowds of people about us! Keep open house! Plunge into something that can deaden and dull our thoughts.

ALLMERS.   Such a life would be impossible for me.— No,—rather than that, I would try to take up my work again.

RITA. [*Bitingly.*]   Your work—the work that has always stood like a dead wall between us!

ALLMERS. [*Slowly, looking fixedly at her.*]   There must always be a dead wall between us two, from this time forth.

RITA.   Why must there——?

ALLMERS.   Who knows but that a child's great, open eyes are watching us day and night.

RITA. [*Softly, shuddering.*]   Alfred—how terrible to think of!

ALLMERS.   Our love has been like a consuming fire. Now it must be quenched——

RITA. [*With a movement towards him.*]   Quenched!

ALLMERS. [*Hardly.*]   It is quenched—in one of us.

RITA. [*As if petrified.*]   And you dare say that to me!

ALLMERS. [*More gently.*]   It is dead, Rita. But in what I now feel for you—in our common guilt and need of atonement—I seem to foresee a sort of resurrection——

RITA. [*Vehemently.*]   I don't care a bit about any resurrection!

ALLMERS.   Rita!

RITA.   I am a warm-blooded being! I don't go drowsing about—with fishes' blood in my veins. [*Wringing her hands.*] And now to be imprisoned for life—in anguish and remorse! Imprisoned with one who is no longer mine, mine, mine!

ALLMERS.   It must have ended so, sometime, Rita.

RITA.   Must have ended so! The love that in the beginning rushed forth so eagerly to meet with love!

ALLMERS.   M y love did not rush forth to you in the beginning.

RITA.   What did you feel for me, first of all?

ALLMERS.   Dread.

RITA.   That I can understand. How was it, then, that I won you after all?

ALLMERS. [*In a low voice.*]   You were so entrancingly beautiful, Rita.

RITA. [*Looks searchingly at him.*]   Then that was the only reason? Say it, Alfred! The only reason?

ALLMERS. [*Conquering himself.*]   No, there was another as well.

RITA. [*With an outburst.*]   I can guess what that was! It was "my gold, and my green forests," as you call it. Was it not so, Alfred?

ALLMERS.   Yes.

RITA.   [*Looks at him with deep reproach.*]   How could you—how could you!

ALLMERS.   I had Asta to think of.

RITA. [*Angrily.*]   Yes, Asta! [*Bitterly.*] Then it was really Asta that brought us two together?

ALLMERS.   She knew nothing about it. She has no suspicion of it, even to this day.

RITA. [*Rejecting the plea.*]   It was Asta, nevertheless! [*Smiling, with a sidelong glance of scorn.*] Or, no—it was little Eyolf. Little Eyolf, my dear!

ALLMERS.   Eyolf——?

RITA.   Yes, you used to call her Eyolf, did you not? I seem to remember your telling me so—once, in a moment of confidence. [*Coming up to him.*] Do you remember it—that entrancingly beautiful hour, Alfred?

ALLMERS. [*Recoiling, as if in horror.*]   I remember nothing! I w i l l not remember!

RITA. [*Following him.*]   It was in that hour—when your other little Eyolf was crippled for life!

ALLMERS. [*In a hollow voice, supporting himself against the table.*]   Retribution!

RITA. [*Menacingly.*]   Yes, retribution!

*(*ASTA *and* BORGHEIM *return by way of the boat-shed. She is carrying some water-lilies in her hand.*

RITA. [*With self-control.*]   Well, Asta, have you and Mr. Borgheim talked things thoroughly over?

ASTA.   Oh, yes—pretty well.

(She puts down her umbrella and lays the flowers upon a chair.

BORGHEIM.   Miss Allmers has been very silent during our walk.

RITA.   Indeed, has she? Well, Alfred and I have talked things out thoroughly enough——

ASTA. [*Looking eagerly at both of them.*]   What is this——?

RITA.   Enough to last all our lifetime, I say. [*Breaking off.*] Come now, let us go up to the house, all four of us. We must have company about us in future. It will never do for Alfred and me to be alone.

ALLMERS.   Yes, do you go ahead, you two. [*Turning.*] I must speak a word to you before we go, Asta.

RITA. [*Looking at him.*]   Indeed? Well then, you come with me, Mr. Borgheim.

*(RITA *and* BORGHEIM *go up the wood-path.*

ASTA. [*Anxiously.*]   Alfred, what is the matter?

ALLMERS. [*Darkly.*]   Only that I cannot endure to be here any more.

ASTA.   Here! With Rita, do you mean?

ALLMERS.   Yes. Rita and I cannot go on living together.

ASTA. [*Seizes his arm and shakes it.*]   Oh, Alfred—don't say anything so terrible!

ALLMERS.   It is the truth I am telling you. We are making each other wicked and hateful.

ASTA. [*With painful emotion.*] I had never—never dreamt of anything like this!

ALLMERS. I did not realise it either, till to-day.

ASTA. And now you want to——! What is it you really want, Alfred?

ALLMERS. I want to get away from everything here—far, far away from it all.

ASTA. And to stand quite alone in the world?

ALLMERS. [*Nods.*] As I used to, before, yes.

ASTA. But you are not fitted for living alone!

ALLMERS. Oh, yes. I was so in the old days, at any rate.

ASTA. In the old days, yes; for then you had me with you.

ALLMERS. [*Trying to take her hand.*] Yes. And it is to you, Asta, that I now want to come home again.

ASTA. [*Eluding him.*] To me! No, no, Alfred! That is quite impossible.

ALLMERS. [*Looks sadly at her.*] Then Borgheim stands in the way after all?

ASTA. [*Earnestly.*] No, no; he does not! That is quite a mistake!

ALLMERS. Good. Then I will come to you—my dear, dear sister. I must come to you again—home to you, to be purified and ennobled after my life with——

ASTA. [*Shocked.*] Alfred,—you are doing Rita a great wrong!

ALLMERS. I have done her a great wrong. But not in this. Oh, think of it, Asta—think of our life together, yours and mine. Was it not like one long holy-day from first to last?

ASTA. Yes, it was, Alfred. But we can never live it over again.

ALLMERS. [*Bitterly.*] Do you mean that marriage has so irreparably ruined me?

ASTA. [*Quietly.*]   No, that is not what I mean.

ALLMERS.   Well, then we two will live our old life over again.

ASTA. [*With decision.*]   We cannot, Alfred.

ALLMERS.   Yes, we can. For the love of a brother and sister——

ASTA. [*Eagerly.*]   What of it?

ALLMERS.   That is the only relation in life that is not subject to the law of change.

ASTA. [*Softly and tremblingly.*]   But if that relation were not——

ALLMERS.   Not——?

ASTA.   ——not our relation?

ALLMERS. [*Stares at her in astonishment.*]   Not ours? Why, what can you mean by that?

ASTA.   It is best I should tell you at once, Alfred.

ALLMERS.   Yes, yes; tell me!

ASTA.   The letters to mother——. Those in my portfolio——

ALLMERS.   Well?

ASTA.   You must read them—when I am gone.

ALLMERS.   Why must I?

ASTA. [*Struggling with herself.*]   For then you will see that——

ALLMERS.   Well?

ASTA.   ——that I have no right to bear your father's name.

ALLMERS. [*Staggering backwards.*]   Asta! What is this you say!

ASTA.   Read the letters. Then you will see—and understand. And perhaps have some forgiveness—for mother, too.

ALLMERS. [*Clutching at his forehead.*]   I cannot grasp

this——I cannot realise the thought. You, Asta——you are not——

ASTA.   You are not my brother, Alfred.

ALLMERS. [*Quickly, half defiantly, looking at her.*]   Well, but what difference does that really make in our relation? Practically none at all.

ASTA. [*Shaking her head.*]   It makes all the difference, Alfred. Our relation is not that of brother and sister.

ALLMERS.   No, no. But it is none the less sacred for that——it will always be equally sacred.

ASTA.   Do not forget——that it is subject to the law of change, as you said just now.

ALLMERS. [*Looks inquiringly at her.*]   Do you mean that——

ASTA. [*Quietly, but with warm emotion.*]   Not a word more——my dear, dear Alfred. [*Takes up the flowers from the chair.*] Do you see these water-lilies?

ALLMERS. [*Nodding slowly.*]   They are the sort that shoot up——from the very depth.

ASTA.   I pulled them in the tarn——where it flows out into the fiord. [*Holds them out to him.*] Will you take them, Alfred?

ALLMERS. [*Taking them.*]   Thanks.

ASTA. [*With tears in her eyes.*]   They are a last greeting to you, from——from little Eyolf.

ALLMERS. [*Looking at her.*]   From Eyolf out yonder? Or from you?

ASTA. [*Softly.*]   From both of us. [*Taking up her umbrella.*] Now come with me to Rita.

{*She goes up the wood-path.*

ALLMERS. [*Takes up his hat from the table, and whispers sadly.*]   Asta. Eyolf. Little Eyolf——!

{*He follows her up the path.*

Act III

~

An elevation, overgrown with shrubs, in ALLMERS'S *garden. At the back a sheer cliff, with a railing along its edge, and with steps on the left leading downwards. An extensive view over the fiord, which lies deep below. A flagstaff with lines, but no flag, stands by the railing. In front, on the right, a summer-house, covered with creepers and wild vines. Outside it, a bench. It is a late summer evening, with clear sky. Deepening twilight.*

ASTA *is sitting on the bench, with her hands in her lap. She is wearing her outdoor dress and a hat, has her parasol at her side, and a little travelling-bag on a strap over her shoulder.*

BORGHEIM *comes up from the back on the left. He, too, has a travelling-bag over his shoulder. He is carrying a rolled-up flag.*

BORGHEIM. [*Catching sight of* ASTA.] Oh, so you are up here!

ASTA. Yes, I am taking my last look out over the fiord.

BORGHEIM. Then I am glad I happened to come up.

ASTA. Have you been searching for me?

BORGHEIM. Yes, I have. I wanted to say good-bye to you——for the present. Not for good and all, I hope.

ASTA. [*With a faint smile.*] You are persevering.

BORGHEIM. A road-maker has got to be.

ASTA. Have you seen anything of Alfred? Or of Rita?

BORGHEIM. Yes, I saw them both.

ASTA.   Together?

BORGHEIM.   No—apart.

ASTA.   What are you going to do with the flag?

BORGHEIM.   Mrs. Allmers asked me to come up and hoist it.

ASTA.   Hoist a flag just now?

BORGHEIM.   Half-mast high. She wants it to fly both night and day, she says.

ASTA. [*Sighing.*]   Poor Rita! And poor Alfred!

BORGHEIM. [*Busied with the flag.*]   Have you the heart to leave them? I ask, because I see you are in travelling-dress.

ASTA. [*In a low voice.*]   I m u s t go.

BORGHEIM.   Well, if you must, then——

ASTA.   And you are going, too, to-night?

BORGHEIM.   I must, too. I am going by the train. Are you going that way?

ASTA.   No. I shall take the steamer.

BORGHEIM. [*Glancing at her.*]   We each take our own way, then?

ASTA.   Yes.

      {*She sits and looks on while he hoists the flag half-mast high. When he has done he goes up to her.*

BORGHEIM.   Miss Asta——you can't think how grieved I am about little Eyolf.

ASTA. [*Looks up at him.*]   Yes, I am sure you feel it deeply.

BORGHEIM.   And the feeling tortures me. For the fact is, grief is not much in my way.

ASTA. [*Raising her eyes to the flag.*]   It will pass over in time—all of it. All our sorrow.

BORGHEIM.   All? Do you believe that?

ASTA.   Like a squall at sea. When once you have got
far away from here, then——

BORGHEIM.   It will have to be very far away indeed.

ASTA.   And then you have this great new road-work,
too.

BORGHEIM.   But no one to help me in it.

ASTA.   Oh yes, surely you have.

BORGHEIM. [*Shaking his head.*] No one. No one to share
the gladness with. For it is gladness that most needs sharing.

ASTA.   Not the labour and trouble?

BORGHEIM.   Pooh—that sort of thing one can always
get through alone.

ASTA.   But the gladness—that must be shared with
some one, you think?

BORGHEIM.   Yes; for if not, where would be the
pleasure in being glad?

ASTA.   Ah yes—perhaps there is something in that.

BORGHEIM.   Oh, of course, for a certain time you can
go on feeling glad in your own heart. But it won't do in
the long run. No, it takes two to be glad.

ASTA.   Always two? Never more? Never many?

BORGHEIM.   Well, you see—then it becomes a quite
different matter. Miss Asta—are you sure you can never
make up your mind to share gladness and success and—and
labour and trouble, with one—with one alone in all the
world?

ASTA.   I have tried it—once.

BORGHEIM.   Have you?

ASTA.   Yes, all the time that my brother—that Alfred and I lived together.

BORGHEIM.   Oh, with your brother, yes. But that is

altogether different. That ought rather to be called peace than happiness, I should say.

ASTA.   It was delightful, all the same.

BORGHEIM.   There now—you see even that seemed to you delightful. But just think now—if he had not been your brother!

ASTA. [*Makes a movement to rise, but remains sitting.*]   Then we should never have been together. For I was a child then—and he wasn't much more.

BORGHEIM. [*After a pause.*]   Was it so delightful—that time?

ASTA.   Oh yes, indeed it was.

BORGHEIM.   Was there much that was really bright and happy in your life then?

ASTA.   Oh yes, so much. You cannot think how much.

BORGHEIM.   Tell me a little about it, Miss Asta.

ASTA.   Oh, there are only trifles to tell.

BORGHEIM.   Such as——? Well?

ASTA.   Such as the time when Alfred had passed his examination—and had distinguished himself. And then, from time to time, when he got a post in some school or other. Or when he would sit at home working at an article—and would read it aloud to me. And then when it would appear in some magazine.

BORGHEIM.   Yes, I can quite see that it must have been a peaceful, delightful life—a brother and sister sharing all their joys. [*Shaking his head.*] What I cannot understand is that your brother could ever give you up, Asta.

ASTA. [*With suppressed emotion.*]   Alfred married, you know.

BORGHEIM.   Was not that very hard for you?

ASTA. Yes, at first. It seemed as though I had utterly lost him all at once.

BORGHEIM. Well, luckily it was not so bad as that.

ASTA. No.

BORGHEIM. But, all the same—how could he! Go and marry, I mean—when he could have kept you with him, alone!

ASTA. [*Looking straight in front of her.*] He was subject to the law of change, I suppose.

BORGHEIM. The law of change?

ASTA. So Alfred calls it.

BORGHEIM. Pooh—what a stupid law that must be! I don't believe a bit in law.

ASTA. [*Rising.*] You may come to believe in it, in time.

BORGHEIM. Never in all my life! [*Insistently.*] But listen now, Miss Asta! Do be reasonable—for once in a way—in this matter, I mean——

ASTA. [*Interrupting him.*] Oh, no, no—don't let us begin upon t h a t again!

BORGHEIM. [*Continuing as before.*] Yes, Asta—I can't possibly give you up so easily. Now your brother has everything as he wishes it. He can live his life quite contentedly without you. He doesn't require you at all. Then this— this—that at one blow has changed your whole position here——

ASTA. [*With a start.*] What do you mean by that?

BORGHEIM. The loss of the child. What else should I mean?

ASTA. [*Recovering her self-control.*] Little Eyolf is gone, yes.

BORGHEIM. And what more does that leave you to

do here? You have not the poor little boy to take care of now. You have no duties—no claims upon you of any sort.

ASTA.   Oh, please, Mr. Borgheim—don't make it so hard for me.

BORGHEIM.   I must; I should be mad if I did not try my uttermost. I shall be leaving town before very long, and perhaps I shall have no opportunity of meeting you there. Perhaps I shall not see you again for a long, long time. And who knows what may happen in the meanwhile?

ASTA. [*With a grave smile.*]   So you are afraid of the law of change, after all?

BORGHEIM.   No, not in the least. [*Laughing bitterly.*] And there is nothing to be changed, either—not in you, I mean. For I can see you don't care much about me.

ASTA.   You know very well that I do.

BORGHEIM.   Perhaps, but not nearly enough. Not as I want you to. [*More forcibly.*] By Heaven, Asta—Miss Asta—I cannot tell you how strongly I feel that you are wrong in this! A little onward, perhaps, from to-day and to-morrow, all life's happiness may be awaiting us. And we must needs pass it by! Do you think we will not come to repent of it, Asta?

ASTA. [*Quietly.*]   I don't know. I only know that they are not for us—all these bright possibilities.

BORGHEIM. [*Looks at her with self-control.*]   Then I must make my roads alone?

ASTA. [*Warmly.*]   Oh, how I wish I could stand by you in it all! Help you in the labour—share the gladness with you——

BORGHEIM.   Would you—if you could?

ASTA.   Yes, that I would.

BORGHEIM.   But you cannot?

ASTA. [*Looking down.*]   Would you be content to have only half of me?

BORGHEIM.   No. You must be utterly and entirely mine.

ASTA. [*Looks at him, and says quietly.*]   Then I cannot.

BORGHEIM.   Good-bye then, Miss Asta.

{*He is on the point of going.* ALLMERS *comes up from the left at the back.* BORGHEIM *stops.*

ALLMERS. [*The moment he has reached the top of the steps, points, and says in a low voice.*]   Is Rita in there—in the summer-house?

BORGHEIM.   No; there is no one here but Miss Asta.

{ALLMERS *comes forward.*

ASTA. [*Going towards him.*]   Shall I go down and look for her? Shall I get her to come up here?

ALLMERS. [*With a negative gesture.*]   No, no, no—let it alone. [*To* BORGHEIM.] Is it you that have hoisted the flag?

BORGHEIM.   Yes. Mrs. Allmers asked me to. That was what brought me up here.

ALLMERS.   And you are going to start to-night?

BORGHEIM.   Yes. To-night I go away in good earnest.

ALLMERS. [*With a glance at* ASTA.]   And you have made sure of pleasant company, I daresay.

BORGHEIM. [*Shaking his head.*]   I am going alone.

ALLMERS. [*With surprise.*]   Alone!

BORGHEIM.   Utterly alone.

ALLMERS. [*Absently.*]   Indeed?

BORGHEIM.   And I shall have to remain alone, too.

ALLMERS.   There is something horrible in being alone. The thought of it runs like ice through my blood——

ASTA.   Oh, but, Alfred, you are not alone.

ALLMERS.   There may be something horrible in that too, Asta.

ASTA. [*Oppressed.*]   Oh, don't talk like that! Don't think like that!

ALLMERS. [*Not listening to her.*] But since you are not going with him——? Since there is nothing to bind you——? Why will you not remain out here with me—and with Rita?

ASTA. [*Uneasily.*]   No, no, I cannot. I must go back to town now.

ALLMERS.   But only in to town, Asta. Do you hear!

ASTA.   Yes.

ALLMERS.   And you must promise me that you will soon come out again.

ASTA. [*Quickly.*] No, no, I dare not promise you that, for the present.

ALLMERS.   Well—as you will. We shall soon meet in town, then.

ASTA. [*Imploringly.*]   But, Alfred, you must stay at home here with Rita now.

ALLMERS. [*Without answering, turns to* BORGHEIM.] You may find it good thing, after all, that you have to take your journey alone.

BORGHEIM. [*Annoyed.*]   Oh, how can you say such a thing?

ALLMERS.   You see, you can never tell whom you might happen to meet afterwards—on the way.

ASTA. [*Involuntarily.*]   Alfred!

ALLMERS.   The right fellow-traveller—when it is too late—too late.

ASTA. [*Softly, quivering.*]   Alfred! Alfred!

BORGHEIM. [*Looking from one to the other.*]   What is the meaning of this? I don't understand——

{RITA *comes up from the left at the back.*

RITA. [*Plaintively.*]   Oh, don't go away from me, all of you!

ASTA. [*Going towards her.*]   You said you preferred to be alone.

RITA.   Yes, but I dare not. It is getting so horribly dark. I seem to see great, open eyes fixed upon me!

ASTA. [*Tenderly and sympathetically.*]   What if it were so, Rita? You ought not to be afraid of those eyes.

RITA.   How can you say so! Not afraid!

ALLMERS. [*Insistently.*]   Asta, I beg you—for Heaven's sake—remain here with Rita!

RITA.   Yes! And with Alfred, too. Do! Do, Asta!

ASTA. [*Struggling with herself.*]   Oh, I want to so much——

RITA.   Well, then, do it! For Alfred and I cannot go alone through the sorrow and heartache.

ALLMERS. [*Darkly.*]   Say, rather—through the ranklings of remorse.

RITA.   Oh, whatever you like to call it—we cannot bear it alone, we two. Oh, Asta, I beg and implore you! Stay here and help us! Take Eyolf's place for us——

ASTA. [*Shrinking.*]   Eyolf's——

RITA.   Yes, would you not have it so, Alfred?

ALLMERS.   If she can and will.

RITA.   You used to call her your little Eyolf. [*Seizes her hand.*] Henceforth you shall be o u r Eyolf, Asta! Eyolf, as you were before.

ALLMERS. [*With concealed emotion.*]   Remain—and share our life with us, Asta. With Rita. With me. With me—your brother!

ASTA. [*With decision, snatches her hand away.*]   No. I cannot. [*Turning.*] Mr. Borgheim—what time does the steamer start?

BORGHEIM.   Now—at once.

ASTA.   Then I must go on board. Will you go with me?

BORGHEIM. [*With a suppressed outburst of joy.*]   Will I? Yes, yes!

ASTA.   Then come!

RITA. [*Slowly.*]   Ah! That is how it is. Well, then, you cannot stay with us.

ASTA. [*Throwing her arms round her neck.*]   Thanks for everything, Rita! [*Goes up to* ALLMERS *and grasps his hand.*] Alfred—good-bye! A thousand times, good-bye!

ALLMERS. [*Softly and eagerly.*]   What is this, Asta? It seems as though you were taking flight.

ASTA. [*In subdued anguish.*]   Yes, Alfred—I a m taking flight.

ALLMERS.   Flight—from me!

ASTA. [*Whispering.*]   From you—and from myself.

ALLMERS. [*Shrinking back.*]   Ah——!

{ASTA *rushes down the steps at the back.* BORGHEIM *waves his hat and follows her.* RITA *leans against the entrance to the summer-house.* ALLMERS *goes, in strong inward emotion, up to the railing, and stands there gazing downwards. A pause.*

ALLMERS. [*Turns, and says with hard-won composure.*] There comes the steamer. Look, Rita.

RITA.   I dare not look at it.

ALLMERS.   You dare not?

RITA.   No. For it has a red eye—and a green one, too. Great, glowing eyes.

ALLMERS.   Oh, those are only the lights, you know.

RITA.   Henceforth they are eyes—for me. They stare and stare out of the darkness—and into the darkness.

ALLMERS.   Now she is putting in to shore.

RITA.   Where are they mooring her this evening, then?

ALLMERS. [*Coming forward.*]   At the pier, as usual——

RITA. [*Drawing herself up.*]   How c a n they moor her there!

ALLMERS.   They must.

RITA.   But it was there that Eyolf——! How c a n they moor her there!

ALLMERS.   Yes, life is pitiless, Rita.

RITA.   Men are heartless. They take no thought—either for the living or for the dead.

ALLMERS.   There you are right. Life goes its own way—just as if nothing in the world had happened.

RITA. [*Gazing straight before her.*]   And nothing h a s happened, either. Not to others. Only to us two.

ALLMERS. [*The pain re-awakening.*]   Yes, Rita—so it was to no purpose that you bore him in sorrow and anguish. For now he is gone again—and has left no trace behind him.

RITA.   Only the crutch was saved.

ALLMERS. [*Angrily.*]   Be silent! Do not let me hear that word!

RITA. [*Plaintively.*]   Oh, I cannot bear the thought that he is gone from us.

ALLMERS. [*Coldly and bitterly.*]   You could very well do without him while he was with us. Half the day would often pass without your setting eyes on him.

RITA.   Yes, for I knew that I could see him whenever I wanted to.

ALLMERS.   Yes, that is how we have gone and squandered the short time we had with Little Eyolf.

RITA. [*Listening, in dread.*]   Do you hear, Alfred! Now it is ringing again!

ALLMERS. [*Looking over the fiord.*]   It is the steamer's bell that is ringing. She is just starting.

RITA.   Oh, it's not that bell I mean. All day I have heard it ringing in my ears.——Now it is ringing again!

ALLMERS. [*Going up to her.*]   You are mistaken, Rita.

RITA.   No, I hear it so plainly. It sounds like a knell. Slow. Slow. And always the same words.

ALLMERS.   Words? What words?

RITA. [*Nodding her head in the rhythm.*]   "The crútch is—flóating. The crútch is—flóating." Oh, surely you must hear it, too!

ALLMERS. [*Shaking his head.*]   I hear nothing. And there is nothing to hear.

RITA.   Oh, you may say what you will——I hear it so plainly.

ALLMERS. [*Looking out over the railing.*]   Now they are on board, Rita. Now the steamer is on her way to the town.

RITA.   Is it possible you do not hear it? "The crútch is—flóating. The crútch is————"

ALLMERS. [*Coming forward.*]   You shall not stand there listening to a sound that does not exist. I tell you, Asta and Borgheim are on board. They have started already. Asta is gone.

RITA. [*Looks timidly at him.*]   Then I suppose you will soon be gone, too, Alfred?

ALLMERS. [*Quickly.*]   What do you mean by that?

RITA.   That you will follow your sister.

ALLMERS.   Has Asta told you anything?

RITA. No. But you said yourself it was for Asta's sake that—that we came together.

ALLMERS. Yes, but you, you yourself, have bound me to you—by our life together.

RITA. Oh, in your eyes I am not—I am not—entrancingly beautiful any more.

ALLMERS. The law of change may perhaps keep us together, none the less.

RITA. [*Nodding slowly.*] There i s a change in me now—I feel the anguish of it.

ALLMERS. Anguish?

RITA. Yes, for change, too, is a sort of birth.

ALLMERS. It is—or a resurrection. Transition to a higher life.

RITA. [*Gazing sadly before her.*] Yes—with the loss of all, all life's happiness.

ALLMERS. That loss is just the gain.

RITA. [*Vehemently.*] Oh, phrases! Good God, we are creatures of earth after all.

ALLMERS. But something akin to the sea and the heavens too, Rita.

RITA. You perhaps. Not I.

ALLMERS. Oh, yes—you too, more than you yourself suspect.

RITA. [*Advancing a pace towards him.*] Tell me, Alfred—could you think of taking up your work again?

ALLMERS. The work that you have hated so.

RITA. I am easier to please now. I am willing to share you with the book.

ALLMERS. Why?

RITA. Only to keep you here with me—to have you near me.

ALLMERS.   Oh, it is so little I can do to help you, Rita.

RITA.   But perhaps I could help you.

ALLMERS.   With my book, do you mean?

RITA.   No; but to live your life.

ALLMERS. [*Shaking his head.*]   I seem to have no life to live.

RITA.   Well then, to endure your life.

ALLMERS. [*Darkly, looking away from her.*]   I think it would be best for both of us that we should part.

RITA. [*Looking curiously at him.*]   Then where would you go? Perhaps to Asta, after all?

ALLMERS.   No—never again to Asta.

RITA.   Where then?

ALLMERS.   Up into the solitudes.

RITA.   Up among the mountains? Is that what you mean?

ALLMERS.   Yes.

RITA.   But all that is mere dreaming, Alfred! You could not live up there.

ALLMERS.   And yet I feel myself drawn to them.

RITA.   Why? Tell me!

ALLMERS.   Sit down—and I will tell you something.

RITA.   Something that happened to you up there?

ALLMERS.   Yes.

RITA.   And that you never told Asta and me?

ALLMERS.   Yes.

RITA.   Oh, you are so silent about everything. You ought not to be.

ALLMERS.   Sit down there—and I will tell you about it.

RITA.   Yes, yes—tell me!

{*She sits on the bench beside the summer-house.*

ALLMERS.   I was alone up there, in the heart of the great mountains. I came to a wide, dreary mountain lake; and that lake I had to cross. But I could not—for there was neither a boat nor any one there.

RITA.   Well? And then?

ALLMERS.   Then I went without any guidance into a side valley. I thought that by that way I could push on over the heights and between the peaks—and then down again on the other side of the lake.

RITA.   Oh, and you lost yourself, Alfred!

ALLMERS.   Yes; I mistook the direction—for there was no path or track. And all day I went on—and all the next night. And at last I thought I should never see the face of man again.

RITA.   Not come home to us? Oh, then, I am sure your thoughts were with us here.

ALLMERS.   No—they were not.

RITA.   Not?

ALLMERS.   No. It was so strange. Both you and Eyolf seemed to have drifted far, far away from me—and Asta, too.

RITA.   Then what did you think of?

ALLMERS.   I did not think. I dragged myself along among the precipices—and revelled in the peace and luxury of death.

RITA. [*Springing up.*]   Oh, don't speak in that way of that horror!

ALLMERS.   I did not feel it so. I had no fear. Here went death and I, it seemed to me, like two good fellow-travellers. It all seemed so natural—so simple, I thought. In my family, we don't live to be old——

RITA.   Oh, don't say such things, Alfred! You see you came safely out of it, after all.

ALLMERS.   Yes; all of a sudden, I found myself where I wanted to be—on the other side of the lake.

RITA.   It must have been a night of terror for you, Alfred. But now that it is over, you will not admit it to yourself.

ALLMERS.   That night sealed my resolution. And it was then that I turned about and came straight homewards. To Eyolf.

RITA. [*Softly.*]   Too late.

ALLMERS.   Yes. And then when—my fellow-traveller came and took him——t h e n I felt the horror of it; of it all; of all that, in spite of everything, we dare not tear ourselves away from. So earth-bound are we, both of us, Rita.

RITA. [*With a gleam of joy.*]   Yes, you are, too, are you not! [*Coming close to him.*] Oh, let us live our life together as long as we can!

ALLMERS. [*Shrugging his shoulders.*]   Live our life, yes! And have nothing to fill life with. An empty void on all sides—wherever I look.

RITA. [*In fear.*]   Oh, sooner or later you will go away from me, Alfred! I feel it! I can see it in your face! You will go away from me.

ALLMERS.   With my fellow-traveller, do you mean?

RITA.   No, I mean worse than that. Of your own free will you will leave me—for you think it's only here, with me, that you have nothing to live for. Is not that what is in your thoughts?

ALLMERS. [*Looking steadfastly at her.*]   What if it were——?

> {*A disturbance, and the noise of angry, quarrelling voices is heard from down below, in the distance.* ALL-MERS *goes to the railing.*

RITA. What is that? [*With an outburst.*] Oh, you'll see, they have found him!

ALLMERS. He will never be found.

RITA. But what is it then?

ALLMERS. [*Coming forward.*] Only fighting—as usual.

RITA. Down on the beach?

ALLMERS. Yes. The whole village down there ought to be swept away. Now the men have come home—drunk, as they always are. They are beating the children—do you hear the boys crying! The women are shrieking for help for them——

RITA. Should we not get some one to go down and help them?

ALLMERS. [*Harshly and angrily.*] Help them, who did not help Eyolf! Let them go—as they let Eyolf go.

RITA. Oh, you must not talk like that, Alfred! Nor think like that!

ALLMERS. I cannot think otherwise. All the old hovels ought to be torn down.

RITA. And then what is to become of all the poor people?

ALLMERS. They must go somewhere else.

RITA. And the children, too?

ALLMERS. Does it make much difference where they go to the dogs?

RITA. [*Quietly and reproachfully.*] You are forcing yourself into this harshness, Alfred.

ALLMERS. [*Vehemently.*] I have a right to be harsh now! It is my duty.

RITA. Your duty?

ALLMERS. My duty to Eyolf. He must not lie unavenged. Once for all, Rita—it is as I tell you! Think it over! Have the whole place down there razed to the ground— when I am gone.

RITA. [*Looks intently at him.*]   When you are gone?

ALLMERS.   Yes. For that will at least give you something to fill your life with—and something you must have.

RITA. [*Firmly and decidedly.*]   There you are right—I must. But can you guess what I will set about—when you are gone?

ALLMERS.   Well, what?

RITA. [*Slowly and with resolution.*]   As soon as you are gone from me, I will go down to the beach, and bring all the poor neglected children home with me. All the mischievous boys——

ALLMERS.   What will you do with them here?

RITA.   I will take them to my heart.

ALLMERS.   You!

RITA.   Yes, I will. From the day you leave me, they shall all be here, all of them, as if they were mine.

ALLMERS. [*Shocked.*]   In our little Eyolf's place!

RITA.   Yes, in our little Eyolf's place. They shall live in Eyolf's rooms. They shall read his books. They shall play with his toys. They shall take it in turns to sit in his chair at table.

ALLMERS.   But this is sheer madness in you! I do not know a creature in the world that is less fitted than you for anything of that sort.

RITA.   Then I shall have to educate myself for it; to train myself; to discipline myself.

ALLMERS.   If you are really in earnest about this— about all you say—then there must indeed be a change in you.

RITA. Yes, there is, Alfred——and for that I have you to thank. You have made an empty place within me; and I must try to fill it up with something——with something that is a little like love.

ALLMERS. [*Stands for a moment lost in thought; then looks at her.*] The truth is, we have not done much for the poor people down there.

RITA. We have done nothing for them.

ALLMERS. Scarcely even thought of them.

RITA. Never thought of them in sympathy.

ALLMERS. We, who had "the gold, and the green forests"——

RITA. Our hands were closed to them. And our hearts too.

ALLMERS. [*Nods.*] Then it was perhaps natural enough, after all, that they should not risk their lives to save little Eyolf.

RITA. [*Softly.*] Think, Alfred! Are you so certain that——that w e would have risked ours?

ALLMERS. [*With an uneasy gesture of repulsion.*] You must never doubt t h a t.

RITA. Oh, we are children of earth.

ALLMERS. What do you really think you can do with all these neglected children?

RITA. I suppose I must try if I cannot lighten and——and ennoble their lot in life.

ALLMERS. If you can do that——then Eyolf was not born in vain.

RITA. Nor taken from us in vain, either.

ALLMERS. [*Looking steadfastly at her.*] Be quite clear about o n e thing, Rita——it is not love that is driving you to this.

RITA. No, it is not——at any rate, not yet.

ALLMERS.   Well, then what is it?

RITA. [*Half-evasively.*]   You have so often talked to Asta of human responsibility——

ALLMERS.   Of the book that you hated.

RITA.   I hate that book still. But I used to sit and listen to what you told her. And now I will try to continue it—in my own way.

ALLMERS. [*Shaking his head.*]   It is not for the sake of that unfinished book——

RITA.   No, I have another reason as well.

ALLMERS.   What is that?

RITA. [*Softly, with a melancholy smile.*]   I want to make my peace with the great, open eyes, you see.

ALLMERS. [*Struck, fixing his eyes upon her.*]   Perhaps, I could join you in that? And help you, Rita?

RITA.   Would you?

ALLMERS.   Yes—if I were only sure I could.

RITA. [*Hesitatingly.*]   But then you would have to remain here.

ALLMERS. [*Softly.*]   Let us try if it could not be so.

RITA. [*Almost inaudibly.*]   Yes, let us, Alfred.

> {*Both are silent. Then* ALLMERS *goes up to the flagstaff and hoists the flag to the top.* RITA *stands beside the summer-house and looks at him in silence.*

ALLMERS. [*Coming forward again.*]   We have a heavy day of work before us, Rita.

RITA.   You will see—that now and then a Sabbath peace will descend on us.

ALLMERS. [*Quietly, with emotion.*]   Then, perhaps, we shall know that the spirits are with us.

RITA. [*Whispering.*]   The spirits?

ALLMERS. [*As before.*]   Yes, they will perhaps be around us—those whom we have lost.

RITA. [*Nods slowly.*] Our little Eyolf. And your big Eyolf, too.

ALLMERS. [*Gazing straight before him.*] Now and then, perhaps, we may still—on the way through life—have a little, passing glimpse of them.

RITA. Where shall we look for them, Alfred?

ALLMERS. [*Fixing his eyes upon her.*] Upwards.

RITA. [*Nods in approval.*] Yes, yes—upwards.

ALLMERS. Upwards—towards the peaks. Towards the stars. And towards the great silence.

RITA. [*Giving him her hand.*] Thanks!